MEDIEVAL AND RENAISSANCE DRAMA IN ENGLAND

Volume 26

Editorial Board

Leeds Barroll
University of Maryland (Baltimore)

Catherine Belsey
*University of Wales
College of Cardiff*

David M. Bevington
University of Chicago

Barry Gaines
University of New Mexico

Jean E. Howard
Columbia University

Arthur F. Kinney
University of Massachusetts

Anne C. Lancashire
University of Toronto

William B. Long
Independent Scholar

Barbara Mowat
Folger Shakespeare Library

Lee Patterson
Yale University

John Pitcher
St. John's College, Oxford

E. Paul Werstine
*University of Western
Ontario*

MEDIEVAL AND RENAISSANCE DRAMA IN ENGLAND

Volume 26

Editor
S. P. Cerasano

Associate Editor
Mary Bly

Book Review Editor
Heather Anne Hirschfeld

Madison • Teaneck
Fairleigh Dickinson University Press

© 2013 by Rosemont Publishing & Printing Corp.

All rights reserved. Authorization to photocopy items for internal or personal use, or the internal or personal use of specific clients, is granted by the copyright owner, provided that a base fee of $10.00, plus eight cents per page, per copy is paid directly to the Copyright Clearance Center, 222 Rosewood Drive, Danvers, Massachusetts 01923. [978-0-8386-4468-3/13 $10.00 + 8¢ pp, pc.]

Associated University Presses
10 Schalks Crossing Road
Suite 501-330
Plainsboro, NJ 08536

The paper used in this publication meets the requirements of the American National Standard for Permanence of Paper for Printed Library Materials Z39.48-1984.

International Standard Book Number 978-0-8386-4468-3 (vol. 26)
International Standard Serial Number 0731-3403

All editorial correspondence concerning *Medieval and Renaissance Drama in England* should be addressed to Prof. S. P. Cerasano, Department of English, Colgate University, Hamilton, N.Y., 13346. Orders and subscriptions should be directed to Associated University Presses, 10 Schalks Crossing Road, Suite 501-330, Plainsboro, New Jersey 08536.

Medieval and Renaissance Drama in England disclaims responsibility for statements, either of fact or opinion, made by contributors.

PRINTED IN THE UNITED STATES OF AMERICA.

Contents

Foreword	7
Contributors	9

Articles

Samuel Daniel's Masque: *The Vision of the Twelve Goddesses*: Texts and Payments JOHN PITCHER	17
"'Batter'd, not demolish'd': Staging the Tortured Body in *The Martyred Soldier* ELIZABETH WILLIAMSON	43
Discovering the Sins of the Cellar in *The Dutch Courtesan*: *Turpe est difficiles habere nugas* SARAH K. SCOTT	60
The "salarie of your lust": Rethinking the Economics of Virtue in Massinger's Plays MATTHEW J. SMITH	75
"The Hall must not be pestred": Embedded Masques, Space, and Dramatized Desire JOHN R. ZIEGLER	97
New Light on Dekker's *Fortunati* JUNE SCHLUETER	120
Eagle and Hound: The "Epitaph" of Talbot and the Date of *1 Henry VI* LAWRENCE MANLEY	136
Richard III's Forelives: Rewriting Elizabeth(s) in Tudor Historiography ALLISON MACHLIS MEYER	156
Heywood's *Silver Age*: A Flight Too Far DAVID MANN	184

New Conversations on "Othello"

Othello's "Malignant Turk" and George Manwaring's *A True Discourse*: The Cultural Politics of a Textual Derivation IMTIAZ HABIB	207

"O blood, blood, blood": Violence and Identity in Shakespeare's
Othello   240
JENNIFER FEATHER

Reviews

Sharon Aronson-Lehavi, *Street Scenes: Late Medieval Acting and Performance*   267
BOYDA JOHNSTONE

Janette Dillon, *The Language of Space in Court Performance: 1400–1625*   269
HEATHER C. EASTERLING

John Astington, *Actors and Acting in Shakespeare's Time: The Art of Stage Playing*   271
LLOYD EDWARD KERMODE

Anne Rochester, *Staging Spectatorship in the Plays of Philip Massinger*   274
CHARLES PASTOOR

Bella Mirabella, ed., *Ornamentalism: The Art of Renaissance Accessories*   276
ERIKA L. LIN

Jerzy Limon, *The Chemistry of the Theatre: Performativity of Time*   279
THOMAS P. ANDERSON

Kristen Poole, *Supernatural Environments in Shakespeare's England: Spaces of Demonism, Divinity, and Drama*   281
D. K. SMITH

Lisa Hopkins, *Drama and the Succession to the Crown, 1561–1633*   283
JOHN E. CURRAN, JR.

Carole Levin and John Watkins, *Shakespeare's Foreign Worlds: National and Transnational Identities in the Elizabethan Age*   285
PATRICIA PHILLIPPY

Linda Woodbridge, *English Revenge Drama: Money, Resistance, Equality*   288
STEPHEN DENG

Jeffrey Knapp, *Shakespeare Only*   290
JAMES P. BEDNARZ

Lene B. Petersen, *Shakespeare's Errant Texts: Textual Form and Linguistic Style in Shakespearean "Bad" Quartos and Co-authored Plays*   292
HUGH CRAIG

Index   297

Foreword

MaRDiE 26 offers a collection of ten essays on both Shakespearean and non-Shakespearean drama. The masque is the focus of studies by John Pitcher and John R. Ziegler, while particular essays concentrate on Shakespeare's contemporaries, and, most specifically, on Thomas Dekker (June Schlueter), Thomas Heywood (David Mann), John Marston (Sarah K. Scott), and Philip Massinger (Matthew J. Smith). Elizabeth Williamson takes Henry Shirley's (?) *The Martyred Soldier*. Shakespeare's history plays are revisited by two contributors: Lawrence Manley (who explores the date of *1 Henry VI*) and Allison Machlis Meyer (who looks back into Tudor historiography and *Richard III*). Imtiaz Habib and Jennifer Feather re-open the critical conversation on aspects of *Othello*.

S. P. CERASANO
Editor

Contributors

THOMAS P. ANDERSON is Associate Professor and Director of Undergraduate Studies at Mississippi State University. He recently finished two essays on Julie Taymor's film version of *Titus Andronicus*—one that looks closely at the film's representation of the play's children and a second that focuses on Taymor's cinematic image of Lavinia as a transformation of the literary blazon. He has also co-edited (with Ryan Netzley) *Acts of Reading: Interpretation, Reading Practices, and the Idea of the Book in John Foxe's* Actes and Monuments, which considers the theoretical implications of the important hypertext edition of *Acts and Monuments*.

JAMES P. BEDNARZ is Professor of English on the Post Campus of Long Island University. He is the author of *Shakespeare and the Poets' War* (2001) and *Shakespeare and the Truth of Love* (2012). He has published widely in international journals and contributed chapters to collections on Shakespeare and his contemporaries.

HUGH CRAIG works at the University of Newcastle, Australia, where he directs the Humanities Research Institute and the Centre for Literary and Linguistic Computing. With Arthur F. Kinney he edited *Shakespeare, Computers, and the Mystery of Authorship* (2009).

JOHN E. CURRAN, JR. is Professor of English at Marquette University. His current book project involves characterization and individuation in English Renaissance drama. The book will corroborate several articles he has recently published on character, including on Chapman's *Byron* plays in *Studies in Philology*, and on the Fletcher-Massinger declamation plays in *MaRDiE*.

STEPHEN DENG is Associate Professor of English at Michigan State University. He is the author of *Coinage and State Formation in Early Modern English Literature* (2011) and co-editor of *Global Traffic: Discourses and Practices of Trade in English Literature and Culture from 1550–1700* (2008).

HEATHER EASTERLING is an Associate Professor in English and Women and Gender Studies at Gonzaga University, a Jesuit University in Spokane, WA.

Her book on Jacobean city comedy and its staging of London (*Parsing the City: Jonson, Middleton, Dekker, and City Comedy's London as Language*) was published in 2007. An article on King James I's royal entry in print currently is under review.

JENNIFER FEATHER is Assistant Professor of English at The University of North Carolina at Greensboro. Her book *Writing Combat and the Self in Early Modern English Texts: The Pen and the Sword* is forthcoming.

IMTIAZ HABIB is a Professor of English and the Graduate Program Director for the M.A. in English at Old Dominion University, where he has been a Burgess scholar and Hixon Research Fellow. The author of several books and numerous articles on Shakespeare and on early modern English literature, culture, and politics, including especially discourses of race, his most recent publications include *Black Lives in the English Archives 1500–1677: Imprints of the Invisible* (2008), a comprehensive archival database and historical analysis of documentary records of black people in sixteenth- and seventeenth-century England. His current research includes a monograph project on *Black Voices in the English Archives and the Problems of Their Reading*.

BOYDA JOHNSTONE is a doctoral student in medieval literature at Fordham University. She has recently published in *Early Theatre* on the subject of an unknown seventeenth-century play, and she has a forthcoming book chapter on the illustrated *Abbey of the Holy Ghost* in BL MS. Stowe 39. Her ongoing interests lie in medieval visual culture, performance theory, and devotional literature.

LLOYD EDWARD KERMODE teaches at California State University, Long Beach. His recent publications include lead editor and introductory essay for a special issue of *Journal of Medieval and Early Modern Studies* entitled "Space and Place in Early Modern English Drama" (Winter 2012/13). He is the author of *Aliens and Englishness in Elizabethan Dram* (2009) and editor of *Three Renaissance Usury Plays* (2009).

ERIKA T. LIN is Assistant Professor of English at George Mason University. She is the author of *Shakespeare and the Materiality of Performance* (2012) as well as essays in *Theatre Journal, New Theatre Quarterly*, and various edited collections. She is currently working on a new project exploring the performance dynamics of seasonal festivities and the commercialization of early modern theater.

LAWRENCE MANLEY, William R. Kenan, Jr. Professor of English at Yale University, is the author of *Literature and Culture in Early Modern London*

(1995) and the editor of *The Cambridge Companion to the Literature of London* (2011). With Sally-Beth MacLean, he is the author of *Lord Strange's Men and Their Plays* (forthcoming).

DAVID MANN was, until his retirement, Principal Lecturer in Drama and Theatre Studies at the University of Huddersfield. His publications include *The Elizabethan Player: Contemporary Stage Representations* (1991), *Shakespeare's Women: Performance and Conception* (2008), and articles for the *Huntington Library Quarterly* ("Sir Oliver Owlett's Men: Fact or Fiction?," Autumn 1991), *Theatre Notebook* ("The Roman Mime and Medieval Theatre," XLVI, 1992), *Early Theatre* ("Female Play-going and the Good Woman," 2007, and "Reinstating Shakespeare's Instrumental Music," (forthcoming). A further article, "William Shakespeare and the Masters of Defence," is currently under consideration for publication, and another book, *Shakespeare and Stage Properties*, is almost completed.

ALLISON MACHLIS MEYER is Assistant Professor of English at Assumption College in Worcester, Massachusetts. Her current research focuses on gender and intertextuality in early modern historiography and history plays.

CHARLES PASTOOR is an Associate Professor of English at John Browns University. He has published a number of essays on inset drama in the works of Ben Jonson, Philip Massinger, and others. He is also the co-author of *Historical Dictionary of the Puritans*.

JOHN PITCHER is an Official Fellow of St John's College Oxford, and University Lecturer in English at Oxford University. Among his recent publications are editions of *Cymbeline* (Penguin Shakespeare) and *The Winter's Tale* (Arden Shakespeare). He served as General Editor of the Malone Society for ten years. He is currently completing the four-volume edition of Samuel Daniel's poems and plays for Oxford University Press.

PATRICIA PHILLIPPY is Professor of English Literature and Creating Writing at Kingston University. Her most recent publications is an edition of Elizabeth Russell's writings, which appeared in the *Other Voice in Early Modern Europe* series in 2011. Her current book in progress is a study of post-Reformation funeral monuments in England.

JUNE SCHLUETER is Charles A. Dana Professor Emerita of English at Lafayette College. Her most recent book is *The Album Amirocum and the London of Shakespeare's Time*. From 1983 to 2003 she co-edited *Shakespeare Bulletin*.

SARAH K. SCOTT is Associate Professor and Chair of the Department of English at Mount St. Mary's University in Emmitsburg, Maryland, where she teaches early modern drama. She is author of essays on Marlowe, Dekker, and Middleton and serves as Assistant Editor of the New Variorum Shakespeare *Julius Caesar* and Associate Editor of *Marlowe Studies: An Annual*.

J. K. SMITH is Associate Professor of English at Kansas State University. He is the author of *The Cartographic Imagination in Early Modern England* (2008) and two novels, *Nothing Diseappears* (2004) and *Missing Persons* (2008).

MATTHEW J. SMITH is a Assistant Professor of English at Azusa Pacific University.

ELIZABETH WILLIAMSON currently teaches at The Evergreen State College. She is the author of *The Materiality of Religion in Early Modern English Drama* (2009) and the co-editor (with Jane Hwang Degenhardt) of *Religion and Drama in Early Modern England* (2011). Her work has also appeared in *Borrowers and Lenders, Studies in English Literature, English Literary Renaissance*, and the *Shakespeare International Yearbook*.

JOHN R. ZIEGLER currently holds a Pre-doctoral Teaching Fellowship at Fordham University.

MEDIEVAL
AND
RENAISSANCE
DRAMA
IN
ENGLAND

Articles

Samuel Daniel's Masque *The Vision of the Twelve Goddesses:* Texts and Payments

John Pitcher

*T*HE *Vision of the Twelve Goddesses* was performed in the Great Hall in Hampton Court on the night of Sunday, January 8, 1604. There was considerable excitement about it in the weeks leading up to the performance. It was to be something special commissioned by the new queen, novel and unusual because she and her ladies-in-waiting would be participants rather than spectators; they were to assume roles and then dance, by themselves and with the men of the court who had been watching them. The masque was scheduled for the very end of the Christmas festivities, a high point on which to conclude the first holiday season of the new reign. No doubt it was expected that matters of state would be alluded to in the masque. Ambassadors from friendly and not-so-friendly countries would be there, trying to decipher any elements of foreign policy they could detect in the ceremonies and welcomes they were shown.

To date there has been no overview of the texts of the masque. Joan Rees concluded that the first, surreptitious edition, published in 1604, contained many printing "mistakes of a kind likely to arise from hasty and not very intelligent reading of a roughly written manuscript."[1] She did not discuss where the "roughly written" manuscript came from—a member of the elite audience, perhaps, or one of the court functionaries?—nor the manuscript from which it was copied. Plainly we need to establish, if we can, whether this source manuscript was the one from which Daniel's authorized edition was printed later in the same year. The recent discovery of the Spanish ambassador's description of the masque[2]—which resembles in many respects the authorized text—also needs to be accounted for. How were these three versions related to one another?

The texts, taken together, tell us a lot about the staging of *The Vision of the Twelve Goddesses,* but there is nothing in them about the actors who played the speaking parts, or the numbers of musicians, or the many preparations needed (building and painting the stage furniture, decorating the hall, cutting and finishing the ladies' dresses). However, an account book recording many of these details—including a payment to Daniel for writing the masque—has been located in the National Archives (formerly Public Record Office). This account and the expenditure listed in it have not examined before. They are discussed below in the section "Payments," which includes extracts from the account book.

It may be helpful to summarize what happened in the masque. The action began in darkness, with Night coming from beneath the earth to the cave of her son, Somnus. She asked him to produce a dream vision to please the assembled court in their "slumber," in which they were to see a Temple of Peace with four pillars and the priestess Sybilla. Night retired, and Somnus slept again. In the vision Iris, messenger of the gods, came down from a mountain to tell Sybilla that the Goddesses were about to appear. Iris gave Sybilla a prospective (a kind of telescope) so that she could see and describe the Goddesses as they descended the mountain afar off. This she did. Iris withdrew and the Goddesses advanced towards the temple, in four ranks of three, led by the Three Graces, each carrying a lit white torch. The Graces sang as the Goddesses one by one presented their gifts at the Temple. Sybilla then said what the gifts represented, and the Goddesses danced with one another. They then danced with certain noblemen among the audience, while the Graces sang another song. At the conclusion of these dances, Iris reappeared to announce that the Goddesses were about to leave. After a short dance, they ascended to the top of the mountain where, unseen, they found Queen Anne and her Ladies. The Goddesses took their forms, "delighting to be in the best built Temples of beauty and honour," and then returned with their faces unmasked.

Texts

Very soon after the performance—no more than a couple of weeks—the masque appeared in print in a small quarto pamphlet, a dozen pages of text fronted with the title-page "*THE* | TRUE DISCRIP- | tion of a Royall | *Masque.* | PRESENTED AT HAMP-| ton Court, vpon Sunday night, be- | *ing the eight of Ianuary.* | 1604. | AND | Personated by the Queenes most Excellent | *Majestie, attended by Eleuen* | Ladies of Honour." The text of the masque was acquired surreptitiously by the stationer Edward Allde and sold at his shop near St. Mildred's Church in Cheapside. We know Allde's edition was not authorized because at some point during 1604 Simon Waterson, Daniel's lifelong publisher, issued another text of the masque, in an octavo entitled "THE | VISION OF | the 12. Goddesses, presented in a | Maske the 8. of Ianuary, at | *Hampton* Court: | *By the Queenes most excellent Maiestie,* | *and her Ladies.*"[3]

Waterson's text was the same in outline as Allde's but superior in detail. It also had prefixed to it a letter from Daniel to Lucy Russell, Countess of Bedford (1581–1627), at whose prompting the Queen had chosen him to write the masque. Daniel began the letter, which serves as a preface, by referring to Allde's edition:

> In respect of the vnmannerly presumption of an indiscreet Printer, who without warrant hath divulged the late shewe at Court . . . and the same verie disorderly set forth: I thought it not amisse seeing it would otherwise passe abroad, to the preiudice both of the Maske and the inuention, to describe the whole forme thereof in all points as it was then performed . . .[4]

Daniel's first aim in the Lady Bedford letter was to defend "the inuention," i.e., the subject and design of the masque, against unnamed critics, one of whom was almost certainly Ben Jonson. His larger purpose was to argue against the tyranny of classical precedent, and the misapplication of ancient literature and philosophy (the preface is discussed further below).

The market appeal of a printed text of the masque was that it recorded an exclusive court event. Allde's surreptitious edition was on sale no later than February 2, 1604. This was the date that Edward, Earl of Worcester (c. 1550–1628), who had attended the masque, wrote to Gilbert Talbot, Earl of Shrewsbury (1552–1616) enclosing a copy of the book:

> Whereas youer Lo. saythe youe wear neuer perticulerly advertised of the Maske, I have been at 6d. charge wth you to send youe the booke, wch wyll inform youe better then I can, having noted the names of the Ladyes applyed to eche Goddes . . .[5]

This copy has survived, as one of the three examples of the Allde edition now in the British Library. It has notes written on sigs. B1v and B2 identifying which ladies performed which roles, in what is most likely Lord Worcester's own hand.[6]

The sixpence Lord Worcester paid for the copy, if this was the normal price, would have brought Allde a good profit on the edition, especially if it sold quickly. This was the price often charged for slim quartos of public stage plays, and *The Vision of the Twelve Goddesses* was much shorter than many plays. The book contained only twelve pages of text, plus a title page with a blank verso. In all, the masque consisted of six speeches and two songs, all but one of which (Somnus' speech) were prefaced by a brief scene direction in prose:

Night's speech	(verse, 23 lines, 170 words)
Somnus' speech	(verse, 10 lines, 70 words)
Iris' first speech	(prose, 24 lines, 280 words)
Sybilla's first speech	(prose, 8 lines, 100 words; verse, 50 lines, 370 words)
The Graces' first song	(verse, 18 lines, 100 words)

Sybilla's second speech	(verse, 10 lines, 80 words)
The Graces' second song	(verse, 12 lines, 80 words)
Iris's second speech	(prose, 17 lines, 200 words)

Thus there were only 172 lines spoken or sung in the masque—and fewer than 1,500 words. Four actors between them spoke 1,270 words (Night, 170; Somnus, 70; Iris, 480; Sybilla, 550), while three singers (the Graces) performed two songs amounting to thirty lines or 180 words (word counts are rounded to the nearest 10).

The relative brevity of the masque gives us a clue about where Allde got the manuscript he printed from. On January 15, 1604, a week after the masque was performed, Dudley Carleton, still at Hampton Court (he had been there since mid-December), wrote a long letter to his friend John Chamberlain. In the first part of the letter he described at length the masques he had seen earlier in January, including *The Vision of the Twelve Goddesses*. His account is well known, particularly the passage about the shortness of the costume the Queen wore. Her clothes, he wrote, "were not so much below the knee but that we might see a woman had both feet and legs, which I never knew before." Less familiar is his description of the procession of the Goddesses, which has a neglected but important phrase in it:

> Their demarche was slow and orderly; and first they made their offerings at an altar in a temple which was built on the left side of the hall towards the upper end; *the songs and speeches that were there used I send you here enclosed.*[7]

It is a reasonable guess that the manuscript Carleton enclosed was related to the one of six speeches and two songs that served as printer's copy for the Allde edition. A handwritten text of 172 lines, even with scene directions, would easily fit into three or four pages of a bifolium sheet, of the kind Carleton may well have sent Chamberlain. The question that follows—where did Carleton get his manuscript?—might tempt us to imagine there was a single original source from which a purloined copy was made, from which other clandestine copies were transcribed in succession. Or that the seven actors and singers, or their handler Robert Payne (see Payments below), combined their parts to make the manuscript text Allde printed, which was distinct from the version Carleton sent Chamberlain.

The truth is probably simpler. It is generally accepted that texts of court masques—manuscript copies as well as printed ones—were often available as souvenirs at performances.[8] *The Vision of the Twelve Goddesses* was early in the development of the masque, but it is fair to suppose that even at this date something similar was planned for the performance on January 8, with several copies of the speeches and songs for dignitaries and VIPs. Daniel too may have wanted manuscript copies at the performance, but for another reason—that the audience might be so caught up with what they were watching that they would fail to listen to what was said.[9] Perhaps he arranged for copies of the speeches and songs to be given to select people as a tactful aide-mémoire as well as a souvenir.

Viewed in these terms, printer's copy for the Allde edition may well have been an inaccurate transcript from a souvenir text, and Carleton's copy a souvenir manuscript he somehow got his hands on. Whoever made the Allde copy did something more, though, inserting details that show he saw the performance. For example, in the 1604 authorized text—which Daniel published because Allde forced his hand—one of the scene directions reads

> Sybilla, *hauing receiued this Message, and the Prospective, vseth these words*

but Allde's version adds an eyewitness phrase:

> Sybilla *deckt* as a Nunne, *in blacke vpon White, hauing receiued this Message, and the Prospective, vseth these words.*

Allde's copyist got many details wrong too, but it is because of him that we can be fairly sure, to take one further example, how the three Graces sang their first song. In the authorized text, the final lines of the first stanza are

> For we deserue, we giue, we thanke,
> Thanks, Gifts, Deserts, thus ioyne in ranke

but in Allde, this appears as

> 1. For I deserue. 2. I giue. 3. I thanke:
> *All.* Thanks, guifts, deserts thus joyne in ranck

thus dividing the song between them. It is entirely possible that the authorized text represents the first version of the song Ferrabosco wrote (see Payments below), which was modified in rehearsal, but which Daniel failed, or chose not to alter in the manuscript he sent to Waterson for publication.

There is no reason to suspect that Daniel from the outset intended to publish *The Vision of the Twelve Goddesses* as a printed book. In the years after the masque, he did not reprint the authorized text or include it in any of his three collected editions (1605, 1607, and 1611).[10] After his death, Simon Waterson and John Danyel did reprint it (not without mistakes) in the 1623 *Whole Workes* collected edition,[11] but they were aiming at a complete text of his poetry and drama, irrespective of what he had felt about masques in print. His views were clear enough in the Preface he wrote to his (second and final) masque, *Tethys' Festival,* performed in June 1610:

> For so much as shewes and spectacles of this nature, are vsually registred, among the memorable acts of the time . . . it is expected (according now to the custome) that I, beeing imployed in the busines, should publish a discription and forme of the late Mask . . . in regard to preserue the memorie thereof, and to satisfie their desires, who could haue no other notice, but by others report of what was done. Which I doe not, out of a desire, to be seene in pamphlets, or of forwardnes to shew my inuention therin . . .[12]

Daniel's reluctance to publish *Tethys' Festival* is apparent throughout the Preface. We may be sure that six years earlier, before masque pamphlets had become "the custome," he was just as disinclined, if not more, to see *The Vision of the Twelve Goddesses* in print.

The text Daniel did publish had two parts of differing lengths. The second part was the masque proper, similar in essentials to Allde's version—same action, same speeches, same songs—but without the minor blunders. The Allde text added staging details in places (see above), but the copyist or compositor (or both) completely messed up certain speeches. Somnus, for example, closes his speech like this in the authorized Waterson text

> from this sable *radius* doth proceed
> Nought but confused shewes, to no intent.
> Be this a Temple; there *Sybilla* stand,
> Preparing reuerent Rytes with holy hand,
> And so bright visions go, and entertaine
> Al round about, whilest I'le to sleepe againe.

In Allde this is printed as

> from this sable *Radius* doth proceed
> Nought but confusd darke shewes, to no intent:
> And therefore goe bright visions, entertaine
> All round about, whilst I'le to sleepe againe.[13]

We should think of Waterson's as the correct text rather than a corrected one. It is inconceivable that Daniel sent Waterson a marked up copy of Allde to print from, especially if he had a souvenir manuscript available (see above), or perhaps his own fair draft of the masque.

The first part of the authorized edition—twice the length of the masque—was the prefatory letter to Lady Bedford, written in twenty-three paragraphs, all in prose except for a few quotations in Latin and Italian. In the letter Daniel mixed freely descriptions of the plot and roles (Paragraphs 4–21) with his views on literature, court entertainments, and classical authorities (1–3, 22–23). As we shall see, it is possible he composed the paragraphs at different stages, some probably in parallel with writing the masque:

Paragraph 1	The reason for publishing the masque
Paragraph 2	A description of the "intent and scope of the project"
Paragraph 3	The liberty to choose between mythologies
Paragraph 4	What the Goddesses represent
Paragraph 5	Goddesses brought "figures of their power" to the Temple of Peace
Paragraphs 6–17	Descriptions of the costume and symbolic gift of each Goddess
Paragraph 18	Night came to her son Sleep, "as the Proem to the Vision"
Paragraph 19	Description of how Sleep was dressed and his symbols
Paragraph 20	Iris gave Sybilla a "Prospectiue" to describe the Goddesses
Paragraph 21	The Goddesses entered, preceded by the Graces; gifts and dances
Paragraph 22	Publishing the masque to justify Lady Bedford's choice of him
Paragraph 23	Answer to "Censurers" who overvalue such "Dreames and showes"

Paragraphs 1–3 and 22–23 amount to a short critical essay in which Daniel develops and adds to some of the ideas in his famous *A Defence of Rhyme,* published the year before. It is almost certain he was answering Ben Jonson in particular, who at the performance and afterwards criticized (as he saw it) Daniel's unscholarly and unforceful way of reading the ancients. Jonson also thought Daniel had failed to grasp how powerful an art form the masque might be. The serious and intelligent answers Daniel gave Jonson are what one might expect from him. In Paragraph 3, he drew attention to his own sources—among them Ovid and Ariosto[14]—but his key quotation (not identified before) was from Pico della Mirandola, *Oratio de hominis dignitate.* There were sensible limits to book learning, so as to avoid a slavish regard for classical authority:

*ingenerosum sapere solum ex commentarijs quasi maioru*m *iuenta industriae nostrae via*m *precluserit, quasi in nobis offaeta sit vis naturae, nihil ex se parere*

[It is unbecoming to know only through notebooks and, as though the discoveries of our ancestors had closed the way to our own industry and the power of nature were exhausted in us, to bring about nothing from ourselves].[15]

Daniel concluded the prefatory Bedford letter with a final fling at "captious Censurers," and their overestimate of the masque, by quoting from Seneca,

"*Ludus istis animus, non proficit*" [*Epistulae Morales,* 111:4: "the mind plays with these things, but gains nothing from them"].

The paragraphs answering Jonson appear to have been written after the performance, as were several of Paragraphs 4–21 (Paragraph 19, for instance, where Daniel, presumably because of criticism from Jonson, defended the attributes he had given Somnus).[16] However, it is possible that certain paragraphs—those describing what the Goddesses wore and the gifts they carried, 6–17—were written beforehand. The figure of the Goddess Concordia in Paragraph 13, for instance, is said to be

> in a partie coloured Mantle of Crimson and White (the colours of *England* and *Scotland* ioyned) imbrodered with siluer, hands in hand, with a dressing likewise of partie coloured Roses, a Branch whereof in a wreath or knot she presented.

In the masque, in the second half of the book, the details of Concordia are similar, but many of them are left unglossed:

> NEXT all in partie-coloured Robes appeares,
> In white and crimson, gracefull *Concord* drest
> With knots of Vnion, and in hand she beares
> The happy joyned Roses of our rest.

The question is, what is the relationship between these two passages? Did Daniel write the note in prose in Paragraph 13 to explain (or to supplement) the verses on Concordia in the masque—perhaps for readers of the authorized edition who, not being at the event, wouldn't know otherwise that the "white and crimson" of Concordia's "partie-coloured Robes" represented England and Scotland "ioyned," or that Concordia's mantle had emblematic clasped hands embroidered in silver on it, along with white and red roses? The function of Paragraphs 4–5 and 18–21 looks very similar to this—that is, that Daniel goes over the action of the masque, in the sequence of the six speeches and songs, filling in details, clarifying, and explicating, all for the sake of readers. Surely Paragraphs 6–17 do just this.

This explanation is convincing until we read the description of the masque sent to King Philip III of Spain by his ambassador the Conde de Villamediana, recently discovered in the Archivo General, Simancas, by Cano-Echevarría and Hutchings. The description, in Spanish prose, was an enclosure in a letter Villamediana wrote to Philip describing diplomatic maneuverings leading up the masque (including disputes over protocol) dated January 20, 1604, that is, twelve days after the performance. Villamediana, who could speak no English, evidently had some kind of text of the masque, which his cousin, Juan de Tassis, translated for him. It is possible that the actors supplied this text clandestinely, or that Daniel prepared it for Villamediana as a special favor. Once again, though, the most likely explanation is that it was a VIP souvenir manuscript that de Tassis worked from, adding details in places that he or Villamediana (or both) had noticed in the performance (including, for example, the time that the Goddesses spent dancing). The outline of the action in Villamediana is the same as in both printed texts, surreptitious and authorized, and most of the speeches and songs are visible beneath their summaries in Spanish. A few details are wrong (at one point about the Graces), either because de Tassis misread the English text or because he misremembered the performance.

However, there is one important difference in Villamediana's version, in the account of what the Goddesses wore, and what their costumes and gifts meant. In both the surreptitious and authorized versions, Sybilla looks through a prospective and describes the Goddesses in turn in four-line stanzas. In Villamediana the sibyl looks through a prospective in the same way, but this time her account of the Goddesses is not as they are described in the masque text but as they are in Daniel's prefatory letter, Paragraphs 6–17. Moreover, alongside each Goddess is written the name of the real Lady who performed the role in the masque. In the case of Concordia, for instance, Villamediana has:

| Concordia: the Countess of Nottingham | With a crimson and white mantle embroidered with figures of hands intertwined to signify the union of England, and would present a white and red rose bush.[17] |

Villamediana's description appears to be a composite, largely drawn from a text of the masque like the one later used for the Waterson printed version,[18] but also from replacement manuscript pages (similar to Paragraphs 6–17) listing the Goddesses, their outfits, and the Ladies who played them.

We can only guess how this came about. One possibility—though there are others—is that Villamediana did have a souvenir manuscript but asked Daniel to supplement the section on the Goddesses with fuller notes—who performed the roles and what the symbols on their dresses signified. When Daniel later came to write the prefatory letter to the authorized edition, perhaps he incorporated the notes, removing the Ladies' names (i.e., Paragraphs 6–17), to explain things to a new audience, of readers.

* * *

Villamediana's account, although it adds significantly to what we know about the masque, is not an infallible guide. There are mistakes in it, and what he (or de Tassis) saw and wrote down needs a proper historical context. A telling instance of this is the prospective or optical instrument (a hand prop) that Iris gave Sybilla.

All but one of the twenty-eight characters in the masque carried an object (a hand prop or torch) at some point in the action. Each Goddess carried her symbolic gift down from the Mountain and left it in the Temple of Peace. The three Graces and nine Torchbearers who accompanied them carried torches in the procession and then probably held these aloft to give light while the Goddesses danced. Of the four speaking parts, Somnus had a white wand or rod made of horn in his right hand, and a black rod (or *"radius"*) in his left. His mother, Night, was the only character not to carry anything, though she did wear a pair of substantial black wings.

The priestess Sybilla's role (the third speaking part) was to receive the symbolic gifts in the Temple, but also to describe the Goddesses as they gathered together supposedly far off on the Mountain before their descent. In terms of the Hall at Hampton Court, Sybilla was at one end, close to the Temple, and to the royal dais and thrones, looking up the long hall towards the screen end where the Queen and her Ladies, the Goddesses, paused as a group, in four ranks of three, on the pathway down. So that Sybilla could see them at this imaginary great distance, Iris, goddess of the rainbow and "messenger of Juno" (the fourth speaking role), descended from the Mountain to give Sybilla (in Daniel's words) "a Prospectiue, wherin she might behold the Figures of their Deities, and thereby describe them." Iris tells Sybilla "take here this Prospectiue, and therein note and tell what thou seest: for well mayest thou there obserue their shadow." To this Sybilla responds—drawing attention to the instrument—"But what Prospectiue is this? or what shall I herein see? Oh admirable Powers! what sights are these?"[19]

Editors have not settled what this "Prospectiue" was. Clearly it was another hand prop, portable and light enough for Iris and Sybilla to carry. Law thought it was a "scroll" in which Sybilla read a description of the Goddesses and the "symbolical meaning of their several attires."[20] Rees, more convincingly, glossed it as "a spy-glass, or perhaps a magic mirror in which distant or future events could be seen."[21] In Villamediana's account in Spanish, Iris gave Sybilla a "prospective mirror" ["espejo prospectiuvo"] where

> (not being permitted to contemplate the goddesses being present) she could see at her pleasure everything that was to happen, and looking in the mirror ["espejo"], the Sybil related the name of the goddesses, their costumes, figures and the blessings they brought with them.

From this, Cano-Echevarría and Hutchings conclude that since "the telescope had yet to be invented," Iris's prospective was undoubtedly "a mirror, and not any other type of perspective device."[22]

At the date of the masque, according to the *OED,* the noun "prospective" had several meanings, among them, the "art of drawing in perspective" or a "view in perspective" (*n.* 2a). It could also be a synonym for a "prospect," that is, a scene or landscape (*n.* 3a). However, its primary meaning was a device that "allows one to see objects or events not immediately present" (*n.* 1a). The *OED* shows that this meaning intrigued Daniel (four of its earliest citations are from his works). In 1585, for instance, in *The Worthy Tract,* his translation of Paolo Giovio's book on imprese, he wrote that "Sunne beames passing through a peece of Christall, beeing so strengthened through their vniting, according to the nature of the Prospectiue . . . burne euery obiect." Twenty years later when he used the word figuratively, in a dedication to the Earl of Hertford, he still had the device in mind. I must "judge," he declared, "as my selfe do stand looking thorow the prospectiue of mine owne imagination."

In the masque, although the prospective had a mirror of some kind, it was still most likely a telescope—but not the "Dutch" refracting telescope (a tube with lenses at each end) that Galileo perfected in 1609 and thereafter. Rather, it was some kind of early reflecting telescope that combined a curved mirror with a lens, where the viewer looked into the mirror to see an image (sometimes the lens and mirror were built into a box, with an eyepiece). The telescopic mirror was the subject of sustained optical speculation in England, though it is a matter of debate whether an instrument of this kind was ever made to work. The theory of the reflecting telescope was in print, however, in Latin, Italian, and English, and the Elizabethan nobility knew about it (the more practically minded ones at least).[23] The mirror instrument Sybilla used to view the Goddesses at long-range was only a model or hand prop (like Pallas's lance and shield), so whether it actually worked was unimportant. The prospective was another symbolic gift, like those the Goddesses left in the Temple, which celebrated the peace and virtue the new reign had brought about, and what was to come. It is worth noting that Queen Anne's father and mother, King Frederick and Queen Sophia of Denmark and Norway, were major patrons of the astronomer Tycho Brahe and his famous observatory and laboratory.[24] Perhaps Daniel intended Iris's telescopic mirror to hint that new scientific knowledge and devices would be of interest to the Queen as well as traditional book learning and the arts.

Payments

Modern literary and historical scholars, according to a recent writer, "do not have very much information about the economics of Queen Anne's court." This is because, the writer explains, the Public Record Office holds

> only about thirty pages out of Anne of Denmark's accounts, relating to the year 1614–15: because her household was dissolved on her death, her accounts, unlike those of the king's household, were not automatically preserved (E101/437/8). [The 1614–15 account] . . . confirms the Queen's financial independence: it gives a large

part of her wages bill, and also details her income from fee-farms, which was nearly £16,000 for that year. Unfortunately, it does not include her wardrobe account for the period; though some textile-related bills turn up in the section on extraordinary expenditures . . .[25]

In point of fact more of Queen Anne's accounts have survived than this, at least for the first years she was in England. Among her household accounts for 1604–5, for instance, there are payments made to "Marie Mountjoy Tyrewoman" and "William Cookesberrie Haberdasher." Charles Nicholl uncovered these in the National Archives, TNA (PRO) SC6/JASI/1646, fo.29, when he was looking into the life of Marie Mountjoy (c.1567–1606), who at one point, famously, was Shakespeare's landlady in Silver Street in London.[26] Marie and her husband Christopher had their home and workshop in Silver Street where they made wigs and ornate headdresses for women of quality. The payment to Marie in the Queen's account would have been for the elaborate head-tires the Mountjoys had created for her out of silver wire and twisted metal thread—of the kind we see her wearing in portraits c. 1605.[27]

The prefix to the PRO manuscript, "SC" for "Special Collections," indicates that this is a gathering of miscellaneous items from various royal departments. Most of the records in SC6 appear to relate to crown lands in different parts of the country. For instance, SC6/JASI/565 contains Lincolnshire accounts, while SC6/JASI/1246 deals with collegiate, chantry, and concealed lands in Yorkshire. At some point the records, largely dealing with land revenues, were arranged by counties, and then, probably artificially, by date. The payments to Marie Mountjoy and William Cooksberry in SC6/JASI/1646 may have been mistakenly copied from the original bills into the SC6 manuscripts for the same period. Alternatively, entries like these— recording settlements of bills—were brought together with land revenues because the Queen's household and entertainment expenses (at least some of them) were being paid out of these revenues. On its title page, SC6/JASI/1646 is described as "The Declaration of the Accompt of Sir George Carew" for "Anglia" for the year "Anno iii^{tio} 1605." The first ten folios list rents and revenues from the Queen's manors in England, followed by folios specifying payments to members of her household and others, including Mountjoy and Cooksberry.

Carew's 1604–5 account has perhaps survived by fluke, and this may well be true of the larger collection of payments in another manuscript in the National Archives, TNA (PRO) LR 6/154/9. This too was the account book of the Queen's Vice-Chamberlain, Sir George Carew (see Extracts below). As its prefix indicates, this account should be concerned with Land Revenues. LR is normally the classification of the audit accounts of receivers of crown lands, but LR 6/154/9, though it does begin with rents and revenues from the Queen's manors, goes on to list many entries relating to her payments and expenses in the first years of King James's reign, 1603-4. It is possible that a clerk simply copied the expenditure in the wrong place, and that when this was discovered the entries were transferred to a more suitable account, such as household and wardrobe payments, E101 (unfortunately the roll covering these dates seems not have survived). More likely, at the beginning of James's reign there was some notion—as there appears to have been with SC6/JASI/1646 and other SC6 accounts—that the Queen's expenditure should be in the same place as the records of her revenue.[28] But however it came about, LR 6/154/9, because of its classification, seems to have escaped the notice of literary scholars.[29]

The payments in LR 6/154/9 are of different kinds and amounts. James Spottiswood, the Queen's Sub-Almoner, was paid by warrant of December 7, 1603 "for soe much by hym to be distributed vnto the poore in her ma^{tes} progresse from wilton vnto Hampton Courte by direccion from her ma^{tes} Lo: Chamberlaine" (fo.26). Neil Nelson, "sometime" the Queen's coachman, received a hundred crowns for his service, "by vertue of her ma^{tes} warrant" of January 27, 1604 (fo.26), while George Hooker, gentleman, was reimbursed for the cost of a "Standard or greate Cheste for her ma^{tes} Treasure" that he acquired in Salisbury on September 8, 1603 (fo.28). William Bell, clerk of the "Jewell Coffers," received wages for looking after the Queen's jewels "at the removing of the Courte to divers places" (fo.30),[30] and Robert Hughes was paid for making and delivering farthingales to "thoffice of her ma^{tes} Roabes" from July 1603 to March 1604 (fo.33).

Rather better-known names appear here and there. An entry on fo.15 records payments for wages and livery to the lutenist and composer Daniel Bacheler (1572–1619), a Groom of the Queen's Privy Chamber. Bacheler also received £13.3s for the cost of a new viol and case along with the mending of another viol and buying a music book and lute strings. The viols, strings and book were "allowed and paid" by a warrant of March 4, 1604 signed by Robert Cecil (fo.28)—which is intriguing given Cecil's keen interest in music, musicians, and musical instruments.[31] There are records of wages paid to ordinary Grooms of the Chamber—Percival Platt, David Penry, and Rees Jones for example (fo.30)—and to Grooms of the Privy Chamber, including Thomas Cardell with two of his servants for "attendance" on the Queen "in her progresse" in the West Country in September and October 1603 (fo.29). John Florio, by this date also a Groom of the Privy Chamber—he was teaching the Queen Italian—was paid an annual wage of £50 (fo.16).

Costs and payments like these are what we would expect of any royal court. In 1603, for the first time for half a century and more, the English had to get used to paying for two courts, that of the Queen as well as the King's. In terms of managing expenditure, the key officers in the Queen's new household were Robert, Baron Sidney (1563–1626), Lord High Chamberlain and

Surveyor General; Sir George Carew (1555–1629), Vice Chamberlain and Receiver General (one of whose general responsibilities as Receiver would have been the account book LR 6/154/9); and William Fowler (1560/1– 1612), Secretary and Master of Requests. Lord Sidney is often alluded to in the entries in LR 6/154/9, as is Audrey, Lady Walsingham (c.1570–1631), who shared the keepership of the Queen's Wardrobe with her husband Sir Thomas Walsingham (1560/1–1630). A fairly typical example of payment concerned two bills presented by the hosier Hugh Griffiths "for Silck Stocking*es*" made for the Queen in 1603. Griffiths had delivered the stockings in batches to Lady Walsingham who vouched that the bills were correct. The bills were then "viewed and rated" by the Queen's officers of the Wardrobe and finally "allowed by the Lo: Sidney and others of her highnes Counsell" (fo.34).

Among the everyday elite payments in LR 6/154/9—for farthingales, silk stockings, and servants" wages—there is a particular set of costs incurred in making and performing the masque *The Vision of the Twelve Goddesses.* The extracts printed below are taken from half a dozen of the manuscript's large folio pages (see below pp. 36–38). The entries cover all aspects of the masque, from writing it and building and painting the stage furniture (a mountain, a temple, and a cave) to the songs and the costumes worn by the boy actors and torchbearers. The bills show payments for satin and other fabrics, for fans and plumes of feathers, for buskins, and for embroidery. Daniel himself is named, as are a dozen others—gentlemen, craftsmen, theater people and suppliers, Marie Mountjoy and the haberdasher William Cooksberry among them. There were seven boy actors and twenty-nine musicians, unfortunately none of them named.

The extracted entries are rich in information about the masque, but they are not a comprehensive list of everything that was paid for and noted in the account. Extract (2) for instance tells us that the embroiderer Christopher Shaw was paid £50 in part payment for the work he did "about her ma[tes] maske." This entry was canceled (vertical strokes were drawn across it), but in another entry, Extract (8), among a list of payments for embroidery from August 1603 to February 1604, covered by four "severall Bills," there is one for the large sum of £346.16s.8d, interlined as "for her ma*tes* maske." Was the £50 paid and set against the £346.16s.8d, or did the total grow as smaller embroidery bills for the masque, not noted separately in the account (one of them for £50), were totted up and presented as a single amount? Cross-referencing between entries left much to be desired, and some bills may well have been duplicated.

There is another problem with entries where suppliers presented bills for goods or services done over a period of time (sometimes six months), in the middle of which there is an item charged for the masque. The charge for it, half-buried in the entry, may have been overlooked and not included in the extracts.[32] On one or two occasions, where a bill only adds an extra detail about the type of purchases made, this has not been transcribed in the extracts. An instance of this is the entry listing bills presented by Abraham Speckart and his wife Dorothy for high-quality fabrics, including eighteen yards of "black sticht cloth*es* florisht wth gold and silver." The Speckarts were also asking for payment for "Tiffanie"—fine transparent silk or perhaps muslin—provided "for her Ma:*tes* maske" (fo.34). This is the same fine material that Richard French supplied for the same purpose (Extract [7]). The Speckart entry would certainly be needed in a thoroughgoing analysis of the Queen's wardrobe but not here. The aim in the extracts is simpler—to show, in headline terms, who supplied the key elements in *The Vision of the Twelve Goddesses* and what they were paid. The overall cost of making and furnishing the masque is touched on below.

Perhaps the biggest surprise in the entries is the part that James Kirton had as "Director & orderer of the work*es* for her ma*tes* maske" (Extract [1]). Kirton (1559–1620) is not someone students of the Jacobean masque will be familiar with; indeed there is no sign he was involved in any other court entertainments before or after *The Vision of the Twelve Goddesses*. The entries show that his task was to finance and manage the building and staging of the masque, for which he was paid £20 ([1], [3] and [5]). We need to recall that this was a full year earlier than *The Masque of Blackness*, "invented" and written by Ben Jonson but performed against backdrops devised by Inigo Jones. *The Vision of the Twelve Goddesses* had nothing like Jones's sets, proscenium arch, and shifting scenery.

Kirton was given his job by the Queen because he was a proven administrator, as the in-house solicitor of Edward Seymour, first Earl of Hertford (1540–1621).[33] The Queen's connection with Lord Hertford is easy to explain. Her two favorites from the moment she arrived in England were Lucy Russell, Countess of Bedford (see above), and Frances Seymour, Countess of Hertford (1578–1639), the latter Lord Hertford's wife. At the beginning of September 1603 the King and Queen stayed with Lord and Lady Hertford at their home, Tottenham Lodge, the Seymour mansion in Savernake Forest in Wiltshire. While they were there, Lord Hertford summoned Samuel Daniel and his brother John (the lute composer), to entertain the visitors, presumably with music and songs or perhaps an interlude. It was James Kirton who arranged for the brothers to be fetched, and for his close friend Samuel Daniel to be paid £4 "for rewarde."[34] A month later the Queen already had it in mind to present a masque at some point in the winter.[35] Her favorites Lady Bedford and Lady Hertford would both be in the masque, and the servants they personally vouched for—the Queen had met them at Tottenham Lodge—would be given the plum commissions, Daniel to write it, Kirton to supervise its preparation and to arrange the necessary short-term finance.

We learn in Extract (1) that Daniel was paid £40 for "his paines & chardges attending the busines of her ma^tes said maske by the space of vj weekes"—which means, if this is correct, that he was at Hampton Court by the beginning of the fourth week of November 1603, that is, three weeks before Lady Arbella Stuart arrived there and wrote that the Queen intended to "make a mask" at Christmas.[36] As we have seen, the text of the masque was very short—only 172 lines, including the songs—but Daniel may have had to oversee the musicians' practicing and the rehearsal of the speaking parts, possibly with Kirton in attendance. The Master of the Revels Edmund Tilney (1535/6–1610) was at Hampton Court at this date, for two months either side of Christmas, doing something similar—overseeing the "rehersalles" and "reforming" of plays brought from the public stage[37] (Tilney's connection with Daniel after the masque is touched on below). The composer Alfonso Ferrabosco the younger (c.1575–1628), who made the songs and had "imploym^t" in the mask, was paid 100 shillings (i.e., £5).[38] He and Daniel may have collaborated in organizing the music (for the procession of the Goddesses, the singing of the Graces, and the dances).

Daniel, Kirton, and Ferrabosco aside, the payments in the extracts were made to two groups of people—craftsmen and suppliers, and performers. The most senior craftsman mentioned in the entries was the carpenter Wiliam Portington, who received 40 shillings "for his paines taken in Directing & seing the said Carpenters busines done about the said maske." Portington, the King's master carpenter, was in demand everywhere for his work (he made the oak paneling and carved screen at Knole in Kent for Thomas, first Earl of Dorset). In 1608 Jonson acknowledged that it was Portington who had made Inigo Jones's scenic machinery ("the motions") work in the *Masque of Beauty*. In Extract (1) the phrase "Directing & seing . . . the busines done" suggests that the 40 shillings was payment for supervising the carpenters. Portington's charge for actually building the stage furniture (noted in a later entry, "the Temple, Rock, and other necessaries," Extract [5]) was £37.20d. The "Rock" or Mountain in particular must have been a very large structure—it took up the full width of the hall at the gallery or screen end and rose well above the gallery into the hammer-beam roof.[39] George Hearne, the craftsman mentioned in Extract (4), charged £73 "for the painting of the frame & other thinges," a considerable sum but one that reflects the work that had to be done in painting and decorating the Mountain (most likely "the frame"), the Temple of Peace (with four pillars and a cupola big enough to hold several musicians), and the Cave of Somnus or Sleep.

Six of the seven other tradespeople in the entries were concerned, in one way or another, with the Ladies' clothes and dressings for their hair. It is well known that the materials for the masque costumes, at least some of them, came from the finest dresses and robes in Queen Elizabeth's wardrobe.[40] These would have needed cutting, reshaping, and tailoring, which is presumably what "James Duncane," the Queen's master tailor, did, and for which he was paid £8.8s.6d (Extract [6]). The most expensive job was the embroidery done by Christopher Shawe, £346.16s.8d ([2] and [8]). In the masque each of the twelve Goddesses wore a mantle, with designs embroidered on it, appropriate to the deity they represented. As Pallas, the goddess of defensive wars, the Queen (in Daniel's words) "was attyred in a blew mantle, with a siluer imbrodery of al weapons and engines of war." In the same way, Lady Hertford was Diana, "in a greene Mantle imbrodered with siluer halfe Moones, and a croissant of pearle on her head," while Lady Bedford was Vesta "in a white Mantle imbrodered with gold-flames."[41] The designs were probably embroidered in gold and silver thread, together with pearls and semiprecious stones—no doubt the reason Shawe charged so much. The insides of the Goddesses' mantles were lined with tiffany or silk gauze, striped with silver (Extract [7]).

It is clear with Shaw that his payment was for materials and work done on all the Goddesses' costumes in the masque, not just the Queen's. This was probably true as well of the "divers ffanes & plumes of fethers" supplied by the haberdasher Cooksberry for £11.16s.8d (Extract [11]), and perhaps also the payment to Mistress Rogers, "the Tyrewoman," who charged 77 shillings and sixpence ([5]), presumably for the headtires, wigs, and hairpieces worn by the Goddesses. As Pallas, the Queen wore something very different, specially made for her by Marie Mountjoy, "an helmett" [10])—what Daniel describes as "a helmet-dressing on her head." In Dudley Carleton's words, she "had a pair of buskins [open-toed lace-up boots] set with rich stones, a helmet full of jewels, and her whole attire embossed with jewels of several fashions."[42] The buskins themselves were relatively cheap at 14s, made by the shoemaker Thomas Wilson ([12]). To complement her outfit, the Queen carried a "Launce & target [a small shield]," which Kirton paid for as a separate item ([5]), but there is no indication of who made them. The seventh tradesman in the account, the draper "Edward fferres" ([9]) presented three bills for fine Holland linen "and other parcells of wares." It is possible these fabrics were for costumes or clothes (noblemen certainly wore Holland linen), but the payment of £51.16s.10d for January 3, 1604 indicates a different use, "to furnish the hall for her ma¹es maske," suggesting decoration of some kind, possibly to embellish or to conceal the scaffolding on which the spectators sat in tiers, or to provide material for seating and cushions.

There were twenty-nine musicians in the performers' group. These were employed, according to the account, "in the Rock, the Temple, and for Dauncinge" (Extract [1]). The phrasing here appears to indicate the three locations in the Hall where they played. Dudley Carleton wrote that "the one end [of the Hall] was made into a rock [i.e., the Mountain] and, in several places, the waits [i.e., musicians playing wind instruments] placed; in attire like Savages." Carleton mistook their outfits—they were dressed as satyrs—perhaps because they sat half-concealed in hollows and holes in the supposed mountainside.[43] A second group of musicians (Daniel describes them as "the Consort Musicke") were hidden in the cupola of the Temple of Peace, which was positioned to one side at the opposite end of the Hall. The Rock and Temple musicians between them in sequence provided the accompaniment when the Goddesses moved in procession down from the Rock and along the Hall to present their gifts in the Temple. A guess at their numbers (twelve satyrs possibly and an ensemble of six in the cupola) suggests there might have been up to a dozen performers who provided the third segment of music of viols and lutes for the dances, playing from one side of the Hall, seated beneath (or alongside) the tiered spectators.

The other performers in the account were theater people. From Extract (1) we learn that seven "Boyes Actors" earned a total of 70 shillings for "theire paines" in the masque. In (3) Thomas Kendall asked for payment of £44.13s.10d, in a bill "entituled the Bill for the Torchbearers" for "the making of Dressings and other necessaries for the Children of her ma^{tes} maske." In (5) Robert Payne presented two bills amounting to £4.3s "for his chardge in bringing to the Courte those boyes wch were speakers & for theire diett and lodging during theire attendance." The masque had four speaking parts (Night, Somnus, Sybilla, and Iris) and three singing parts (the Graces), so it is almost certain the seven boy actors played these roles. Thomas Kendall (c.1563–1608) was a haberdasher and one of the five members of a new partnership formed in April 1602 that put on plays at the Blackfriars Theatre performed by the company of boy players, The Children of the Queen's Chapel Royal.[44] The presence of Kendall in the entries is a sure sign that the boy actors in the masque belonged to this company. The statement of charges he presented, "the Bill for the Torchbearers," evidently covered costumes and wigs worn by the speakers and singers (six of whom played female characters), but also, it appears, the outfits "and other necessaries" of the Torchbearers. There were nine of these, dressed, as Carleton put it, as "pages in white satin loose gowns, set with stars of gold; and their torches of white virgin wax gilded."[45] In the procession down from the Mountain, the three Graces led the way "in siluer Robes with white Torches," followed by the Goddesses, similarly in threes. Between "euery ranke of Goddesses," there marched," in Daniel's words, "three Torch-bearers in the like seuerall colours, their heads and Robes all dect with Starres."[46]

The Torchbearers neither spoke nor sang, so they weren't among "those boyes wch were speakers" whom Robert Payne brought to Hampton Court and housed and fed. It is possible the Torchbearers really were pages, but more likely they were additional boys from the Children of the Chapel, paid for (perhaps on a casual basis) under Kendall's "Bill for the Torchbearers." It is intriguing that in the Kendall entry, the payment is said to be "for the Children of her ma^{tes} maske," almost as if this were an established company, with the Queen as patron. Perhaps the clerk who wrote it (in January 1604) had in mind that a new acting company was just then being formed, out of the disbanded Children of the Chapel, with Kendall and Payne (d. 1623) as two of its shareholders. This was the Children of the Queen's Revels, granted a royal patent on February 4, 1604 (the company's license was made out a little earlier, on January 31).[47]

Daniel later claimed that it was through his efforts that Kendall and Payne and their partners obtained the patent. His own reward was the unusual stipulation in the patent that the new company should only present plays—either before the Queen herself or on the public stage—with "the approbation and allowaunce of Samuell Danyell" whom it was the Queen's pleasure "to appoynt for that purpose." This made Daniel the company's licenser, an innovation that encroached on the office of Edmund Tilney, the Master of the Revels, whose job it was to license public stage plays. As we saw, Tilney was at Hampton Court at the date of the masque and the creation of the company. Presumably this was when he agreed (or was obliged to agree) to the new post for Daniel. For the first year or so, the arrangement may have provided Daniel with a small income, but after that his association with the company was disastrous. He was still caught up in a lawsuit with the shareholders as late as May 1609, and it is more than likely that it was the Children of the Queen's Revels that put on his controversial play, *The Tragedy of Philotas*, which nearly ruined him.[48]

The entries and payments in LR 6/154/9 help to fill in our picture of *The Vision of the Twelve Goddesses*—how much music there was and who performed the speaking roles—but they do not tell us what the masque cost as a whole. Later in 1604, in December when probably all the bills had been presented, the Privy Council estimated that the cost of the next Christmas masque (were it to happen) would be £4,000.[49] No matter how we count up the masque payments in LR 6/154/9 the total is nowhere as much as that. This must be because many of the charges simply were not entered in this account. One omission in particular makes the point. On December 23, two weeks before the performance, Sir Thomas Edmonds wrote from Hampton Court to Gilbert, Earl of Shrewsbury (see above), reporting the plans to have two masques, the "younge Lordes and chief Gentlemen of one parte, and the Queene and her Ladyes of the other parte." And because "there is use of invention therein," Edmondes explained,

> speciall choice is made of M[r.] Sanford to direct the order and course of the Ladyes, which is an occasion to staie him here till that busyness be donne.[50]

This was Hugh Sanford (d. 1607), formerly tutor to William Herbert, Earl of Pembroke (1580–1630). Sanford, "learned in all arts, sciences, knowledge, humane and divine," was evidently chosen because of his Pembroke connections at Wilton House[51]—where the King and Queen had stayed in August

1603, not long before their visit to Lord and Lady Hertford's home nearby in Savernake Forest (see above). Sanford's part in the preparations for the Queen's masque was either as director in charge of everything—"the order and course of the Ladies [masque]"—or as the person who supervised how the Ladies marched and danced within the masque [their "order and course"]. Either way, it was an important role, given to someone of the rank of Kirton and Daniel. Yet it appears there is no mention of any payment to Sanford in LR 6/154/9. Unless one is found—with Sanford's name entered but horribly misspelled—one can only assume that he was not paid for his service (which is unlikely) or that his payment passed through some other account, now either lost or unexamined.

* * *

Extracts

Extracts relating to the masque *The Vision of the Twelve Goddesses* from the account book of Sir George Carew, Vice-Chamberlain and Receiver General of Anne of Denmark, 24 June 1603 to Michaelmas 1604, TNA (PRO) LR 6/154/9.

(1), fo. 26; (2) and (3), fo. 27; (4) and (5), fo. 28; (6), fo. 33; (7), (8) and (9), fo. 34; (10) and (11), fo. 36; (12), fo. 37

(1) James Kirton gent Director & orderer of the workes for her ma^{tes} maske at Hampton Courte on Sondaie the viijth of Januarie 1603 for soe much money by to him Ree de*l*i*v*ered, as p*ar*cell of ccxliij^{li} xvj^s ij^d by vertue of A warrante signed by her hignes bearing date the xxth daie of Ianuarie 1603 & heereafter in the title of ex*tra*ordinarie paym^{tes}. likewise advouched aswell for him selfe as divers others hereafter menc*i*oned viz for m^r Samuell Daniell for his paines & chardges attending the busines of her ma^{tes} said maske by the space of vj week*es* xl^{li} The said James Kirton for his travaile & paines about the said maske xx$^{li.}$ The musicc*i*ons imploied in the Rock, the Temple, and for Dauncinge in the said maske being in number xxix$^{tie:}$ xx$^{li.}$ Alphonso fferabosco for making the song*es* and his imploym^t in the said maske cs. vij Boyes Actors in the said maske for theire paines lxxs & for willi*a*m Portington m^r Carpenter for his paines taken in Directing & seing the said Carpenters busines done about the said maske xls. heere allowed and paid by vertue of the said warrante seene & examined & nowe called in & remaining among the remembranc*es* of this Accompt amounting in all to ^{xx}iiij x^{li} x^s

(2) [*left margin*] this is to be sett of in Sup. Confession.
Christofer Shawe Imbroderer for soe much money by him received of this Accomptant by waie of Imprest and [in] parte of payment for work*es* & Im-

broderies to be done by him about her ma^(tes) maske & heere allowed to this Accomptant by warrant vnder the hand of the right ho:^(ble) Roberte Lo: Sidney & william ffowler esquire two of her ma^(tes) Councell dated the xxxth of Decembre 1603 together wth thacq^(tes) of the said Christofer Shawe seene & examined & nowe called in and remaininge wth the rest of the remembrances of this Accompt in the Bagge of the particulers thereof above menconed L^(li)

(3) Thomas Kendall for the making of Dressings and other necessaries for the Children of her ma^(es) maske as appeareth by his bill of the particulers therof entituled the Bill for the Torchebearers signed by the said Thomas Kendall amounting to the some of xliij^(li) xiij^s x^d & heere allowed and paid ⌈as followeth⌉ viz to the said Thomas Kendall by waie of imprest by warrant from the Lo Sidney & william ffowler esquire ⌈two of her ma^(tes) Counsell⌉ dated the xxxth of Decembre 1603 x^(li) and to James Kyrton gent as parcell of ccxliij^(li) xvj^s ij^d by him rec by vertue ⌈of⌉ a warrante signed by her ma^(tie) bearinge date the xxth daie of Ianuarie 1603 xxxiij^(li) xiij^s iiij^(d.) In all as appeareth by the said warrantes & theire acq^(tes) nowe called in and remaining as aforesaid xliij^(li) xiij^s iiij^d

(4) [*margin*] Extraordinarie paymentes paid to
George Hearne Painter for the painting of the frame & other thinges about her ma^(tes) maske as appeareth by his bill of the particulars therof entituled the painters Bill signed by the said George Hearne amounting to the some of Lxxiij^(li) & heere allowed & paid as heareafter followeth viz to the said George Hearne by waie of imprest by warrant from the Lo: Sidney & william ffouler esquire dated the xxxth of Decembre 1603 x^(li.) And to thabove named James Kirton gent as parcell of the said Some of ccxliij^(li) xvj^s ij^d by him Rec by vertue of the warrant above menc*i*oned Lxiij^(li.) In all as appeareth by the said warrantes & theire acq^(tes) called in and rem*aining* as aforesaid   LXXiij^(li)

(5) ⌈The said⌉ James Kirton gent who had the Directing and ordering of the woorkes in the aforesaid maske for soe much money by him Rec, as parcell of the ⌈fore⌉ said Some of ccxliij^(li) xvj^s ij^d aswell for him selfe as for divers others according to theire Bills of the particulers therof seene & examined viz for m:^(ris) [*blank*] Rogers the Tyrewoman her bill amounting to Lxxvij^s vj^(d.) Roberte Payne for his chardge in bringing to the Courte those boyes w^(ch) were speakers & for theire diett and lodging during theire attendance as appeareth by his two bills amounting to iiij^(li) iij^(s.) The said James Kirton for the Launce & targett vsed by the Queenes ma:^(tie) & for the Satines habittes & other necessaries for the said maske as appeareth by his bill vnder his hand xj.^(li) x^(s.) viij^(d.) William Portington m^r Carpenter for the making of the Temple, Rock, and other necessaries meete for her ma^(es) ⌈said⌉ maske at Hampton Courte as appeareth by his bill vnder his hand amounting to xxxvij^(li) xx^(d.) All w^(ch) said Somes of money are heere allowed and paid by vertue of ma^(tes) warrante above menc*i*oned ⌈bearing date the xxth of Ianuarie1603⌉ and doe ⌈heere⌉ amount to ⌈the Some of⌉ lvj^(li) xij^s x^d

(6) James Duncane m^r Tayler to the Queenes Ma:^tie for his workmanshippe and makinge of divers Roabes for her hignes. . . . [*including*] for her ma^*tes* maske at *Christ*emas 1603 viij^li viij^s vj^d . . .

(7) Richarde ffrench Haberdasher for divers p*a*rcells of ware . . . for her ma^*tes* vse . . . [*from 26 July 1603 to 20 March 1604, including*] the third of Ianuarie 1603 for Tiffanie stript [*i.e.* striped] wth silver to line mantles for her ma^*tes* maske xxiiij^li xii^s . . .

(8) Christopher Shawe Imbroderer for divers p*a*rcells of ⌈work of⌉ imbroderie by him done for her ma:^*tes* ⌈vse &⌉ s^ervice as appeareth by iiij^or severall Bills thereof vouched ~~and recevd by~~ ⌈by⌉ the La: Walsingh*a*m and allowed by the right honorable the Lo Sidney and others of her ma^*tes* Counsell . . . [*including*] the iiijth of Ianuarie 1603 ⌈for her ma^*tes* maske⌉ CCCiiij^xxvi^li xvi^s viii^d . . .

(9) Edward fferres Linen drap*er* for Holland and other p*a*rcells of wares by him delivered for her ma^*tes* service as appeareth by his iij bills vouched by the La: Walsingham viewed and rated by th*o*fficers of her ma^*tes* Roabes & allowed by the said Lo: Sidney and others of her ma^*tes* Counsell . . . [*including*] the third of Ianuarie 1603 to furnish the hall for her ma^*tes* maske lj^li xvjs xd . . .

(10) Marie mountioye ~~of London~~ Tyrewoman for an helmett for her Ma:^tie, and divers Tryminges for the La: in ⌈of⌉ her ma:^*tes* maske at Twelfetide 1603 as by her bill vouched by the La: Walsingh*a*m signed and allowed by the Lo: Sidney and two others of her hignes Counsell maie appeare LIX^li. wch bill is now called in seene and examined ⌈&⌉ rem*a*ine as aforesaid together wth a warrant signed by iiij^or of her ma^*tes* said Counsell dated the vijth of August 1604 for the paym^t of xviij^li xiij^s vij^d in p*a*rte of payment of the said Some and an acq:^*tes* of the said marie mountioy for the re:^t of the same in p*a*rte of paym^t as aforesaid besides xl^li vij^s v^d yet vnp*a*id due vnto her xviij^li xiij^s vij^d

(11) Willi*a*m Cookesberie ~~of London~~ Haberdasher for divers ffanes & plumes of fethers by hym delivered to the La: Walsingh*a*m and the La: Carey[52] viz the third of Ianuarie 1603 [*for the masque*] xj^li xvj^s viij^d . . .

(12) Thomas Wilson Shomaker for Shooes pantoffles[53] & Buskins . . . for her ma^*tes* vse & service at sondrie tymes . . . [*from 25 July to 4 March 1604, including*] Buskins for her ma^*tes* maske xiiijs . . .

Notes

1. Joan Rees, ed., *The Vision of the Twelve Goddesses* by Samuel Daniel, in T. J. B. Spencer and Stanley Wells, ed., *A Book of Masques in Honour of Allardyce Nicoll* (Cambridge: Cambridge University Press, 1967), 17–42 (38).

2. Berta Cano-Echevarría and Mark Hutchings, "The Spanish Ambassador and Samuel Daniel's *Vision of the Twelve Goddesses:* A New Document," *English Literary Renaissance* 24 (2012): 223–57.

3. The surreptitious edition, *The True Discription,* is STC 6264, 4⁰: A-B⁴; the authorized edition, *The Vision,* is STC 6265, 4⁰: A-B⁸.

4. *The Vision,* sig. A3r.

5. John Nichols, ed., *The Progresses, Processions, and Magnificent Festivities, of King James the First,* 4 vols. (London 1828), i.317.

6. This is the British Library copy, 161.a 41 (the BL copies of Allde, 161.a 41, C.21.c.69 and C.33.e.7.(21.) are the only ones recorded in the STC). The manuscript notes in 161.a 41 were identified as Lord Worcester's in Ernest Law, ed., *The Vision of the Twelve Goddesses: a Royall Masque* (London: B. Quaritch, 1880), 50–51.

7. Maurice Lee, ed., *Dudley Carleton to John Chamberlain, 1603–1624: Jacobean Letters* (New Brunswick, NJ: Rutgers University Press, 1972), 55 (emphasis added).

8. The evidence is reviewed in Lauren Shohet, *Reading Masques: the English Masque and Public Culture in the Seventeenth Century* (Oxford: Oxford University Press, 2010), 88–92, 123.

9. This is connected to the reason Daniel had Sybilla describe the Goddesses at a distance before the audience saw them close up—"that the eyes of the Spectators might not beguile their eares, as in such cases it euer happens, whiles the pompe and splendor of the sight takes vp all the intention without regard what is spoken" (prefatory letter to *The Vision,* sig. A7).

10. Lauren Shohet is mistaken about this in *Reading Masques,* 94.

11. STC 6238.

12. *Tethys' Festival,* part of *The Order and Solemnitie of the Creation of . . . Prince Henry* (published by John Budge in 1610, STC 13161), sig. E1r. The masque was never reprinted.

13. Waterson edition *The Vision,* sig. B2v; Allde edition, *True Discription,* sig. A3v.

14. The lines beginning "*Execussit tandem sibi se*" on sig. A4r are from Ovid, *Metamorphoses,* 11:621–22. On the same page the lines beginning "*Intanto soprauenne*" and "*Il sonno viene*" are from Ariosto, *Orlando Furioso,* 25:80 and 25:93 respectively.

15. Sig. A4r. Pico wrote "Profectum ingenerosum est, ut ait Seneca, sapere solum ex commentario et, quasi maiorum inventa nostrae industriae viam praecluserint, quasi in nobis effeta sit vis naturae, nil ex se parere, quod veritatem, si non demonstret, saltem innuat vel de longinquo." (Giovanni Pico della Mirandola, *Oratio de hominis dignitate,* ed. Eugenio Garin (Pordenone: Edizioni studio tesi, 1994), 56.

Daniel glosses Pico: "[it may well seem] that there can be nothing done authenticall, vnles we obserue al the strict rules of the booke." Daniel also refers to Pico in *A Defence of Rhyme;* see Gavin Alexander, ed., *Sidney's "The Defence of Poesy' and Selected Renaissance Literary Criticism* (London: Penguin, 2004), 219.

16. Somnus or Sleep, Daniel wrote, "is brought in, as a body, vsing speech & motion: and it was no more improper in this forme to make him walke, and stand, or speake, then it is to giue voyce or passion to dead men, Ghosts, Trees, and Stones:

and therefore in such matters of Shewes, these like Caracters (in what forme soeuer they be drawne) serue vs but to read the intention of what wee would represent. . . ." preface to *The Vision,* sig. A6.

17. The translation is by Cano-Echevarría and Hutchings, "The Spanish Ambassador and Samuel Daniel's *Vision of the Twelve Goddesses,*" 250.

18. Certain details in Villamediana are in the authorized text of the masque as well but missing in the surreptitious version, e.g., the numerals in the lines Iris speaks interpreting the Goddesses' gifts (Cano-Echevarría and Hutchings, "The Spanish Ambassador and Samuel Daniel's *Vision of the Twelve Goddesses,*" 251, and *The Vision,* sig. B6r).

19. *The Vision,* sig. B3v.

20. Law, ed., *Vision of the Twelve Goddesses,* 42.

21. Rees, ed., *The Vision of the Twelve Goddesses* by Samuel Daniel, 41.

22. Cano-Echevarría and Hutchings, "The Spanish Ambassador and Samuel Daniel's *Vision of the Twelve Goddesses,*" 249.

23. See Sven Dupré, "William Bourne's Invention: Projecting a Telescope and Optical Speculation in Elizabethan England," in *The Origins of the Telescope,* eds. Albert Van Helden, Sven Dupré, Rob van Gent and Huib Zuidervaart (Amsterdam: KNAW Press, 2010), 129–45, and Albert Van Helden, *The Invention of the Telescope,* Transactions of the American Philosophical Society 67 (1977): 1–67.

24. Leeds Barroll, *Anna of Denmark, Queen of England: A Cultural Biography* (Philadelphia: University of Pennsylvania Press, 2001), 16.

25. Jane Stevenson, "Texts and Textiles: Self-Presentation among the Elite in Renaissance England," *Journal of the Northern Renaissance* 3 (2011): paragraph [12]. The extraordinary expenditures in the 1614–15 account include a payment to Richard Miller of £135 for "stuffes," a bill which, Stevenson says, "stands out, for its size, in a general context of such miscellaneous expenditures as £10 to firework makers, £10 to her players for a play performed on December 17, 1615, and £30 to an Italian poet."

26. Charles Nicholl, *The Lodger: Shakespeare on Silver Street* (London: Allen Lane, 2008), 143–44, 156–57, Illustration 23 (see p. xvii).

27. See Nicholl, *The Lodger,* Illustration 24.

28. LR 6/154/9 is headed "The Declaration of the Account of S:r George Carewe." It comprises forty folios in three sections: fos.1–12, preamble, and rents and revenues from Queen Anne's manors; fos.13–38, payments to individual officers of the household and others, with a summing up and totals on fos.38–39r; fos.39–40 unpaid debts, specified by person or groups (usually tenants). LR 6/154/9 is not foliated, so folio numbers have been supplied throughout this essay.

29. Helen Payne informed me about the payments to Daniel and Kirton in LR 6/154/9, which led me to examine it. Andy Boyle took photographs and transcribed portions of the manuscript. I am most grateful to them for their help and advice.

30. There is no mention of William Bell in Diana Scarisbrick, "Anne of Denmark's Jewellery Inventory," *Archaelogia* 109 (1991): 193–238.

31. See Lynn Hulse, "The Musical Patronage of Robert Cecil, First Earl of Salisbury (1563–1612)," *Journal of the Royal Musical Association* 116 (1991): 24–40. Perhaps more to the point, Cecil was Lord High Steward of the Queen's household and would want to keep an eye on expenditure.

32. My hope is that nothing significant has been missed, but LR 6/154/9 is a large manuscript, crammed with interlineations, cancellations, and added phrases, which may contain minor details about spending on the masque.

33. Lord Hertford had at least two servants called James Kirton, possibly three: James Kirton the elder (c.1559–1611) of the Middle Temple, a lawyer who worked for the Earl occasionally; his cousin James Kirton the younger (1559–1620) of Almsford, Somerset—the Earl's servant who was paid to organize *The Vision of the Twelve Goddesses*—and another James Kirton, also of the Middle Temple, possibly connected with Sir William Cavendish, and perhaps the man described as Hertford's solicitor by the Countess of Shrewsbury's servant involved in the plan Arbella Stuart hatched in 1602 to marry Edward Seymour, Hertford's grandson. James Kirton the younger entered Hertford's service by 1592, and was, according to his own testimony in 1615, employed by the Earl "in matters of greatest charge and trust" between 1599 and 1608 ("History of Parliament" online). Kirton was not Hertford's steward—this was Sir Gilbert Prynne.

34. John Pitcher, "Samuel Daniel, the Hertfords, and a Question of Love," *Review of English Studies* 35 (1984): 449–62 (459).

35. Barroll, *Anna of Denmark,* 77.

36. In a letter of December 18, 1603 from Hampton Court, Arbella Stuart wrote that "The Queene intendeth to make a mask this Christmas to which end my Lady of Suffolk and my Lady of Walsingham have warrants to take of the late Queenes best apparel out of the Tower at theyr discretion." (Sara Jayne Steen, ed., *The Letters of Lady Arbella Stuart* [New York: Oxford University Press, 1994], 197.)

37. W. R. Streitberger, ed., "Jacobean and Caroline Revels Accounts, 1603–42," *Malone Society Collections* 13 (Oxford: Oxford University Press, 1986), 5.

38. At Queen Elizabeth's court, Ferrabosco received £50 a year from 1601. He was made an Extraordinary Groom of the Privy Chamber from Christmas 1604, specifically to teach music to Prince Henry. Perhaps Ferrabosco wrote the songs for *The Vision of the Twelve Goddesses* because of his connection with Lord Hertford, James Kirton's employer. Aubrey said that Ferrabosco served the Earl, visiting him in Amesbury and Wolfhall in Wiltshire (*ODNB*).

39. Glynne Wickham in *Early English Stages 1300 to 1660,* 3 vols. in 4 (London: Routledge and Paul, 1959–81), II. Part 1.269 offers in a diagram a "conjectural reconstruction of the arrangements in the hall" of the Rock (Mountain), Temple and Cave. The Rock—which in Wickham's diagram is far too small and is shown as freestanding—was probably attached to the screen wall, across its full width. This would have allowed the Queen and her Ladies access to the top of the Mountain via the gallery and the staircase that led up to it.

40. See the excerpt from Arbella Stuart's letter quoted in n. 36.

41. *The Vision,* sig. A5r.

42. Lee, ed., *Dudley Carleton to John Chamberlain, 1603–1624,* 55.

43. Ibid.

44. Lucy Munro, *Children of the Queen's Revels: A Jacobean Theatre Repertory* (Cambridge: Cambridge University Press, 2005), 18.

45. Lee, ed., *Dudley Carleton to John Chamberlain, 1603–1624,* 55.

46. *The Vision,* sig. A7v.

47. The license for the company, a docquet dated 31 January, is TNA (PRO) SP 38/7/65.
48. See Munro, *Children of the Queen's Revels*, 20 (199, n. 39), 140–42, 188.
49. Barroll, *Anna of Denmark*, 99–100.
50. Quoted in Law, ed., *Vision of the Twelve Goddesses*, 10–11.
51. For Sanford, see "History of Parliament" online and *ODNB*.
52. This was Elizabeth Lady Carey, wife of Sir Robert Carey (1560–1639), a Lady of the Queen's Privy Chamber and Mistress of the Sweet Coffers, responsible for the care of the Queen's gowns and in charge of cosmetics and perfume.
53. Corrected from "pantables" ("ables" crossed through and "offles" written above).

"'Batter'd, not demolish'd': staging the tortured body in *The Martyred Soldier*

Elizabeth Williamson

How does torture work on the stage? And how does that work align with, or provide room for a critique of, the work that torture does for the state? This essay takes up these questions through a close reading of Henry Shirley's *The Martyred Soldier,* first performed at the Red Bull Theater around 1618. This play has recently gained critical attention because of its miraculous conversions and other special effects.[1] It is also noteworthy because it falls in the middle of a group of plays first performed in the late 1610s and early 1620s that consistently revisit narratives from early Christian history, using visual and aural effects to heighten the audience's appetite for familiar religious themes.[2] What interests me here, however, is the way *The Martyred Soldier* interrogates both religious ideology and state power. In a recent analysis of *King Lear,* John D. Staines argues that tragedy "makes an audience experience the violence of its culture."[3] *The Martyred Soldier* is ambiguously tragic—its protagonists die enthusiastically, like all good martyrs—but it does present an anatomy of torture that complicates religious narratives of transcendent suffering. Its staging of martyrdom pushes the Christian tradition to the limits of its own logic before exposing the ways in which state power both relies upon and effaces martyred bodies.

My approach to *The Martyred Soldier* draws on the work of Nova Myhill and Holly Crawford Pickett, whose analyses of the spectacular martyrdoms in Jacobean drama reveal the limitations of attempting to label these moments as either Catholic or Protestant. To borrow Pickett's elegant formulation, "[o]ne need not be pro-Catholic in order to be anti-torture."[4] Instead, these scholars demonstrate the importance of analyzing stage martyrdoms as theatrical events created by using systems of signification particular to the stage. Like the medieval plays described by Jody Enders, Jacobean stagings of torture invited playgoers "to interpret what is already subject to interpretation," i.e., the spectacle of the body in pain.[5] Myhill locates a similar kind of awareness in the staging of early modern drama, arguing that public theater audiences were constantly reminded, by the recognizable conventions of the repertory system, that it was their own reception of the play that determined its significance. She focuses in particular on Dekker and Massinger's *The Virgin Martyr*, suggesting that its heroine's suffering "allows for multiple readings simultaneously, based not on Dorothea's body, which reveals nothing, but through the generic conventions of martyrdom and the stage play."[6] The result is that spectators have a variety of options available to them: they can read the events depicted on stage mimetically according to a variety of ideological positions, or they can view them as "mere" spectacle.

Extending Myhill's argument about *The Virgin Martyr* to a series of other Jacobean plays, including *The Martyred Soldier*, Pickett makes the claim that these texts "seem to carve out a space within their culture's definition of mainstream Christian orthodoxy . . . for theatrical spectacle."[7] Complicating Michael O'Connell's influential assertion that the theater existed as a reaction against an anti-visual Protestant culture, Pickett finds in the plays' self-consciousness not just ideological flexibility but also a defense of the theatrical apparatus itself: "they admit to their own ostentation," she concludes, "without conceding the power of that ostentation to improve."[8] In Pickett's reading, the plays implicitly argue that theatrical spectacle was not so different from the kinds of spectacle that religion itself deployed.

The overt staginess of *The Martyred Soldier* lends itself naturally to readings such as Pickett's and Myhill's, which reveal that theater was always pointing first and foremost to its own mechanisms. The play begins with a typically bloody pagan crusade against a small but stalwart group of Christians. After the Vandal king's death, his son inherits the throne and continues the campaign against the Christians, but his star general, Bellizarius, is soon converted after being visited by an angel. To make matters worse, the most ambitious of the Vandals, Hubert, is turned Christian by Bellizarius's daughter, Bellina. When the king is mortally wounded in a boar hunt, the Christian bishop Eugenius performs a miraculous cure, but the king breaks his promise to free the Christians in return for this service, and his hubris is revenged when he is struck dead by thunder in the final act. The play ends with two Christian couplings: the onstage martyrdom of Bellizarius and his wife Victoria, and the crowning of Hubert and Bellina as the new rulers of the kingdom. At first glance, there appears to be a strangely artificial gap between what should be the play's culminating event, the shared death of the Christian martyrs, and the extensive political deliberations that follow it. In the final section of the essay I will suggest that it is precisely this interruption in the audience's attention that prompts spectators to draw a connection between the martyrs' deaths and the establishment of the new regime.

During this period in history, the English state was busy disavowing the practice of torture, which had never been formalized as part of its jurisprudence. Francis Bacon, for instance, differentiated between the use of force to discover information about treasonous plots and the use of force to secure evidence against the accused. John Langbein accepts Bacon's distinction, insisting that state-sponsored punishment was only torture when designed to produce evidentiary proof.[9] According to Langbein, the standards of proof for declaring guilt were so minimal that prosecutors did not have to rely upon evidence gleaned from torture. James Heath, whose seminal study followed soon after Langbein's, does define what Bacon helped to legitimate as torture, and carefully catalogs various instances of it from the twelfth century to the Civil War.[10] Despite Heath's slightly more scientific approach, there seems to be a scholarly consensus that torture, which was primarily used (or at least documented) in cases involving treason and other issues of national importance, declined significantly after the second half of the Elizabethan era—a period that "featured the greatest use of torture in English history."[11] Langbein speculates that torture became less frequent during James's reign because of an overall increase in political stability, with the succession secured and the Spanish threat somewhat diffused.[12] Yet Curtis C. Breight, who urges literary scholars to pay closer attention to the detailed lists of torture warrants collated by historians such as Heath, also points out that strict enumeration is not the only measure of torture's effects. "[T]error," he writes, "can be induced by a discourse of torture so long as there are enough tortured bodies . . . to ground that discourse in material reality."[13] One key feature of torture, then, is its effect on bodies other than that of the torture victim. But the most noteworthy feature of English torture during this period was that it was governed not by law but by the dictates of "political necessity."[14] In what follows I argue that *The Martyred Soldier* takes up both of these features, illustrating the former through the on-stage representation of martyrdom and the latter by linking the founding of a new government to the threat of violence materialized in the martyr's dead bodies.

My goal in invoking the history of English torture is not to argue that the play is making a direct political intervention, but to suggest that it offers us a way of understanding the relationship between martyrdom and torture, between religious ideologies and the mechanisms of state power that depend on those ideologies. By examining these connections I hope to contextualize *The Martyred Soldier* within a broader set of historical dynamics while highlighting the particular way in which these dynamics might play out in performance.

* * *

The first four acts of *The Martyred Soldier* are built around an apparent clash of ideologies—the unequal contest between religious faith and overwhelming military power—which eventually gives way to a more nuanced analysis of the demands that martyrdom makes upon the human body. The play begins at the bedside of the dying Vandal king, whose last moments are spent gleefully recounting all the Christians he has killed. Eugenius, one of the newest victims of the king's campaign, is brought on stage, eagerly anticipating his journey to heaven; the king, however, insists that he live so that the Vandals can attempt to convert him through torture.[15] This opening scene, which also includes a lengthy debate about which of the Vandals has proved himself most heroic on the battlefield, succinctly lays out the play's thematic opposition between the Christians' battle for souls and the Vandals' struggle for political supremacy.

The bloodshed described as music to the dying king's ears in act 1, scene 1 is notable both for its brutality and for the sheer numbers of its victims. "[U]nclaspe that booke, / Turne o're that Monument of Martyrdomes," the king begs. "Read there how *Gonzerick* has serv'd the gods, / And made their Altars drunke with Christians blood."[16] His servant dutifully reads, listing "[f]ive hundred broyl'd to death in Oyle and Lead. . . . Seven hundred flead alive. . . . Thirty faire Mothers big with Christian brats. . . . Foure hundred virgins ravisht" (B1v-B2r). The point of this enumeration, apart from the pleasure the king takes in it, is to demonstrate the Vandals' overwhelming use of force. During this recounting, the king references the importance of burning the bodies and scattering the ashes to the wind, "[t]o show that of foure Elements, not one had care / Of them, dead or alive" (B1v). Ironically, the joy he takes in lingering over the material details of their suffering allows them to live in fame as martyrs. The very fact that he is still reading about their deaths, in a volume that self-consciously references Foxe's *Acts and Monuments,* undermines his claim that their bodies are inconsequential. The plot of the play repeatedly bears out the fact that killing Christians is no way to eliminate the religion, since martyrdom will always inspire new converts. Yet the overall effect of the play is to provide an alternative to martyrology that both resists and calls attention to the tyrant's need to efface the bodies of his enemies.

Bellizarius's first monologue describes in detail the impression the Christians have already had on him. They are, Bellizarius remarks, "as resolute / And full of courage in their bleeding falls, / As should they tryumph for a Victory" (C1v). Their displays of exultation in turn lead him to question his own worldview: why should Christian martyrs sue for death if there were no afterlife to be had? This questioning leads to the angel's visitation and to Bellizarius's conversion, upon which he immediately embraces the martyr's conventional eagerness for death:

> Centuple all that ever I have done,
> Kindle the fire, and hacke at once with swords,
> Teare me by piece-meales, strangle, and extend
> My every limbe and joynt; nay, devise more
> Than ever did my bloody Tyrannies.
>
> (C2v–3r)

Not yet fully understanding the value of Christ's sacrifice, Bellizarius believes that he must somehow undo the evil he has done by suffering more than his victims ever suffered. But his speech also points to the importance, in martyrological narratives, of sharing the experience of that sacrifice in order to better understand its value.

The excesses of the suffering depicted in these narratives are echoed in the latter scenes of the play as the new king struggles to find innovative forms of physical coercion that will compel the Christians to recant. When he attempts to stone Eugenius, for instance, the rocks become "soft as spunges," forcing the king to call for "[n]ew studied tortures" that will somehow succeed where other torments have failed (F4v). This trope—which parallels the pressure on the playwright to surpass previous stage depictions of martyrdom—is extended throughout the play. "Our power is mockt by magicall impostures," the king complains in the middle of the final scene, "[t]hey shall not mocke our tortures" (I1r). Calling for Victoria's death, he first imagines a new kind of beheading, and then immediately reverses himself, as if his imagination had reached its limits: "Let her braines be beaten on an Anvill: / For some new plagues for her" (I2v). The excessive onstage violence in *The Martyred Soldier* often turns back upon those who seek to inflict it, providing one more indication that they are on the wrong side of the ideological battle. But the play is not merely an attack on tyranny. Drawing on contemporary martyrologies, *The Martyred Soldier* ultimately invites audiences to re-examine those narratives and the contradictions at the heart of their depiction of the suffering body. Specifically, the details of Victoria's torture and death put pressure on the Christians' moral triumph by overtly staging the paradox of martyrdom: if faith is all that matters, then how can the body experience pain and fragmentation, and if the body cannot experience pain and fragmentation, how will the sufferer commune with Christ? The answer is that the body must first feel pain, and then demonstrate God's power by expressing a certain kind of inertness in the face of that pain. The body must suffer in an extraordinary fashion, yet it must also persist, serving as proof of God's favor.

The faith of all Christian martyrs, including those who suffered death in Reformation-era England, was rooted in elements of doctrine that conceptualized the body as both mired in sin and the only available evidence of the triumph of the soul.[17] Susan Zimmerman aptly summarizes this paradoxical condition as a consequence of life after the Fall:

> Fundamentally, the transfigured self of the Christian subject in heaven represented a state of plenitude or fulfillment. . . . It was, therefore, in the earth-bound, unredeemed and post-lapsarian subject, contaminated by original sin, that the relationship between material and spiritual practices was necessarily unstable.[18]

To continue Zimmerman's paraphrase, "the final state of wholeness—whether that of the resurrected Christ, his saints, or the ordinary Christian—

was meaningless without prior mutilation and/or fragmentation."[19] Bodily suffering confirmed, and was explained by, the limitations of material existence; it also pointed to the prospect of salvation, which would miraculously re-unify the martyr's scattered limbs. Indeed, the violent separation of body parts was a kind of anticipatory proof of the restorative miracle of the resurrection. The body was both an inadequate means of accessing the divine and the only grounds upon which the divine could be conceived of in the first place.[20] The suffering of the martyr, caught between the baseness of her material body and the immanence of her salvation, comes into view as a powerful instantiation of Christianity's conflicted reliance on the body as an ideological construct. Her pain both manifests her connection to Christ and yet, as long as she is alive, it keeps her from fully experiencing His mercy.

The body of the female martyr, theorized most thoroughly by Caroline Walker Bynum, was the site of a particularly profound anxiety about human vulnerability; it was also the most compelling example of spiritual triumph over that vulnerability. Narratives describing the death of early Christian virgin martyrs consistently foregrounded the materiality of the body and were typically constructed as follows:

> The virgin is threatened, then incarcerated, stripped naked, publicly flogged, lacerated, burnt and boiled, and dismembered in some way. . . . Her conduct during all this remains impeccable, her ability to reason unimpaired, and, to the frustration of the tyrant, her bearing and her arguments frequently convert his attendant soldiery and populace whom he then has to martyr as well. Finally, when the virgin and God have displayed enough of God's supreme rule over the world, she concludes her passion by going to formal execution by beheading."[21]

More so even than her male companions, the female martyr was celebrated for her passivity; she triumphed not by conquering her enemies but by foiling their attempts to penetrate her body and thus mar her chastity, which was the primary token of her spiritual superiority. Analyzing the links between the gendered body and the threat of religious conversion, Jane Hwang Degenhardt explains that "resistance to physical torture conveys the inviolable nature of [the martyr's] body itself. . . . In other words, the physical itself constitutes the sign of constancy."[22] The virgin martyr's stoicism allowed her to conquer not only her persecutors but also the supposed limitations of her own body, and her torture lasted just long enough to sustain real tension about whether her body could endure long enough to protect her spirit. This may help explain why, in the late medieval narratives Bynum examines, there are so few references "to the fact that being cut apart might hurt."[23]

The protagonists in early modern martyrologies are also frequently valorized for being inert to physical pain. Alexander Briant, a Catholic associate of Edmund Campion's, reports that despite his suffering, he "continued still with perfect and present senses, in quietness of hart, and tranquilitie of mind," prompting his captors to "racke me againe the next day following after the same sorte" in hopes of producing a more dramatic form of submission.[24] Even more pointedly, Anne Askew, memorialized by Protestant martyrologists John Bale and John Foxe, affirms that "bycause I laye styll and ded not crye, my lorde Chauncellour and master Ryche, toke peynes to rake me their owne handes, tyll I was nygh dead."[25] In both cases, the body of the martyr is extraordinary not only because it suffers, but because it endures. And in both cases, the prisoner's refusal to register the bodily effects of pain prompts the torturers to increase their efforts. These accounts capture a kind of perverse dialectic that serves both the aims of the state and the motives of the martyr: by extending the torture, the interrogator is able to continue exerting physical dominance over the subject, and the martyr is able to continue demonstrating the remarkable effects of God's love.

Like her virgin predecessors and her contemporary counterparts, Victoria's suffering is extended as long as possible within the fiction of the play.[26] Her torments begin when, having been commanded to save her husband's life by convincing him to re-convert, she instead publicly celebrates his refusal to abandon his new faith. Victoria's rhetoric simultaneously outmatches the king's threats and embarrasses him for allowing her this privileged moment of proclaiming her Christian fortitude. In his rage, the king calls for a camel driver to rape her in front of Bellizarius, attempting to provoke as much humiliation as he himself has suffered. Urging her to maintain her conviction, Eugenius tells Victoria not to fear the threat of sexual violence: "be / Thou a chaste one in thy minde," he promises, "thy body / May, like a Temple of well tempered steele, / Be batter'd, not demolish'd" (H1r). Eugenius's statement is full of contradictions; the whole point of the martyr's death was to eradicate the possibility of losing her chastity, yet by focusing on the battering she will receive, he draws attention to the persistence of her mortal body, rather than her release from its constraints. It is here that the play begins to undermine the theological underpinnings of Christian martyrology.

Having invoked the threat of violence, the scene temporarily suspends it in favor of a moment of comic relief, doubling and then tripling the joke played on the king. The first camel driver is prevented from raping Victoria by being struck mad; he is followed by another who goes first blind and then deaf (the resulting stage business, in which the king's servants attempt to help the would-be ravisher find his prey, is especially ridiculous). The final two camel drivers barely have time to open their mouths to express their obedience to the king's request before hurrying off stage together, dancing *"antiquely"* (H2r). Later, after Victoria has been imprisoned in a cave, the jailor asks whether any of his prisoners has succumbed to death. The Clown, who plays a vital role in the play's commentary on martyrdom, replies:

> Dead? yes;
> And five more come into the world, instead of one:
> These Christians are like Artichoaks of Ierusalem,
> They over-runne any ground they grow in. (H2v)[27]

The analogy reinforces the idea of the Christians' moral superiority, but it also pokes fun at them by comparing them to vegetables. When asked whether Victoria has survived her prison ordeal, the Clown responds that he did his best to kill her by dumping scalding porridge on her head (H3v). The description conjures up a disturbing image, but by introducing something as typically English as boiled oats (a send-up of boiling oil), it also undermines the seriousness of the act of torture.

The Clown is by no means a proponent of Christian fortitude; in other scenes he mocks Eugenius for refusing earthly food in favor of heavenly desserts and lays out a callous comparison between the ways in which martyrs of various national origins catch fire when being burned. But his fooling opens up a space for considering the preposterousness of the act of torture, as well as the improbability of its victims' survival. As Degenhardt has argued in relation to similar moments in *The Virgin Martyr,* "the combined effects of the comedic tormentors, the scene's self-reflexive theatricality, and the representation of an authentic miracle also serve to sustain a tension between the threat of bodily penetration and the comforting assurance that Christian resistance will prevail."[28] In other words, the play straddles the line between reinforcing certain basic religious and cultural norms and providing a sufficient amount of dramatic suspense. I would argue, however, that *The Martyred Soldier*'s use of comic violence does more than ease the dramatic tension; when coupled with the improbable stage business surrounding Victoria's martyrdom, it provokes fundamental doubts about the miracles the martyred body is being asked to produce.

In the play's final scene, Victoria bursts from the cave robed in white and accompanied by the singing of angels. There is no way to read this moment as anything other than a kind of resurrection; she has been so fully transfigured that the king fails to recognize her and falls promptly in love. When he threatens to complete the task his camel drivers failed to carry out, Victoria forcefully asserts her invulnerability, confirming the lyrics sung by the angels who accompanied her entrance:

> All my mortality is shaken off,
> My heart of flesh and blood is gone,
> My body is chang'd, this face
> Is not that once was mine;
> I am a Spirit, and no racke of thine
> Can touch me.
>
> (I3r)

Victoria's resurrection appears to materialize Eugenius's earlier promise that her faith will transform her, making her more spirit than body.

And yet even this new state of being, authenticated by the angels as well as by the king's failure to recognize her, does not fully secure her chastity.[29] When the king asserts his desire not to rack her but to bed her, she expresses her fear in a way that seems out of keeping with her transfigured state. "Oh that some rocke of Ice, / Might fall on me, and freeze me into nothing," she prays, begging to be rematerialized as something no longer resembling a body.[30] The king calls for charms to put her to sleep but the angels beat him to the punch, and he finds himself wooing a corpse "[a]s frozen as if the North-winde had in spight / Snatcht her hence from you" (I3v). The literal-mindedness of the imagery in this scene seems clumsy, but in light of the play's desire to reveal the paradox at the heart of the martyrological narrative I would suggest that it is highly deliberate. Marked as imperfect from the moment of her conversion to the Christian faith—her husband initially accuses her of being physically incapable of salvation, because, unlike her virgin daughter, she is "too much o're growne with sinne and shame" (D3r)—her body becomes transfigured, though still vulnerable to the king's sexual advances. In fact the transitional state Victoria occupies in this scene is a fascinating inversion of the typical condition of martyrdom: rather than being miraculously alive, despite torments which should have killed her, Victoria appears to be dead, and yet she remains subject to the tyrant's threats. Her sexual vulnerability both challenges the conventions of the martyr narrative and points to a more profound problem: if the martyr can experience genuine terror during the moment of her suffering, how can we build our faith on her sacrifice?

The centrality of a non-virginal heroine appears to be a crucial part of the play's strategy to question the status of the perfectly inert body at the heart of the martyrological narrative, but Victoria's vulnerability is also a crucial element of her dramatic appeal. Similarly, the intimate details of Foxe's accounts routinely emphasize the actual terror experienced by those about to suffer martyrdom; these were real human beings overcoming their fear, rather than semi-divine figures immune from it altogether.[31] Foxe's narratives are powerful in part because of their striking theatricality; they address their audience through visual conventions and cues.[32] But the drama of these narratives also comes from their emphasis on human frailty, the reality of which was made palpable in theatrical stagings of the torture and death of martyrs.

Despite the inherently compelling nature of its visual spectacles, the early modern theater was not particularly well suited to producing realistic depictions of torture and death. What it could do, as Myhill suggests, was open up space for an interpretation of the *performance* of martyrdom. *The Martyred Soldier* accomplishes this by demonstrating the sheer impossibility of the martyrologist's demand that the body be "batter'd, not demolish'd," but it also addresses the power, and the limitations, of acting more generally. When Bellizarius tells the king, "[y]ou cannot act so much as I will suffer," he is reconfirming the classic dynamic in which the virgin martyr's passivity is represented as her ultimate weapon (D2r). In valorizing his own *passio,* Bellizarius seems to imply that military deeds and acts of violence—the kind of actions he has built his identity upon—are, by contrast with the transcendent quality of his suffering as a Christian, hopelessly superficial. But the metatheatrical resonances of this line are also worth noting: if what you want is a body that will appear to suffer and yet survive, what you want is an actor.

Stage suffering is a particular kind of special effect: self-consciously narrated, often miraculously averted, it actively raises the issue of how the theater can represent life realistically in the first place. It also draws attention to an already difficult question—namely, whether we can understand another person's experience of pain—by watching an actor counterfeit that experience. In his account of the classical theories of acting that carried over into the early modern period, Joseph Roach explains that acting was thought to be a way of literally translating spirit or *pneuma* through the actor's body to his audience.[33] Because of the high-stakes nature of transmitting such powerful energies, the actor's body was also a vulnerable body. This vulnerability, powerfully summarized by Anthony Dawson, gave a particular emotional emphasis to the actor's speech and gestures in the moment of performance:

> It is precisely the material imperfections of performance, its reliance on actors' bodies and movements, with whatever heaviness and hesitation the actors bring with them, that ground and enable the strange kind of transcendence that theater aims at and occasionally delivers. Of course any such uplift was temporary and provisional; triggered by connection to fictional persons, it allowed a brief breaking away from the everyday towards something that felt bigger and more important, though that larger sense was grounded in, and inseparable from, the profane everyday.[34]

The dynamic Dawson identifies made the actor ideally suited to representing, however provisionally, the martyr's imperfect body. Both displayed virtuosic abilities, but their very ability to endure extremes of pain and emotion also inevitably brought them, and their audiences, up against the limitations of material existence.

These limitations lend poignancy to *The Martyred Soldier*'s critique of torture, the religious narratives that support it, and the political ideologies that depend upon it. Though the actor could never evade his personal vulnerability, he could achieve a momentary respite from it within the conventions of performance. Likewise, Victoria's suffering is compelling precisely because, as long as she is alive, she can never fully escape the constraints of her own body. Both the actor and the martyr draw their symbolic power from the very source of their vulnerability: their transitional existence between two states of being. To borrow Francis Barker's formulation, the play emphasizes not Victoria's transcendence but her participation in "a materiality that is fully and unashamedly involved in the process of domination and resistance which are the inner substance of life."[35] Through the imperfect device of the actors who played their parts, the theater brought into clearer view the otherwise invisible ideologies bearing down on women's bodies.

As Bynum reminds us, however, the ideological weight that women were made to bear in Christian Europe did not emerge from some innate set of notions about gender. Rather, those categories were shaped and inflected by the more fundamental threat of decay and dissolution, which both religious narratives and governmental authority seek to redress by theorizing a transcendent corporate body: the "Christian people" or the "English nation."[36] What is dramatically powerful about the final act of *The Martyred Soldier* is the connection between the martyr's body and that of the actor, but what is tragic (in Staines's sense of the term) about the play's ending is its deliberate staging of the formation of a new government built upon—while wholly ignoring—the dead Christians.

* * *

Christine Peters has suggested that the early modern period marked a shift in the martyrological narrative "from the experience of martyrdom itself to the experience of imprisonment and interrogation," which brought the competition over the meaning of the martyr's death to the forefront of these texts.[37] No longer merely a catalog of torments, accounts promoted by writers such as Foxe allowed the sufferer significant room to speak on her own behalf and, if read sympathetically, could stand as a viable response to official accounts of the martyr's treasonous behavior. Such narratives suggest that the state's increasing focus on interrogation was both an exercise of its overwhelming power and a demonstration of its inability to completely control the meaning of the martyr's death. According to Elizabeth Hanson, the moment at which the torturer broke from legal convention to inflict violence on the prisoner's body "marked the limit of his discursive hegemony," literally rendering him "inarticulate" in relation to existing languages of power.[38] The ultimately incommunicable nature of the "truth" of pain gave martyrs and other torture victims room to describe their suffering on their own terms—at least as long as their supporters were able to exert some control over the proliferation of narratives that appeared after their death.[39]

Hanson's research suggests an intriguing contrast between the relatively arbitrary nature of the state's use of torture and the profoundly influential collective investment in its power as a truth-producing mechanism. Both victims and interrogators sought meaning in the act of torture, but both, arguably, were subject to a more powerful inertia, which Hanson would describe as the epistemology of truth, and which I would call the momentum of the state, working to preserve itself by whatever means necessary. In what follows, I turn to the final moments of *The Martyred Soldier,* suggesting that in these moments the play goes far beyond its initial critique of religious doctrine to engage more fully with the question of how state power operates—and depends—on the body.

After Victoria and Bellizarius are pronounced dead, the dialogue continues for several more pages as the Vandal lords deliberate and finally elect Hubert to be their king. As Hubert lobbies for the throne, he works to convince the lords that it is their authority that cements his rule, all the while reassuring Eugenius that he will not forsake his new faith. Here, it seems, the audience is witnessing the formation of a new regime built on policy rather than war mongering. "Violent streames," Hubert proclaims, "[m]ust not bee stopt by violence" (K1v). His future ministers, whose "bagges are emptied in these warres," are more than eager for an end to the bloodshed, and Hubert promises to plant them like vines "round about my throne" (K2r). Despite the strong biblical resonances of this final line, the dialogue evokes nothing so much as the founding of a modern, secular state. Hubert strategically avoids the question of whether his subjects must all convert to Christianity, and Eugenius does not press the point—in fact he becomes increasingly less prominent as the scene progresses. And yet the threat of violence is never far from Hubert's mind in this scene: he repeatedly reminds the lords that if they had denied him the throne he would have seized it by force. Will this be a regime that eschews torture and conquest? Such a possibility might be very attractive to English playgoers exhausted by the extraordinary violence of past decades, including the dramatic increase in the use of torture in the second half of Elizabeth's reign. The play, however, makes it clear that for all his rhetoric about policy and peace Hubert reserves the right to deploy violence in the name of "national security."

Breight has recently chided New Historicists for their attachment to the notion of a weak Elizabethan state, vulnerable to foreign attack and incapable of coercing its subjects into obedience. He argues that the state in early modern England was more than just the monarch; it was a network of forces centered on maintaining power through militarism and surveillance:

> Hence the state is not simply an ideological project or a fiction, but a means of organizing aggression, largely for the greater glory and profit of a small minority. . . . We must understand that the state is not static, not the "established order," but an often violent process in which allied individuals exert power to establish an institutional order largely favorable to the few comprising the political nation.[40]

Breight complains that literary scholars, beginning with E. M. W. Tillyard, have unconsciously inherited an imperialistic point of view when it comes to the "golden age" of Great Britain, and that in seeking to find traces of individual agency, particularly among Shakespeare's audiences, we have overlooked the extent to which the Cecils, Burghleys, and Walsinghams of the world were consciously working to keep the members of the population docile by alternately torturing and conscripting them. Power, Breight suggests, can be theatrical without losing its efficacy.

In its staging of Hubert's ascension, *The Martyred Soldier* emphasizes the drive toward ensuring "institutional order," for though Hubert's actions do not precipitate the tyrant's death, he exerts his right to rule the kingdom vigorously once the political vacuum has been created. He describes himself as God's champion, the virtuous convert whose merit must appear obvious to the people, yet he continually harangues the lords as they deliberate: "Will you consent or no? be quick in answer; / I must be swift in execution else. . . . Have you done? / So long chusing one Crowne?" (K1r). He even questions whether the lords have the authority to choose the next king, since "[t]he Tree upon whose boughs your honours grew . . . is falne to th' ground" (I4v). The absence of a biological heir to the dead tyrant opens up the political field completely, such that the lords are forced to "stand on [their] owne strength," that is, the sheer necessity of the state's continuance (I4v). When they finally sound drums and trumpets to announce Hubert king he proclaims, rather redundantly, "I have it, then, as well by voice as sword; / For should you holde it back it will be mine. / I claime it then, by conquest" (K1r). Similarly, he asserts his will over Bellina, Victoria's daughter, ignoring her desire to remain a virgin by declaring the necessity of founding a new line of Christian rulers. Through his actions and implied threats, Hubert performs, almost didactically, a wide variety of forms of political control under the rubric of peace.

Though he reassures the lords that he will "lay by the conquest," there is never any doubt about what Hubert is willing to do to maintain power, and his threats are made palpable by the corpses that remain on stage, disregarded by everyone but the audience, throughout this scene (K1r). Bellizarius's body has been hung up by the arms, with lead weights pulling down on his feet (he has literally been racked to death, but in an upright position for better visibility), while Victoria is displayed on a bed, surrounded by angels. In this newly politicized context, the martyrs' corpses, together with that of the dead tyrant, manifest the risk posed to the population by war and social upheaval. At the same time, Hubert offers himself as the leader who will replace chaos with security, indiscriminate slaughter with targeted violence. This is the image of the enlightened Christian ruler, who will torture not for the joy of torturing but in order to minimize risk; he is less interested in disciplining individuals than in what Peter Spierenburg calls "general prevention."[41] In this precarious moment of rebuilding the government, he needs the lords to be aware of the evil he is saving them from, as well as the threat they themselves will face if they choose non compliance. Perhaps, the play leads us to wonder, the cessation of torture under James was not so much a deliberate end to state-sponsored coercion as it was a re-branding campaign. Having never committed itself to torture as a mechanism of the judiciary process, the state continued to reserve the right to practice it—when necessary.

The Martyred Soldier's depiction of state power is, like the depiction of sexual and economic oppression in *Taming of the Shrew,* "a kinde of history."[42] Viewing it as such does not necessarily provide remedies or alternatives, but it does remind us that state power is a construction, not a natural phenomenon—it helps us see how things get put together, so that we can eventually tear them apart. But what of the phenomenology of the stage? What does it look like to give this kind of history a theatrical form? Drawing in part on Foucault's *Discipline and Punish,* James Robert Allard and Mathew M. Martin suggest that the staging of pain might have the potential for "generating outrage and disgust in the spectators, who might then intervene and halt the theater of cruelty unfolding before their eyes."[43] Enders, however, warns us that catharsis does not always produce empathic results. "Sometimes," she argues, "dramatic rhetoric may even convince audiences that they are being entertained when they are being coerced."[44] Similarly, the bodies left on stage at the end of *The Martyred Soldier* reveal the violence behind Hubert's political maneuvering, blocking his ability to completely control the meaning of their deaths by allowing the audience to see them as part of a broader political picture.

What is most radical about the ending of *The Martyred Soldier* is the way in which the audience's invitation to identify with or take voyeuristic pleasure in the martyrdom of Victoria and Bellizarius is immediately interrupted by a very different sort of narrative—an intimate exploration of the process whereby state power reproduces itself. This interruption provides an opportunity for the audience to look critically at both the religious ideology that supports torture and the "institutional order" built upon the threat of future violence. Even more importantly, the play allows us to begin to glimpse the techniques of power that link martyrdom with nation building. For early modern audiences, the break in theatrical convention opened up an interpretative space, a respite from political reality that led back, inevitably, to political reality.

Notes

I wish to express my gratitude to the participants in the 2011 Shakespeare Association of America seminar on "Prosthetics and Performance" for providing feedback on an earlier version of this essay. I am particularly indebted to Thomas P. Anderson, Jennifer Roberts-Smith, and Nicola M. Imbracsio, all of whom offered generous and generative written comments.

1. See Jane Hwang Degenhardt, *Islamic Conversion and Christian Resistance on the Early Modern Stage* (Edinburgh: Edinburgh University Press, 2010), Nova Myhill, "Making Death a Miracle: Audience and the Genres of Martyrdom in Dekker and Massinger's *The Virgin Martyr*," *Early Theatre* 7, 2 (2004): 9–31, and Holly Pickett, "Angels in England: Idolatry and Transformation at the Red Bull Playhouse," in *Thunder at a Playhouse: Essaying Shakespeare and the Early Modern Stage,* eds. Peter Kanelos and Matt Kozusko (Selinsgrove, PA: Susquehanna University Press, 2010), 175–99.

2. These include: *The History of the Trial of Chivalry* (1601); Anthony Brewer, *The Lovesick King* (1607–17?); John Day, George Wilkins, and William Rowley, *The Travels of Three English Brothers* (1607); William Rowley, *A Shoemaker a Gentleman* (1608); *The Second Maiden's Tragedy* (1611); Thomas Heywood, *The Four Prentices of London* (1615); Thomas Dekker and Philip Massinger, *The Virgin Martyr* (1620); and *The Two Noble Ladies* (1621). Anthony Dawson has suggested that, for early modern playwrights and playgoers, early Christian history provided a refuge from contemporary sectarian strife. Like other scholars who have recently drawn attention to the ideological complexities of *The Virgin Martyr,* he finds in its combination of referentiality and allegory a compelling case for the theater's conscious swerve away from any kind of straightforward history of the Reformation. See "The Secular Theatre," in *Shakespeare and Religious Change,* eds. Kenneth J. E. Graham and Philip D. Collington (Houndmills, Basingstoke, Hampshire: Palgrave, 2009), 238–60.

3. John D. Staines, "Radical Pity: Responding to Spectacles of Violence in *King Lear*," in *Staging Pain, 1500–1800,* eds. James Robert Allard and Mathew R. Martin (Farnham, UK: Ashgate, 2009), 75–92.

4. "Dramatic Nostalgia and Spectacular Conversion in Dekker and Massinger's *The Virgin Martyr*," *SEL* 49, no. 2 (Spring 2009): 437–62, 449.

5. Jody Enders, *The Medieval Theater of Cruelty: Rhetoric, Memory, Violence* (Ithaca, NY: Cornell University Press, 1999), 46.

6. Myhill, "Making Death a Miracle," 12.

7. Pickett, "Angels in England," 188.

8. Ibid., 189.

9. John H. Langbein, *Torture and the Law of Proof: Europe and England in the Ancien Régime* (Chicago: University of Chicago Press, 1977), 76–77.

10. James Heath, *Torture and English Law: An Administrative and Legal History from the Plantagenets to the Stuarts* (Westport, CT: Greenwood Press, 1982), 159.

11. Curtis C. Breight, *Surveillance, Militarism, and Drama in the Elizabethan Era* (New York: St. Martin's Press, 1996), 5.

12. Langbein, *Torture and the Law of Proof*, 87, 138–39.

13. Breight, *Surveillance, Militarism*, 76.

14. Elizabeth Hanson, "Torture and Truth in Renaissance England," *Representations* 34 (Spring 1991): 53–84, 59.

15. Eugenius is named for the historical bishop of Carthage, and the play is apparently based on the 1605 English translation of St. Victor of Vita's *The memorable and tragical history of the persecution in Africke* (Degenhardt, *Islamic Conversion*, 104).

16. Henry Shirley, *The martyr'd souldier* (London, 1638), B1v. Subsequent references to the quarto will be given parenthetically in the text.

17. Both Catholic and Protestant writers sought to draw a connection between the protagonists of their accounts and the early Christian martyrs who suffered at the hands of Romans. See, for instance, John R. Knott, *Discourses of Martyrdom in English literature, 1563–1694* (Cambridge: Cambridge University Press, 1993), 35, and Lisa McClain, *Lest We Be Damned: Practical Innovation and Lived Experience among Catholics in Protestant England, 1559–1642* (New York: Routledge, 2004), 238ff.

18. Susan Zimmerman, *The Early Modern Corpse and Shakespeare's Theatre* (Edinburgh: Edinburgh University Press, 2005), 26–27.

19. Ibid., 39.

20. "However problematic body was to late medieval Christians, however clearly a locus of temptation and pain, it was also the place where divine power was met" (Caroline Walker Bynum, "Bodily Miracles and the Resurrection of the Body in the High Middle Ages," in *Belief in History: Innovative Approaches to European and American Religion,* ed. Thomas Kselman [London: Notre Dame University Press, 1991], 68–106, 70).

21. Jocelyn Wogan-Browne, "Saints' Lives and the Female Reader," *Forum for Modern Language Studies* 27, no. 4 (October 1991): 314–32, 314–15.

22. Degenhardt, *Islamic Conversion*, 87.

23. Bynum, "Bodily Miracles," 79.

24. William Allen, *A briefe historie of the glorious martyrdom of xii reverend priests* (Rheims, 1582), ed. J. H. Pollen (London, 1908), 53.

25. Elaine Beilin, ed., *The Examinations of Anne Askew* (Oxford: Oxford University Press, 1996), 127.

26. Given Protestantism's renewed emphasis on the home as a microcosm of the Christian state and on the godly wife as the locus of household stability, it makes sense that playgoers might be asked to identify with a married protagonist. But the genuine threats posed to Victoria's chastity in act 5 fail to match up fully with Foxe's narratives, which emphasize "spiritual endurance" over "sexual or physical constancy" (Degenhardt, *Islamic Conversion*, 100).

27. The Clowne's simile strongly echoes Foxe, who in turn is quoting Tertullian: "The more . . . we are mown down of you, the more rise up. The blood of Christians is seed" (quoted in Knott, *Discourses of Martyrdom*, 37).

28. Degenhardt, *Islamic Conversion*, 94.

29. The angel's lyrics deliberately work to bolster the sense that Victoria has become untouchable: "No Tyrant shall confine / A white soule that's divine" (H4r). The contradictions that remain unresolved in the play's depiction of Victoria's "resurrected" body may be inspired by the contradictions in Christ's post-resurrection appearances to his disciplines: he eats and has wounds that can be penetrated, yet he is not enfleshed; he is himself, yet they fail to recognize him.

30. Knott, *Discourses of Martyrdom*, 43. The rack and the manacles were the primary instruments of torture used by the royal authorities in London; Langbein claims that Elizabethan interrogators used mainly the latter, whereas the rack was more prevalent in the Jacobean era (84–85).

31. Knott, *Discourses of Martyrdom*, 80–81.

32. See Huston Diehl, *Staging Reform, Reforming the Stage: Protestantism and Popular Theater in Early Modern England* (Ithaca: Cornell University Press, 1997).

33. Joseph R. Roach, *The Player's Passion: Studies in the Science of Acting* (Newark: University of Delaware Press, 1985), 27. This translation was itself a kind of sacrifice, for if the actor did not adequately control the emotions he summoned up, they might take over his body. See also Paul Menzer's more recent argument about acting as a triumph of physical restraint: "The Actor's Inhibition: Early Modern Acting and the Rhetoric of Restraint," *Renaissance Drama* 35 (2006): 83–111.

34. Dawson, "The Secular Theater," 244.

35. Francis Barker, *The Tremulous Private Body: Essays on Subjection* (London: Methuen, 1984), 25.

36. Bynum, "Bodily Miracles," 85.

37. Christine Peters, *Patterns of Piety: Women, Gender, and Religion in Late Medieval and Reformation England* (Cambridge: Cambridge University Press, 2003), 273.

38. Hanson, "Torture and Truth," 61.

39. "In the discursive economy of English torture the body functioned amphibiously, giving truth a basis in material reality that made it susceptible to discovery, while, in the intense subjectivity of its pain, making truth inaccessible to all but the sufferer" (Ibid., 56). Susanna Monta notes that writers on both sides of the sectarian divide "were at pains to validate their martyrs' smiling countenances with references to their inwardly held, and thus presumably genuine, faiths" (*Martyrdom and Literature in Early Modern England* [Cambridge: Cambridge University Press, 2005], 163).

40. Breight, *Surveillance, Militarism*, 21–22.

41. *The Spectacle of Suffering: Executions and the Evolution of Repression: From a Preindustrial Metropolis to the European Experience* (Cambridge: Cambridge University Press, 1984), 201. Spierenburg concludes that the spectacle of public suffering was designed to achieve "a certain degree of stability" and to reinforce a set of institutionalized power relations—a *raison d'état*—that were "not yet entirely taken for granted" (201–2).

42. This line, the boy actor's description of the play presented to Sly, is taken from the second induction, l. 135. The spelling is from the folio; line numbers are cued to Stephen Greenblatt, Walter Cohen, Jean Howard, and Katharine Eisaman Maus, eds. *The Norton Shakespeare* (New York: W.W. Norton, 1997).

43. Allard and Martin, *Staging Pain*, 6.

44. Enders, *Medieval Theater of Cruelty*, 183.

Discovering the Sins of the Cellar in *The Dutch Courtesan: Turpe est difficiles habere nugas*

Sarah K. Scott

THE *fabulae argumentum* of *The Dutch Courtesan* declares that the "difference betwixt the love of a courtesan and a wife" is the scope of the drama, but Marston's plotlines devoted to the courtesan Franceschina and the vintner Mulligrub complicate this simple formulation, along with the play's related epigraph, *"Turpe est difficiles habere nugas."*[1] Through a series of episodes, the playwright demonstrates that the two urban characters are not as unlike one another as one may initially think, given the behaviors they exhibit and the various forms of moral, economic, and social corruption they promote and, conversely, endure themselves at the hands of two self-styled "virtuous" citizen tricksters, one a city gentleman and the other a gallant knave, each claiming to act for the common good. Marston invites us to understand the similarity between Franceshina and Mulligrub in the double entendre he suggests that we should associate with them, literally embodied in the "seller" and "cellar" homonym.[2] The typesetter of the earliest edition of the play (1605) prints "sellar" (A4), which M. L. Wine modernizes to "cellar" (1.1.40) to mean "Mulligrub's wine cellar."[3] Marston's notorious punning would suggest "sellar" to mean a literal "storehouse" or "storeroom," thus making sense of the opening sequence, as well as a figurative "small vessel" that anticipates the introduction of Franceschina in the following scene.[4] Both "sell" and trade in "cellars," Mulligrub the wine merchant with his architectural space, Franceshina the courtesan with her analogous biological femaleness.

Yet the play makes important distinctions between them. Cocledemoy decries the vintner, a "spigot-frigging jumbler of elements" (3.2.38–39), for polluting the wine vessels and falsifying customers' accounts. Franceschina, shown to be the weaker vessel, is strangely stronger, more productive, and more honest than the thieving merchant (for she is honest about who she is), sells the cellar itself. Marston's representation of the perils of wine and women therefore reveals a kind of double vision, a way of seeing that leads one to understand a thematic element in the play that has been rarely discussed: the idea of moral relativity, in spite of protestations to the contrary by those characters who fancy themselves more virtuous than their fellows as well as by those critics who argue the play is narrowly moralistic and even censorious. Marston demonstrates his *humanitas* and ethic of social tolerance in his sensitive and sympathetic vision of essentially powerless women oppressed by a society of self-interested urban men.

Many scholarly treatments of *The Dutch Courtesan* have examined its moral vision, especially in the mid-twentieth century, when this was common practice, just as current criticism focuses on topics such as national identity and urban economies, both sexual and commercial, in early modern London, typical of our own time. Morse Allen (1920) and Samuel Schoenbaum (1952) argue that the morality of the play and playwright is perverse. Similarly, Paul Zall (1953) reasons that Marston's confused ethical perspective, "concerned more with titillation than with reformation," compromises the unity of his comedy, an idea that has persisted in studies of this work, such as that of Michael Scott (1978).[5] This obsession with morality, unsurprisingly, led to studies of *The Dutch Courtesan* in the lineage as a descendant of the moral play such as Robert K. Presson (1956), Brian Gibbons (1968), G. K. Hunter (1978), and George L. Geckle (1980).[6] Others such as Anthony Caputi (1961) think that the play is less didactic yet still "censorable" for its "coarse scatological references," or, as Wine (1964) claims, in the tradition of *Measure for Measure,* which ends with "healthy laughter and a conclusion that forgives mankind its follies."[7] More recent critical studies by Jean E. Howard, Garrett A. Sullivan, and Marjorie Rubright shift their focus away from direct discussions of morality and have redirected scholarship on the play toward social history.[8]

The Dutch Courtesan has a moral purpose as scholars aver, but it can no more be described as narrow in its vision of human behavior than it can be said to encourage audiences to indulge in carnality for its own sake. As city comedy, the play's satirical purpose is to expose and excoriate harmful social conditions, as well as those who create and perpetuate them. To this end, Marston presents a complex study of dual-perspective portraits to reveal to audiences the idea that what differentiates the good and the bad, the morally right from the wrong, can be difficult to determine, for such judgments depend on one's view and biases. He implies that audiences should understand that in this play of unrestricted free will, the words of flawed people make plenty of sense if one listens carefully enough, especially in this social milieu.

To find Franceschina as a grotesque embodiment of corrupt commerce whose gorgeous exterior superficially conceals her "filthy cellar" is to misread her. Cocledemoy describes her "as false, as prostituted and adulterate, as some translated manuscript" (4.3.6–8), which aligns her with the common Protestant complaint that Roman Catholic texts are corrupt and, as a consequence, spiritually and morally misleading. Mary Faugh's epithet for

Franceschina, "naughty belly," creates a metonym for a diseased cosmopolitan London that concocts and spills discord, for she allows the bawd to market the use of her body to an international clientele, including a Spaniard, an Italian, an Irishman, a German, a Frenchman, and an Englishman (2.2.23, 11–18). This has misled some critics to describe Franceschina's jumbled accent as "ridiculous," as it is "a helter-skelter of Germanic, French, Italian, as well as pure English," an outward expression of internal corruption and signal of the "viciousness of her nature."[9] Schoenbaum, for example, finds her to be a "ferocious" symbol of "sheer animalism."[10] Such a way of thinking about the courtesan resembles the image of the Bahktinian grotesque, described by Peter Stallybrass and Allon White as a "mobile, split, multiple self, a subject of pleasure in processes of exchange," one that is "never closed off from either its social or ecosystemic context."[11] For audiences to take Freevill and Franceschina at their words is to view her as a metonym for a riotous, destabilizing marketplace, a "money-creature" and "mangonist" (1.1.90–91), cause of social and economic ills. This thinking, then, transforms the courtesan into the scapegoat that Freevill and Faugh wish for her to be but that Marston's moral vision does not.[12]

What these critics and others do not seem to take into account is the playwright's subtle differentiation in terminology to describe Franceschina's profession, which signifies his sympathetic understanding of who she is. Marston uses *courtesan* in the name of the play to identify her, a term that is different than *whore*. The designation stands in contrast to those dramas of the period that use *whore* in their titles, such as Thomas Dekker's and Thomas Middleton's *The Honest Whore: Parts I and II,* Dekker's *The Whore of Babylon,* and John Ford's *'Tis Pity She's a Whore.* Perhaps critics have been misguided by the negative comments about Franceschina by the play's less savory characters without understanding Marston's irony. These judgments are apparently affected by the language of the play's characters who are clearly biased against her. Even as Freevill reproaches Malheureux for calling his divorced mistress a "whore," for instance, we know to take his defensive language as an offense against Franceschina: "Whore? Fie whore! You may call her a courtesan, a cockatrice, or (as that worthy spirit of an eternal happiness said) a suppository. But whore! Fie! 'tis not in fashion to call things by their right names" (1.2.97–100). Freevill's crass quip to Malheureux reveals a callous attitude toward his one-time mistress, implying clearly that he still thinks of her as a "whore," and his apparent ability to embrace another love, the chaste Beatrice, in a completely different manner. Such descriptions clash with conventional images of the courtesan. Even at this early stage of the satire, Marston expects us to know better, even if Freevill is hardly capable of expressing capaciousness.

The playwright, perhaps subversively, clearly implies another way of thinking about his title character. Much in the play suggests that Franceschina is a sophisticated, cosmopolitan "lady of the evening" and "an exotic mistress of the sensual arts" in the fashion of Continental courtesans, as Andrew Fleck argues, and as a woman reputed for her beauty as even Freevill and Malheureux attest.[13] Any worldly gentleman gallant might enjoy her company very much. Franceschina is clearly a very beautiful woman as Freevill indicates: "pretty, nimble-eyed," "an honest soft-hearted impropriation," "soft, plump, round-cheek'd" (1.1.140–42). She is also a skilled musician and singer, as well as well-versed in what Ovid immortalizes as the avowedly physical art of love in the *Ars amatoria.* Malherureux's estimation, "Beauty entirely choice" (2.2.101), summarizes Franceschina perfectly.

Despite her obvious attractiveness, Marston undercuts this sophistication, albeit sympathetically, with the malapropisms and comic misunderstandings that her Dutch accent causes. The possible sexual allure of her intriguingly "foreign" pronunciation of certain words collides with frequent cursing combined with impassioned revenge, which paint the courtesan as either a comic villain or a very angry woman. The language employed by other characters, such as Cocledemoy, undermines Franceschina's status as well. As the knavish city companion praises her wealthy customers, for instance, he degrades them, and by extension, vitiates her. The courtesan's clientele are not "base corn-cutters or sowgelders," but most "rare wealthy knights and most rare bountiful lords" (1.2.40–41), an obvious irony, since Freevill was her most recent client. While no rustic, he is certainly no "bountiful lord" either. These competing perspectives of Franceschina lead us to sympathize with Franceschina's plight as a foreigner and as a woman with little choice but to work within her social status and condition.

The courtesan's embodiment of sexuality and commerce contributes to the satirical elements of the play, but Marston stresses that she is more victim than victimizer. Her "cellar" may very well be adulterated by disease, but she has undoubtedly been "tampered" with by her bawd's machinations and Freevill's conduct, as well as by that of Malheureux and her international clients. Although several previous critics imply that Franceschina's "impurity" is her fault and that Marston is condemning her, the dramatist is not as disdainful of her as some commentators suggest. For instance, she appears to have been victimized by the sex trade in England due to political conflicts between the Spanish in the Low Countries, as Freevill's defense of prostitution implies: "I would have married men love the stews as Englishmen lov'd the Low Countries: wish war should be maintain'd there lest it should come home to their own doors" (1.1.62–65). Combined with the multinational clients that Mary Faugh lists in 2.2, she herself is a kind of new England, a mix of many people, a potential source of danger and delight. Franceschina seems to have been an impoverished refugee, as expressed indirectly by her bawd's account of their relationship:

I ha' kept counsel for thee. Who paid the apothecary? Was it not honest Mary Faugh? Who redeem'd thy petticoat and mantle? Was't not honest Mary Faugh? Who helped thee to thy custom, not of swaggering Ireland captains nor of two-shilling Inns o' Court men, but with honest flat-caps, wealthy flat-caps, that pay for their pleasure with best of any men in Europe, nay, which is more, in London?

(2.2.25–31)

In these lines, Mary foolishly fancies herself a successful professional tradeswoman who proudly maximizes her profit in human traffic as she, ironically, remonstrates Francheshina for complaining that *she* has been demeaned, for the bawd takes pride in selling virginity "like a great merchant by wholesale" (1.2.38–39) as jesting Cocledemoy submits. Absurdly, the bawd protests that she is the victim in the relationship, which she likens to a mother-daughter bond: "I ha' made as much o' your maidenhead—and you had been mine own daughter, I could no ha' sold your maidenhead oft'ner than I ha' done" (2.2.10–12). Moreover, the courtesan's desire for revenge on Freevill, who at no place in the play acknowledges "any responsibility for or complicity in her prostitution" as Susan Baker avers, may not appear to be quite so villainously cliché as it might seem if one understands Franceschina to be a courtesan in the fashion of Cassio's domestic companion Bianca who wishes to be his wife.[14] The outrage she voices to Mary at loosing Freevill suggests as much: "You ha' brought mine love, mine honor, mine body, all to noting!" (2.2.7–8). So does her disgust for Malheureux, the allegorical embodiment of unhappiness or bad fortune: "Go, go go! I can no more of love. No, no, no!," and later, "Oh mine forsaken heart! (2.2.14, 117–18). Franceschina's feelings certainly interfere with her chances of financial stability or to be cared for in a way that that a woman kept by a wealthy man would. By refusing to find another patron she predictably becomes a scorned woman left "to the world" (2.2.3) since she has lost Freevill and, accordingly, finds herself seemingly without free will, due to the force of the collective constraints upon her. Franceschina's description of herself as an agent of the devil, "Dere sall be no Got in me but passion, no tought but rage, no mercy but blood, no spirit but divla in me" (4.3.40–42), while an intense articulation of her anger, strikes one as not so strange, given the situation. In this sense, then, Marston provides a naturalistic account of her plight, and shows his minute understanding of the social conditions that he presents in his portrayal of the sex trade and the corresponding commodification of women.[15]

The character Freevill, whose name and behavior carries many associations pertinent to the idea of moral relativism, functions as the play's catalyst and serves as mocking commentary on the folly of young male citizens. He shows the importance of the concept, and to some extent a lack of free will. He also brings to mind the theological concept of free will, which in some respects he exhibits, and his name implies that the other characters in many respects have this—no one is making them do what they are doing. As an allegorical figure, Freevill alludes to the philosophical concept of the will, the engine of Plato's tripartite soul, and related too are all the early modern English connotations of the will as sex drive, or even the male thing itself, as in the second line of Shakespeare's Sonnet 135 ("will in overplus") and *All's Well that Ends Well* ("fleshes his will in the spoil of her honor"), all of which Marston employs freely in the play.[16] Finally, "vill" is the way that a Dutch person, such as Franceschina, would likely pronounce "will." Marston presents Freevill as the very embodiment of the biological and therefore somewhat involuntary male drive that necessitates the courtesan and oppresses her married and respectable sister.[17] Apparently unaware that he acts purely out of self-interest rather than for the betterment of others, he pushes Franceshina to the brink of madness, relegating her to "extremest whip and jail" (5.3.59), and he fakes his own death on the evening of the masque that celebrates his marriage contract with his "second love" (3.1.224) Beatrice, also a victim, who subsequently collapses in despair and later contemplates suicide rather than endure his absence.[18] Freevill claims to stage all of this confusion to correct Malhereux's concupiscence that Freevill introduced him to, so as to force his friend to *avoid* the brothel by leading him to narrowly escape the "vildest of dangers" (4.2.35), public hanging, albeit only after his friend contemplates murdering him to win the bed of Franceschina. The convoluted plan is hardly a virtuous one, as he acknowledges in an aside: "Now repentance, the fool's whip, seize thee! / Nay, if there be no means I'll be thy friend," adding a few lines later, "But is this virtue in me? No, not pure; / Nothing extremely best with us endures" (4.2.31–32, 38–39). Such private scheming clearly demonstrates egotistical engagement in that which provides amusement regardless of the feelings or well-being of others. His justification for the plot, that the resulting good will justify the means taken to achieve it, "The end being good, the means are well assign'd" (4.2.46–47), reveals him to be a libertine utterly devoid of *caritas*. Even foulmouthed Cocledemoy, who unrelentingly schemes to "fiddle" Mulligrub "till he fist" (4.5.70–1) restores the objects he steals from the vintner. Marston depicts the pathological scourge who pretends to possess moral standards while operating on pure pretense all the while throughout the drama, and especially near its close. When Franceschina is punished with "severest prison" (5.3.55), audiences are led to seriously doubt the sincerity of his actions that incited his former mistress to attempted double murder: "I wrought the feigned, [death] suffering this fair devil / In shape of woman to make good her plot; / And, knowing that the hook was deeply fast, / I gave her line at will till, with her own vain strivings, / See here she's tired" (5.3.43–50).[19] They also must question his punishing test of Beatrice's chastity. Crispinella, who is the closest thing to a surrogate of Marston in the play, summarizes his person and the role of free will in the satire when she sharply retorts "Sir, all I can yet say of you is, you are uncivil" (5.2.27), declaring candidly a few lines later, "you have wronged us" (5.2.58).[20] To be sure, his actions against his fiancée and his courtesan are patently cruel. Marston's Freevill is clearly not the virtuous and idealized protagonist of city comedy, but the realistic embodiment of hypocrisy and malice who oppresses women by exploiting them, hardly the "virtuous gentleman" that some have called him.[21]

The playwright employs Freevill as object and agent of satire, an ironic chorus who enunciates the hypocritical platitudes of his society without understanding how empty they are.[22] His commentary conveys the theme of the play, such as "The sight of vice augments the hate of sin," an ironic repetition of the aphorism first spoken by Malheureux and repeated twice by Freevill (1.1.153, 154; 1.2.153). The commonplace becomes all the more satirical as the actions and tableaus build to reveal the libertine as anti-hero and citizen-villain. It encapsulates one of the central moral lessons of the drama, for it points to the problems of a society managed by self-interested individuals lacking virtue. Even *sententiae* that he uses to bespeak Franceschina's character would be better applied to himself, such as the expression "Nothing is defamed but by his proper self" (3.1.231).

Not much difference exists between Freevill's fundamental attitude toward the courtesan and his fiancée who is doomed to marry him, given his brutish love test, blind chauvinism, and aphorisms, one of which even quotes part of the first phrase of the *Metamorphoses*. Freevill's indictment against Franceschina, "*In nova fert animus mutatas dicere formas!*" (3.1.213) ("My spirit compels me to tell of forms changed into new . . .") bespeaks his moral relativity.[23] His omission of the word "corpora," from the famous line from the master of love not only identifies but indicts him, for it is the epitome of changeability, which Freevill is. That he changes it himself by leaving off one word shows him to be even more shifty and indirect, blown sideways as he is: "Then let my course be borne, though with side wind" (4.2.46). Crispinella's avowal, "Things hop'd with fear and got with strugglings are men's high pleasures when duty pales and flats their appetite" (4.1.36–38), certainly applies to the drive of unrestrained licentious freedom of the will and to Freevill, who seeks the hand of the chaste Beatrice after having grown weary of Franceschina. Moreover, the audience is nowhere shown that he will be faithful in his marriage regardless of his Platonic pronouncements of love, which Crispinella considers empty obsequy, motivating her to opine to her sister, "There is no more affinity betwixt virtue and marriage than betwixt a man and his horse" (3.1.82–83). We have every reason to expect that he will be a version of the stereotypical husband that Crispinella characterizes in her mocking exchange with Tysefew. To her suitor's claim that she "wilt marry shortly" for she "growest somewhat foolish already," she sarcastically rejoins, "Oh, in faith, 'tis a fair thing to be married, and a necessary" (4.1.28–30). In the speech that follows, she describes women's position in marriage, arguing that it is a state of which to be leery, for "If our husbands be proud, we must bear his contempt"—no matter how "proud," "noisome," or foolish they may be (4.1.31–32). Beatrice's sister also complains of the difference in status between spouses: whereas husbands "may" choose whether or not to obey to their wives, women "must" care for their men (4.1.36). Her pronouncements of the disparity of obligation invite audiences to compare the statuses of wives to husbands and courtesans to bawds and clients to observe that there is little difference between the positions of women in either bond.[24] By pointing to the potential perils of marriage for women, especially to individuals such as Freevill, who asserts his male sexual privilege at will and provides little evidence of genuine sympathy to others, Marston satirically proposes that there may not necessarily be much "difference *betwixt the love of a courtesan and a wife.*"

The playwright's moral outlook is less concerned with differentiating between conceptions of love and lust and chastity and whoredom than with negating the difference between them. Such dichotomies are laughably invalid in the society he depicts so empathetically. Another character who illustrates this concept, in spite of her protestations to the contrary, is Mistress Mulligrub, although she is hardly a paragon of goodness whose unshakable credibility gives her the authority to make pronouncements.[25] Geckle has observed that she is morally "not much different" than Franceschina, for she resembles the courtesan who is a "serious threat" to temperance, "the unifying concept" of the play. I would say instead that the wife is not employed by Marston to this end, but as a figure contributing in an additional sense to Marston's compassionate view of women. She is a product of her environment and behaves accordingly, an idea that the playwright emphasizes as he creates several parallels between Mistress Mulligrub and Franceschina. Just as Mary Faugh treats the title character herself as commodity, the vintner suggests the same about his wife when he cries "Wife! My money! Wife!" (2.3.81–82), an expression merging women and material goods ontologically in a fashion resembling the exclamations of Barabas, "O my girl, My gold, my fortune, my felicity" (*The Jew of Malta* 2.1.48–49), and Shylock, "My daughter! O my ducats!" (*The Merchant of Venice* 2.8.15).[26] Mistress Mulligrub unknowingly suggests as much about herself when she promises to Cocledemoy to keep on continual offer at the tavern "a piece of mutton and a featherbed" (5.3.93), typically unaware of the sexual innuendo she broadcasts in witness of her husband as he faces public hanging.[27] Yet in the world Marston dramatizes, such a statement becomes quite sensible if one considers the necessity of retaining customers, no matter how undesirable, for economic survival. Her marriage, the only conjugal relationship in the play, resembles that characterized by Crispinella, for the vintner is indeed "proud," "noisome," and foolish (4.1.31–34). Moreover, their membership to the Familist religious sect, the "Family of Love," well-known for is associations with licentiousness, clearly associates the Mulligrubs' house and tavern with Franceschina's brothel, which Cocledemoy designates at the opening of the play as "a house of salvation," "the Family of Love" (1.1.137, 139–40).[28] It elides Franceschina's promiscuity with Mistress Mulligrub's double entendre and her husband's piercing of "profane vessels," leading, according to Cocledemoy, "to the subversion, staggering, and overthrow of many a good Christian" (5.3.103, 9–10). The expression "Cheaters and bawds go together like washing and wringing" (3.3.124) finds an additional subject in the Mulligrubs' relationship, for despite her pretensions to moral superiority, she obeys her husband's charge to "score false with a vengeance" (2.3.12–13) on their customers' accounts, even while admitting their wrongdoing: "We do wink at the sins of our people, our wines are Protestants" (2.3.8–11). Collectively, these instances give further expression to Freevill's dictum, "Every man must follow his trade, and every woman her occupation" (1.1.94–95), for the commonplace applies equally both to Franceshina and Mistress Mulligrub, thus creating another instance of double vision. Marston's satirical portrayal of the vintner's wife and the similarities she bears to the courtesan express the idea that what constitutes morality depends upon one's condition. How can we judge Franceschina if she simply does what Mrs. Mulligrub says she does, or would do, herself, given the circumstances?

To make his strongest argument that we should not believe in the misogynist moral judgments that some characters in the play make, Marston uses women themselves to explain the hypocrisy and oppression that they suffer. He designs Crispinella's disquisition with Beatrice to communicate this idea through a series of aphoristic statements on the nature of sexual relations, perhaps the central passage of the dramatic text. It can be divided into four different parts. First, Marston's agent in the play asserts: "We pronounce boldly robbery, murder, treason, which deeds must be far more loathsome than an act which is so natural, just, and necessary as that of procreation" (3.1.29–32). This most reasonable and honest person speaks with candor to argue that sex is not a crime but a pleasurable, "natural, just, and necessary," and useful good, and that as such, those women who enjoy it hardly deserve to be punished. It would be both unnatural and unjust to do so. Her next comment, "You shall have an hypocritical vestal virgin speak that with close teeth publicly which she will receive with open mouth privately" (32–34), explains the social and moral consequences of subverting nature. Here Crispinella argues that narrow formulations of morality absurdly force even the most celibate of women into hypocrisy, implying too that sexual longing possesses a sacred quality, despite it being a public taboo, for it is desired and privately relished by women renowned for possessing the highest moral standards. Although she does not say so, procreation is the intended happy result of marital relations, the sacred injunction of God to Adam and Eve in Genesis 1:28. Her third statement proposes an alternative to forced feminine hypocrisy, with herself as an example: "For my own part, I consider nature without apparel; without disguising of customs or compliment, I give thoughts words, and words truth, and truth boldness" (3.1.34–37). In a moment of self-definition, she expresses the belief that what is natural to humanity is good and true, and therefore should be made visible rather than painted over by popular social conventions and empty posturing by individuals such as Freevill, who do much to mar the inherent beauty of sex. And finally, she merges the general and the personal:

> She whose honest freeness makes it her virtue to speak what she thinks will make it her necessity to think what is good. I love no prohibited things, and yet I would have nothing prohibited by policy but by virtue; for, as in the fashion of time, those books that are call'd in are most in sale and request, so in nature those actions that are most prohibited are most desired.
> (3.1.37–44)

Crispinella's concluding statement, cleverly reversing the gender of the usual argumentative gambit from "he" to "she," states the theme of the play and expresses the playwright's point of view, as does her earlier remark, "Let's ne'er be ashamed to speak what we be not ashamed to think; I dare as boldly speak venery as think venery" (3.1.26–27). It provides a personal example that relies on the four previous statements to argue that for women to refrain from sexual activities as a matter of "policy" leads to the most deleterious effect of all. If what should be licit is made illicit, then all women run the risk of being judged "adulterate" (4.1.7) manuscripts. As she addresses the problems of social formations of sexuality, Crispinella presents an ethic of social tolerance as well as a sympathetic attitude toward all women. As it watched the boy actor portraying Beatrice's well-to-do sister, it is likely that Marston's male audience would have been all the more receptive to this sensitive portrait of *humanitas* since this persona more closely resembled their mothers, sisters, or wives than a courtesan such as Franceschina.

Crispinella's sensitive and intelligent defense of women and sexuality against the conventions of narrow-minded morality is one Marston would have us understand as entirely reasonable. She argues, essentially, that Franceschina and other women who are similarly disenfranchised should be treated like those women that hypocritical men judge to be respectable, for whoredom is a relative, socially constructed concept. Prostitution would not be the necessity that Freevill avers if censorious attitudes such as his weren't the governing ones.[29] Surely women—and men—would be happier with more freedom to express themselves in such a manner. Her sister's cautioning that she be less vocal on such matters, for "the world would censure" her since "truly severe modesty is women's virtue" (3.1.46–47), clearly expresses the strictures of the milieu. In this morally restrictive environment, audiences are little surprised to find Franceschina preyed upon by dishonest city gallants who publicly demean her as a "whore" with a diseased "cellar," but who privately praise the courtesan for her remarkable beauty and lovemaking skills. Marston's semi-naturalistic portrait of the fallen woman asks his audiences to witness a desperate woman hopelessly entangled in an array of disparate relationships. Franceschina, a victim of her circumstances, will never realize her desire to become a loving wife or to be part of any legitimate family at all. The playwright's ultimate satirical goal is not to ridicule her, as some critics have argued, but to revile Franceschina's Janus-faced victimizers by exposing the cruel conditions that they create and that she must accept.

Examination of *The Dutch Courtesan*'s *fabulae argumentum* reveals the playwright's intention to expose and excoriate hypocritical attitudes toward women to explain there is not much "difference betwixt the love of a courtesan and a wife" within the social context. Marston's sympathetic treatment of women in this dramatic world asks audiences to question the moral dictates of those who censure them, which in turn leads to a questioning of the claims of those critics who have been misled by the play's insincere characters. The play's challenge to the idea of woman as commodity circulates around the entire play, much like the richly symbolic ring that represents this dynamic as it passes between Beatrice to Freevill and from Freevill to Malheureux to Franceschina and back to Beatrice. Its movement suggests, in still yet another sense, that for the playwright to depict the "difference *betwixt the love of a courtesan and a wife*" is to expose the "difficult nonsense" to which the drama's epigraph alludes, at least judging from the array of morally relativistic viewpoints that Marston provides his audience.

Notes

1. *The Dutch Courtesan,* ed. M. L. Wine, Regents Renaissance Drama (Lincoln: University of Nebraska Press, 1965) 3, 5. Wine's translation of the epigraph: "It is shameful to achieve difficult nonsense." All references to the play follow this edition, and are indicated by act, scene, and line numbers in parentheses.

2. For a discussion of the double entendre and the sexual pun in Marston's play, but one that does not discuss the cellar / seller homonym, see Richard Scarr, "Insatiate Punning in Marston's Courtesan Plays," in *The Drama of John Marston: Critical Re-Visions,* ed. T. F. Wharton (Cambridge: Cambridge University Press, 2000), 82–99.

3. *The Dutch Curtezan. As it was Playd in the Black-Friars, by the Children of her Maiesties Revels* (London: T. P. for Hodgets, 1605). Wine, n. 40. See also *The Dutch Courtesan,* ed. David Crane, The New Mermaids (London: A & C Black, 1997) 1.1.44, which follows Wine's modernization.

4. See "cellar" n. and "cellar," n.1, *OED*.

5. Allen complains that the *Courtesan* is humorless satire and comprises "more than the coarseness of the age; it is lecherous and filthy." See *The Satire of John Marston* (New York: Haskell House, 1965), 142, originally "The Satire of John Marston" (PhD diss., Princeton University, 1920). To Schoenbaum, Marston's play is "turbulent and irrational," reflecting his "disordered fantasies and half-acknowledged impulses that rankled within him." See "The Precarious Balance of John Marston," *PMLA* 67 (1952): 1069–78; 1077. Zall contends that the play's characterization shows "the results of restrictions on natural behavior: perversion on the one hand, inordinate passions on the other, both fundamentally potentially tragic." See "John Marston, Moralist," *English Literary History* 20 (1953): 186; 186–93. Scott argues that Marston's misuse of Montaigne demonstrates his inability to reconcile "dramatic structure and credibility and theatrical convention" or to base it successfully on "moral philosophy." See *John Marston's Plays: Theme, Structure, and Performance* (London: Macmillan, 1978), 47. William Hamlin contends the opposite, that Marston's reading of the *Essais* in John Florio's translation, especially "Of Custome," demonstrates a sophisticated, "mediated" understanding of Montaigne that the play reflects, especially regarding the title character: "The rehabilitation of Florio's Montaigne within the genesis of" *Courtesan* "contributes to the rehabilitation of Franceschina within the play's moral dynamic." See "Common Customers in Marston's *Dutch Courtesan* and Florio's Montaigne," *Studies in English Literature 1500–1900* 52 (2012): 421, 407–24. Wine lists forty-five instances of borrowing from Montaigne in *Courtesan* ("Appendix A," 112–20).

6. Robert K. Presson, "Marston's 'Dutch Courtezan': The Study of an Attitude in Adaptation," *Journal of English and Germanic Philology* 53 (1956): "a late but legitimate descendant of the *Psychomachia* literature," 407; 406–13. Gibbons argues the play is "a didactic *exemplum*," narrowly concluding as a "satiric comedy rather than tragedy." See *Jacobean City Comedy: A Study of Satiric Plays by Jonson, Marston, and Middleton* (London: Rupert Hart-Davis, 1968), 119. Hunter, *Dramatic Identities and Cultural Tradition: Studies in Shakespeare and His Contemporaries* (New York: Barnes and Noble, 1978): the drama is "braced by a rigid Morality framework" (130). Geckle claims that Marston's "unifying concept" is *temperantia,* for the play interrogates "the very principle of morality and practical rules of conduct that both classical and Christian teachers found in temperance." See *John Marston's Drama; Themes, Images, Sources* (Rutherford, NJ: Fairleigh Dickinson Press, 1980), 150, 172.

7. Wine, xxiii; Caputi, *John Marston, Satirist* (Ithaca, NY: Cornell University Press, 1961), 239.

8. For Rubright, see "Going Dutch in London City Comedy: Economies of Sexual and Sacred Exchange in John Marston's *The Dutch Courtesan* (1605)," *English Literary Renaissance* 40 (2010): 88–112. Sullivan investigates Marston's use of social and architectural spaces to express complex commercial exchanges and the "problematic relationship between the brothel and the shop." See "'All Thinges Come into Commerce': Women, Household Labor, and the Spaces of Marston's *The Dutch Courtesan,*" *Renaissance Drama* 27 (1996): 21; 19–46. Howard examines the city comedy's "complicated engagement with the realities" of a cosmopolitan London populated with diverse groups of peoples. See "Mastering Difference in *The Dutch Courtesan,*" *Shakespeare Studies* 24 (1996): 109; 105–17.

9. Wine, xix, n. 15 xix. Rubright, "Going Dutch in London City Comedy," argues Franceschina's accent is early modern "'stage Dutch,'" a combination of "part-Dutch and part-English" that associates "Dutch women with sex work" (97). Howard, "Mastering Difference in *The Dutch Courtesan*," finds the courtesan's "hybridized speech" a result of dwelling in a culturally cosmopolitan city: "when she talks she is a monster of deformity, a hybrid creature who masters no one language but roils about in a mixture of many" (112).

10. Schoenbaum, "The Precarious Balance of John Marston," *Publications of the Modern Language Association* 67 (1952): 1075, 1069–78: "Women become symbols of sheer animalism, a tendency culminating in the ferocious Franceschina of *The Dutch Courtezan*."

11. Peter Stallybrass and Allon White, *The Politics and Poetics of Transgression*. (Ithaca, NY: Cornell University Press, 1986), 22. It also is similar to some of the language used to describe her by several other critics, such as Alfred Harbage, who finds Marston's portrait a "venomous" one that counters typical tolerant dramatic treatments of prostitutes as "amiable creatures" who are "fubbed off in marriage as part of the concluding mirth." See *Shakespeare and the Rival Traditions* (New York: Macmillan, 1952), 196. David Crane argues she is a common whore, "easy to lust after without inconvenience, without real consequence": "Franceschina is Dutch, foreign, as well as being a whore, and so she is double expendable, doubly incapable of secure status, and by the same token easy to lust after without inconvenience, without real consequence." He goes on to suggest that moral confusion would follow by the middle of 2.1. See "Patterns of Audience Involvement at the Blackfriars Theatre in the Early Seventeenth Century: Some Moments in Marston's *The Dutch Courtesan*" in *Plotting Early Modern London: New Essays on Jacobean City Comedy,* ed. Dieter Miehl, Angela Stock, and Anne-Julia Zwierlein (Aldershot: Ashgate, 2004) 102; 97–107. These ideas sometimes inform interpretations of the play's moral framework as well. Allen, *The Satire of John Marston,* describes her as "one of the wickedest little persons in Elizabethan drama" and the play completely unsentimental (142). Wine avers Franceschina is "a grotesque, even an absurd, figure," not a symbol of vice or a victim but a comedic character "ridiculously vicious," which contributes to the overall sentimental tone of the play (xix).

12. Or, as Hamlin says, "Marston designs his play in such a way that we cannot ultimately sever Freevill's happiness and moral triumph from Franceschina's alienation." See "Common Customers," 420.

13. See Andrew Fleck, "The Custom of Courtesans in John Marston's *The Dutch Courtesan.*" *American Notes and Queries* 21 (2008): 11, 11–19.

14. Susan Baker, "Sex and Marriage in *The Dutch Courtesan*," in *In Another Country: Feminist Perspectives on Renaissance Drama,* ed. Dorothea Kehler and Susan Baker (Metuchen, NJ: Scarecrow Press, 1991), 224–25. See *Othello* 3.4.169–200 and 4.1.108–44 in *The Riverside Shakespeare,* 2nd ed., ed. G. Blakemore Evans (Boston: Houghton Mifflin, 1997). All references to Shakespeare's works follow this edition.

15. Adaptations of the play in the 140 years following its 1605 publication exhibit a marked preference for the subplot's comedy over the satirically dark qualities of the drama's upperplot, for Franceschina's character assumes a more romantic, sentimen-

talized treatment, or she is omitted entirely. The underplot's inclusion in *The Wits* (1673), a collection of drolls, as *The Cheater Cheated* attests to its popularity, as do the adaptations that followed. In *The Revenge; or, A Match in Newgate* (1680), Thomas Betterton thought Franceschina's punishment too cruel. Instead the adaptor created a melodrama that omits the Dutch accent of the Franceschina character (Corina) and that concludes with the courtesan marrying Sir Empty, therefore removing one aspect of Marston's unsettling close for another. Christopher Bullock's melodrama *Woman's Revenge: or, a Match in Newgate* (1715), also delivers an alternative sentimental ending by featuring the Freevill character (Trueman) providing Franceschina (Corinna) money so long as she abandons her trade. This play was subsequently fashioned into the ballad opera *Love and Revenge; or, The Vintner Outwitted* (1729). *Trick for Trick* (1739), and *The Vintner Trick'd* (1746) neglected the upper plot entirely to feature solely the Mulligrub plot. Marston's play was restaged in 1954 at the Theatre Workshop, Stratford East (dir. Joan Littlewood) with Avis Bunnage playing Franceschina "as a real woman and not a stage slut,'" and in 1959 it was revived by the same director at the same theater with Ann Beach presenting the courtesan as "Babyish in her endearments, groveling in tantrums when discarded." See Scott, *John Marston's Plays: Theme, Structure, and Performance* (London: Macmillan, 1978), 105–11 and Leo Hughes and Arthur H. Scouten, "Some Theatrical Adaptations of a Picareque Tale," *Studies in English* 25 (1945–46): 98–114.

16. *All's Well That Ends Well*, 4.3.16–17. See Carol W. Pollard, "Immoral Morality: Combinations of Morality Types in *All's Well That Ends Well* and *The Dutch Courtesan*," *Cahiers Élisabéthains* 25 (1984): 53–59, for a discussion of similarities between the two plays.

17. Wine describes Freevill as "the central intelligence of the main plot" (xvii). Philip J. Finkelpearl considers him to be a critic of "bad conduct and false morals." See "*The Dutch Curtezan:* 'Rich Sence' and 'Bad Language,'" in *John Marston of the Middle Temple: An Elizabethan Dramatist in His Social Setting* (Cambridge, MA: Harvard University Press, 1969), 215, 195–215. Gustav Cross argues that Freevill is "Montaigne's 'natural man,' forerunner of the libertine or *honnête homme* who features so largely in later seventeenth-century literature." See Gustav Cross, "Marston, Montaigne, and Morality: *The Dutch Curtezan* Reconsidered," *English Literary History* 27 (1960): 36.

18. Considering Freevill's actions toward Beatrice, Alexander Leggatt finds "Freevill's use of disappearance and disguise . . . has its evil side. He savors her [Beatrice's] display of grief too smugly," adding that "even the moral agent who tests and corrects the other characters is examined and found wanting." See *Citizen Comedy in the Age of Shakespeare* (Toronto: University of Toronto Press, 1973), 123.

19. Compare to Mark Thornton Burnett, "Calling 'things by their right names': Troping Prostitution, Politics, and *The Dutch Courtesan*," in *Renaissance Configurations: Voices/Bodies/Spaces, 1580–1690*, ed. Gordon McMullan (New York: St. Martin's Press, 1998): "Franceschina functions as a scapegoat: the abusive treatment of the prostitute permits a range of anxieties to be conveniently discharged" (174).

20. Geckle also finds that she "serves as Marston's female satiric commentator" to "satirize contemporary practices of courtship" and "takes a natural and realistic view of sex." She also "inveighs against the domination of husbands over wives in the

manner of Shakespeare's Beatrice in *Much Ado About Nothing.*" See *John Marston's Drama; Themes, Images, Sources,* 165. Allen holds an alternate view: "Freevil [*sic*] generally expresses the author, having many resemblances to Planet [in *Jack Drum's Entertainment*]." See Allen, *The Satire of John Marston,* 146.

21. For example, Howard, "Mastering Difference in *The Dutch Courtesan,*" 108.

22. Caputi briefly mentions by the idea of Freevill as a "choral character." See *John Marston, Satirist,* 234.

23. Wine's translation: "In new situations the mind prompts the utterance of altered sentiments."

24. See also Baker, "Sex and Marriage in *The Dutch Courtesan*": "In her own temperate way, Beatrice is allied with Franceschina—both women object to Freevill's easy recourse to totalizing stereotypes of woman-as-deity or woman-as-whore. The play exposes the inseparability of these stereotypes" (226).

25. Geckle, "Temperance in *The Dutch Courtesan,*" is judgmental, excoriating Mrs. Mulligrub for her lack of temperance, her weak "sense of justice," and low morals generally, especially in speaking about her "sexual exploits" (166).

26. Christopher Marlowe, *The Jew of Malta,* ed. James R. Siemon, The New Mermaid Series (London: A & C Black, 2006).

27. Geckle, 166, avers the wife is fully aware of her double meaning, although I am doubtful. Even though she is silly, she is not heartless.

28. Familists were derided for promoting inclusivity and egalitarianism, exemplified by the lines from Dutch merchant Hendrik Niclaes's *Evangelium Regni* (Cologne: Printed by N. Bohmberg, 1575?) 3–4,wherein he calls on all "lovers of [God's] . . . Truth, here and there, wheresoever . . . of what Nation and Religion soever they be, Christians, Jews, Mahomites or Turks and heathen" to come together to interaffilitate in love and peace. For a detailed discussion of the Familist sect see Christopher Marsh, *The Family of Love in English Society, 1550–1630* (Cambridge: Cambridge University Press, 1994). See also Rubright, "Going Dutch in London City Comedy," 102–6. She observes moreover that the play presents "four concepts of 'family': idealized patriarchal household, common bawdy house, banned religious sect, and the commercialized home-tavern," 94. See also Sullivan, "'All Things Come into Commerce': Women, Household Labor, and the Spaces of Marston's *The Dutch Courtesan,*" n.10, 42.

29. Vivienne Cottrell's 1990 London production emphasized the idea that women's social positions result not from some aspect of their "essential being" but from environmental conditions, an argument by underscored by the actors playing Beatrice and Franceschina who exchanged roles during the course of the performance. See Peter Womack, "John Marston, *The Dutch Courtesan*[:] Children of the Queen's Revels, Blackfriars (1605)," in *English Renaissance Drama,* ed. Peter Womack (London: Blackwell, 2006), 171; 168–73.

The "salarie of your lust": Rethinking the Economics of Virtue in Massinger's Plays

Matthew J. Smith

DEBT, suspicion, and obligation are perhaps the most pervasive of all thematic conflicts in Philip Massinger's many plays. The recurring trope is of characters' foolhardy indebtedness depriving them of the ability to exercise virtue, often leaving financial obligation and moral decay as interdependent. A valuable and as of yet unappreciated context for understanding this conflict is recent work in economic history that challenges the older diachronic depiction of seventeenth-century England as an origin of secularized contract economics; recent scholarship suggests that the early seventeenth century is more than a mere transition from a community-driven and religiously informed market to one of secular individualism.[1] Craig Muldrew redraws the lines of economic transition by describing the early seventeenth century as distinctly reliant on credit relations and a commercial ethic built around reputation rather than debt.[2] A reader of Massinger will receive this historical frame with interest since it suggests a more promising perspective for interpreting Massinger's suspicion of indebtedness as a meaningful statement about the ethical implications of the market setting in theater. Yet a reading of Massinger's treatment of economic virtue is incomplete without also accounting for his steadily eccentric treatment of religion. In T. A. Dunn's opinion, "Alone of all the Elizabethan and Jacobean dramatists he displays an almost constant religious bias," even if, I would add, this bias is difficult to pin down.[3] Massinger freely employs an untidy mixture of Catholicism, Protestantism, and ancient Christian forms, without expressing exclusive favor for any one religious mode, and scholars have long debated the possibility of Massinger being a Roman Catholic.[4] While searching for Massinger's personal religious views is of limited value to realizing the cultural engagements of his plays, what is relevant is that his characters' reclamations of virtue often take the form of religious penitence, sometimes in disparate ways, and certainly too dynamically to deem his plays "undenominationally Christian."[5]

Against the critical trend to view his plays as merely conventional, this essay proposes that Massinger's fixations with financial obligation and religion emerge as serious respective engagements when read through one another. Massinger criticism—underrepresented but growing—has only recently begun to treat his handling of economics seriously, but such studies rarely explore the relation between economics and religion in depth.[6] For Massinger, stifling indebtedness goes hand-in-hand with spiritual depravity, and the developments in early seventeenth-century economics and theology suggest that Massinger is not alone in this opinion. Theological evolutions in the English church confront problems similar to those faced by the market, namely, the desire to move away from debt-centered theology toward a greater reliance on credit. Massinger's treatment of indebtedness draws attention to the ethical problems that arise in this transition. In short, he censures the kind of remedial virtue that occurs when a character acts to repay a debt, theological or financial; while conversely, he commends virtuous activity that aims at an ethical standard transcending the strictures of the marketplace. Using parallel characters and settings in several of his plays, I will argue that Massinger reacts to the sizeable shifts in the market and church in the early seventeenth century, and I will show how a new perspective on virtue and economic obligation enriches what is traditionally seen as Massinger's merely generic and conventional assessment of virtue and vice.

* * *

The importance of debt in early modern England is due in large part to its centrality as a moral concept. The most prominent cultural statement of this is the "Lord's prayer" with its central binding statement, "forgive us our debts, as we forgive our debtors," translated as "debts" rather than "trespasses" in the 1611 Authorized Version as well as in Cranmer's earlier "Great Bible."[7] Ceri Sullivan observes that early modern English theology had an intricate "theology of debt" founded upon an understanding, at least from the pulpit, that money is a common social possession and that its use is always subject to a common good.[8] This attitude toward money exchange and obligation prioritizes the personal, a characteristic that has its roots in medieval English law where legal cases of debt were examined *in personam* and not *in rem*.[9] Here, the legal object in a contract was the person and not the money or items owed, making the legal impetus of debt obligation more ethical than contractual. As DeLloyd Guth puts it, in the late middle ages "'to owe' and 'to ought' are two sides of the same debt."[10]

Beginning with this late medieval emphasis on the personal ethics of debt, economic historians traditionally tell the story of debt in the English Renaissance as a movement through two main phases. Roughly, through the Tudor dynasty, the ethics of debt remained much as they were in the fifteenth century, with debt always implying a moral duty and often serving as a metaphor for moral responsibility.[11] Guth describes the Tudor period as an "age of debt" due to its distinct localism, held in balance between common law and ecclesiastical jurisdictions.[12] Gradually, however, economic and theological changes caused a growth in self-interest and a decline in the social agreement that personal economic activities were always subject to the common good. This is the well-known legacy of Weberian Protestant economics: Protestantism drove individuals' attention inward where they were to take account of their work as evidence of election, causing a secularization of economic activity. No longer was the common good of chief worth to an individual whose eternal soul depended only on self-gain. The result is an alleged economic sea change from an age of debt to a more capitalistic age of contract, usually dated with the English Civil War. The old assumption that a relation of lending and debt between two people was one of personal obligation gave way to an economic obligation increasingly *in rem,* not ethical as much as contractual, concerned with the initial thing lent and the terms of the promise to repay.

Expectedly, the tidy trajectory of this story has incited many amendments. One recent alteration to the history redraws the line between the age of debt and the age of contract, or more accurately, it suggests that the transition between the two constitutes a time that is more than mere transition but an age in itself—an age of *credit,* so to speak, surfacing in the early seventeenth century. This position has been proffered by Muldrew's *The Economy of Obligation* in which he argues that, before a period of increasingly secularized debt, arose a period when greater significance was placed on one's local credit and reputation. Muldrew tells the story of the decline of the age of debt not through Weber's spiritual causes but primarily through economic forces. The growth of production and the movement away from land-oriented economics caused the debt system to deteriorate: "Increasing consumption and investment in the expansion of production meant that household debt loads grew to levels at which financial failure was an increasingly common experience."[13] When the currency of debt failed, the "currency of reputation" replaced it and served as an "indirect spur to competition."[14]

Massinger's plays are acutely aware of the problems of a debt-based society and the potential promises of credit- and reputation-based economics. The majority of his extant plays in some way use economic failure or economic obligation to create rising conflict. For example, his popular *A New Way to Pay Old Debts* is premised on the protagonist Welborne's loss of landed fortune at the hands of a usurer; Welborne experiences a dramatic decline in social position due to the immobilizing impossibility of repaying Giles Overreach. *The City Madame,* similarly, builds its conflict when Luke comes under economic obligation to his brother, Sir John Frugal, who pays his debts only to experience Luke's ungratefulness; here, Luke completely disregards the duty of the debtor that was thought to have characterized financial obligation in the fifteenth and sixteenth centuries. Another example among many is the hopeless state that befalls the foolhardy Bertoldo in *The Maid of Honour,* both when his war ransom is too high and when his own king, Roberto, forbids anyone to pay it; Bertoldo finds himself in a state of impossible indebtedness. A fourth example is from *The Emperor in the East* where Theodosius grants universal forgiveness of his realm's debts with the stated aim of later turning usurer and demanding their obedience. Theodosius takes the economic stimulus off of the debtor but foolishly fails to model the qualities of a good creditor.

In addition to the problems of debt, Massinger's plays also speak to the promises of credit, as their characters are often entreated to value a creditor's reputation above the satisfaction of a loan. This logic resonates in *A New Way* where Overreach restores Welborne's reputation—albeit duplicitously—by improving his outward appearance despite his outstanding debt: "I will redeeme 'em, and that no clamor, / May taint your credit for your petty debts."[15] In a similar way, *The City Madame*'s antagonist, Luke, successfully gains the confidence of his brother's debtor by convincing John to forgive his debts for the sake of bettering his "reputation with good men" (1.3.84). What sells the honest Sir John on this plan is that his reputation as a creditor is, in fact, of more importance in society than the satisfaction of his debtors' loans.

As is evident in these examples from Massinger's plays, the importance placed on reputation in early seventeenth-century England was intertwined with moral standards. Condemnations of usury, abusive lending practices motivated by self-gain and apathetic towards the debtor's well being, were extremely frequent in sermons, tracts, and legal writings during the period, but little has been said about how the language of ethics changed in light of a distinct period of time focused instead on the currency of reputation between the ages of debt and contract.[16] What seems clear is that, unlike the age of contract characterized by historians as a secularization of economics, the age of credit is highly charged with religious moral imperatives. A significant amount of moral focus was transferred from the sixteenth-century debtor to the early seventeenth-century creditor. Increasingly, the creditor became the focus of business ethics, and his reputation became an ethical commodity. Sullivan demonstrates the pains of this transition, noting how borrowers began to be depicted as victims of debt rather than as moral agents:[17]

> One may speculate too about the reception that lenders gave such a criticism [of creditors]. . . . Clearly merchants who deal in debt and spend their energies in circulating credit-worthy packages are not going to agree with the argument that they abandon a commercial possessive individualism to see their products—themselves—as a communal resource.[18]

Sullivan fills out Muldrew's depiction of credit-based society by showing how creditors resisted the notion that they acted merely out of self-interest.

The picture that emerges is of a society that (a) realizes that the debtor has, in fact, become the impotent victim of debt, (b) knows also that credit can act as a new medium for a commerce that circumvents some of the trappings of household debt, and (c) is trying to feel out a new community ethic that both suspects *and* respects the moral prerogative of the creditor. Francis Bacon's essay *On Usury* illustrates this point. He views usury, defined here as simply lending with interest, as a necessary evil. On the one hand, usury causes fewer and poorer merchants, and it "it doth dull and damp all industries, improvements, and new inventions, wherein money would be stirring."[19] On the other hand, "usury is a 'concessum propter duritiem cordis'; for since there must be borrowing and lending, and men are so hard of heart, as they will not lend freely, usury must be permitted."[20] So, to Bacon's mind, a creditor's use of interest is a concession on account of hardness of heart—not the hardness of the individual's heart but the hardness of humanity's heart as a result of the fall.

The uneasy tone of Bacon's essay shows how this transition out of debt-centered economics left an indeterminate moral gap. This is nowhere more apparent in Massinger than in the opening scene of *A New Way* in which the once-landed Welborne has lost credit at a local tavern for which he had provided the start-up capital.[21] Welborne hits rock bottom when the bartender Tapwell refuses to serve him for his lack of financial and moral credit: "Ale, or Beere, they are things I take it / You must no more remember, not in a dreame Sir" (1.1.21–22). To Welborne's angry retort that Tapwell was "Borne on my fathers land, and [previously] proud to bee / A drudge in his house," Tapwell sharply informs him that "What I was Sir, it skills not, / What you are is apparent" (1.1.27–30). Both characters remember a time when land determined "What you are" despite one's credit, and, even more, Tapwell asserts that he owes no obligation to Welborne's past generosity because the borrower and the lender have traded roles: "Your land gone, and your credit not worth a token, / You grew the common borrower" (1.1.54–55). This ethical deterioration is compounded by the fact that Tapwell's snub is actually directed by the vicarious hand of Overreach who bribes a justice to threaten Tapwell. The gap of ethical anxiety sits between a memory of Tapwell's moral responsibility as a debtor and the corruption of the play's most conspicuous creditor, Giles Overreach.

In fact, one can read Massinger's pervasive treatment of economic failure and corruption as a search for an ethic of credit. While the main plot of *The City Madame* follows the tempting and uncovering of John's ungrateful brother's treachery, Massinger sets the scene of John's household as a kind of microcosm of economic change where, in the words of the play's last lines, the ethics of "the City" and "the Court" clash. An argument early in the play between two suitors of John's daughters demonstrates this conflict. The exchange involves Lacie, a figure of land and inherited wealth, and one of

Plenty's pages—Plenty being a self-made wealthy merchant. Lacie requests that Plenty not "passe the *Merchants* threshold" until Lacie himself has made his choice between which of the daughters he prefers (1.2.9). Plenty arrives on the scene, and, despite Massinger's more ridiculous portrayal of Plenty, the argument turns to violence. Importantly, the "*Merchants* threshold" is not a limit of economic advancement but more so the limit of a merchant's economic reputation. Massinger creates friction between the old and new roles of the merchant's reputation, drawing from the fact that rural economies became critically reliant on merchants' increasing activity based on credit.[22] Although Plenty's motivation might strike the modern audience as entrepreneurial, Massinger portrays him as cut-throat and bullying. He brags about his profits and is accompanied by three thuggish "*Serving-men*." However, Massinger does not portray Plenty with complete dishonor. When it comes to matters of economic responsibility, the merchant appears more favorably than the gentleman. Lacie ridicules Plenty by noting "What a fine man / Hath your Taylor made you"; while Plenty coolly retorts:

> I have made my Taylor, for my cloaths are pai'd for
> Assoon as put on, a sin your man of title
> Is seldom guiltie of, but Heaven forgive it.
> I have other faults too very incident
> To a plain Gentleman. I eat my Venison
> With my neighbours in the Countrie, and present not
> My phesants, partridges, and growse to the userer,
> Nor ever yet paid brokage to his scrivener.
>
> (1.2.43–52)

This scene shows additional changes in the ethics that underlie the transition from inherited wealth to merchant wealth. Plenty is aware of this tension and confidently rejects Lacie's appeal to title on the grounds that his own reputation is spotless. Lacie and Plenty's mutual distrust illustrates a society of divided interests, at once dubious of and grateful for the rise of a merchant class, attempting to find a singular ethic of reputation that can judge the court as well as the city.

* * *

To understand more fully Massinger's depiction of an economic society that he views as morally deficient one should examine not only representations of economic conflict but also his use of controversial religious language and characters that accompany such conflicts. In Massinger's plays, for almost every moral conflict there is economic baggage, and for virtually every instance of economic discord there is a notable religious element hovering in context. For instance, *The Renegado*'s Turkish Donusa drives the merchant-disguised Vitelli to spiritual despair after she comes into his debt and seduces him. As well, *The City Madame* links devil worship and "worldly honours" to Luke's harsh and unmerciful treatment of debtors (5.1.26–27). Similarly, Lord Lovell's condemnation of Overreach's usury in *A New Way* regrets that the religious action of corrupt creditors is to "leaue Religion, and turn Atheists" (5.1.380). And, in the opinion of *The Maid of Honour*'s Camiola, King Roberto's refusal to allow the payment of Bertoldo's ransom is "to breake / Th'Adamant chaines of nature and religion, / To binde up Atheisme, as a defence / To his darke counsailes" (3.3.144–47). It is also notable that these religious elements are usually identifiably Catholic. For instance, Vitelli's spiritual mentor is a Jesuit priest, and Luke is referred to as a "beads-man" that is said to mumble *pater noster*s (3.2.2, 9).

Massinger criticism has attempted to explain these frequent religious notes and their Catholic characteristics, often focusing on *A New Way* and *The Virgin Martyr*—the latter a collaboration with Dekker that includes Catholic ritual, miracle, martyrdom, and iconoclasm. Behind Massinger's many representations of Catholicism is an old curiosity about his own religious affiliation, especially since he had some Roman Catholic friends and family. Yet on the more relevant question of the plays' representations of religion, critics tend to offer one of two answers. The first suggests that Massinger had little knowledge of Catholicism and no real literary interest in religion at all.[23] The second view recognizes that Massinger did, in fact, intend to say something about religion but such scholars tend to restrict discussion to examining only the most explicit religious language and activities in the play. Doris Adler and Benedict Robinson take the contrary view and claim that Massinger did, in fact, intend to say something about religion, and both see the frequent Christian-pagan conflicts in his plays as analogies for Catholic-Protestant conflicts, "taking Islam [in *The Renegado*] as a stand-in for Catholicism."[24]

I suggest that a fuller explanation of Massinger's handling of religion can be appreciated by looking beyond only explicit religious references and expecting more theological synthesis from Massinger, the kind of synthesis that recognizes and integrates issues in religious, social, political, and especially economic areas. Moreover, better sense can be made of Massinger's preoccupation with economic discord by exploring its theological valences. Scholars have long studied the interconnections between economics and theology, but very little has been written on the theological causes and consequences of a reputation-based economy. Muldrew touches on the subject and observes that with the Reformation and the emergence of the age of credit "Protestant theology's emphasis on faith was mirrored by an increasing emphasis on trust *within* everyday social relations."[25] However, Muldrew's treatment of the relations between theological and economic credit limits the economic meanings of a believer's "trust" merely to trust in God for salvation, as opposed to a believer's trustworthy reputation. Likewise, Sullivan's chapter on "The

Theology of Credit" focuses on theological attacks against usury and on the different metaphors used to describe usurers in religious writings.[26] While greatly opening up discussion about credit and language in early seventeenth-century England, neither scholar examines the most theologically central meanings of credit, those that evolved from Anselm's debt-based model for salvation.

In Massinger's plays, there is more to a "theology of credit" than is found in rhetoric against usury, and there is more *theology to credit* than the believer's activity of trusting that God is faithful. In addition to theology informing the ethics of economics, the reverse is also true: economics informed the way that theology was conceptualized. Valerie Forman argues, in the only in-depth study of economics and religion in Massinger to date, that *The Renegado* is tragic-comical insofar as it proffers a "logic of investment" that redeems money exported to foreign markets with the expectation of "prosperous return."[27] I suggest, however, a less optimistic reading of Massinger's use of economics, contending that Massinger has serious qualms with depicting Christian redemption economically.

Namely, Massinger engages a changing theology of reputation and credit that developed concurrent to, and perhaps in conjunction with, parallel economic changes. As discussed above, when the debt-based society of the sixteenth century fell to crisis, the wake was also felt in religious experience, and when society turned to credit and reputation for a standard of economic stability, theological conceptions of the sinner as debtor were affected by the failings of financial indebtedness. One result of this, and that which Massinger regularly dramatizes, is that society's ethic of economic practice found itself grasping for a foothold between the old moral obligation of the debtor and the suspicion of creditor usury. Thus, while closely tied by the shared cultural territory of ethics, religion and economics were also in conflict. Peter Stallybrass argues that the early modern period developed anxiety about Christianity's reliance on economic concepts and observes a growing insecurity with what he describes as the economic essence of theology.[28] He claims that pushing against concepts of debt and repayment threatens the very foundation of Christianity, and he points to the various sacred and secular meanings of words like *credere* and *debita* that early modern England sought to separate.[29] However, what Massinger's representation of the conflict between economics and theology shows is the pursuit of theological understanding outside of the confines of certain culture-specific economic frameworks. Massinger also implies that the multiple meanings of *credere* and *debita* do not indicate an undeniable adherence to a financial understanding of salvation but rather that such economic language is merely a powerful metaphor for approaching an ultimately incomprehensible spiritual concept. Massinger is not attempting to purify Christianity from economics but to dramatize religious identity beyond indebtedness.

An illustration of this conflict between economics and religion is *The City Madame*'s Luke. Luke is a former debtor whose debts were paid by his brother John, and as a result, John forces him to work as a servant in his house. As is expressed by numerous characters, this is anything but a clear-cut state of redemption. Lord Lacie, for instance, takes offense at Luke's relegation from a brother to a servant and attributes it to John's poor reputation: "I have heard / In the acquisition of his wealth, he weighs not / Whose ruines he builds upon" (1.2.137–39). Lacie's complaint is that one should not demand the same humbled obligations that are expected from a forgiven debtor when that debtor is family. In Lacie's opinion, and consistent with the period's shifting emphasis toward credit, John's reputation as creditor, and not Luke's obligation as debtor, should determine his conduct. Later, Lacie confronts John directly and accuses him of religious misconduct:

> Your charity to your debtors
> I do commend, but where you should expresse
> Your pietie to the height, I must boldly tell you
> You shew your self an Atheist.
>
> (1.3.123–26)

Notably, the difference between a generous creditor who shows "pietie" and one who is an "Atheist" is that the atheist limits satisfaction to the economic sphere. John pays what Luke owes in order to satisfy his debts but prevents Luke from any kind of employment that might allow him to rebuild his fortune. In other words, John shows "charity" in satisfying Luke's debt, but he shows atheism by restricting this charity to the economic sphere.

Still, the troubled relation between economics and religion in the character of Luke is complicated by the fact that, in the end, Luke is the one who turns out to be the atheist. He describes his servile employment in a religious voice, but his theologically figured indebtedness is brought into question when Luke is exposed to be a hypocrite. Luke says his brother treats him:

> Beyond my merit, I think his goodnesse for't.
> I am a Freeman, all my debts discharg'd,
> Nor does one Creditor undone by me
> Curse my loose riots. I have meat and cloaths,
> Time to ask heaven remission for what's past;
>
> (1.3.126–30)

In this response, Luke channels the theological meanings of substitutionary satisfaction, liberty outside of one's own "merit." However, Massinger puts this language of Protestant orthodoxy in the voice of a character who does anything but turn from "what's past." Somewhat more than implicitly, Massinger calls into question Reformational soteriology, or at least the ethical effectiveness of the commonplace faith-versus-works binary framework. Massinger's problem with this combination of economic and religious language is further refined by the fact that, in Lacie's terms, the "height" of "pietie" for the creditor is not the forgiveness of debt but the extension of grace beyond the realm of economic satisfaction, a theologically remarkable critique when one considers that the creditor is Christ, according to the metaphor.

Massinger's point in mixing an economic-heavy *sola fide* soteriology with hypocrisy is that true religious conduct should not be restricted to the economics of debt, satisfaction, and obligation. For Massinger, the potential hypocrisy of *sola fide* economics is the central issue for developing an understanding of social ethics appropriate to an age of credit, and this is also a position that receives considerable treatment in the theological writings of early seventeenth-century English theologians, particularly the so-called Caroline Divines. One might conceptualize the parallel changes in economics and theology by associating the rising problems of debt with the growing dissatisfaction over the strictures of the faith-versus-works binary. Massinger's theological age began to challenge strictly forensic and economic metaphors for salvation and their role as virtually the only frameworks for understanding one's spiritual state. This subtle yet significant theological change is a response to decades of obsession over how a Christian attains, and knows he has attained, saving faith. Protestant theological perspectives in England evolved from locating more objective sacramentally mediated signs of salvation to the very subjective and introspective salvation anxiety of more extreme Calvinists. These developments in theology were attempts to fill out and apply Protestantism's original contention—heavily influenced by Anselm—that one cannot repay the debt of sin owed to God and therefore must rely on the currency of Christ and the receipt of faith. However, this broad story of theological change does not explain Massinger's critique of debt-centric theology and ethics. The fact remains that the theological authority of Luke's expression of repentance problematically supplies him with the economic vocabulary to be an "Atheist."

Massinger's theology of credit is better situated next to the ways that early seventeenth-century English theologians sought acutely to revise England's reliance on a faith-versus-works binary. In recent decades, religious historians have taken a greater interest in different forms of religious continuity. This is a revisionist challenge to the assumption that the English Reformation was as radical as had been claimed.[30] Even more recent discussions of continuity go as far as to claim that Catholicism survived in England even into the seventeenth century as *part of* and not just *aberrant to* the English church.[31] Nonconformists were, in a sense, also conformists. Church papists were "papists" but were also part of the English "church." One aspect of this discussion revisits the Caroline Divines within this context, asking how they were motivated not just by defining English theology but by redefining the English Church's relationship to Catholicism and to catholicism—lower-case "c." When read in this light, we can see the theological developments of the early seventeenth century not as primarily interested in the old faith-versus-works contest but as emphasizing what is catholic rather than what is *protest*ant about Anglicanism.

One of the central concerns of theologians like Hooker, Davenant, and Downame—theologians influential during Massinger's time—was to reevaluate the points on which England diverges from Rome, on which England agrees with Rome, and those matters considered "things indifferent." Such conversations were sparked by the Council of Trent and by the writings of Bellarmine. The major theological contention of the Divines in relation to justification is the question of the formal cause(s) of salvation.[32] They ask what *form* salvation takes and where it resides. Is the formal cause of a Christian's salvation the economic transaction of Christ, the righteousness of Christ, or the righteousness of the believer? Trent maintained that the formal cause of salvation is the righteousness of the Christian believer, a reaffirmation of the Thomistic doctrine of infused righteousness and a rejection of the Protestant notion that righteousness is solely alien to the Christian: "the alone formal cause is the justice of God, not that whereby He Himself is just, but that whereby He maketh us just, that, to wit, with which . . . we are not only reputed, but are truly called, . . . receiving justice within us, . . . according to each one's proper disposition and co-operation."[33] English Protestants would agree that God's—i.e., Christ's—justice is the formal cause of salvation but would reject the language that Christ "maketh" Christians just and that they cooperate for salvation. The Divines' nuanced reaction to Trent embraces the opportunity to redefine salvation outside of strictly economic and forensic frameworks. At the heart of this change, according to Hooker, was the growing awareness that both Protestants and Catholics affirm that Christ merits the justification of a penitent believer.[34] Thus, while Trent contends that saving righteousness is found in the Christian, the Divines counter that righteousness exists in two forms, infused and imputed, within and without of the believer.[35] The vocabulary of imputed righteousness (*imputatio* and earlier *reputatio*) articulates the Protestant doctrine that believers are justified by the alien righteousness of Christ. Infused righteousness is also not new to the Divines but is given new importance as a doctrinal continuity with Catholicism and as an extra-economic way of describing the good works of sanctification. To this end, the main thrust of Downame's *A Treatise of Justification* is the assertion that the formal cause of salvation is not the satisfaction of debt but the righteousness of Christ.[36] Thus, he stresses that the form and realization of salvation is not an economic transaction but an imputation of righteousness. Davenant, moreover, mitigates potential worries by reminding Protestants that holding the economic faith-versus-works binary less tightly does not lead to a works-based doctrine of salvation—as he says Catholics do—since human works are never truly good.[37]

On the other hand, although they are not the formal cause, Davenant maintains that good works are still part of justification. Good works, he says, are concurrent with God's imputation of righteousness as the penitential "work of true conversion" and also "after justification is obtained" as proof of salvation.[38] Thus, there is a sense in which these technical qualifications, when viewed circumspectly, seem more contiguous than consistent. Even amid the Divines' careful scholarship, one can see the creative use of grammar, metaphorical vocabulary—including economic—and law, a creativity that one might expect to find in theology during a period of steady economic and ethical change. This creativity is evident at another point in Davenant's treatise *On Justification* where he surprisingly clarifies that the form of justification is, in fact, found in good works but just *not necessarily so:*

> We grant the form of justification to be that, by which man is not only accounted and pronounced [or imputed] justified before God, but is made or constituted [or infused as] so. But because man is said to be justified in the passive term, . . . it is not absolutely necessary that this term be derived either from an inherent form, or that it should imply an inherent form.[39]

Therefore, a believer's actual change is the form of justification only insofar as it is a passive activity *upon* man, as long as it is an alien gift—"by which man." The result of Davenant's nuance is the positioning of good works as centrally within the structure of salvation as possible *without* slipping into Trent's economic language of "receiving justice within us." One's infused righteousness, the Divines argue, is not just a receipt that confirms a forensic transaction; infused righteousness is still righteousness and is saving in its own right.[40] The effect of decentering the financial exchange model of salvation in favor of the Divines' revised theology of *imputatio* is that the justified believer acts freely as a moral agent and not always as a debtor.

A simple way to put Massinger's interaction with these theological developments is that he embraces the movement away from a strictly economic and transactional model for salvation, and although Massinger rarely shows interest strictly in theology, he often couples spiritual depression with extreme indebtedness. As is the case with England's material economy, Massinger's perception of England's spiritual economy is that it is in need of a stronger reliance on reputation and on ethical creditors. It should be noted, however, that this never takes the form of an utterly generous creditor who forgives debts without question. Instead, Massinger uses the theological balance between imputed and infused righteousness to roughly outline the shape of an ethical creditor who attends both to economic status and to real moral activity.

The clearest illustration of this is the corruption and loss that results from Theodosius's irresponsible generosity in *The Emperor in the East,* when he loses his newly converted wife, Athenais, to his policy of absolute imputed satisfaction. The complication that Massinger introduces in Theodosius's character is the mixture of generosity with intended usury, as Theodosius intends to extort his pardoned subjects. In this, Massinger is carving out an alternative ethic of forgiveness that is located somewhere between an easily corruptible blind forgiveness and the outright usury exercised by characters like Giles Overreach. Massinger does something similar in *The Maid of Honour* with Camiola's generosity toward Bertoldo, a knight who is guilty of breaking his religious vow and is consequently captive to an extortionate ransom. Exhibiting her exemplary ethic of imputed forgiveness, Camiola pays for the freedom of Bertoldo with the condition that he will marry her. Yet she demonstrates a higher moral obligation—differentiating her from Theodosius—when she chooses not to marry him and instead to join a convent, charging Bertoldo to move beyond his imputed freedom and to "Redeeme your morgag'd honor" by proving to be a good soldier (5.2.288). Camiola frees herself as well as Bertoldo from moral confines of debt obligation. Additionally, the separation of imputed and infused justness lies behind Luke's treachery in *The City Madame.* Before he is exposed, Luke conveys a strong theological line when he suggests to his brother John that by showing generosity to his debtors he makes them "beads-men" and will "Write you a good man in the peoples hearts" (1.3.101, 07). Here, Luke is arguing that the ethical practice of the creditor is greater than the ethical obligations of a debtor, that one's reputation can be built on imputing credit to others, but while he duplicitously warns against "our devotions" being "but words," he later regrets that "what's done, with words / Cannot be undone" (5.3.146–47). The problem with Luke's forgiven state—perhaps as the Divines might summarize it—is that his own alien righteousness never becomes actual righteousness.

This last example from *The Maid of Honour* urges the question of the connection between the play's imperative ethic that is defined outside the boundaries of economic transaction and the play's Roman Catholic characteristics. Besides the aforementioned equation of redemption with "beads-men," another overt Catholic component is John's pretended retreat to a monastery in "Louvain." The university in Louvain was a European center for Catholic education and was the first university to denounce Luther's works. It had a strong representation at the Council of Trent and was a site of religious infamy in the Protestant English mind. While the details of Massinger's religious affiliation are not the subject of this essay, such insistent Catholic presence is too heavy-handed *not* to be viewed as more than a negligible quirk. Whether Maurice Chelli is right in judging Massinger's knowledge of Catholicism to be inaccurate is of almost no importance to whether he means something by it.[41] Moreover, I would also direct suspicion toward Mullany's position that religion is in no way a topic of Massinger's plays but merely "lends an aura of seriousness and suggests the capacity for choice by characters facing dilemmas."[42] Mullany treats religion, in other words, only as a tool for which to "move audiences," but how could Massinger count on religion to convince audiences of real dramatic conflict without representing a character's religion with some kind of conviction or, at least, perspective?[43]

The Maid of Honour is a case in point that religion and the eccentric elements of Catholicism are represented meaningfully. In this case, Luke and John's false Catholic piety—though performed in entirely different ways—is not a proscription against hypocritical greed but is a kind of overreaching mark of asceticism that points back to an ethical balance between the two extremes. Just as Luke's *pater nosters* serve as an exaggerated guise to John, so does John's pretended retreat to Louvain exaggerate his total relinquishment of fortune to Luke. Catholicism, here, is not a flat characteristic of Massinger's protagonist. Rather, Massinger takes advantage of Catholicism's stereotypical asceticism, bordering on superstition, to put what he takes to be an overly materialized theology of debt into perspective. Catholicism works dynamically in *The Maid of Honour* to reflect on the type of transactional salvation that is easily corrupted by Luke.

The Renegado expresses this treatment of Catholicism as a check—not an answer—to the problems inherent to a debt-centric religious ethic in a conversion scene that pits extreme indebtedness against a Catholic-styled form of penance. This tension gets its first expression in the words of the clownish Gazet who rejects ecclesiastical extremes, proclaiming that he does not want "To feed vpon poore Iohn, when I see Pheasants / And Partidges on the Table"; nor does he favor "The other that allowes vs to eate flesh / In the Lent . . . rather then bee / Thought superstitious" (1.1.26–30). A more serious engagement of theology involves Grimaldi, the play's title character, who is a renegade from Venice where he famously committed two heinous crimes, first desecrating the Eucharistic host and then abducting Paulina, the sister of Vitelli, to sell her in Tunis. Despite Grimaldi's somewhat peripheral importance to the play's main action, act 4 includes a long conversion—or reconversion—scene. The first part of the scene depicts Grimaldi alone with a book of penance about which he complains that only

> he that restores trebble the value,
> Makes satisfaction, and for want of meanes
> To doe so, as a slaue must serue it out
> Till he hath made full payment.
>
> (4.1.49–52)

The soliloquy quickly takes on a defeated tone when Grimaldi considers the impossible sacrifices required to purchase "a full remission" from his "cruell creditors" and particularly when he concedes that his desecration of the sacrament is too "fiendlike" to be forgiven (4.1.59, 75). At this moment Grimaldi is interrupted by the Jesuit priest Francisco, "*in a Cope like a Bishop,*" who grants him immediate absolution:

> Tis forgiuen,
> I with this tongue (whom in these sacred vestments
> With impure hands thou didst offend) pronounce it,
> I bring peace to thee, see that thou deserue it
> In thy fayre life heereafter.
>
> (4.1.80–84)

Within the context of Venetian Catholicism, two soteriological models are on display. The first is an inflated version of economic and forensic penance, but when, in unsurprising Protestant fashion, Grimaldi realizes that these requirements would be impossible for him to perform, this model is replaced by one of forceful sacramental mediation. With some theological imprecision, and apparently unaware that priests in copes were not imitating bishops, Massinger dramatizes a conversion that takes its cue from the Divines in looking outside the confines of debt repayment for salvation. It is clear that Catholic penance fails to deliver him from spiritual debt, but it is equally notable that the "holy and religious fineness" that Francisco applies is very far from the didactic Calvinist approach to spiritual despair where a priest would simply read to the sufferer from the tenants of election-based salvation (4.1.45).[44] The emphasis in Grimaldi's subsequent monologue is on the fact that his imputed status of righteousness—"celestiall balme, / I feele now pour'd into my wounded conscience"—affords him the freedom to demonstrate "strong proofes" through "good deede" (4.1.88–89, 98, 96). Salvation is by faith in Francisco's absolution, but it does not abandon the saving "balme" of good works.

In effect, the imputation of righteousness through Francisco makes Grimaldi capable of pursuing the works of penitence that were formally impossible. It is important to the tension in this conversion scene that statements such as Francisco's command to "Purchase it [Grimaldi's salvation], / By zealous vndertakings, and no more / Twill be remembred" hint at Catholic works-based righteousness, but the scene's dramatic force compels a reading always in light of the failed transactional atonement depicted before Francisco's entrance (4.1.86–88). The result is a distinctly conservative Protestant-feeling conversion to Catholicism. The theology of Grimaldi's conversion resists Catholicism through its focal point of imputed righteousness, but, conversely, it resists a works-versus-faith binary through its insistence on the consequence of infused righteousness.

* * *

Admittedly, *The Renegado* is not a play about theology. The methodology I am using, though, understands religious changes to inform and multiply the meanings of culture's "secular" ethical axes, such as indebtedness and reputation. The reverse is also true: the economic changes of the early seventeenth century allow Massinger to do much more than theologize when he creates such a remarkable and irreducible conversion scene. Still, Massinger's plays are also not primarily about economic change. More than anything else, and consistent with tragicomic patterns, they are about virtue, or more accurately, they stage various contests between the ethical, the seemingly ethical, and the outright corrupt. As is the case with Massinger's use of Catholicism, the conflict is sometimes between two extremes, pointing out the direction toward virtuous economic practice or true religion without actually manifesting it. In each of the five plays that I have examined here, this "direction" begins as a patent virtue-shaped hole lying in the middle of the social scene. Economically speaking, this gap partly results from financial crisis, the movement of economic stability from debt to credit, and the nascent and fungible ethic that begins to replace the duty of debt. Theologically, this gap is the void between faith and works that the Divines attempt to close by rethinking the "form" of salvation.

Recent readings interpret *The Renegado*'s Catholicism as a symbol of unity among disparate Christian traditions, a "negotiation of . . . Protestant and Catholic models of faith" in order to ward off Islam.[45] However, such interpretations have difficulty accounting for the theological specificity on display in Grimaldi's central conversion and, moreover, fail to account for indebtedness being the major cause of conflict. Reading the play as recovering a lost bedrock for virtue better explains both the play's confusing religious vision as well as its intertwining of theology and economics. In this way, Massinger uses Catholicism as a reference point that both distances his audience from what he takes to be problematic about seventeenth-century Protestant theology and also pushes away from the economic indebtedness of Catholic penance. Consequently, the controversially Jesuit Francisco is really an advocate of extra-economic virtue, concluding that "Good actions are in themselues rewarded" (4.1.129).

Massinger represents the need for a clearer, reputation-based, and religiously informed form of virtue by vilifying the marketplace. I do not mean, as some economic historians might, that he secularizes the marketplace. On the contrary, he shows the sphere of debt and exchange to be a place that has deteriorated from its intended moral standard. This is akin to Bacon's recognition of the necessity of usury but also of the need to sharply differentiate between personal gain and the higher value of reputation. Such is the case in *The Renegado* where the spiritual fall of the protagonist, Vitelli, is initiated by a descent into the marketplace in an opening setting that Michael Neill observes is out of character for a tragicomedy.[46] Vitelli has traveled to Tunis disguised as a merchant of touristy Catholic trinkets in order to save his sister, Paulina, who was kidnapped from Venice by Grimaldi. The fake art and religious tokens that he and his servant Gazet sell look pitiably misguided in contrast to Paulina's "Relique" that has real power to protect her from sexual violence. Although well intentioned, the market seems to be the wrong venue for Vitelli to protect his sister's virginity. Nonetheless he descends deeper into the corrupt ethics of the market when he scandalizes another virgin's chastity. Vitelli's affair with the Tunisian noblewoman Donusa is set in the language of economic bondage. After Donusa literally descends from the palace into the market, also in disguise, she becomes enraptured by Vitelli and purposely puts herself into his debt by smashing some glasses at Vitelli's stall, demanding that he come to the palace for repayment. Donusa describes the emotional experience as the loss of her "boasted freedom" as a virgin and as a betrayal of her "libertie," and Vitelli is stunned when she exclaims to him: "You wake; your debtor tells you so, your debtor" (2.1.25, 44).

In the palace seduction scene that follows, Donusa takes on the vocabulary of debt and satisfaction, nearly to the point of parody. She playfully rejects the notion that her seduction is mere "Sport" and instead insists that she is demonstrating to Vitelli an "example, to make satisfaction / For wrongs vniustly offer'd," referring to her breaking of "some poore pettie trifles" (2.4.71,78–79, 81). She continues by offering him the "tender of / My selfe" as satisfaction, reasoning that "in that guift / Full restitution of that Virgin freedome / Which thou has rob'd mee of" (2.4.101–4). The meaning of her "restitution" is twofold, suggesting that she offers her virgin freedom as restitution for breaking his glasses and that by offering herself to him she is making satisfaction and regaining the virgin freedom that he took from her. What is most striking in the exchange is Donusa's dual internment: her financial indebtedness is worsened by the captivation of her passions. Indebtedness is figured as imprisonment. In their next meeting, Vitelli becomes aware of how the economy of vice has, in turn, robbed him of his own freedom. He responds to Donusa's demand that he act upon his obligation "and denie alleageance, / Where you stand bound to pay it" by invoking that which he has lost, conjuring: "Vp my vertue" (3.5.18–19, 37):

> That I could with that ease
> Redeeme my forfeit innocence, or cast vp
> The poyson I receiu'd into my entrayles,
> From the alluring cup of your inticements
> As now I doe deliuer backe the price,
> And salarie of your lust

(3.5.44–49)

The economy of obligation to Donusa's virginity, he continues, "teares off / Our flesh, and reputation both together" (3.5.53–54). In a rejection of Machiavelli's notion that virtue often requires the beast in man to govern the rational faculty, as illustrated in his invocation of the centaur, Vitelli articulates his spiritual despair in the language of debt but pronounces his spiritual health in the language of reputation's triumph over "flesh."[47]

In this and other plays, Massinger consistently condemns the corruption of virtue that he believes follows indebtedness. For Massinger, pretended virtuous activity that only repays what is owed is the opposite of true virtue. Thus, Vitelli's final words in the seduction scene recall the treachery of *The City Madame*'s Luke, saying "now I finde / That Vertue's but a word, and no sure garde / If set vpon by beauty, and reward" (2.4.135–37). In this way, Massinger's debtors are always incontinent moral agents, or, at least, his debtors are morally incontinent when seen through their indebtedness and not through their reputations and the virtue of their creditors. *A New Way*'s Welborne, for example, is in moral decay until he restores his reputation with Lady Alworth and not merely until he repays his debts. It is noteworthy as well that when Welborne finally restores his fortune to match his restored reputation, he departs from the society of debt and usury and joins Lovell's military, declaring resolutely that now "is a time of Action" (5.1.395). Action is precisely what Welborne could not practice when he was in extortionate debt, and active virtue is explicitly differentiated from the kind of remedial virtue that only serves as repayment. So in a manner similar to *The Renegado*'s penitent Grimaldi, Welborne realizes the preeminence of reputation above financial status:

> there is something else
> Beside the repossession of my land,
> And payment of my debts, that I must practise.
> I had a reputation, but 'twas lost
> In my loose course; and 'till I redeeme it
> Some noble way, I am but halfe made vp.
>
> (5.1.388–94)

The language of payment, indebtedness, reputation, and redemption culls from the seventeenth century's economic and theological attempts to turn away from debt and toward reputation. Massinger's point is to use tragicomedy's conventions of fall and surprise redemption to draw out unexpected shapes of a new kind of virtue.

Massinger's revised form of virtue is extra-economic in the sense that its highest standard of action is reputation. The difference between an identity that is based on debt as opposed to reputation is that reputation is able to act virtuously for its own sake. Reputation is experienced in action, just as the Divines posited that forensic justification is actively experienced through infused, actual righteousness and not merely through theologically economic status. Thus, for Camiola—as we have seen with *The Renegado*'s Vitelli and *The City Madame*'s Luke—virtue is more than a mere word: "I stand here, mine owne advocate; and my truth / Deliver'd in the plainest language, will / Make good it selfe" (5.2.75–77). The reason why Camiola ultimately leaves Roberto's kingdom for a convent is that she deems his emotional governing through obligation to be the activity of "Tyrants, not Kings" who "By violence, from humble vassals force / The liberty of their soules" (4.5.63–65). Roberto is portrayed as a corrupt creditor, as it were, whose own actions are governed by the obligation of the debtor and not by the virtue that is inspired by good reputation. What Camiola, on the other hand, exemplifies is no generic and undenominational "assertion of the supremacy of the good, the religious, the Christian," but a distinct restructuring of salvation and Christian virtue.[48] For Massinger, only when virtue is inspired by reputation is a debtor credited with the freedom of enterprise outside of the confines of repayment and satisfaction. Massinger's ethic mirrors the theology of *imputatio* and *reputatio* by not treating economic satisfaction as the end of virtue but as the beginning.

This extra-economic ethic of *imputatio* offers a new perspective on what has been called Massinger's moral escapism for the sake of "theatrical excitement."[49] That Massinger's virtuous characters tend to disappear, or at least pretend to disappear—Camiola, John Frugal, Welborne, Paulinus, the entire recently converted *Renegado* party—is no mere tragicomic convention or refusal to expose vice. Massinger's virtuous characters disappear in protest against their fictional societies where virtue is indebted to economic satisfaction, where virtue is not rewarded for itself. At the same time, the very characters that one might view as escaping moral conflict are those who, in fact, value an ideal of freely virtuous action above the confines of virtue as an act of reconciliation. Thus, characters leave societies of indebtedness because, in Massinger's opinion, a debtor is not a moral agent.

Notes

1. Valerie Forman's recent study reads Massinger's use of tragicomedy as a generic tool for representing economic redemption on the international scale, a view with which I contend below. See *Tragicomic Redemptions: Global Economics and the Early Modern Stage* (Philadelphia: University of Pennsylvania Press, 2008), 146–85.

2. Craig Muldrew, The Economy of Obligation*: The Culture of Credit and Social Relations in Early Modern England* (New York: St. Martin's, 1998).

3. T. A. Dunn, *Philip Massinger: The Man and the Playwright* (London: Thomas Nelson and Sons, 1957), 176.

4. For Massinger's religious identify and possible Catholicism, see Dunn, *Philip Massinger*, 176–91, and also Donald S. Lawless, *Philip Massinger and His Associates* (Muncie, IN: Ball State University Press, 1967), 8–9, 63–64.

5. Dunn, *Philip Massinger*, 177.

6. Besides Forman's (n. 1), other recent studies by Michael Neill and Benedict Robinson observe a tension between the market and Massinger's religious ethic, but their observations are brief, treat only *The Renegado,* and serve ulterior arguments. Michael Neill, "Turn and Counterturn: Merchanting, Apostasy and Tragicomic Form in Massinger's *The Renegado,*" in *Early Modern Tragicomedy,* ed. Subha Mukherji and Raphael Lyne (Cambridge: D. S. Brewer, 2007), 154–74; Benedict S. Robinson, *Islam and Early Modern English Literature: The Politics of Romance from Spenser to Milton* (New York: Palgrave Macmillan, 2007), 115–43; Robert Y. Turner, "Giving and Taking in Massinger's Tragicomedies," *SEL* 35, no. 2 (1995), 361–81.

7. Matthew 6:12, Authorized Version, and *The Byble in Englyshe that is to saye the content of al the holy scrypture, both of ye olde, and newe testament . . . Thomas, Archbysshop of Cantorbury* (London: Printed by Edward Whytchurche, 1540).

8. Ceri Sullivan, *The Rhetoric of Credit: Merchants in Early Modern Writing* (Madison, NJ: Fairleigh Dickinson University Press, 2002), 44–45.

9. DeLloyd J. Guth, "The Age of Debt, the Reformation and English Law," in *Tudor Rule and Revolution: Essays for G. R. Elton from His American Friends,* ed. by D. J. Guth and J. W. McKenna (Cambridge: Cambridge University Press, 1982), 74.

10. Guth, "The Age of Debt," 69.

11. Ibid., 82.

12. Ibid., 70. An especially influential book on the age of contract is P. S. Atiyah, *The Rise and Fall of Freedom of Contract* (Oxford: Clarendon Press, 1979). Atiyah calls this pre-contractual early modern period one of "property" instead of debt but, like Guth, differentiates it from the age of contract by its focus on individual responsibility.

13. Craig Muldrew, *The Economy of Obligation,* 16–17.

14. Ibid., 2–3, 17.

15. Philip Massinger, *A New Way to Pay Old Debts,* in *The Plays and Poems of Philip Massinger,* 4 vols., vol. 1, ed. Philip Edwards and Colin Gibson (Oxford: Clarendon Press, 1976), 3.3.65–66. Subsequent references to Massinger's plays will appear parenthetically in the text in this format—act, scene, line.

16. See Norman Jones, *God and the Moneylenders: Usury and the Law in Early Modern England* (Oxford: Blackwell, 1989); and J. T. Noonan, *The Scholastic Analysis of Usury* (Cambridge: Harvard University Press, 1957).

17. Sullivan,*The Rhetoric of Credit,* 52–53.

18. Ibid., 53.

19. Richard Whately and Fraklin Fiske Heard, eds., *Bacon's Essays with Annotations* (Boston: Lee and Shepard, 1884), 417.

20. Ibid., 416.

21. Nancy Leonard observes a "gap" between rhetoric and action in *A New Way,* prompting us to question how rhetoric, rather than action, shapes dramatic movement. While very different, my identification of a moral gap is similar to Leonard's insofar as there is a disparity between active and inactive virtue: "Overreach at Bay: Massinger's *A New Way to Pay Old Debts,*" in *Philip Massinger: A Critical Reassessment,* ed. Douglas Howard (Cambridge: Cambridge University Press, 1985), 174.

22. Margaret Spufford, *Contrasting Communities: English Villagers in the Sixteenth and Seventeenth Centuries* (Cambridge: Cambridge University Press, 1974), 80.

23. See Maurice Chelli, *Le Drame de Massinger* (Lyon: Audin, 1923), 328–31, who claims that Massinger's cursory knowledge of Catholicism reflects his cursory interest, and also several works by Peter Mullany who says that religion is marginal to Massinger's real interest in emotional conflicts: "Religion in Massinger's *Maid of Honour*," *Renaissance Drama* 2 (1969): 143–56; "Religion in Massinger and Dekker's *The Virgin Martyr*," *Kosmos* 2 (1970): 89–97; "Massinger's *The Renegado*: Religion in Stuart Tragicomedy," *Genre* 5 (1972): 138–52.

24. Doris Adler and Benedict Robinson both see the frequent Christian-pagan conflicts in his plays as analogies for Catholic-Protestant conflicts, "taking Islam [in *The Renegado*] as a stand-in for Catholicism." Adler adds that Massinger's interest in Catholicism and Protestantism is primarily a moral interest in the "struggle between temporal sensual pleasures and eternal long-proven verities," and Michael Neill reads Massinger's religious content as informing social ethics, especially attacking ambition and vanity. Benedict Robinson, "The Turks, Caroline Politics, and Philip Massinger's *The Renegado*," in *Localizing Caline Drama: Politics and Economics of the Early Modern English Stage, 1625–1642*, ed. Adam Zucker and Alan B. Farmer (New York, Palgrave Macmillan, 2006), 224; Doris Adler, *Philip Massinger* (Boston: Twayne, 1987), 57. Michael Neill, "'Tongues of Angels': Charity and the Social Order in *The City Madam*," in *Philip Massinger: A Critical Reassessment*, ed. Douglas Howard (Cambridge: Cambridge University Press, 1985), 193–220.

25. Muldrew, *The Economy of Obligation*, 132.

26. Sullivan, *The Rhetoric of Credit*, 44–70.

27. Forman, *Tragicomic Redemptions*, 13–16, 147.

28. Peter Stallybrass, "The Value of Culture and the Disavowal of Things," in *The Culture of Capital: Property, Cities, and Knowledge in Early Modern England*, ed. Henry S. Turner (New York: Routledge, 2001), 275–92.

29. Stallybrass, "The Value of Culture," 280. On the changing meanings of *credere*, see also John Parker, "God Among Thieves: Marx's Christological Theory of Value and the Literature of the English Reformation" (Ph.D. diss., University of Pennsylvania, 1999).

30. The most prominent argument for a continuing Catholic community is John Bossy, *The English Catholic Community, 1570–1850* (London: Oxford University Press, 1975). Other arguments for Catholic continuity, some of which contend with Bossy, include: Eamon Duffy, *The Stripping of the Altars: Traditional Religion in England, 1400–1580*, 2nd ed. (New Haven, CT: Yale University Press, 1992); Christopher Haigh, *English Reformations: Religion, Politics, and Society under the Tudors* (Oxford: Clarendon, 1993); Michael Questier, *Conversion, Politics, and Religion in England, 1580–1625* (Cambridge: Cambridge University Press, 1996).

31. See Alexandra Walsham, *Church Papists: Catholicism, Conformity, and Confessional Polemic in Early Modern England* (Rochester, NY: Boydell Press, 1993); Michael Questier, "Conformity, Catholicism, and the Law," in *Conformity and Orthodoxy in the English Church, c. 1560–1642*, ed. Peter Lake and Michael Questier (Woodbridge: The Boydell Press, 2000); Ethan Shagan, ed. *Catholics and the "Prot-*

estant Nation": Religious Politics and Identity in Early Modern England (New York: Manchester University Press, 2005).

32. For a classic study of formal causality in English theology see the reprinted C. Fitzsimons Allison, *The Rise of Moralism: The Proclamation of the Gospel from Hooker to Baxter* (Vancouver, BC: Regent College Press, 2006).

33. *Canons and Decrees of the Sacred and Ecumenical Council of Trent,* trans. J. Waterworth (Whitefish, MT: Kessinger, 2003), 35.

34. Corneliu C. Simuţ?, *The Doctrine of Salvation in the Sermons of Richard Hooker* (Berlin: Walter de Gruyter, 2005), 228.

35. See *Alister E. McGrath,* Iustitia Dei: *A History of the Doctrine of Justification, vol.* 2 (New York: Cambridge University Press, 1986), 104.

36. Allison, *The Rise of Moralism,* 16.

37. Ibid., 13.

38. John Davenant, *A Treatise on Justification,* vol. 1 (Birmingham: Hamilton, Adams, 1844), 274–75.

39. Ibid., 232.

40. I do not mean to ignore differences between the Divines, Davenant's claim that justification is "made or constituted" in man being one instance when he treads closer to Trent than Hooker or Downame. Nevertheless, the emphasis on the necessary imputation rather than the infusion of justice as the formal cause of justification is consistent.

41. See note 23.

42. Mullany, "Religion in *The Maid of Honour,*" 155.

43. Ibid., 145.

44. More Reformed English theologies direct pastors to engage those who suffer from spiritual melancholy in doctrinal discussion. Burton describes his approach to such scenarios: "To such persons I oppose God's mercy and his justice; *Judicia Dei occulta, non injusta:* his secret counsel and just judgment, by which he spares some, and sore afflicts others again in this life; his judgment is to be adored, trembled at, not to be searched or inquired after by mortal men: he hath reasons reserved to himself, which our frailty cannot apprehend." Robert Burton, *The Anatomy of Melancholy: What it is with All the Kinds, Causes, Symptoms, Prognostics, and Several Cures of It* (London: Chatto and Windus, 1883), 734. See also Jeremy Schmidt, *Melancholy and the Care of the Soul: Religion, Moral Philosophy, and Madness in Early Modern England* (Aldershot: Ashgate, 2007), 50–53.

45. Jane Hwang Degenhardt, "Catholic Prophylactics and Islam's Sexual Threat: Preventing and Undoing Sexual Defilement in *The Renegado,*" *Early Modern Cultural Studies* 9, no. 1 (2009), 63. A similar argument is made by Robinson, *Islam and Early Modern Literature,* 139–43.

46. Neill, "Merchanting," 157.

47. Niccolò Machiavelli, *The Prince,* ed. Quentin Skinner and Russell Price (Cambridge: Cambridge University Press, 1988), 61. For a discussion of Machiavelli's animal virtue, see Felix Gilbert, *Machiavelli and Guicciardini: Politics and History in Sixteenth-century Florence* (Princeton, NJ: Princeton University Press, 1965), 197.

48. Dunn, *Philip Massinger,* 183.

49. Mullany, "Religion in *The Maid of Honour,*" 155.

"The Hall must not be pestred": Embedded Masques, Space, and Dramatized Desire

John R. Ziegler

IN Philip Massinger's *The City Madam,* Anne, daughter of the prideful Lady Frugal, itemizes her conditions for marriage to her suitor Lacy. Among them is a "friend to place me at a masque" (2.2.115).[1] The play locates masques and their audiences within a nexus of fashion, emulation, self-display, social ambition, and theatergoing, pointing to the masque as an object of desire, especially for the upwardly mobile.[2] Yet while someone like Anne might be able simply to buy a box for herself and her retinue at the Blackfriars, she could not as easily attend a masque. Entrance to a masque could not be purchased, and the average Londoner had a much better chance of hearing the cry "A hall, a hall! Let no more citizens in there" at the door than of being admitted to the performance (3.2.81).[3] This line, spoken by a gentleman usher in George Chapman's *The Widow's Tears* (c. 1605?; printed 1612), neatly sketches the tensions surrounding masquing spaces.[4] Because access to spaces where masques were performed was so restricted, the embedded masques contained in a significant number of early modern English plays, most of them Jacobean and early Caroline, could sell a class-based voyeurism—with varying combinations of valorization and critique—to audiences in the commercial playhouses. Such voyeurism, which operates on the same principles as the more commonly discussed sexual voyeurism, lent an eroticism to the space of masque performance, whether actual or represented.

Between the 1590s and 1642, around ninety plays included some version of a masque. As a point of comparison, nearly eighty commercial early modern plays contained dumbshows. However, more than half of these appeared before 1611, after which dumbshows experienced a precipitous and permanent drop-off. Embedded masques, on the other hand, while somewhat less common in each of the two decades between 1611 and 1630, not only maintained consistent numbers following their initial popularity, but actually became more widespread again from 1631 onwards. Despite the enduring and pervasive presence of embedded masques, scholarship to date has dealt with them in almost wholly aesthetic terms and made almost no attempt to account for the social and economic factors underpinning their use. This essay begins to address that lack by outlining some of the mechanisms by which embedded masques and their productions of space both responded to and participated in the turbulent changes to ideas of social order in early modern London.

Many playgoers would never see a masque in the court or a great house. Admission to a court masque, for instance, depended upon having sufficient rank and connection to the court (for the most part, being an aristocrat or government official), and attendance was technically by invitation only. Even within Patricia Fumerton's picture of audiences growing increasingly large "as rich merchants and common gentry infiltrated the aristocratic elite," court officials enforced, to the best of their ability, restrictions on access.[5] Mere wealth did not guarantee entry, nor did rank, as Fumerton herself notes regarding James's "response to complaints from ambassadors when they were not invited: 'a Masque is not a public function,' grumblers were informed, and therefore 'his Majesty is quite entitled to any Ambassador he may choose.'"[6] Of course, court masques were always a mix of public and private. They were "private" by virtue of their restricted admission, but they were simultaneously "public" in the sense of participating in state matters and including persons of consequence in public life. Plays featuring masques stressed the former at the expense of the latter in a bid to increase their perceived exclusivity (along with the theater's perceived importance—it could provide access to the hidden practices of public persons), making masques "public" in the second sense: part of the market and available to anyone who could pay for them. Those admitted to actual masques always remained a subset of those who attempted or desired admission. But those not on any guest list might instead go to the theater to watch an impersonation of a masque, to experience the event and its space vicariously. The audience at a performance of *The Widow's Tears*, for example, would have seen a "private" nuptial masque including music, a speaking part for Hymen of more than 20 lines, and a dance featuring Sylvans, Hymen, and the bride, Eudora.

The interest of London audiences in voyeuristic representations of the elite was driven by significant increases in the wealth and population of the city during roughly the last quarter of the sixteenth and first half of the seventeenth centuries. The increased wealth infusing London during this period expanded the possibilities for upward social mobility, which stimulated widespread curiosity about the socioeconomic elite, their fashion, and their behaviors: in short, how to emulate them.[7] It was the era of courtesy manuals, knighthoods for sale, and the eventual abandonment of sumptuary laws. Not coincidentally, embedded masques became a popular device in the first decade of the seventeenth century.[8] They participated in the populuxe market as described by Paul Yachnin: a market composed of "popular, relatively affordable versions of deluxe goods."[9] Populuxe goods could be practices and cultural output as well as material objects, and the "theater was one of the originating institutions of the market in populuxe cultural goods, where consumers could enjoy experiences that were redolent of the lives of their social betters."[10]

The impressions of masques that audiences brought to the theater could come from various sources. As Lauren Shohet observes, masques worked "in a diffuse and complex nexus of elite and quasi-public culture." They might, for example, be digested in ballads or have a progress component visible to anyone along the route.[11] In both her recent and previous work on masque reception, she usefully stresses that masques were the objects of both "insider" and "public" gossip and that their texts were distributed both in print and in manuscript, and she cautions us to remember that manuscripts too were sold in bookstalls.[12] She concludes from records of reprintings and complaints of piracy that printed texts of masques produced "lively commercial interest" and retained that interest over time; they were also comparatively cheap—between 2*d* and 4*d*, as compared to 1*d* for a loaf of bread or 6*d* for many unbound books.[13] Ownership appears to have been widespread, and some texts even included music, encouraging a type of partial in-home recreation.[14] Audiences could also take ideas about masquing from texts like Thomas Middleton's satirical pamphlet *The Nightingale and the Ant* (1604), which paints the social-climbing dissolution of a prodigal landlord come to London by specifying that he "had been at court and at least in five masques" over Christmas.[15] The final two sections of Thomas Dekker's prose work *A Strange Horse Race, At the end of which, comes in The Catch-Pols Masque* (1613) use mock descriptions of a masque—apparel, props, torchbearers, dance, and banquet—for satiric ends as well.[16]

Importantly, even those plays that didn't feature onstage masques also helped to create and circulate images of masques as signals of social achievement. Like *The City Madam,* another of Massinger's plays, *A New Way to Pay Old Debts* (1621–25?; printed 1633), associates masques with social advancement. Here, the wealthy citizen Giles Overreach is led to believe that his scheme to marry his daughter to a lord is succeeding and that the lord's "marriage at court [will be] celebrated / When he has brought your honour up to London" (4.3.97–98).[17] He is told that the "due pomp" of marking his daughter's entry into the gentry will include "running at the ring, plays, masques, and tilting" (4.3.95). This makes sense to Overreach: "He tells you true; 'tis the fashion on my knowledge" (4.3.99–100). To Lady Haughty in Ben Jonson's *Epicoene* (1609–10; printed 1616), not to have a wedding masque is an offense against ceremony for a bridegroom who has "suck'd the milke of the court" (3.6.78).[18] In fact, it caps her list of missing "markes of solemnitie": "I must insinuate your errours to you. No gloues? no garters? no skarfes? no *epithalamium?* no masque?" (3.6.83, 87–89). Jonson's *Poetaster* (1601; printed 1602) comments on masques in a similar way. It features Chloe, a "gentlewoman borne," who says she that she became "a citizens wife; because I heard indeed, they kept their wiues as fine as ladies" (2.1.29–31).[19] She taunts her husband, who tries to decorate his residence to appear "courtly," with her superior social abilities: "Alas man; there was not a gentleman came to your house I' your tother wiues time, I hope? nor a ladie? nor musique? nor masques?" (2.1.127, 63–65). Plays that actually included embedded masques—which are almost always identified by onstage characters *as* masques—helped to perpetuate and benefited from the notion of masque participation or attendance as a mark of fashionability and status, for the already elite as well as the socially ambitious. To put it another way, these plays simultaneously fashioned and exploited one of many overlapping theatrical publics.

The masque made its debut on the commercial stage in an atmosphere of increasing wealth and social possibility. At first, from the 1590s through 1611, the majority of plays with embedded masques were performed by boys' companies in indoor playhouses, venues that attracted a higher grade of spectator, one with more potential for social mobility, than did the open-air amphitheaters.[20] Boys' companies had traditionally provided entertainment to the court, and had begun their movement toward commercialization and professionalization by charging spectators to attend "private" rehearsals for court productions.[21] So it makes sense that representing masques, the kind of entertainment most inseparable from court culture, first became widespread in children's troupes. By the time that the Children of the Queen's Revels first performed *The Widow's Tears,* probably in 1610–11 at the Blackfriars and then the Whitefriars, the trend had spread to the adult companies as well, which often played in the less expensive amphitheatres, and so to an even wider audience. The same play, of course, might be performed in both types of venue, as was *The Widow's Tears,* with different types of audience response resulting from the different types of space.[22] Later, under Charles I, masques retained their importance in and identification with court life, and so a new generation of playwrights continued to employ the embedded masque until the closing of the playhouses in the 1640s.

Throughout the decades in which the embedded masque was used, the voyeurism it offered entailed a desire to witness not just elite bodies, dress, and behaviors but those bodies, dress, and behaviors *within certain types of space.* Voyeurism is a way of looking in which the spectator seeks to satisfy desire and exercise (perceived) control over the object(s) of his or her gaze. It is the intention behind the gaze rather than its object or content that defines an instance of looking as voyeuristic, and so the absence of explicitly sexual content does not signal the absence of a voyeuristic impulse.[23] Inequalities of power characterized the voyeuristic desire of the playhouse audience in the same way that they do sexual voyeurism, and these inequalities, in turn, influenced how plays constructed the space of masque performance itself as an object of desire—as eroticized space.[24] This eroticism in turn helped to construct the theater as a more public space (in the sense of a space of social consequence) by placing spectators in a position of perceived power and control. The erotics of space made possible by the dynamics of the audience's voyeuristic impulse occurs at the point at which wealth, space, and desire entangle. Erotic impulses result from a desire for the inaccessible, and the spaces of the wealthy were not in most cases freely accessible. Michel de Certeau, discussing heterological writing—writing that engenders its "products by means of a passage through or by way of the other" in what he labels a sexual process—asserts that it is precisely the condition of partial failure due to "the inaccessibility of its 'object'" that formulates it as an erotics.[25] His formulation of erotic dynamics applies equally to (inaccessible) space as the object of desire.

In the case of the embedded masque, the inaccessible includes not only the private spaces and entertainments of the elite but also the social ranks to which wealth—that of a successful merchant, say—could not always buy entry. The erotics of the masquing space therefore involves both the failure of the aspiration to see more than representations of the desired space and behaviors and, for some, the failure of economic status to correspond completely to social status.

Embedded masques capitalized on these frustrated (and thus perpetuated) desires. They offered an opportunity to gaze at or watch both aristocrats—or at least representations of aristocrats—*and* what aristocrats themselves watched. Spectators, especially in indoor theaters, might also have had the chance to watch actual aristocrats watching images of themselves, perhaps even in close physical proximity, a situation which would have helped to blur the distinction between on- and offstage audiences. In these situations, the theater itself would have resembled an actual masquing space, a mixture of public and private. Conceptually, the plays produced versions, attractive though not unreservedly positive, of restricted elite space in the commercial space of the playhouse. Their masques repositioned entertainments normally performed in spaces to which access was constrained by rank in spaces restricted only by the market, and offered them for consumption to a wider range of spectators. To borrow from Yachnin's description of populuxe goods, they provided audience members "an opportunity to play at being their social 'betters' and a limited mastery of the system of social rank itself."[26] In doing so, they also taught theatergoers something about the artificiality of how elite space was produced. However, this purchased play was transitory. Thus, the space of the theater became a site of incompletely fulfilled desire; the object of desire—the experience of the masque and its attendant spaces, bodies, and behaviors—could then be sold to the consumer again and again.

One of the most fascinating ways by which plays with embedded masques commodified voyeurism was actually to dramatize the desire for the inaccessible space of the masque. Plays that did this held out to spectators the added pleasure of a kind of success where many onstage characters failed, and so too a kind of power and superiority: characters were shown struggling for or being denied entrance to masque performances while the audience was permitted (a simulated) access, and allowed to experience those spaces as paying voyeurs.

In order to examine the different ways in which the world of the audience intersects with the world of the play, the remainder of this essay will consider examples of plays that staged and capitalized on desire for the elite space of the masque. *The Maid's Tragedy* (c. 1610?; printed 1619), performed at an indoor playhouse, and *The Two Merry Milkmaids* (1619?; printed 1620), performed at an amphitheater playhouse, both depict the struggle over access to space, and both stress the private, secret nature of that space over its public component.[27] Significantly, the former presents the successful enforcement of spatial boundaries, and the latter portrays the successful penetration of elite space by an everyman figure. In these plays, representations of elite spaces and behaviors remain conflicted even as they are marketed to playhouse audiences; their attractiveness is attended by anxiety about increased accessibility and by an undercurrent of critique directed at the very things that they market as desirable.

The Maid's Tragedy, by Francis Beaumont and John Fletcher, is one of a number of commercially staged plays that dramatize the basic conflict over access to and control over the space of masque performance: the masses desire to get in (and to look), and the elite labor to keep them out (and to keep them from looking). Early in the play, Calianax, a courtier, and his assistant Diagoras work to preserve the space of the court from unwanted onlookers.[28] They are engaged in preparations for a wedding masque to be played before the King of Rhodes, and Calianax knows that "the King will rail" if they regulate access poorly (1.2.2). Aside from the placement of the spectators, which must follow proper hierarchical etiquette, Calianax's primary concern is that Diagoras "look to the doors better" so as not to "let in all the world," a description evoking a fearful jumble of heterogeneity (1.2.1–2). The two men preserve the integrity of the space where the masque will be performed by keeping the doors shut against "such youths and their trulls" as would violate its social and spatial boundaries (1.2.33). After all, such boundaries performed an important social function: one's status allowed entry to the royal space and constructed it as desirable, and occupying that space in turn constructed and/or reinforced that status. The space at court chosen for the masque is "no place" for them (1.2.33).

Even among the elite of Jacobean society, such spatial access could be strictly limited, as the play dramatizes. For instance, after Melantius, brother to Evadne, the bride, identifies himself through the closed door, Diagoras's next concern is to enforce the exclusivity of admittance: "I hope your lordship brings no troop with you, for if you do, I must return them" (1.2.25–26). His somewhat ambiguous choice of words—does "troop" signify a large group of hangers-on or, given Melantius's military calling, other soldiers, a group potentially more clearly marked by class stratification?—allows for multiple identifications of the excluded and reinforces the sense of a fear of a private space being overrun by "all the world." Either way, only Melantius and his Lady are ultimately permitted to enter, and like the King, the Lady remains nameless, emphasizing her position.

So central is the fear of losing control over spatial boundaries that Calianax frames the entire scene by voicing it. He resents that "the King will have the show i' th' court" because it makes his task more difficult, likely because the location is more public and thus attracts a greater number of potential spectators (1.2.3). After he temporarily exits, Diagoras attempts to verify the identities of invitees by yelling to them through the closed doors and dispenses threats to the rest of the offstage crowd: "Stand back there! Room for my lord Melantius! Pray bear back . . . ! Let the doors shut again! Ay, do your heads itch? I'll scratch them for you! . . . So, now, thrust and hang!" (1.2.32–35). His wish for the speedy return of his partner suggests that stronger measures might well be taken to protect the masquing space from interlopers: "Would he were here! He would run raging amongst them, and break a dozen wiser heads than his own in the twinkling of an eye!" (1.2.37–39). Maintaining the physical boundary between those whose status allows them to occupy the royally coded space and the remainder of the excluded crowd more than warrants physical violence.

If one did breach the boundary that set off the masquing space (which embedded masques allowed the playhouse audience to do, at least ocularly), one would encounter further sets of boundaries inside, extending the social repercussions of space into the performance area. The importance of precedence in seating at court masques has been well-documented, and Beaumont and Fletcher reproduced that concern on the commercial stage.[29] The entrance and seating of Melantius's Lady highlights the importance of hierarchy not just in gaining entry to an elite space but in how that space is then internally arranged. Diagoras explains that the "ladies are all placed above," except those who are of the King's party (1.2.28–29). The monarch acts as the focal point of the court masque, and so the closer one's proximity to him, the greater the status that proximity confers. In other words, proximity to the public figure of the king in this nominally private space measures one's public importance. In the second quarto of the play, Diagoras continues, "The best of Rhodes sit there, and there's room," offering a seat above with the rest of the ladies (1.2.29). In the first quarto, however, the text reads "there is no room," in which case the referent of "there" is the space nearest the King. Therefore, while the Lady ends up "placed"—a word with significant social echoes—in the gallery, in both cases, the Q1 reading constitutes a deliberate snub of Melantius (1.2.30).[30]

Calianax uses the same tactic shortly thereafter to attack Melantius, whom he considers his enemy.[31] His verbal assault exploits both the internal ordering and construction of space and the social construction of persons through their access to and place within certain spaces. Power over space (and so what can or cannot be seen by others) translates into social power and vice versa. An attempt to deny Melantius entry by virtue of his office having failed, Calianax denigrates him by questioning the right of his Lady to occupy a space "So near the presence of the King" (1.2.59). He asserts that "she must not sit there" because that "place is kept for women of more worth" (1.2.60–61).[32] The multiple meanings of "place" again, appropriately, overlap in these insults. Its frequency and continued oscillation of meaning as the exchange continues suggest a conscious play on the interaction between location and rank in constructing persons and spaces:

MELANTIUS More worth than she? It misbecomes your age
And place to be thus womanish.
. . .
CALIANAX Why, 'tis well
If I stand here to place men's wenches.

(1.2.62–66)

After Calianax's insinuation that Melantius's Lady is available for "placing," Melantius angrily rejoins that he "shall quite forget this place, thy age, my safety" and murder Calianax for his insults (1.2.67–69). "Place" here describes both spatial and social coordinates, which are mutually constitutive, while it moves denotatively from Calianax's social position, to the Lady's location, to the entire royal masquing space. The ideological importance of "place" resurfaces later in the action, when Melantius turns Calianax's insults against him before the King: "Mark his disordered words, and at the masque. / Diagoras knows, he raged and railed at me / And called a lady 'whore'" (4.2.189–91). Calianax's disrespect of place, in both senses of the word, is enough to discredit him.

His disrespect of place is also, however, significantly bound up with his sexual disrespect of Melantius's Lady (her "worth," or lack thereof, is simultaneously social and sexual), and Melantius's attack on Calianax is similarly sexualized. That the "place" held by Calianax in his authority over space participates in a sexualized economy of power is signaled by Melantius's identification of his behavior as "womanish." Calianax's reply, with its bawdy pun on "stand," adds a sexual dimension to placing men's wenches and reasserts the masculinity challenged by Melantius. Spatial and sexual access overlap, and placing others acquires a gendered coding. The ability to include or exclude others from, and organize them within, a desired space intersects with other types of "masculine" power, becoming another variety of virility and another mark of status.

Following its representations of courtiers maintaining control of access to the masquing space, keeping out those below them in rank, and worrying about their own placement within that space, *The Maid's Tragedy* then presents to the Blackfriars audience an embedded masque of nearly 150 lines, comparable to the length of some actual masques. This masque, as Michael Neill argues, "prefigures[s] the development of the whole elaborate artifice of structural and rhetorical conceits" throughout the rest of the play, an artifice composed of "a symmetry of inversions and opposites—love and death, marriage and adultery, appearance and reality."[33] To that list, I would add watching and being watched.

In the opening speech of the masque, Night asks Cynthia for light "*By which I may discover all the place / And persons, and how many longing eyes / Are come to wait on our solemnities*" (1.2.119–21). Night's request illuminates the importance of looking in the economies of status and power and the multiple vectors of the gaze. It also reminds the playhouse audience of its privileged position as watchers. Night, a performer in the masque, returns the gaze of the audience and wishes to distinguish "*all the . . . persons*" in the audience, presumably to gauge their collective social standing. She comments on the "*beauty*" (1.2.123) of the audience members, and Cynthia marvels that they look "*as if thyself and I / Had plucked our reins in and our whips laid by / To gaze upon these mortals, that appear / Brighter than we*" (1.2.130–33). For these showpiece figures of immortality, the elite audience is the real show, and the offstage audience exercises the power of watching both.

When it takes the onstage audience as its subject, the embedded masque, as here, reproduces the voyeuristic imagining that the players represent actual (elite) people on the stage. It thus puts theatergoers (and the various physical areas of the theater) into a relationship of proximity with (representations of) public figures on the stage, and maybe to real aristocrats in the audience, just as would happen for spectators at an actual masque. In doing so, it intensifies the "realism" of the voyeuristic experience and the illusion of access. If characters recognize allusions in a masque to other onstage characters, "real" people within the world of the play, that recognition validates the audience doing the same. That sense of realism may also have been intensified by the artificiality of the onstage masque and its performers, which could have caused the onstage audience to appear all the more real by comparison. Ronald Bedford notes that surviving direct performance accounts "always stress the inalienable world of characters and events as if they were real."[34] He makes a case for defining real in a way that takes into account "the mingled social and theatrical performativity of life in early modern England":[35]

No doubt exactly what is meant by *real* here is . . . problematic: but *real* can very adequately mean 'in conformity with experience or with the observable world,' and in that sense the observable world of Elizabethan London and the experience of its citizens may well have been that their individual selves were for the most part publicly and emblematically represented rather than privately and subjectively conceived and that the performance of a character onstage conformed closely enough to the conditions of social performance operating in real life and hence could be described as 'natural,' 'lifelike,' and 'real.'[36]

In Nathan Field's *A Woman is a Weather-cocke,* Scudamore, comparing his own lover to one onstage, enacts precisely the mingling of "real" and theatrical that Bedford describes:

What an internall ioy my heart has felt,
Sitting at one of these same idle playes,
When I haue seene a Maids inconstancie
Presented to the life; how my glad eies
Haue stole about me, fearing lest my lookes
Should tell the companie conuented there,
The Mistris that I had free of such faults.

(3.2.148–54)[37]

Scudamore uses stage versions of women—verisimilitudinous versions, in his view, "Presented to the life"—as benchmarks against which to judge his own "Mistris." He concludes that his own woman, and thus his own social identity, is superior to those presented on stage, and his "internall ioy" testifies to the validation that he derives from the act of comparison.

While audience members might not always end up feeling as superior as Scudamore does, they could compare and contrast themselves and their own lives with the onstage objects of their voyeuristic desire and/or imagine correspondences with actual aristocrats in the same way that Scudamore compares dramatic and actual mistresses, thus strengthening their feeling of connection with the elite. Playgoers with an emulative streak might be especially prone to such behavior.[38] Drawing on pamphlets, stage comedies, and archival evidence from the Bridewell Court Books, Cristine M. Varholy explains that some spectators took from such playhouse comparisons "a desire to touch the fabrics they saw at a distance and to bed the upper-class women whom they saw portrayed."[39] The result was the use, both in brothels and marriage beds, of opulent clothing in erotic role play that allowed people to pretend to belong to a higher class or to experience sexual encounters with their betters. Their enjoyment depended on the thrill of touching taboo fabrics, but also on the illusion of touching taboo bodies, normally out of reach because of their status.[40] The same erotic cross-class dynamic applies as well to the onstage masque. It created a relationship of the audience and the different areas it occupied in the theater to the stage space that compromised the use of spatial boundaries to enforce traditional socioeconomic categorizations by allowing entry to a "masque" performance to non-aristocratic consumers. It also undermined one psychological class barrier of secrecy—"pursuing a mysterious life behind closed doors" to differentiate aristocratic from non-aristocratic classes—by allowing the audience to imaginatively construct itself in close relation to or even as aristocrats.[41]

When class secrecy is breached on the stage, the next step might be to dramatize a surrogate for audience members accessing elite space, providing them a character onto whom they can project their imaginative self-constructions. *The Two Merry Milkmaids* takes this step. It was likely performed in 1619, after embedded masques had made their way into the repertoire of the adult companies, and it presented to its amphitheater audience a modified version of the struggle over space, one in which a character from a lower class—in this case, Smirk the clown—successfully infiltrates the aristocratic masquing space. His infiltration places an everyman figure within the masque itself, a figure who functions as a kind of ultimate participant-spectator.

Attributed on the title page to I.C., likely John Cumber, a chief actor and a sharer in Queen Anne's Company (known until the accession of James I as the Earl of Worcester's Men), the play displays the same concern as *The Widow's Tears* and *The Maid's Tragedy* with encroachment upon what is presented as the secret, private life of the elite. The usual enforcement of restricted access plays out, with a breakdown of what happens to the different classes of people who try to gain entry to the revels. Like Chapman's play, Cumber's also contains a social climbing plot. The Duke is passing through the countryside, and, in a scene that echoes the later masque sequence, Lord Raymond asks the men to "keepe off the Countrey People, that doe swarme / As thicke as doe the Citie multitude / At sight of any rare Solemnitie" (1.3.291–94). The language of "swarm" and "multitude," common class-inflected terms, betrays the same anxieties about the socially inferior as Diagoras and Calianax's descriptions in *The Maid's Tragedy,* while "rare Solemnitie" recalls Night's description of its masque as "our solemnities."[42] There is also an echo of *A Midsummer Night's Dream,* in which Hippolyta reassures Theseus that it is but four days until the moon will "behold the night / Of our solemnities" and Theseus includes as part of "this solemnity / In nightly revels" the inset entertainment staged by Bottom and his fellows and mocked by its onstage audience of elite spectators (1.1.10–11, 5.1.352–53).[43] Smirk the clown's response furthers these parallels in attitude, as he threatens violence to preserve the physical barrier between the Duke and the lower classes: "Keepe back there, keepe back, or Ile make your Leather Pelches cry twango else" (1.3.295–96). Dorigene, whose ambition tells her, "Be an Empresse Wench, a Queene, or Duchesse," disguises herself as a milkmaid to "ieere the Courtiers" as they pass, takes her first opportunity to negotiate an earldom for her father, and quickly turns that into a marriage (up the social ladder) to the Duke (1.2.171, 116).

By the time that the masque occurs, in the fifth and final act, the social climbing—and the play proper—are basically over. What remains are revels conducted to commemorate the Duke's (second) reconciliation with his wife and to offer an annual stipend as the prize to whoever most delights the Duchess. The exclusivity of admission is established by an exchange between Ferdinand and Cornelius, two courtiers and servants of Lord Raymond. Cornelius asks, "May I not vnder your protection, / Behold the sports[?]" (5.1.30–31). Ferdinand's response is less than encouraging: "I cannot tell, I will not promise you, / For my Lord's very strickt, Ile do my best" (5.1.32–33). The usual watch is set on the door by Lord Lodwicke, with specific instructions to admit only those of sufficient status: "Pray giue 'hem great charge at the outward dores / They admit none but such as are Courtiers, / The Hall must not be pestred" (5.1.59–61). Lodwicke's use of "pestred" communicates both a sense of the doors being besieged by crowds trying to get in and of their status as pests. (A character in *The Malcontent* (1602–4; printed 1604), by John Marston, uses almost exactly the same phrase leading up to that play's masque, prodding, "Oh fool, will ye be ready anon to go with me to the revels; the hall will be so pestered anon" [5.2.10–11]).[44] Smirk enumerates the treatments of different pests, describing how he enters "when Lords and Ladies stand waiting this officer and tother officer, country gentlemen their pates broke, & citizens wiues thrust vp and downe in euery corner, their husbands kept out with flame and Torch, glad to fetch a nap i'th Cloysters" (5.1.77–82).[45]

The admission of the citizen wives who are "thrust vp and downe in euery corner" highlights another dimension of the ordering of the spatial hierarchy. They are permitted to act as boundary crossers on the basis of their sexual appeal. The erotics of the space dictates that the husbands, like the playhouse audience, desire to see and enter the space, and the women increase its desirability.[46] The masquing space is given an erotic charge for the elite as well, by the promise of association with sexually available (middling) women rather than with other courtiers.[47] This scene also makes the erotic attraction of and the desire to be in elite space very literal, by concretely sexualizing it.

The husbands of these sexual and sexualized women, as we have seen, are barred entry as part of maintaining physical—and thus conceptual and social—barriers against such encroachment. According to Smirk, they would be "kept out with flame and Torch." What, for the courtiers, justifies such violence (which, incidentally, staged how badly people want to enter these spaces of private performance)? Why would male citizens be willing to risk having "their pates broke," as happened to poet and member of Gray's Inn Thomas May at *The Triumph of Peace* (1634), when the Lord Chamberlain, unaware of who he was, broke a staff over the perceived interloper?[48] What is this struggle about? One answer is that the violent vigilance at the doors represents an elite assertion of power in the face of female citizens crossing a boundary into nobly coded space. It affirms control against those who "crowd" the hall, the pestering press. While the wives might gain some power as boundary crossers, repelling the husbands both emphasizes that the wives enter only with the assent of the elite males, and, significantly, that the elite males have the upper (class) hand when it comes to the sexual control of the citizens' wives.

As stage representations of struggle at the doors to a masque imply, access to real masques was necessarily limited, restricted to professional players, ticketholders or invitees connected to the court, and, in some situations, servants of those performing or invited.[49] While access to masques, like the citizen wives' onstage boundary-crossing, remained under the control of the elite, representation of masques in the commercial theaters relocated versions of these exclusive (semi-) private entertainments to spaces where persons from a much greater variety of socioeconomic positions could purchase the privilege of spectatorship. It allowed some segments of the audience in commercial theaters to see what their onstage counterparts could not. Staging the masque in the space of the playhouse, as Emily Isaacson argues, "reappropriate[s] the masque for the public to some extent," thereby questioning the exclusivity of aristocratic dominion over the masque genre.[50] The stage clown was as popular and populist a figure as any, and the penetration of Smirk, the everyman, and his actions in the masquing space take on additional significance as regards the public (unrestricted except by the market) re-appropriation of the masque, in this case in an amphitheater playhouse. Such re-appropriation would have made a claim for the increased importance of the theater as a public sociopolitical space.

Smirk uses a ring that makes the wearer invisible to sneak into the entertainments that comprise the last act of the play. As room is made at the door with "oaths" and "Trunchions" for the lords and ladies to pass, Smirk slips inside "like the aire" (5.1.93–94, 77).[51] While he is invisible, he contemplates living "like a Gentleman," in part because, he thinks, "And for cloathes, 'tis nomatter [*sic*] how I go" (5.1.40, 57–58). The boundaries created by sumptuary customs both helped create social division on their own and interacted with spatial boundaries by marking who did or did not belong in a certain space, who could or could not enter or occupy it. Smirk's dream of living the gentleman's life does depend on access not only to spaces like the masquing hall but also to those like the one where he has stolen beef and beer earlier in the day. After Envy and Pleasure have passed over the stage and the masque is about to begin, Smirk pockets the ring to avoid losing it and, becoming visible, he is immediately and insultingly ("How now sirrah, what make you here?") turned out by the Groom: "And get you gone quick-ely, or you shall feele——I see you, go, begone this is no place for such as you" (5.1.105, 107–9). Fallen from his temporary status as invisible gentleman, he is "become a wretch againe" (5.1.110).

However, he shortly figures out that he owes his invisibility to wearing the ring and re-enters the masquing space. Seeing but unseen, he becomes a very literal voyeur to the proceedings. Having again crossed this threshold, he can again construct himself as having attained a nobility of rank. In fact, he has now risen in his own mind from being "like a Gentleman" to the rank of royalty. When the Duke tries to claim the ring, Smirk protests, "For being inuisible, I am a Prince, / And being a Prince no hands is to be laid upon me" (5.1.179–80). His self-identification as a prince points to not only his feeling of enhanced status due to being within the masquing space but also the power of the voyeur vis-à-vis those whom he observes. One aspect of that power is his ability to judge those upon whom he gazes and their actions (in this case, their revels). Smirk rapidly concludes that, as "the miracle" of the kingdom who can "doe wonders," he is in fact more entertaining than the masque and other revels (5.1.129, 132). He wonders, "Is this all the deuices, sports, and delights, the Duke shall haue for his money: . . . ist all come to a dull Masque?"; so, he determines to "shew his Grace some sport" himself with the help of his magic ring (5.1.121–25).

As a voyeur and someone who comes to feel superior to his superiors, Smirk offers the perfect surrogate for many socially ambitious audience members. He conceives of himself as above both his betters and their behavioral choices, and his reaction to the revels allows for more and less sympathetic audience interpretations. On the one hand, it is his ability to observe without being observed that gives him the power to construct himself as superior and to see the masque as dull. On the other hand, his reaction may also mark him as of the wrong class to enjoy a masque, thus ultimately endorsing the social boundaries that he at first violates. Finally, though, Smirk undeniably retains at least some degree of the power he gains by entering the masquing space. The masque is followed by contests in prose, poetry, and song before a dance closes the revels, and, having gained access to the space as a voyeur, Smirk manages to remain there by imitating and even excelling the other invitees in these gentlemanly exercises and "winning" the revels. In other words, Smirk's emulation meets their standards better than their own behavior does.[52] Whether this means that he has successfully boundary-crossed and bettered them or merely exposed the boundaries as ineffective failures is open to audience interpretation, but either conclusion would likely have satisfied much of the Red Bull audience.[53]

While Smirk's initial characterization of the masque as dull did not necessarily diminish its attraction for the audience, it does call attention to the range of potential reactions to and perceptions of masquing. To discuss the masque as if it were universally perceived both unproblematically and positively, even in plays that present attendance as desirable, would be erroneous. The spectrum of responses to the masque outside the playhouse, from admiration to condemnation, created tensions that necessarily affected its depiction inside the playhouse.

Plays containing embedded masques, therefore, did not present the aristocracy merely as templates for emulation. Because of the socioeconomic variations in audiences between the higher-priced citizen playhouses and the more affordable amphitheaters, as well as the heterogeneous makeup of the audience within any one playhouse, these plays walked a line between encouraging emulation and criticism of the upper classes.[54] While some, like *The Maid's Tragedy,* offer longer, complete scenes that basically replicate court entertainments in miniature, others, like *The Revenger's Tragedy* and *Women Beware Women,* include masques that are aborted at various lengths—most popularly, due to abduction or murder. Some few present the masque as a straightforward celebratory moment, many more as an ironic comment on characters, themes, and/or masquing itself and the lifestyle it represents. The opening scene of *The Maid's Tragedy,* for example, tells the audience how to interpret the masque as a structural component of the play. The gentleman Strato is asked his opinion because he has "some skill in poetry" (1.1.5), allowing him to be seen as a surrogate for the commercial playwright (a role often ascribed to Prospero in *The Tempest,* which I do not discuss here for reasons of space). According to him, the entertainment will be only "as well as masques can be" (1.1.7):

> Yes, they must commend their King, and speak in praise
> Of the assembly, bless the bride and groom,
> In person of some god; they're tied to rules
> Of flattery.
>
> (1.1.7–11)

The nuptial masque is indeed flattering to the bride, groom, and assembled guests, but ironically so.[55] It is part of the structural importance of the masque that its exaltation of the newly married couple and their love is badly misplaced. The King has married Evadne to Amintor merely to conceal his affair, and the rites of the marriage bed celebrated in the masque will be refused the new groom by his unchaste bride. This disjunction between the terms of the celebration and what it honors creates a censorious connection between the masque and other things that go on behind closed/locked doors, in secret. Control over space becomes about control over eroticism. The King and Evadne have carried on their affair in private spaces, control over which derives from their (public) status. Their control over these spaces, in turn, allows them to maintain their status and power by maintaining the secrecy surrounding their behavior there. Privacy and power mutually reinforce one another by means of concealment. The nuptial masque takes place in another private space and functions as another mechanism of concealment, one illusion (the masque) lending authority to another (Amintor and Evadne's marriage). When viewed in this context, the play critiques court culture and values via the practice of the masque, which was indeed tied to certain generic rules of flattery.

A similar tension plays out in *The Widow's Tears,* a play concerned, like *The Two Merry Milkmaids,* with the socioeconomic self-advancement of inferior characters.[56] Tharsalio, a younger brother and page to the deceased husband of Countess Eudora, decides to better himself by aggressively courting the widow, who at first tells him to occupy the kennel with her dogs rather than his preferred space of her bed. Eudora's command after his first suit is to "Shut doors upon him" and post a guard if he shall "dare to come again" (1.2.149–50).[57] However, her protests that she will not "stoop to make my foot my head" (2.4.160) or be caught "to give any glance to stooping to my vassal" are overcome; Tharsalio's confidence (interpreted, perhaps correctly, by Eudora as brazenness) wins out, and in the next act, his promise to give his nephew Hylus a part in his nuptial show comes to pass (2.4.155–56).[58] In a version of the wordplay on space and rank in *The Maid's Tragedy,* Eudora invites Tharsalio, "Take your place, worthiest servant" (3.2.79). Earlier, one of his competitors in love tells him that he escapes assault only because of "the place," which belongs to Eudora, to which Tharsalio replies, "Lord Rebus, the place is never like to be yours / that you need respect it so much"; now he assumes two of the multiple places suggested by his rejoinder: as her husband and in the seat of honor at the masque (1.2.97, 105, 120–22). Some of the tension generated by this masque comes from the potentially problematic motivations of the couple. The masque praises the union as "noblest nuptials," but a skeptical spectator might call to mind Tharsalio's stated aim of social climbing or consider Eudora to merely typify the lustful widow, pursuing the young man in the new suit (3.2.97).[59]

The great majority of embedded masques traffic in some balance between offering themselves as a glimpse, however distorted, into the desirable private lifestyle of the elite (or at least into a particular aspect of it) and critiquing that same elite lifestyle. Janette Dillon observes that commercial theater often feels "the need to reprove the audience for enjoying such display for its own sake" while profiting from this very enjoyment.[60] In the case of embedded masques, such reproof is grounded in something more immediate and more concrete than a moral disapproval of empty show. With the embedded masque, there exists an underlying tension between the attractiveness of the masque form itself, what it represents—and, perhaps more importantly, what access to it as a spectator represents—in terms of socioeconomic status, on the one hand, and condemnation of the onstage participants in the masque or their unwholesome uses of it on the other. This tension echoes the manner in which court masques sometimes simultaneously (covertly) critique and praise royal power and/or behavior.

Smirk's triumphs over his betters at their own pastimes and Tharsalio's marriage to Eudora, whose page he had been, make the intangibles of elite behavior, as well as their successful emulation, more accessible by staging them. Tharsalio's marrying upwards is perhaps the most successful because the most permanent. However, even as these plays map social-climbing behaviors, they still register—and work to some degree to assuage—the anxieties arising from socioeconomic emulation. The fakers, by and large, make it only temporarily: Smirk loses the ring that allowed him entrance to the revels. Even Tharsalio justifies his marrying upward by claiming service as a disguise for his "honorable" descent from a "decay'd" house (2.4.169, 3.1.47). On the other hand, he also assures the pandress Arsace that her own social origins can be elided, that a marriage to "some one knight or other" would "bury thy trade in thy lady- / ship" (2.3.32–33). Additionally, the Captain in *The Widow's Tears* describes the Governor as an "upstart," "unworthy beast" of "dull apprehension" who was raised from "mean condition . . . / by Fortune's injudicious hand, / Guided by bribing courtiers . . . / To this high seat of honor" (5.1.140–52). Whether Tharsalio's rise to his own "chair of honor" at his nuptial masque in truth contrasts with or reproduces the Governor's, whether or not his claims to pedigree are legitimate, the possibility is made available to the audience to view his social climbing as less transgressive than it would at first appear (3.1.126). These plays temper the potential threats of the eroticization and increased accessibility of elite behavior and elite spaces that public representation offered, consistently exhibiting tension about the attainment of what they present as desirable. They leave the audience the choice to condemn or to covet, or maybe, like themselves, to do both. The onstage failures of upward mobility parallel the failures that always accompany the audience's voyeurism, the inability to experience the real behavior and space and not the representation or to make social and economic status synonymous—in other words, the unfulfilled desires that spectators continued to pay for and that plays continued to market to them.

Notes

Thanks to Mary Bly, Stuart Sherman, Eve Keller, and all of the participants in the 2010 SAA seminar "The Publics of the Public Stage," particularly Paul Yachnin and Rebecca Lemon, for reading and providing valuable feedback on this essay in its various stages.

    1. All references to Philip Massinger, *The City Madam,* ed. T.W. Craik (London: Ernest Benn Limited, 1964).

    2. Anne's requirement to be placed at masques is directly followed by demands

for the "private box took up at a new play / For me and my retinue" and "a fresh habit / (Of a fashion never seen before) to draw / The gallants' eyes that sit upon the stage upon me" (2.2.115–19). The play also condemns "hopes above their birth, and scale" (1.1.17) of Anne and her sisters by observing that "there are few great ladies going to a masque / That do outshine ours in everday habits" (1.1.26–27). It similarly condemns their mother's social-climbing by, among other things, naming her desire to know the "what shape this countess / Appear'd in the last masque, and how it drew / The young lords' eyes upon her" (4.4.96–98).

Throughout, I use "masque" as an umbrella term that includes anti-masques, not to make any distinction.

3. All references are to George Chapman, *The Widow's Tears,* ed. Ethel M. Smeak (Lincoln: University of Nebraska Press, 1966).

4. Argus's name seems not unimportant here, given his function of monitoring the entrance to the masquing space. Earlier in the play, Sthenia remarks, with Argus present, "Nay, 'twould trouble Argus with his hundred eyes to descry the cause" of Eudora's "solitary humor" (2.4.14–15, 10). The play as a whole is much concerned with both spying and social climbing, themes that resonate with the appeal of embedded masques.

5. Patricia Fumerton, *Cultural Aesthetics: Renaissance Literature and the Practice of Social Ornament* (Chicago: University of Chicago Press, 1991), 161.

6. Ibid., 140. Fumerton goes on to examine how masques at the Banqueting House were involved in both the creation and "transgression of private space" and made James' "privacy disappear even as it appeared" (148, 156). See Martin Butler, *The Stuart Court Masque and Political Culture* (Cambridge: Cambridge University Press, 2008), 27–57 for further discussion of masque audiences and admission.

7. The expenditure necessary to better one's station of course entailed the complimentary possibility of downward social mobility.

8. I use the term "embedded" masque advisedly. It usefully suggests the inclusion within a play of a distinct unit that is recognizably a masque, but it does not convey the sense that the inclusion is always also a transformation, never only an insertion.

9. Paul Yachnin, "'The Perfection of Ten': Populuxe Art and Artisinal Value in *Troilus and Cressida,*" *Shakespeare Quarterly* 56, no. 3 (2006), 315.

10. Ibid., 315.

11. Lauren Shohet, *Reading Masques: The English Masque and Public Culture in the Seventeenth Century* (Oxford: Oxford University Press, 2010), 10, 46, 71–2.

12. Lauren Shohet, "The Masque as Book," in *Reading and Literacy in the Middle Ages and Renaissance,* ed. Ian Frederick Moulton (Turnhout, Belgium: Brepols, 2004), 146, 155.

13. Ibid., 156, 161–62. See also Shohet, *Reading Masques,* 81–102 for a detailed discussion of masque texts and their markets.

14. Ibid., 162, 167.

15. Thomas Middleton, *The Nightingale and the Ant* and *Father Hubbard's Tales,* ed. Adrian Weiss, in *Thomas Middleton: The Collected* Works, eds. Gary Taylor and John Lavagnino (Oxford: Clarendon, 2007), 160.

16. It is worth noting that the early portion of Dekker's text says that it is making

room until the masque and banquet, and it also identifies itself as a building. Later examples of printed texts providing images of masquing are Francis Lenton's verse collections *The Innes of Court Annagrammatist: or, The Masquers Masqued in Anagrams* (1634) and *Great Britains Beauties, or, The Female Glory Epitomized, In Encomiastick Anagramms, and Acrosticks, Upon the highly honored Names of the Queenes most gracious Majestie, and the Gallant Lady-Masquers in her Graces glorious Grand-Masque* (1638).

17. All references are to Philip Massinger, *A New Way to Pay Old Debts*, ed. T.W. Craik (1964; reprint, New York: New Mermaids, 1999).

18. All references are to Ben Jonson, *Epicoene*, in *Ben Jonson*, vol. 5, eds. C. H. Herford and Percy Simpson (1937; reprint, Oxford: Clarendon, 1965), 139–272. There is some chance that the play was also printed in a 1612 quarto, now lost.

19. All references are to Ben Jonson, *Poetaster*, in *Ben Jonson*, vol. 4, eds. C. H. Herford and Percy Simpson (1932; reprint, Oxford: Clarendon, 1966), 185–326.

20. Sarah P. Sutherland, *Masques in Jacobean Tragedy* (New York: AMS, 1983), 23.

21. Indeed, their successful commercialization depended on "their reputation as purveyors of dramatic entertainment to the court and nobility" and the "wider distribution of a product previously reserved for limited audiences of courtiers and aristocrats." Michael Shapiro, *Children of the Revels: The Boy Companies of Shakespeare's Time and Their Plays* (New York: Columbia University Press, 1977), 1–2, 22.

22. See Janette Dillon, *Theatre, Court, and City, 1595–1610: Drama and Social Space in London* (Cambridge: Cambridge University Press, 2000), 35–39.

23. For his caution against focusing on content at the expense of intention when considering voyeurism, see Jonathan M. Metzl, "From scopophilia to *Survivor*: a brief history of voyeurism," *Textual Practice* 18, no. 3 (2004): 416–17.

24. Metzl calls voyeurism "culturally pathological, imbued with power, gender and other types of non-chemical imbalances" (ibid., 428). To this we can add social and economic imbalances.

25. Michel de Certeau, *The Practice of Everyday Life*, trans. Steven Rendall (Berkeley: University of California Press, 1988), 161–62. In Anthony B. Dawson and Paul Yachnin, *The Culture of Playgoing in Shakespeare's England* (Cambridge: Cambridge University Press, 2001), Yachnin sees eroticism as part of the populuxe: "the experience of social masquerade was in general pleasurable for the Elizabethans, even erotically pleasurable" (61). However, the eroticism he discusses is more literally sexual, "especially the way masquerade reaps pleasure from the doubleness of submission and mastery" (61).

26. Dawson and Yachnin, *The Culture of Playgoing*, 41.

27. *The Maid's Tragedy* was first performed in 1611 at the Blackfriars Theatre (and possibly the Globe) by the King's Men, but not printed in quarto until 1619. All references to *The Maid's Tragedy* to Francis Beaumont and John Fletcher, *The Maid's Tragedy*, in *Four Jacobean Sex Tragedies*, ed. Martin Wiggins (Oxford: Oxford University Press, 1998), 75–160. All references to *The Two Merry Milkmaids* to I.C., *The Two Merry Milkmaids*, ed. G. Harold Metz (New York: Garland, 1979).

28. The play is in most ways built around what goes on behind closed doors be-

coming known. In an analog to the audience breaching the privacy of the masque, the secret of Evadne's illicit sexual relationship with the King, which we later learn is not a secret to the privileged Gentlemen of the Bedchamber, becomes known. It moves from Evadne to her new husband, Amintor, to Melantius, and so on, setting in motion the wheels of revenge and the various deaths to follow. Secrecy is of course also closely related to the maintenance of honor and reputation.

29. See Allardyce Nicoll, *Stuart Masques and the Renaissance Stage* (New York: Beaufort, 1938); John H. Astington, *English Court Theatre: 1558–1642* (Cambridge: Cambridge University Press, 1999); and Stephen Orgel, *The Illusion of Power: Political Theater in the English Renaissance* (Berkeley, University of California Press, 1975) on seating at masques.

30. Melantius's phrase, "When I have seen you placed, madam" (1.2.30), hints at the role that visibility plays in the construction of status through space.

31. Evadne, Melantius's sister, has replaced Calianax's daughter Aspatia as bride to courtier Amintor.

32. Cf. *The Two Merry Milkmaids:*' Lord Lodwicke to a "Lady": "Here Madame you shall face the Duke and Duchesse, 'tis the best place to see in all the Hall" (5.1.86–87).

33. Michael Neill, "'The Simetry, Which Gives a Poem Grace': Masque, Imagery, and the Fancy of *The Maid's Tragedy, Renaissance Drama,* n.s. 3 (1970): 135, 134.

34. Ronald Bedford, "On Being a Person: Elizabethan Acting and the Art of Self-Representation," in *Early Modern Autobiography: Theories, Genres, Practices,* eds. Ronald Bedford, Lloyd Davis, and Philippa Kelly (Ann Arbor: University of Michigan Press, 2006), 55.

35. Ibid., 58.

36. Ibid., 55.

37. All references to Nathan Field, *A Woman is a Weather-cocke,* in *The Plays of Nathan Field,* ed. William Perry (Austin: University of Texas Press, 1950), 57–142.

38. Charles Whitney makes the case that early modern aesthetics was not separate from praxis and that audiences applied drama or dramatic texts directly to their real world concerns, lives, and behaviors in *Early Reponses to Renaissance Drama* (Cambridge: Cambridge University Press, 2006), for ex., 68, 104, 115. Jeremy Lopez similarly notes the "striking . . . correspondence between defenders of and detractors from the stage in their assessment of the theatre's effects—precisely their inability, or perhaps unwillingness to separate 'the real and the imaginary'" and argues that "if both the Puritans and their adversaries were willing to argue publicly that a play could affect reality and the lives of its audience, it seems more than safe to assume that this is the kind of assumption playgoers would have brought with them to the playhouse" in *Theatrical Convention and Audience Response in Early Modern Drama* (Cambridge: Cambridge University Press, 2002), 31–32.

39. Cristine M. Varholy, "'Rich like a Lady': Cross-Class Dressing in the Brothels and Theaters of Early Modern London," *The Journal for Early Modern Cultural Studies* 8, no. 1 (2008), 27.

40. Ibid., 6.

41. Frank Whigham, *Ambition and Privilege: The Social Tropes of Elizabethan Courtesy Theory* (Berkeley: University of California Press), 64–5.

42. The equivalence between spectacle-loving country and city swarms and their love of spectacle also suggest an affinity between city entertainments like the masque and procession or progress, as well as the portability of the rules of spatial order and hierarchy

43. All references to William Shakespeare, *A Midsummer Night's Dream,* in *The Norton Shakespeare,* eds. Stephen Greenblatt, Walter Cohen, Jean E. Howard, and Katherine Eisaman Maus (New York: Norton, 1997), 805–64.

44. John Marston, *The Malcontent,* ed. W. David Kay (New York: New Mermaids, 1998).

45. A similar situation occurs in John Fletcher's *A Wife for a Month* (1624; printed 1646). Tony, King Frederick's fool, is assigned to "Looke to the doore" because he "may'st do mischiefe lawfully" (2.4.39–40). The men regulating access to the masque employ the standard terminology of being overwhelmed by the numbers of the lower classes. A servant admonishes, "Looke to that back doore, and keep it fast, / They swarme like Bees about it" (2.6.3–4), while Tony professes amusement at "how they flock hether, / And with what joy the women run by heapes / To see this Marriage!" (2.4.31). He then elucidates the makeup of the crowd for the King, who says that he "will have no such presse" (2.4.60):

Some come to gape, those are my fellow fooles;
Some to get home their wives, those be their own fooles;
Some to rejoyce with thee, those be the times fooles;
And some I feare to curse thee, those are poore fooles,
A sect; people calls them honest.

(2.4.46–50)

Tony's categorization, it should be noted, makes room in the masquing space for the critique of power, as court masques sometimes did, albeit subtly and within the generic constraints of praise. It also marks an important parallel with Smirk's enumeration in Cumber's play: the exception apparently made for citizens' wives—the pretty ones, anyway. Tony bargains with these women about their desire to be "put . . . in" (2.4.1) and see the wedding and "the brave Masque too" (2.4.12). The wives must, and do, agree not to "squeak" "if a young Lord offer [. . .] the courtesie" or "grumble, / If . . . thrust up hard" (2.4.17–20). The women say that they "know the worst" and are told, "Get you two in quietly then, / And shift for your selves" (2.4.21–22). All references to John Fletcher, *A Wife for a Month,* in *Beaumont and Fletcher: Dramatic Works,* vol. 6, ed. Robert Kean Turner (Cambridge: Cambridge University Press, 1985), 355–482.

Jonson's *Cynthia's Revels* (1600; printed 1601) also depicts both regulation against "THE THRONG," as the stage direction reads, and the exceptions made for citizen wives. One character, Asotus, requests, "Cousin Morphides, assist me, to make good the doore with your officious tyrannie" and instructs, "Knocke that simple fellow, there" in reference to a citizen, while Morphides himself gives the order, "Knocke those same pages there" (5.3.4–5, 41, 25). The women, both ladies and the citizen's wife, are allowed to enter, but Asotus explains that "Husbands are not allow'd here in truth" (5.3.46). All references are to Ben Jonson, *Cynthia's Revels,* in *Ben Jonson,* vol. 4, eds. C.H. Herford and Percy Simpson (1937; reprint, Oxford: Clarendon, 1965), 1–184.

46. See Mark Albert Johnston, "Prosthetic Absence in Ben Jonson's *Epicoene, The Alchemist,* and *Bartholomew Fair,*" *ELR* 37, no. 2 (2007) for remarks on the "erotic equivalence between boys and women" (412). He cites Stephen Orgel's observation that boys and women "are treated as a medium of exchange within the patriarchal structure, and both are (perhaps in consequence) constructed as objects of attraction for adult men." (See Stephen Orgel, *Impersonations: The Performance of Gender in Shakespeare's England* [Cambridge: Cambridge University Press, 1996], 103). Such an equivalence—here and in boys' company performance—would have lent an extra erotic charge to the embedded masque for the boy's company audience, since not only the women but also the men onstage were actually boys. See also Heather Anne Hirschfeld, *Joint Enterprises: Collaborative Drama and the Institutionalization of the English Renaissance Theater* (Amherst: University of Massachusetts Press, 2004), 166, who says, "There has not been enough attention given to the erotics (both same and opposite sex) of the masque, to the possibilities of sexual innuendo and real activity. The banquets before and after the masques were scenes of voluptuousness. Masques themselves hinted at the sexual potential of the masque even as they idealized or platonized it."

47. *A Wife for a Month* provides further evidence that the female citizens would have been perceived to be sexually available. Camillo, a lord, orders, "Keepe back those citizens, and let their wives in, / Their hansome wives" (2.6.5–6). Since they "must have no old women, / They are out of use," "pretty women" are used to stock the hall, and these women are tagged as sexually voracious (2.4.21–23). When Menallo suggests that the courtiers "Take the women aside, and talk with 'em in privat, / Give 'em that they came for," Tony objects that "The whole Court cannot do it" (2.6.8–9). This erotic charge worries Tony, who claims a danger beyond sexual insatiability: "Besides, the next Maske if we use 'em so, / They'l come by millions to expect our largesse" (2.6.10–11). His anxiety about increasing numbers of middling women works both literally and as a metaphoric comment on the potential for encroachment on the nobility.

48. Astington, *English Court Theatre,* 177. See 175–77 for other evidence of the use of violence in creating and maintaining order at masques.

49. It should be noted that the masquing spaces represented onstage always seem to have doors, to be spaces that can be locked or sealed, that can become hermetic. For a discussion of the use of tickets for admission to masques, see Astington, *English Court Theatre,* 171. For an example of masque performance including family, friends, and some household servants, see Marion O'Connor, "Rachel Fane's May Masque at Apethorpe, 1627," *ELR* 36, no. 1 (2006) on masques performed at the Fane household in the 1620s, written by daughter Rachel.

50. Emily Isaacson, "Relocating Devices: The Masque in Middleton's *Your Five Gallants,*" *Discoveries: South Central Renaissance Conference News and Notes* 21, no. 1 (2004): 11.

51.

52. The full title of the play, *A Pleasant Comedie, Called The Two Merry Milkmaids. Or, The Best Words Weare the Garland* demonstrates the importance

placed on of the scene of Smirk's victory at the revels. G. Harold Metz, Introduction to *The Two Merry Milkmaids* (New York: Garland, 1979), lxxxviii, calls Smirk the "authentic representative of the rising middle class—he began life as a stainer and at the end of the play is a gentleman." Metz too notes that the clown makes "fools of his social betters" (lxxxviii) but focuses on the roles that his intelligence, resolve, and wit play in his triumphs (lxxxviii–ix).

53. For a brief summary of the Red Bull repertory and reputation as a "citizen" playhouse, see Andrew Gurr, *The Shakespearean Stage* (Cambridge: Cambridge University Press, 1992), 14–18. James Knowles calls it "the most downmarket of the amphitheatres" in his "Insubstantial Pageants: *The Tempest* and Masquing Culture," in *Shakespeare's Late Plays: New Readings,* eds. Jennifer Richards and James Knowles (Edinburgh, Scotland: Edinburgh University Press, 1999), 114.

54. Voyeurism itself can be seen as both an assertion of power and an admission of anxiety, as noted in Metzl, "From scopophilia to *Survivor,*" 417.

55. See Hirschfeld, *Joint Enterprises,* 72–77 for the masque in *The Maid's Tragedy* as a satire of the genre and "an exposure of the frailties of masque distinction and distinguishing" (73). Such an interpretation need not replace or negate viewing the masque scene itself as a pleasurable/aspirational/desiring look behind the closed doors of aristocratic spaces.

56. All references are to George Chapman, *The Widow's Tears,* ed. John Hazel Smith (Lincoln: University of Nebraska Press, 1970).

57. She later has a similar reaction to Arsace the bawd, an impulse to control access to her space: "keep you her out" (2.2.35–36). Still later, in dialogue that closely echoes the conversations at the doors of the masque in *The Maid's Tragedy,* Argus (along with Clinia) are reminded to "guard her approach from any more intruders," and Argus asserts that he will beat out Tharsalio if necessary (2.2.63–64). After she rejects Tharsalio again, this becomes laying an ambush at the "next threshold pass'd" (2.2.254).

58. His promise to marry that nephew to Eudora's daughter Laodice also is made good at the end of the play. Eudora, after the masque, disappears from the play until the final scene during which this new marriage is announced.

59. Some tension also arises from the fact that Tharsalio's nephew, in the person of Hymen, praises these newlyweds just after Tharsalio and Lysander have made plans for testing the fidelity of Tharsalio's virtuous sister-in-law Cynthia, who represents the viewpoint that women should never remarry and is eventually, though problematically, proven to be "the only constant Wife" (5.1.706). In contrast to the discussions of Cynthia's constancy, the countess validates the misogynistic picture of weak, false, changeable woman advocated by Tharsalio.

60. Dillon, *Theatre, Court, and City,* 78.

New Light on Dekker's *Fortunati*
June Schlueter

To scholars of English literature, the best-known rendering of the story of Fortunatus and his magical purse and wishing hat is Thomas Dekker's *The Pleasant Comedie of Old Fortunatus,* published in 1600.[1] But *Old Fortunatus* was not the first English Fortunatus play; indeed, *Fortunatus* has an interesting, if elusive, history. *Henslowe's Diary* contains six entries concerning receipts for performances of *Fortunatus,* dated February 3, 10, and 20, 1595, April 14, 1596, and May 11 and 24, 1596, the first of these recording the play as "the j p of fortewnatus" (*The First Part of Fortunatus*). There are three additional entries in November 1599 (9, 24, 30) for payments to Dekker, as playwright, for "the hole hystory of ffortunatus" (*The Whole History of Fortunatus*), the last of these specifying "in full payment." Two other entries concerning payments to Dekker follow, the first on [*sic*] November 31, 1599 "for the altrenge of the boocke of the wholl history of fortewnatus" (for the altering of the book of *The Whole History of Fortunatus*), the second on December 12, 1599 for payment "for the eande of fortewnatus for the corte" (for the end of *Fortunatus* for the court).[2] The text that we know today, *The Pleasant Comedie of Old Fortunatus,* is the text Dekker prepared for court performance—the altered *Whole History of Fortunatus*—which, according to its title page, was performed by the Admiral's Men before the Queen during the Christmas season 1599.

There is also a Fortunatus play, in German, in a volume published in Leipzig in 1620. Compiled by Frederick Menius, *Engelische Comedien und Tragedien,* in addition to two Pickelherring plays and six interludes, collects eight plays—*Esther and Haman, The Prodigal Son, Fortunatus, A King's Son of England and a King's Daughter of Scotland, Sidonia and Theagenes, Nobody and Somebody, Julio and Hyppolita,* and *A Very Lamentable Tragedy of Titus Andronicus*—all performed by English actors in towns and at courts in Germany.[3] Menius, who was public notary at Wolgast in Pomerania from 1617 to 1621, may have seen the English actors perform there, for Philip Julius, Duke of Pomerania, nephew to Heinrich Julius of Braunschweig, hosted several troupes of *englische Komödianten* at the Wolgast court between 1606 and 1623. Menius apparently took pride in the volume: not only did he publish the plays but he did so in a form that would enable them to be

easily acted ("dass sie gar leicht darauss Spielweiss widerumb angerichtet
... können"), and he made the point that none of the plays in the collection
had been previously published (i.e., in German).

But *Fortunatus* had been previously performed; indeed, on the Continent
it appears to have been a staple of the English actors' repertory. A letter from
the Archduchess Maria Magdalena to her brother, Archduke Ferdinand (later
Emperor Ferdinand II), documents a performance during *Fasching* 1608 in
Graz, Austria,[4] when a visiting English troupe presented ten plays: the play
about the prodigal son, about a pious lady of Antwerp, Doctor Faustus, about
a Duke of Florence who fell in love with a nobleman's daughter, about nobody and somebody, Fortunatus's purse and wishing hat (*"von des fortunatus peitl und Wünschhietel"*), the play about the Jew, another play about the 2 brothers King Ludwig and King Friderich of Hungary, about a King of Cyprus and a Duke of Venice, and about the rich man and Lazarus.[5] Prior to that performance, in the winter of 1606/1607, a Fortunatus play was performed in Kassel, along with other plays in the Graz repertory and two plays that appear in the 1620 collection.[6] And on July 11, 1626, a Fortunatus play (*"von Fortunato Wünschhütlein"*) was presented in Dresden, which, over nine months, saw English actors perform numerous plays, including four others that are also in the 1620 volume.[7]

The performances in Kassel, Graz, and Dresden were almost certainly of the play published in 1620; hence we need to ask what the relationship is between that text and Dekker's *The Pleasant Comedie of Old Fortunatus*. In 1886, Charles H. Herford, asking that question, studied both versions. Although he dismissively called the 1620 *Fortunatus* and other German prose versions of English plays "barbarous pieces," he was sure that the German *Fortunatus* published in 1620 derived from Dekker's play, stating that although the German text "is a meager epitome of its original," it is "undoubtedly Decker's play,"[8] a conclusion that Paul Harms endorsed in 1892.[9] I do not wish to challenge Herford's and Harms's observations concerning the indisputable kinship between these two plays. But I do wish to redraw the genealogy tree and propose that the *Fortunatus* published in German in 1620 may, through its English original, antedate *Old Fortunatus*. That is, the *Fortunatus* published in 1620 may derive not from Dekker's *The Pleasant Comedie of Old Fortunatus*, published in 1600, but from the lost *Whole History of Fortunatus*, which Dekker was paid to write and re-write in 1599.

The story of Fortunatus and his sons Andelocia[10] and Ampedo is a rags-to-riches tale with a sorry end. Its first known printing was in Augsburg, Germany, in 1509, when an anonymous author placed this folk hero at the center of a prose narrative that enjoyed considerable popularity.[11] As Debra Prager reports in "*Fortunatus:* 'Aus dem Künigreich Cipern': Mapping the World and the Self," the *Volksbuch* was published in multiple editions—twenty in the sixteenth century, eleven in the seventeenth, and nine in the eighteenth—

and was translated into thirteen languages. Moreover, at the Frankfurt Fair in 1569 one vendor sold nearly two hundred copies of the *Fortunatus* chapbook—more than any of his other books.[12] The popularity of this early prose version of the story may well have inspired Hans Sachs in 1553 to create the first dramatic version of the tale, *Der Fortunatus mit dem Wunschseckel,* "Tragedia mit zweiundzwanzig personen und hat fünf actus" (*Fortunatus with the Wishing Purse,* Tragedy with twenty-two persons and five acts), in rhymed couplets.[13]

Several late nineteenth- and early twentieth-century German scholars have compared the various texts of *Fortunatus,* documenting Dekker's debt to the *Volksbuch.*[14] There is little doubt that Dekker knew the *Fortunatus* of the *Volksbuch,* for, as Alexis F. Lange points out, both the 1509 Augsburg edition and the 1551 Frankfurt edition resonate in his play.[15] In 1599, however, when Dekker was writing *Old Fortunatus,* there may not yet have been an English translation: at least none is now known to have existed. Moreover, it is unlikely that Dekker's use of the *Volksbuch* was indirect, i.e., through the now lost *First Part of Fortunatus,* for, given its title, that play was unlikely to have dramatized events beyond Fortunatus's death, as *Old Fortunatus* and, presumably, *The Whole History of Fortunatus* do. In search of Dekker's source, a number of scholars have proposed that Dekker read the story in Dutch translation (several of his plays suggest his familiarity with that language).[16] But here, too, there is a problem, for the first known edition of *Fortunatus* in Dutch dates from the seventeenth century. Without extant sixteenth-century English or Dutch editions, we can only assume, without evidence, that Dekker read the *Volksbuch* in the original German.

Even as the question of the playwright's access to the *Volksbuch* remains unresolved, it is clear that his *Old Fortunatus* and the *Fortunatus* published in the 1620 collection are closely related. In all four versions of the story—the *Volksbuch,* Hans Sachs, the play published in 1620, and *Old Fortunatus*—the impoverished Fortunatus is alone in the wood when Fortune appears, but Echo, who repeats fragments of Fortunatus's lament, is "present" only in *Old Fortunatus* and the 1620 text. Conversely, the Hermit who helps Fortunatus remove his horns appears in the *Volksbuch* and Sachs but not in the two later texts. And it is only in these two later plays that the two lords, after eating the apples Andelocia peddles, grow horns—unwelcome additions to their hairlines that provide a motive for their cruelty toward Andelocia.

Most noticeable are the otherworldly characters—especially the condemned Spirits and Virtue and Vice—who appear only in the two later plays. In *Old Fortunatus,* such characters participate in the grand spectacle that turns an unhappy tale into *A Pleasant Comedy.* Mary Leland Hunt describes the extravagance: "Fortuna mounting to her throne on the necks of chained and conquered kings, the fairy troops, Vice and Virtue and their trees, the dance of satyrs about the dead Fortunatus, together with considerable song and music."[17] Although the supernatural characters' roles are not nearly so prominent in the 1620 text, there, too, they provide moral weight and theatrical appeal. Indeed, the title page of the German play—*Comœdia von Fortunato und Seinem Seckel und Wünschhütlein / Darinnen Erstlich Drey Verstorbenen Seelen als Geister / Darnach die Tugendt und Schande Eingeführet Werden* (*Comedy of Fortunatus and His Purse and Wishing-Hat, in Which First Three Dead Souls as Spirits Appear, and Afterwards Virtue and Shame*)—advertises their role.

Even as *Old Fortunatus* and the 1620 text share deviations from the *Volksbuch,* so also do they differ from one another. In *Old Fortunatus,* Fortunatus's deliberations on which of Fortune's gifts to choose—Wisdom, Riches, Strength, Health, Beauty, or Long Life—are lengthy; in the 1620 text, they are brief. (In the *Volksbuch* and Sachs, Fortunatus immediately chooses Riches.) There are fewer courtiers in the 1620 text, and the King's daughter, Agripyna, has fewer suitors. But Andelocia's disguise as a jeweler, devised to gain entrance into Agripyna's chamber, occupies a full scene in act 4 of the 1620 text, while the situation is embedded in a choral narration in *Old Fortunatus.* In both plays, Andelocia and Ampedo die as a consequence of the actions of the murderous lords, but in the 1620 text concern for his brother's fate causes Ampedo's death. Similarly, in both, the offending lords are condemned by the King, but in *Old Fortunatus* Vice commutes their sentence.

The most telling distinctions are in the resolutions of the plays' respective supernatural subplots. In the 1620 text, where that subplot is nascent, the King and his daughter kneel before Fortune, asking blessing from the goddess who, like her counterpart in the *Volksbuch,* reigns supreme. In *Old Fortunatus,* Fortune, speaking metatheatrically, calls on the assembled court of moral judges to decide the otherworldly competition, and a triumphant Virtue addresses Queen Elizabeth: "Vertue alone lives still, and lives in you, / I am a counterfeit, you are the true" (v.ii). While the final scene of *Old Fortunatus,* as Herford remarks, "corresponds, not only to nothing in the *Volksbuch,* but to nothing in the rest of the play,"[18] the final scene of the 1620 text brings closure to a leaner Virtue/Vice subplot—the plot, in short, that Dekker created before he was commissioned to alter the play.

Interestingly, both Harms and Cyrus Hoy (who supplied the commentary to Fredson Bowers's edition of Dekker's plays) provide technical explanations for the differences between *Old Fortunatus* and the 1620 text. Harms expresses doubt that the author of the German version had the printed text of the "English original" in front of him. He even proposes that the several insertions of Pickelherring appearances in the 1620 play occur at points when the German author, who, he assumes, was reconstructing a performance by the English actors, could not recall what happens next.[19] Similarly, Hoy, observing that "The first two-and-a-half acts of the German *Comœdia* are clearly a redaction of Dekker's play," proposes that "as the reporter found his memory failing as he proceeded in his attempt to reconstruct the stage action, he was forced to turn to other sources [i.e., the *Volksbuch*] for help."[20] Unequivocally, he states that the German *Fortunatus* is a "reported" text, i.e., a memorial reconstruction. But both Harms and Hoy assume that the 1620 play derives from Dekker's *Old Fortunatus* rather than *The Whole History of Fortunatus*. When one posits instead that the 1620 text, with its borrowings from the *Volksbuch*, was, in its original form, the source of *Old Fortunatus*, it becomes clear that the "author" of the German version did have the text in front of him. But the text was not *Old Fortunatus;* it was *The Whole History of Fortunatus*.

However corrupt that text became by 1620, in its restored position on the genealogy tree it provides insights into Dekker's revisions for the court. Scholars have long agreed that the playwright's embellishments included the Prologue and Epilogue, which are explicit in their identification with the court and their praise of Gloriana; the allegory of Virtue and Vice; and, taking their cue from *Henslowe's Diary*, the ending. With the 1620 play representing *The Whole History*, we can not only confirm these assumptions but also employ a more considered perspective on Dekker's "altrenges."

Clearly, Dekker's revisionary efforts were heavily invested in the supernatural subplot, a minor but precipitating structure in his source. In the earlier play, Three Spirits, condemned to wander in chains until the end of the world, appear as Fortunatus deliberates on his choices. Each had encountered Fortune, and each, for a time, had known power, the first as King of Spain, the second as a mighty Kaiser. (The third merely complains, anonymously, of his misery.) To Fortune, they are fools, whom she promptly dismisses before turning to Fortunatus for his decision. In *Old Fortunatus*, the Spirits, still in chains, now represent four kings, each with a broken crown. Here Fortune's contempt takes physical form: the proud goddess treads on the supine kings as she ceremoniously ascends to her throne, boasting of her power to destroy. This is the goddess who has made and broken the German and French Emperors of the Holy Roman Empire—Henry V [*sic*—IV], Frederick Barbarossa, Lewis the Meek—and Bajazet, the Ottoman Sultan. And this is the Accursèd Queen of Chance who set an idiot's cap on Virtue's head.

Dekker's revised play includes several scenes in which supernatural characters play a prominent role. Before act one of *Old Fortunatus* ends, the playwright takes us to a Cyprian wood, where he introduces the Triumvirate, each in costume: Vice and her retinue with a tree of gold with apples on it; Virtue and her nymphs carrying a tree with green and withered leaves and little fruit; Fortune with her nymphs, one carrying her wheel, the other her globe. The occasion is a tree planting: Virtue searches for the rare plot of soil that will nourish her tree; Vice is ready to plant hers and to watch it flourish. The apples of the 1620 text, which have the power to grow horns and remove them—and do so in the mortal world—are now also part of Dekker's otherworldly scheme. Fortune may be impartial—she destroys the good and the wicked alike—but by the end of act one, the competition between Virtue and Vice and within the Triumvirate of goddesses is in place.

Dekker brings Fortune on stage again in act 2, along with the Three Destinies, to tell Fortunatus that his life is ending; shortly, she enters with a company of Satyrs to carry off his body (in the 1620 text, the sons carry Fortunatus off). Unique to *Old Fortunatus,* the two moments add to the spectacle that will unfold before the Queen. When the Triumvirate returns in act 4, each of the goddesses comments on what has just occurred: Andelocia has eaten an apple from the tree of Vice and grown two forkèd horns. Speeches and song advance not only the play's moral lessons but also the supernatural competition.

Finally, Dekker earns the 40 shillings he was paid "for the eande of fortewnatus for the corte." In the text published in 1620, Virtue and Vice do not plant their trees until act 4, and though Andelocia, led by Fortune, eats fruit from Virtue's tree to rid himself of his horns, the goddesses themselves do not reappear. Even Fortune, after instructing Andelocia to return to London with apples from both trees, does not materialize again until the final passages of the play. Then she retrieves the magic purse from the King and, upon identifying herself, presides over the monarch and his daughter, who, kneeling before her, pray for their kingdom. Although Virtue and Vice, through the fruit of their respective trees, each tries to control Fortunatus, there is no power play within the supernatural world. In this play, the reign of Fortune, more benign than her counterpart in *Old Fortunatus,* remains unchallenged.

But in *Old Fortunatus,* Dekker needed to return to the Triumvirate to resolve their conflict. Midway into act 5, he assembles a large cast of characters—Virtue, Vice, and Fortune included—and orchestrates the play's grand finale. By now, Andelocia and Ampedo are dead, and their murderers, whose horns were removed by Virtue, have discovered that the purse no longer yields coins. As in the earlier play, Fortune enters to reclaim her purse and to pardon the King and Agripyne. But in the play for the court, there is much talk of punishment for Longavile and Montrosse: at one point, Vice has jurisdiction, at another Fortune, at yet another the King. And though the King would have one lord tortured on the wheel, the other drawn and quartered, Vice intervenes to reverse the sentence, setting them free but assuring them they will be tormented by conscience. In the competition between Virtue and Vice, Vice concedes, leaving in misery, even as Fortune yields her supremacy to Virtue and the Queen: "Kneele not to me, to her transfer your eyes, / There sits the Queene of Chance, I bend my knees, / Lower then yours":

> dread goddesse, tis most meete,
> That *Fortune* fall downe at thy conqu'ring feete.
> Thou sacred Empresse that commandst the Fates,
> Forgive what I have to thy handmaid don,
> And at thy Chariot wheeles *Fortune* shall run,
> And be thy captive and to thee resigne
> All powers which heav'ns large Patent have made mine.
>
> (v.ii)

As Hoy points out, the end of *Old Fortunatus* "does not altogether accord with the moral scheme of the play as Dekker seems to have conceived it before alteration for court performance was decreed."[21] With Herford, he finds it disconcerting that Fortune, who begins as "the supreme arbiter of the world, bringing the destinies in her train, and overthrowing greatness at her good pleasure, suddenly falls into the position of one of a Triumvirate."[22] Nonetheless, Hoy's conclusion is apt: "the rules of courtly compliment required a tribute to the Queen, and the allegorical scheme which Dekker adopted for the management of this required a triumph of Virtue over Fortune."[23] It may seem a muddled ending—certainly it is complicated—but Dekker's goal must surely have been to please the Queen; and, even at the cost of inconsistency, his embellished subplot succeeded in honoring the true Virtue that sat on England's throne. The differences between acts 4 and 5 of the 1620 text and acts 4 and 5 of *Old Fortunatus,* then, have little to do with a failure of memory and everything to do with Dekker's commitment to the supernatural subplot.

In revising *The Whole History,* Dekker also needed to be sure that his moral scheme encompassed the mortal characters. Hence Fortunatus deliberates at length on each of Fortune's gifts; Andelosia, having lost his purse and hat to Agripyna and acquired horns, laments his soul's deformity; Longavile and Montrosse suffer the torments of conscience; and moral *sententiae* caution against the folly of seeking gold ("O what treacherie / Cannot this Serpent gold intice us to?" [iv Chorus]).[24] Perhaps the most interesting of Dekker's changes in the moral mortal world is his judgment of Ampedo. For although the *Volksbuch* preordained the death of Fortunatus's elder son, in the moral environment of *Old Fortunatus,* that death needed to be rationalized. Yet the playwright's efforts here left much to be desired. In all four versions of the story, Andelocia, the gad-about, repeatedly misbehaves, while Ampedo, the stay-at-home, is kind and forgiving. But in the final act of *Old Fortunatus,* Dekker not only allows the benign brother to suffer his cruel death; he also has Virtue offer a surprising assessment of "those that (like him) do muffle / Vertue in clouds" (v.ii). Of Ampedo, she complains, "He made no use of me, but like a miser, / Locked up his wealth in rustie barres of sloth: / His face was beautifull, but wore a maske, / And in the worlds eyes seemd a Blackamore" (v.ii). Sounding more like the contemptuous Fortune than the glorious Virtue—and basing her judgment on nothing that is dramatized in the play—Virtue expresses disdain for Fortunatus's elder son: "The Idiot's cap I once wore on my head, / Did figure him . . ." (v.ii). Formally, the brothers now are part of Dekker's moral scheme. As Hoy puts it, in *Old Fortunatus* (or at least in its final moments), each brother exemplifies an extreme: "Andelocia is the prodigal, squandering his gifts, and Ampedo is the niggard who makes no use of his."[25] For whatever reason—perhaps haste—Dekker made no adjustments to Ampedo's character earlier in the play, but his rationalization of Ampedo's death is surely a part of the "insistent morality"[26] that distinguishes *Old Fortunatus* from its source.

I would also propose that the second Prologue and the Choral narratives preceding acts 2 and 4 were Dekker's revisions. In two cases, the playwright uses these narratives to economize, i.e., to keep to a reasonable length a play already extended by additions. The first instance (act 2) is a digest of Fortunatus's travels as they appear in the *Volksbuch;* the second (act 4) is the episode in which Andelocia, disguised as a jeweler, reclaims his purse and hat and carries Agripyna away. In general, though, the playwright employs the Chorus to summarize, to anticipate, and to state the developing "argument" of the play. One could contend that this would have been appropriate to *The Whole History* as well, but the 1620 text shows no residue of a Chorus. Moreover, in two places, the Chorus references events peculiar to *Old Fortunatus.* The first, in the second Prologue, occurs when the Muse sings "Of *Loves* sweete war," anticipating Dekker's elaborate, though unfinished plotting of Agripyna's suitors—Orleans, the Prince of Cyprus, and Andelocia—a love contest he apparently planned to feature in order to win favor at court. The second occurs when the fourth act Chorus speaks of Andelocia's theft of the wishing hat from his brother and his (broken) pledge to seek misery and die: in the 1620 text, Ampedo willingly gives the hat to his brother, not so he can seek misery but so he can try to recover the purse. Finally, these three Homeric narratives are formally of a piece, each entreating the audience to extend the actors' art through their thoughts: imagine the many miles Fortunatus, then Andelocia traverses; imagine the Asian shores, Tartar's palace, the courts of the barbarian kings; and, when Andelocia and Agripyna are transported to a wilderness in England, "Imagine this the place." Clearly, Dekker had the court performance in mind when he added the Chorus, and clearly he was intent on building a relationship not only between players and audience but, more practically, between the Admiral's Men and the Queen.

Other changes to *The Whole History of Fortunatus* must have been made for aesthetic or practical reasons—the cameo role for Insultado, the Spanish dancer, for example—but it is difficult to say with certainty what these were. For not all the differences between the 1620 text and *Old Fortunatus* can be attributed to the playwright. If the text published in 1620 follows the pattern of other plays performed by the *englische Komödianten* in Germany, we would expect that the exigencies of performance would result in a legion of changes. Moreover, changes that are the consequence of performance are ongoing. If we had scripts of every continental performance of a particular English play—*Hamlet* and *Der Bestrafte Brudermord,* for example, or *Nobody and Somebody,* or even the three known performances of *Fortunatus*—we could track the adjustments the actors themselves made, for reasons associated with the composition of the troupe, the venue, lessons learned from previous performances, or personal preferences. Surely the several insertions of Pickelherring in the 1620 text occurred after the play reached Germany, quite possibly as a substitute for the brothers' comic companion. Shadow's absence from the 1620 text may imply that Dekker added this comic character to *Old Fortunatus* to amuse the court. Or it may be that Shadow was in both *The Whole History of Fortunatus* and *Old Fortunatus* but met his demise in Germany, for what troupe of savvy English actors would not have played to the German audience's love of Pickelherring, their legendary clown?

Translation, too, is responsible for changes, particularly because the verse of English plays was typically rendered in German prose. Because that prose was simple and "ungermanic," some have speculated that it was the actors themselves—or one of them with some knowledge of German—who did the translations. William J. Thoms, in *Three Notelets on Shakespeare,* implies this was the case when he observes that the plays in the 1620 volume are

> translated into the very commonest German prose, printed very incorrectly, and in a language which seems to have been written down from the recitation of unskilful actors, being filled with uncouth phrases and words misapplied—the construction of the sentences any thing but German, and the whole abounding with coarse equivoques and obscene allusions.[27]

Yet he concludes that, even in this "wretched translation," *Nobody and Somebody,* one of the plays in the volume, is "the same piece which was printed in London in 1603."[28] Although Thoms is undoubtedly correct, continental records have not yet yielded information that would allow us to identify the translators of English plays. That at least one of the English actors was bilingual, however, is confirmed by a November 26, 1599 record from a performance, in English, in Münster:

> Sie hetten bei sich einen schalkes naren, so in duescher sprache vielle bötze und geckerie machede under den ageren, wann sie einen neuen actum wollten anfangen und sich umbkledden, darmidt ehr das volck lachent machede . . .

> They were accompanied by a clown, who, when a new act had to commence and when they had to change their costume, made many antics and pranks in German during the performance, by which he amused the audience. . . .[29]

Albert Cohn, whose work on the English actors in Germany is seminal, thought it "probable that all these English players soon acquired a familiarity with the German language."[30]

Translation and performance, then, are key to understanding the differences between continental plays and their English counterparts. But in the case of the plays in the 1620 collection, additional consideration must be given to the editor, who undoubtedly also made changes. It was almost certainly the editor who styled the title page of *Fortunatus,* presenting the play as one of six "*Comœdia*" in the volume[31] and singling out the features that were most likely to please: the purse and wishing hat, the Three Spirits, and Virtue and Shame. To express his esteem for the *englische Komödianten,* by then in Germany for three decades, and to give the volume further appeal, he included a foreword that places the English actors in a line of descent from orators and writers of ancient Greece (Æsop) and Rome (Cicero, Livy, Publilius Syrus, Macrobius). Most important, he presented the plays in a form that would enable them to be easily acted, which meant he provided stage directions, compulsively. When Fortunatus first meets Fortune, for example, a stage direction notes that he falls on his knees and speaks. But it comes just before Fortunatus begs forgiveness and Fortune tells him to stand up (133),[32] dialogue plainly indicating how the actor should behave. Similarly, in act 2, Fortunatus, wearing the Sultan's wishing hat, wishes himself to his ship and vanishes, even as the Sultan cries "O weh"; nonetheless, a stage direction explains that Fortunatus flies away (141). In act 4, Fortune tells Andelocia to eat the fruit of the tree of Virtue, after which Andelocia exclaims that his horns have disappeared; yet there is a stage direction stating that he eats the apple and the horns fall away (173). Later, Andelocia wishes himself to the cloister in Hibernia where Agripyne is sequestered, then announces that he is there; still, a stage direction makes doubly sure we know he has arrived (195). In the final act, when Ampedo declares his intent to burn the wishing hat, then comments on it as it is burning, the stage direction notes that he tosses it in the fire (201). This pattern of redundancy persists throughout the 1620 text of *Fortunatus* and, for that matter, every play in the volume. In *Titus Andronicus,* for example, we have these instances of dialogue and stage direction, along with many others: "Now let me throw off these old rags" / "*He takes off the old mantle*" (21);[33] "I now place the crown upon your head" / "*Sets the crown on her head*" (22); "But what an astonishing thing do I see now—the Empress all alone and hurrying toward us!" / "*Empress approaches them*" (26).[34] Such editorial additions may have been intended to help actors perform the plays, but, as William B. Long points out in his essay on the eighteen surviving playbooks from the Elizabethan / Jacobean / Caroline theaters, only an amateur would think that "the way to aid the players was to tell them how to do their jobs."[35] Belaboring the obvious, Menius, well-meaning but misguided, clearly contributed his share to the evolving text of *Fortunatus.*

If the German Fortunatus play, then, is *The Whole History of Fortunatus* as transformed on the Continent by actors, translator, and editor, we need to ask whether it is reasonable to believe that this English play found its way to Germany within a few years of its composition in 1599. In fact, its migration to the Continent should not be surprising, for dozens of English plays from the Elizabethan and Jacobean period, some considered lost, are extant, in title or in text, in German prose translations. In the late sixteenth and early seventeenth century, there were no fewer than 112 English actors on the Continent,[36] assembled in troupes intent on capitalizing on the thriving theatrical market abroad. Continental records document the many performances by these troupes, the stipends they were awarded, the geographical range of their activity, and their warm reception. Fynes Moryson may have scoffed at the "pieces and Patches" of plays the English actors performed at the Frankfurt Fair in 1592,[37] but at least one late sixteenth-century report suggests that his countrymen "returned home rewarded, and loaded with gold and silver."[38] Just what arrangements enabled plays that were typically the property of London companies or, in some cases, individual actors—*Fortunatus, Nobody and Somebody, Doctor Faustus, The Jew of Malta, Titus Andronicus,* for example—to travel from England's stages to Germany's is yet an unanswered question.

To conclude this discussion of Dekker's *Fortunati,* I offer the following summary: (1) In late 1599, Dekker revised his recently completed *The Whole of Fortunatus,* turning it into *The Pleasant Comedy of Old Fortunatus* for presentation at court; (2) within a few years, *The Whole History of Fortunatus* was in Germany, where someone (possibly an English actor) translated it into German; (3) the "corrupt" text of *The Whole History of Fortunatus* published in the 1620 German collection is the product of translation, editing, and performance, each entailing simplifying, pruning, adding, and adapting; and (4) although the text of *The Whole History of Fortunatus* is lost, the German version provides good indications of how Dekker changed his play for performance at court. Side-by-side, then—if one considers the German text, *in its English original,* to be the earlier—the two extant plays tell the story recorded in *Henslowe's Diary* in the final weeks of 1599: upon additional payments for altering *The Whole History of Fortunatus,* including the ending, Dekker delivered *The Pleasant Comedie of Old Fortunatus* for performance before the Queen.

I end this essay with a postscript concerning a little-known manuscript of yet another Fortunatus play. The manuscript, in German, is in the Landesbibliothek und Murhardsche Bibliothek der Stadt Kassel, Germany (8° Ms. theatr. 4), among numerous documents associated with the Landgrave Moritz, who hosted English actors at his Kassel court from the early to mid-

1590s to at least 1613.[39] It is bound with a manuscript of *Ariodante und Ginevra,* also in German, and in the same hand. (Richard Mulcaster's Merchant Taylors School boys performed *Ariodante and Genevora* at court on February 12, 1583.)[40] Harms, who studied the several texts of *Fortunatus* in 1892 and supposed that the Kassel manuscript dates from between 1610 and 1620, concluded that this version, which begins with the father of Fortunatus, derives not from Dekker's play but from Hans Sachs's.[41] Given the ready availability of Hans Sachs's play, though, it is curious that such a manuscript, with line-by-line parallels with the earlier play but not identical to it, would exist at all. More importantly, given the sustained association of the Kassel court with the *englische Komödianten,* it would be surprising if this manuscript were not related in some way to the English players. Kassel was, after all, the site of the 1606/1607 performance of the *Fortunatus* published in 1620, and the troupes that presented that play in Graz in 1608 and in Dresden in 1626 were led by a member, or former member, of the Landgrave's players. John Green, who had traveled in France in 1603–5 with actor/manager Robert Browne, the Landgrave Moritz's sometime agent, had played at the Frankfurt Fair in 1606 and 1607, and he was identified then as a member of the *Fürstliche Hessiche Comoedianten,* i.e., the actors in the service of the Landgrave Moritz. However intriguing another early seventeenth-century manuscript of *Fortunatus* may be, the origin and purpose of the Kassel manuscript remains a mystery.

Finally, no discussion of Dekker's *Fortunati* would be complete without mention of the seventeenth-century German *Puppenspiel,* for the text of the Fortunatus puppet play clearly derives from Dekker. As Carl Engel points out in his 12-volume anthology, *Deutsche Puppenkomödien,* in Germany during the Thirty Years' War and in England during the parliamentary closing of the theaters, puppet plays, performed at fairs or in the privacy of homes, helped satisfy the public taste for theatre.[42] In Germany, these productions enabled the repertory of the *englische Komödianten* to continue, even as fewer English actors sought employment in the war-torn cities and courts of northern Europe. Engel's anthology presents some two dozen puppet plays, including *Geneveva,* four versions of *Doctor Faust,* and four of the plays published in the 1620 collection: *Haman and Esther, The Prodigal Son, A King's Son of England and a King's Daughter of Scotland,* and *Fortunatus (Glückssäckel und Wünschhut).* Each of the puppet plays that derives from the 1620 collection closely follows its source, though the puppet play of Fortunatus surprises with a revised, happy ending. Interestingly, one of the players who presented the *Puppenkomödien* may have been Robert Browne who, following an early career with the Worcester's Men (1583–85), was the most prominent actor/manager on the Continent. The last we hear of him is in 1620, when he completed a two-year tour that included performances in Prague before the Winter King. His wife's remarriage in 1622 suggests Browne's demise, but it may be that he and Cecilie divorced, for the name Robert Browne appears in a 1638 Coventry record concerning a "motion" (or puppet play) and in a 1639 Norwich petition to "shewe an Italian Motion." This was surely not Browne's son, who died in 1625, and not the Browne of the Boar's Head, who died in 1603. The possibility that it was the Robert Browne who toured the Continent is strengthened by the names of those who were with him: Richard Jones and George Hall in Coventry and Hall in Norwich—both players who had been with Browne in Germany. Might "old Browne," who by the 1630s would have been in his seventies, have turned to puppetry, offering his motions in the provinces he had known as a member of the Worcester Men? And, in the 1620s and earlier 1630s, when there are no known records of him, might he have been in Germany restaging familiar English plays as "motions"? Whoever the puppet master, the Fortunatus *Puppenspiel* testifies to the still evolving afterlife of Dekker's lost *Fortunatus*.

Notes

1. The title page reads: *The Pleasant Comedie of Old Fortunatus. As it was plaied before the Queenes Maiestie this Christmas, by the Right Honourable the Earl of Nottingham, Lord high Admirall of England his Servants.* London, Printed by S.S. for William Aspley, dwelling in Paules Church-yard at the signe of the Tygers head. 1600.

2. Quotations are from *Henslowe's Diary,* 2d ed., ed. R. A. Foakes (Cambridge: Cambridge University Press, 2001), 34–37, 126–27, 127–28.

3. Although the volume does not identify the editor, I have accepted Gustaf Fredén's argument that it was Menius. See *Friedrich Menius und das Repertoire der Englischen Komödianten in Deutschland* (Stockholm: P. A. Palmers, 1939). (Fredén's work extends that of Johan Nordströom, "Friedrich Menius. En aventyrlig Dorpatprofessor och hans glömda in sats I det engelska komediantdramats historia," *Samlaren* 3 [1922]: 42–91.) The title page of the 1620 collection reads: *Engelische Comedien und Tragedien Das Ist: Sehr Schöne / Herrliche und Ausserlesene / Geist- und Weltliche Comedi und Tragedi Spiel / Sampt dem Pickelhering / Welche wegen Ihrer Artigen Inventionen, Kurtzweiligen auch Theils Warhafftigen Geschicht Halber / von den Engelländern in Deutschland an Königlichen / Chur- und Fürstlichen Höfen / auch in Vornehmen Reichs- See- und HandelStädten Seynd Agiret und Gehalten Worden / und Zuvor Nie im Druck Aussgangen. An Jetzo / Allen der Comedi und Tragedi Liebhabern / und Andern zu Lieb und Gefallen / der Gestalt in Offener Druck Gegeben / dass Sie gar Leicht Darauss Spielweiss Widerumb Angerichtet / und zur Ergetzligkeit und Erquickung des Gemüths Gehalten Werden Können. Gedruckt im Jahr M. DC. XX.* (*English Comedies and Tragedies, i.e. Very Fine, Beautiful and Select, Spiritual and Worldly Comedy and Tragedy Plays, with the Pickelherring Clown, Which on Account of Their Fanciful Inventions, Entertaining and Partly True Histories, Have Been Acted and Given by the English in Germany at Royal, Electoral, and Princely Courts, As Well As in the Principal Imperial-Sea- and Commercial*

Towns, Never before Printed, but Now Published To Please All Lovers of Comedies and Tragedies, and Others, and in a Form That Would Enable Them To Be Easily Acted for the Delight and Recreation of the Mind. Published in the year 1620). The volume is available in the Folger Shakespeare Library (PR 1246 G5 E59 Cage); for a modern reprint, see *Spieltexte der Wanderbühne*, ed. Manfred Brauneck, 4 vols. (Berlin: Walter de Gruyter, 1970), vol. 1: *Engelische Comedien und Tragedien*.

4. The letter was first published in Friedrich Hurter, *Geschichte Kaiser Ferdinands II. und Seiner Eltern, bis zu Dessen Krönung in Frankfurt*, 11 vols. (Schaffhausen: Hurtersche Buchhandlung, 1852), vol. 5, 311–16. For an English translation, as well as a discussion, see Orlene Murad, *The English Comedians at the Habsburg Court in Graz 1607–1608* (Salzburg: Institut für Englische Sprache und Literatur, Universität Salzburg, 1978), 4–11. Also see Irene Morris, "A Hapsburg Letter," *The Modern Language Review* 69, no. 1 (1974): 12–22. The original letter is in Vienna at the Haus-, Hof- und Staatsarchiv, Familienkorrespondenz A. Karton 6, fol. 312–15.

5. The list reflects Murad's translation of the Archduchess's letter, pages 6–7. Murad, who makes the point that the Archduchess's letter provides descriptions rather than titles, identifies plays that may fit Magdalena's descriptions.

6. See Hans Hartleb, *Deutschlands Erster Theaterbau: Eine Geschichte des Theaterlebens und der Englische Komödianten unter Landgraf Moritz dem Gelehrten von Hessen-Kassel* (Berlin: Walter de Gruyter, 1936), 79.

7. See Moritz Fürstenau, *Zur Geschichte der Musik und des Theaters am Hofe zu Dresden*, 2 vols. (Dresden: Rudolf Kuntze, 1861), vol. 1, 96–97.

8. Charles H. Herford, *Studies in the Literary Relations of England and Germany in the Sixteenth Century* (Cambridge: At the University Press, 1886), 218.

9. Paul Harms, *Die deutschen Fortunatus-Dramen und ein Kasseler Dichter des 17. Jahrhunderts* (Hamburg and Leipzig: Leopold Volz, 1892), 3–17.

10. For Andelocia's / Andolosia's and Agripyne's / Agrippina's names, I have used the spelling in *Old Fortunatus*.

11. For a modern edition of the *Volksbuch*, see *Fortunatus: Studienausgabe nach der Editio Princeps von 1509*, ed. Hans-Gert Roloff (Stuttgart: Philipp Reclam, 1981). The seventeenth century saw English translations of the *Volksbuch* that do not concern us here. Thomas Churchyard's [or Thomas Coombe's] *The Right, Pleasant and Variable Tragical History of Fortunatus*, issued in 1676 and again in 1682, indicates that the text was "First Penned in the Dutch Tongue" (although "Dutch" may mean "Deutsch"). *The History of the Birth, Travels, Strange Adventures, and Death of Fortunatus*, by an anonymous author, was published in 1682. This, too, is a translation, with "several new Additions which was not in the Original Copy from whence it was Translated." Finally, *The Comical and Tragical History of Fortunatus* of 1700, extant in the seventh edition, also by an anonymous author, abridges the text "for the benefit of young men and women, whose impatience will not allow them to read the larger volume." All are prose narratives, their source the *Volksbuch Fortunatus*. The British Library holds a manuscript of *The History of Fortunatus. Translated from the Dutch* (Cat. No. 12410. Bb. 8), tentatively dated c. 1650.

12. Debra Prager, "*Fortunatus:* 'Aus dem Künigreich Cipern': Mapping the World and the Self," *Daphnis: Zeitschrift für Mittlere Deutschen Literatur und Kultur der Frühen Neuzeit (1400–1750)* 33.1–2 (2004): 123–24.

13. For a modern edition of Hans Sachs's play (in seven acts), see *Dichtungen von Hans Sachs, Dritter Theil. Dramatische Gedichte,* ed. Julius Tittmann (Leipzig: F. A. Brockhaus, 1871), 112–55.

14. See, for example, *The Pleasant Comedie of Old Fortunatus* by Thomas Dekker, ed. Hans Scherer (Erlangen: A. Deichert'sche Verlagsbuchh. Nachf. [Georg Böhme], 1901), 1–14.

15. Alexis F. Lange, "On the Relation of *Old Fortunatus* to the *Volksbuch,*" *Modern Language Notes* 18, no. 5 (May 1903): 141–44. The earliest extant Frankfurt edition is 1547; Lange uses the 1551 edition.

16. See, for example, *Old Fortunatus: A Play written by Thomas Dekker,* ed. Oliphant Smeaton (London: J. M. Dent and Co., Aldine House, 1904), xi–xii; Mary Leland Hunt, *Thomas Dekker: A Study* (New York: Columbia University Press, 1911), 16; and Julia Gasper, "The Anglo-Dutch Alliance in Dekker's Early Works," in *The Dragon and the Dove* (Oxford: Clarendon Press, 1990), 16–43.

17. Mary Leland Hunt, *Thomas Dekker,* 34.

18. The quotation continues: "with the exception of two other scenes of the same stamp. In these three scenes, which bear the evident character not only of an afterthought, but of an after-thought conceived in just such circumstances as have been described, the two figures of *Vertue* and *Vice* appear as the rivals of Fortune in her originally unaided work." Charles H. Herford, *Studies in the Literary Relations of England and Germany,* 211–12.

19. Paul Harms, *Die deutschen Fortunatas-Dramen,* 4–5, 6–10.

20. Cyrus Hoy, *Introductions, Notes and Commentaries to Texts in The Dramatic Works of Thomas Dekker Edited by Fredson Bowers,* 4 vols. (Cambridge: Cambridge University Press, 1980), vol. 1, 90.

21. Ibid., 86.

22. Charles H. Herford, *Studies in the Literary Relations of England and Germany,* 216.

23. Cyrus Hoy, *Introductions, Notes and Commentaries,* 87.

24. For an analysis of the play's treatment of gold, see William H. Sherman, "'Gold is the strength, the sinnewes of the world': Thomas Dekker's *Old Fortunatus* and England's Golden Age," *Medieval and Renaissance Drama in England* 6 (1993): 85–102.

25. Cyrus Hoy, *Introductions, Notes and Commentaries,* 85.

26. Ibid., 85.

27. William J. Thoms, *Three Notelets on Shakespeare* (London: John Russell Smith, 1865), 8.

28. Ibid., 10.

29. Melchior Röchell, *Die Münsterischen Chroniken von Röchell, Stevermann und Corfey,* ed. Johannes Janssen (Münster, 1852), quoted in Albert Cohn, *Shakespeare in Germany in the Sixteenth and Seventeenth Centuries: An Account of English Actors in Germany and the Netherlands and of the Plays Performed by Them During the Same Period* (1865; New York: Haskell House, 1971), CXXXV.

30. Albert Cohn, *Shakespeare in Germany,* CXXXV.

31. Six of the plays are called comedies, two tragedies. While the term "*Comœdia*" was used to specify genre, it was also used more generally to indicate that the piece was a play. Hence the English "*Komödianten,*" or players of plays.

32. Page references are to the German text in *Spieltexte der Wanderbühne,* ed. Manfred Brauneck.

33. Page references are to the English translation in Ernest Brennecke, in collaboration with Henry Brennecke, *Shakespeare in Germany 1590–1700, With Translations of Five Early Plays* (Chicago: The University of Chicago Press, 1964). The corresponding pages in Brauneck are 466, 469, and 476.

34. See June Schlueter, "Rereading the Peacham Drawing," *Shakespeare Quarterly* 50, no. 2 (1999): 171–84.

35. William B. Long, "'Precious Few': English Manuscript Playbooks," in *A Companion to Shakespeare,* ed. David Scott Kastan (Oxford: Blackwell, 1999), 427.

36. In "Bilingual *Hamlet: Der Bestrafte Brudermord* in the 21st Century," to appear in a 2013 issue of *Shakespeare Bulletin*, Christine Schmidle credits Edwin Nungezer, *A Dictionary of Actors* (1929; New York: Greenwood Press, 1968); David Kathman, *Biographical Index of English Drama before 1600,* http://www.shakespeareauthorship.com/bd/index.html; and Judith Milhous and Robert D. Hume, "New Light on English Acting Companies in 1646, 1648, and 1660," *The Review of English Studies,* new series, 42, no. 168 (November 1991): 487–509.

37. *Shakespeare's Europe: A Survey of the Condition of Europe at the end of the 16th century. Being unpublished chapters of Fynes Moryson's Itinerary (1617).* With an Introduction and an Account of Fynes Moryson's Career by Charles Hughes, 2d ed. (1903; New York: Benjamin Blom, 1967), 304.

38. Erhardus Cellius, *Eques auratus Anglo-Wirtembergicus* (Tübingen: Typis Auctoris, 1605), quoted, in English translation, in *England as Seen by Foreigners in the Days of Elizabeth and James the First. With Extracts from the Travels of Foreign Princes and Others,* ed. William Brenchley Rye (1865; New York: Benjamin Blom, 1967), cvi–cvii.

39. See June Schlueter, "English Actors in Kassel, Germany, during Shakespeare's Time," *Medieval and Renaissance Drama in England* 10 (1998): 238–61.

40. E. K. Chambers, *The Elizabethan Stage,* 4 vols. (1923; Oxford: At the Clarendon Press, 1967), vol. 2, 99; vol. 4, 99 and 159. For an analysis of the German *Ariodante und Ginevra* manuscript, see Paul Harms, *Die deutschen Fortunatas-Dramen,* 54–79. The Kassel library also holds a manuscript of *I Gelosi* (*Comedia molto piaceuole p[iena] d'ogni gelosia et amore*) (8º Ms. theatr. 3), also in German and in the same hand.

41. Paul Harms, *Die deutschen Fortunatas-Dramen,* 28–54.

42. *Deutsche Puppenkomödien,* 12 vols, vol. 2: *Der verlorene Sohn. Der Raubritter oder Adelheid von Staudenbühel,* ed. Carl Engel (Oldenburg: Druck und Verlag der Schulzeschen Buchhandlung, C. Berndt & A. Schwartz, 1875), VII–VIII. For the Fortunatus play, see vol. 7: *Glückssäckel und Wünschhut. Rosa von Tannenburg,* ed. Carl Engel (Oldenburg: Schulzesche Hof-Buchhandlung und Hof-Buchdruckerei [C. Berndt & A. Schwartz], 1878), 7–48.

Eagle and Hound: The "Epitaph" of Talbot and the Date of *1 Henry VI*

Lawrence Manley

A REASON sometimes given for attributing *1 Henry VI* to Lord Strange's Men is the "epitaph" in which Sir William Lucy delivers what turns out to be a posthumous tribute to the English hero Sir John Talbot, who, unknown to Lucy, has died in battle some twenty-eight lines earlier:

> But where's the great Alcides of the field,
> Valiant Lord *Talbot,* Earle of Shrewsbury?
> Created, for his rare successe in Armes,
> Great Earl of *Washford, Waterford,* and *Valence,*
> Lord *Talbot* of *Goodrig* and *Vrchinfield,*
> Lord *Strange* of *Blackmere,* Lord *Verdon* of *Alton,*
> Lord *Cromwell* of *Wingefield,* Lord *Furniuall* of *Sheffeild,*
> The thrice-victorious Lord of *Falconbridge,*
> Knight of the Noble Order of S. *George,*
> Worthy S. *Michael* and the *Golden Fleece,*
> Great Marshall to *Henry* the sixt
> Of all his Warres within the Realme of France.
>   (4.7.60–71; Folio TLN 2295–305)

Noting that Thomas Nashe's tribute to a play depicting Talbot's death appeared in *Pierce Penilesse* (1592), a work which praises Ferdinando Stanley, Lord Strange of Knokyn, scholars have often picked "Lord Strange of Blackmere" from this list of titles as evidence that *1 Henry VI* is the "harey the vj" that, according to Philip Henslowe's theatrical diary, was performed at Henslowe's Rose Theatre in 1592–93 by "my lord stranges mene."[1] Michael Hattaway, for example, states that Ferdinando Stanley was "a descendant of the Lord Talbot who appears in the play." Michael Taylor observes, in connection with Talbot's title "Lord Strange of Blackmere" that "the current Lord Strange was patron" of the company that performed "harey the vj." Roger Warren argues that "Lord Strange may have commissioned a play about Talbot, an earlier Lord Strange." Paul J. Vincent states that "Lord Strange, the patron of an acting company which first performed *harey the vi,* was a descendant of the play's protagonist, Lord Talbot," and he suggests that "the playwright(s) were concerned to flatter the patron of the commissioning acting company." I have helped to perpetuate this error by referring in an earlier essay to Talbot as Ferdinando Stanley's "titular ancestor."[2] It is the purpose of what follows to correct this error, but in a way that nevertheless makes it clear that act 4 scene 7, which most scholars attribute to the hand of Shakespeare, must have been written for Lord Strange's Men in 1592.

Ferdinando Stanley, Lord Strange of Knokyn, was not a descendant of John Talbot, and "Lord Strange of Blackmere" was not among his titles. From the early fourteenth century there had in fact been two different baronages of Strange. Both baronages, Knokyn and Blackmere, originated among the Lestranges, lords of the Shropshire marches. Roger Lestrange, eldest son of John (III) Lestrange of Knokyn, Shropshire became the first baron Strange when summoned to Parliament in 1295. This title became "Lestraunge de Knockyn" when John (V) Lestrange was summoned in 1309. When Joan Lestrange, ninth holder of the title, married George Stanley, the son of Thomas Lord Stanley and first Earl of Derby, the Strange of Knokyn title entered the Stanley line.[3] Ferdinando Stanley (1559–94), son of Henry Stanley and later fifth earl of Derby, became the thirteenth Lord Strange of Knokyn.

In distinction to the Strange of Knokyn title, the title of Lord Strange of Blackmere was created in 1309 for Fulk Lestrange of Longnor, Shropshire, and Blackmore, Herefordshire. Following the death of the fifth Lord Strange of Blackmere, the title passed through female descendants until it was inherited in 1421 by John Talbot, later first earl of Shrewsbury and the hero of *1 Henry VI*. The title of Lord Strange of Blackmere remained with the Talbot earls of Shrewsbury and was held from 1590 by Gilbert Talbot (1552–1616), seventh earl of Shrewsbury.[4] That the direct line of ancestry from the fifteenth-century Talbot descended to the seventh earl of Shrewsbury rather than the Stanleys should be obvious from comparison of Gilbert Talbot's titles with those of Ferdinando Stanley in Ralph Brooke's *Catalogue and succession of the Kings, Dukes, Marquesses, Earles, and Viscounts of this Realme of England* (1619):

Ferdinando Lord *Stanley*, *Strange*, and of the *Isle of Man* . . . the fift Earle of *Derby*
(p. 72)

Gilbert Talbot, . . . seuenth Earle of *Shrewsbury*, . . . Lord *Talbot, Furniuall, Verdon* and *Strange* of *Blackmer,* . . . Knight and Companion of the Noble Order of the Garter.
(p. 199)

Clearly the titles of Gilbert Talbot, not those of Ferdinando Stanley, are the ones which connect with the "epitaph" of Sir John Talbot in *1 Henry VI.* Lucy's speech might conceivably have been added to "harey the vj" at any time before 1623, the date when *1 Henry VI* was published in the first folio. The year 1596 is sometimes suggested as the earliest possible date, based on a publication many believe to be a source for Sir William Lucy's speech, *An Armor of Proofe* (1596), dedicated by Roger Cotton to Gilbert Talbot, "earle of Shrewsburie, Lord Talbot, Furniuall, Strange of Blackmeare, Verdon and Louetofte, Knight of the most noble Order of the Garter." In his dedication, Cotton pays tribute one of Gilbert Talbot's "most noble progenatours," the "worthy peere" who

> together with his valiant Sonne the Lord Lisle, in that sore battle fought at *Castilion* in *Fraunce* their sweete lyues did ende: where a monument of the Earle remayneth vnto this day, and this inscription following, ingrauen thervpon:
>
>   *Heere lyeth the right noble Knight* Iohn Talbot *Earle of Shrewsburie, Earle of Washford, Waterforth, and Valence, Lorde Talbot of Goodritche and Vrchingfeilde: Lord Strange of Blackmeare, Lord Verdon of Alton, Lord Crumwell of Wingfeilde, Lord Louetoft of Worsoppe, Lord Furniuall of Sheffeilde, and Lord Falconbridge, Knight of the most noble orders of S. George, S. Michael, and the Golden Fleece, Great Marshall to King* Henrie *the sixt of his Realme of Fraunce, who dyed at the battle of Castilion neare Burdeaux, Anno.* 1453. (sig. A3v)

A similar epitaph appears in Richard Crompton's *Mirror of Magnanimitie* (1599), where it is said to have been "ingrauen" on the "Tombe" where Talbot was "interred" in France (sigs. E3v-E4). By the time of Ralph Brooke's *Catalogue and Succession* (1619), Cotton's "monument" on the battlefield of Castillon and Crompton's "Tombe" had become "A Tombe at *Roane* in *Normandy,* whereon this Epitaphe"—one virtually identical to those in Cotton and Crompton—was said to be written (p. 196). This "Tombe"—often, following Brooke, located at Rouen—became a staple of subsequent chronicles,[5] and it has continued to be credited by eminent Shakespeareans from Edmund Malone to John Dover Wilson, J. P. Brockbank and Emrys Jones.[6]

The supposition that the list of titles first found in Cotton and Crompton originates from an actual epitaph has been offered as evidence that, barring discovery of an earlier source, Sir William Lucy's tribute must derive from Cotton and Crompton and so represents revisions to 4.7 much later than the debut of "harey the vj" at the Rose in February, 1592 or the demise of Lord Strange's Men in December 1593. Thus Tucker Brooke, who knew of Compton (1599) but not Cotton (1596), used the "epitaph" to argue for a theory of later Shakespearean revision of the play.[7] Allison Gaw, also aware of Crompton but not Cotton, argued on the basis of then-current knowledge that revision of this portion of the play could not be placed "earlier than 1599."[8] Josephine Pearce, who subsequently discovered the earlier version of Talbot's titles in Cotton, suggested that "the reviser of *1 Henry VI* could have availed himself of this material" with the publication of *An Armor of Proofe* in 1596.[9]

Pearce, asserting that Cotton "had not been to France" and that "the nature of the epitaph would suggest the source was printed," cautioned that "there is no reason to doubt a source available to Roger Cotton would also be available to the reviser, indeed, perhaps the original author of *1 Henry VI*" (p. 329). Subsequent commentators have also cautioned that "it is of course likely that Cotton is repeating a formula that could have existed in many sources now lost."[10] It is this earlier source that we are looking for.

That the formula must indeed have come from a source earlier than Cotton and, more importantly, could not have originated from an epitaph at Rouen or from any historical epitaph of the hero Talbot is underlined by Augustine Vincent's attack on Ralph Brooke in *A Discouerie of Errovrs in the first Edition of the Catalogue of Nobility* (1622). Citing Brooke's version of the epitaph, Vincent demolishes several of its elements as fiction:

> Doe you thinke so to gull vs, as to make vs beleeue that there is such an Epitaph at *Roan* in *Normandy,* for this great Earle of *Shrewsbury* as here you have cited? I question it, not as doubting of his worth, but youre wisedome, in regard you haue puffed it vp with titles, (by him assuredly) not once thought of, and which any of reasonable iudgement will blush at.
>
> First in stiling him *Earle of Valence,* when you cannot but know, & therefore you ought to confesse, that there neuer was any Earle of VALENCE as yet in *England.* . . .
>
> Secondly, you say he was *Lord Talbot of Goodrich and Orchenfield,* the one I confesse, the other *Irchenfield* I confidently deny, onely grant him to be Lord (I meane the owner) but not Baron thereof. . . .
>
> Fourthly, that hee was *Lord Cromwell of Wingfield.* I say *Cromwell* was Baron of *Tastehale* in *Lincolnshire,* and that *Wingfield* . . . neuer was a Barony. . . . If you take but some paynes to search further into it, you shall find that *Ralph* Lord *Cromwell* was liuing, both then and after.
>
> Fiftly, that he was Lord *Falconbridge:* surely you are a widower of wit, otherwise you would haue remembred that about this time the Lord *Fauconbridges* heire had inuested this *Barony* into the family of the *Neuils,* by marrying *William Neuill* in her right Lord *Fauconbridge,* and after created Earle of *Kent.*
>
> Lastly, that hee was *Knight of the Order of Saint Michael.* . . . Did you neuer reade that painfull and iudicious labour written by Sir *William Segar,* Garter? if you haue not, then now looke, and you shall learne, that the Order of Saint *Michael* was not instituted vntill the yeare 1469. . . . This Earle of *Shrewsbury* died (as I haue said before) a. 1453. the Order of Saint *Michael* begunne a. 1469. so that by this account you make him a Knight and Companion thereof sixteene years before that order was deuised. A word or two about the *place of his Bvriall; Yorke* says at *Roane in Normandy,* but vndoubtedly hee was buried at *Whitchurch* in *Shropshire,* where his Monument is extant, for *Roan* was surrendred to the French 3. or 4. years before his death, therefore vnlikely to haue his Sepulture there. Learned *Camden* . . . deliuers the epitaph truely, as it is to be seene at *Whitchurch,* in these words.
>
> (pp. 464–65)

The epitaph that Vincent cites from William Camden, in a form much simpler than the versions discussed so far, commemorates "the right Noble Lord, Sir John Talbot, sometimes Earle of Shrewsburie, Lord Talbot, Lord Furnivall, Lord Verdon, Lord Strange de Black-Mere, and Mareshall of France."[11] None of the other "puffed . . . vp" titles found in *1 Henry VI,* Cotton, and the other treatments of Talbot, appear.

Georges Lambin, who in 1971 pointed out Vincent's 1622 corrections to Brooke (mistakenly identifying them as corrections made by Brooke himself), explained in some detail why Talbot could not have been buried at Rouen, which was occupied continuously by the French from 1449 through the unsuccessful English siege of 1591–92. Lambin also examined the probable circumstances surrounding the disposal of Talbot's mortal remains—the rendering of the flesh from the bones near the site of his death at Castillon in the south of France, the contemporary burial of his embalmed heart under the porch of the church of St Alkmund at Whitchurch, and the repatriation of his bones some forty years later by his grandson, Sir Gilbert Talbot, to Whitchurch, where an effigy and inscription were erected.[12] This was all in keeping with the terms of Talbot's will of 1452, which directed that his body should be entombed at Whitchurch on the right-hand side of the chancel. The chancel tomb was damaged when the church collapsed in 1711, and although the church was rebuilt, the tomb of Talbot was not restored until the later nineteenth century, following the exhumation and examination of Talbot's bones. No inscription survived, but as Lambin noted, the version of the inscription cited by Daniel Defoe in 1724 agrees with the one cited in Camden's *Britannia* and subsequently produced in Vincent's attack on Brooke.[13]

Despite his sympathy with Vincent's debunking of Brooke's version of the epitaph as "puffed . . . vp" fiction, and despite his explanation of why no tomb of Talbot could have been located at Rouen, Lambin went on, in the absence of any shred of evidence, to construct a notional now-lost tomb for Talbot at Falaise. It is not impossible, of course, that some such early tomb or monument existed;[14] but the sixteenth-century antiquarian André Thevet, the earliest writer I can find attesting to the "Chapelle de Talbot" (a monument erected at Castillon by Charles VII), writes skeptically of rumors that Talbot was buried at Bordeaux.[15] I have found no contemporary French chronicle source that attests to the existence of a Talbot tomb,[16] and if such a tomb had existed, it is odd that the reported "epitaph" does not include any of the French titles of nobility to which Talbot laid claim—count of Clermont and lord of Graville, Heugeville, Thouars, Longempre and Bretteville sur Laize.[17] It is odd, too, that it would have been "puffed . . . vp" with all the historical errors cited by Vincent.

In seemingly sensible contravention of his own bizarre attempt to recreate the missing tomb and its "puffed . . . vp" epitaph, Lambin did supply, in the middle of his analysis, a much better explanation of the missing "source" for the list of titles repeated in Cotton, Crompton, and Brooke: "c'est 'Shakespeare!'"[18] Taking note of the most egregious error in the reports,

Knight of the most noble orders of S. George, S. Michael, and the Golden Fleece
(Cotton, sig. Aa)

Knight of the most noble order of S. George, S. Michaell, and the Golden Fleece
(Crompton, sig. E4)

Knight of the Noble Order of S. George, S. Michaell, and the golden Fleece
(Brooke, 196)

Lambin noticed that unlike these reporters, Sir William Lucy, though guilty of rhetorical excess and anachronism, is innocent of falsely reporting Talbot's membership in the orders of St. Michael and the Golden Fleece. He is merely declaring, in the teeth of the French and Burgundian victors, that Talbot, knight of "the noble Order of Saint George," or more likely "the noble Order of Saint George" itself, is "*Worthy* Saint Michael and the Golden Fleece." On the basis of this reading, however, Lambin went on to argue that Shakespeare was merely channeling, by means unknown, a lost report of Talbot's "tomb" in France. He proceeds to construct a hypothetical epitaph, which he places at Falaise, and then argues it was defaced, in its final lines, by a later (hypothetical) English patriot who must have attributed worthiness to Talbot himself in the following manner:

> HERE LYETH THE RIGHT NOBLE KNIGHT IOHN TALBOT
> EARLE OF SHREWSBURY EARLE OF WASHFORD WATERFORD
> AND VALENCE LORD TALBOT OF GOODRICH AND ORCHENFIELD
> LORD STRANGE OF BLACKMERE LORD VERDON OF ALTON
> LORD CROMWELL OF WINGFIELD LORD LOVETOFT OF WORSOP
> LORD FURNIVALL OF SHEFFIELD LORD FALCONBRIDGE
> KNIGHT OF THE MOST NOBLE ORDER OF St GEORGE
> *worthy st. michaell and the golden fleece*
> GREAT MARSHALL TO KING HENRY THE SIXT
> OF ALL HIS WARS WITHIN THE REALME OF FRANCE

This is a weirdly elaborate and speculative way of accounting for the defiant rhetoric of Sir William Lucy, especially since it misses the point that it was not Augustine Vincent in 1622 but Joan of Arc in *1 Henry VI* who was the first to recognize the "puffed . . . vp" semi-fictional nature of Sir William Lucy's tribute:

Puc. Heere's a silly stately stile indeede:
The Turke that two and fiftie Kingdomes hath,

Writes not so tedious a Stile as this.
Him that thou magnifi'st with all these Titles,
Stinking and fly-blowne lyes heere at our feete.

(4.7.72–76; TLN 2306–10)

So far, then, is *1 Henry VI* from borrowing from Cotton or Crompton, or from any real epitaph of John Talbot, that the play's own language actually explains where, by way of later misinterpretation, Talbot's anachronistic status as a Knight of St Michael and the Golden Fleece originated. It originated at the Rose with "harey the vj."

There is further evidence for this in Cotton's wording, which introduces his version of the "epitaph" with the statement that Talbot "together with his valiant Sonne the Lord Lisle, in that sore battle fought at Castilion in Fraunce *their sweete lyues did ende*" (italics mine). Edward Hall, from whose account of the battlefield deaths of the Talbots later ones derive, notes that Talbot, "desirynge the life of his entirely and welbeloved sonne the lord Lisle, willed, advertised and counsailled hym to departe out of the fielde." But Hall focuses his account on Talbot's speech of dissuasion, not on the deaths of father and son; of the latter events, Hall merely states drily that along with Talbot "there dyed manfully hys sonne the lord Lisle."[19] As Nashe's celebration of Talbot in *Pierce Penilesse* (1592) suggests, it was not in the pages of Hall but on the stage that Talbot had "his bones new embalmed with the teares of ten thousand spectators at least (at seuerall times), who, in the Tragedian that represents his person, imagine they behold him fresh bleeding" (1:212). There is every likelihood that Cotton referred to the Talbots ending "their sweete lyues" because he, a London draper, had been among those "ten thousand spectators" first shedding tears over Talbot's final, stirring battle cry:

Then follow thou thy desp'rate Syre of Crete,
Thou Icarus, thy *Life* to me is *sweet:*
If thou wilt fight, fight by thy Fathers side,
And commendable prou'd, let's dye in pride. *Exit.*

(4.6. 54–57; TLN 2225–28, italics mine)

If Sir William Lucy was committing an anachronism, then, by invoking the order of St Michael some fourteen years before it was created, this was not a citation of "fact" in support of claims about Talbot's actual titles but a rhetorical move in support of the hero's—and really the play's—defense of Talbot heroism and the glory of the Order of the Garter. Talbot's battle cries are "Saint *George* and Victory"(4.6.1; TLN 2172) and "God and Saint George, Talbot and "God, and S. *George, Talbot* and Englands right" (4.2.55; TLN 2006) England's right" (4.2.55).[20] When Talbot tears the Garter from the leg of the cowardly Sir John Fastolfe, he delivers a praise of the Order:

> When first this Order was ordain'd, my Lords,
> Knights of the Garter were of Noble birth;
> Valiant, and Vertuous, full of haughtie Courage,
> Such as were growne to credit by the warres:
> Not fearing Death, nor shrinking for Distresse,
> But alwayes resolute, in most extreames.
> (4.1.27–44, TLN 1779–84)

That the "the noble Order of Saint George" is an order "worthy Saint Michael and the Golden Fleece," a claim that Lucy upholds in defiance to his addressees, the princes of France and Burgundy and thus patrons of the two foreign orders (the play's Burgundy is the very same Philip the Good who created the Order of the Golden Fleece in 1430), is part of the play's celebration of the Talbot Shrewsbury earldom and the Order of the Garter. If we were looking for a "source" for this "anachronistic" portion of the epitaph, we might find it in William Harrison's *Description of England* in Holinshed (I, fol. 162), where "The noble order of the Toison Dor or golden fléese" and "that of saint Michaell and his one and thirtie knights" are linked together in the story about the founding of the Order of the Garter by Edward III. This passage, and the similar account given under the reign of Edward III (II, fol. 686), have been suggested as possible sources for another contemporary Garter play, *Edward III,* and especially for the Countess of Salisbury scene, in which Shakespeare had a hand.[21]

As for the rest of Talbot's epitaph in *1 Henry VI,* its most likely source is not the epitaph of the first earl, which had been inscribed on a brass plaque in the porch at Whitchurch, but that of the sixth earl, George Talbot, who died November 18, 1590 and was buried in a splendid tomb in the Shrewsbury Chapel at St Peter's Church Sheffield on January 13, 1591. A lengthy Latin epitaph by John Foxe, amounting to a small essay but not resembling Lucy's tribute, remains inscribed to this day on the wall above the effigy.[22] But according to the seventeenth-century antiquarian Roger Dodsworth (1585–1654), an English epitaph, recorded at Sheffield cathedral on August 17, 1620 but no longer extant, was displayed "on a table hanging in the south quier builded by Georg erle of Salope a little before his death." Recording an event at the earl's funeral (it is the tomb in the south choir, not the tablet, that is being said to have been built "a little before" the earl's death), it read in part:

> George Earle of Shrowsbury, Washford and Waterford,
> Earle Marshall of England, Talbot of Goodridge, Lord
>   Verdone of Altoun, Furniuall of Sheffield, Lord
>   Luftot of Worksopp, Lord Crumbwell of Wingfeld,
>
> Lord Strange of the Blackmeere, and Justice by Northtrente
> Of forrestes and chases, a councellor, president

> Unto the Soueraigne Quene & c. for his loyaltye
> Knyght of the Garter, eke these titles all had hee:

[solemnly proclaimed] by heraldes that daie when was his funerall.[23]

Here, just in time to have inspired Lucy's epitaph in 1592, are the titles awarded to the hero Talbot in *1 Henry VI,* including those contested by Vincent as unhistorical for the first John Talbot, with the exception of "Falconbridge," a name with its own impressive pedigree as theatrical fiction.[24] "Urchinfield," Vincent had noted, was a mere misspelling of part of the Goodridge title. Lord Cromwell of Wingfield, "liuing, both then and after" John Talbot's death in France, died in 1456, and the Wingfield manor was then purchased by the second John Talbot earl of Shrewsbury, hence the Wingfield title descended from the second to the sixth and seventh earls, but never belonged to the first. "Valence," which Vincent protests was not "as yet" a barony in England, does not appear in the (presumably wooden) tablet epitaph, but it does appear prominently quartered in stone on the shields above the sixth earl's tomb and in two other places in the chapel.[25] Only the fictional Falconbridge title and the misunderstood mention of St Michael and the Golden Fleece remain unaccounted for at the Sheffield tomb itself; these remaining "fictional" elements are, in effect, the traces that allow us to track all the subsequent versions of Talbot's "epitaph" in Cotton, Crompton, and Brooke back to their theatrical original at the Rose.

These same playhouse traces can be found also in a version of the epitaph that as early as 1598 had apparently migrated to the site of John Talbot's burial in Whitchurch, Shropshire. Elias Ashmole's notes taken at Whitchurch August 31, 1663 state that there was no epitaph to go with the effigy of Talbot in the south wall of the chancel (the brass plaque at the porch of the church, under which Talbot's heart was buried, was also by then missing). Ashmole added, however, that

> in a MS. there shewed me, wherein (15 July, 1598) there were entered some extracts out of the old Church Register, this Epitaph is to be seen:—
>
> "Here lyeth the right noble knight, John Talbot, Earle of Shrewsbury, Earl of Washford, Waterford, and Valence, Lord Talbot of Goodrich and Urchinfield, Lord Strange of Blackmere, Lord Verdon of Alton, Lord Crumwell of Wingfield, Lord Levetoft of Worsoppe, Lord Furnivall of Sheiffield, and Lord Fauconbridge, Knight of the most Noble Order of St. George, Saint Michaell and the Goulden Fleece, Great Marshall to King Henry the Sixt of his realme of Fraunce, who dyed at the battaile of Castilion, nere Bourdeaux. An° 1453."[26]

Ashmole's 1663 report of this 1598 manuscript is confirmed by Sir William Dugdale's 1663 *Visitation of Shropshire,* in which Dugdale conjectures that this manuscript epitaph "was heretofore written, as I guess, on some tablet hanging neere this tomb."[27] Originating in 1590 in Sheffield, on a tablet which purported to record the speech act of a herald at the funeral of the sixth earl of Shrewsbury, next supplemented by some rhetorical flourishes added in Sir William Lucy's adaption of it in *1 Henry VI,* then crucially misconstrued on the score of St Michael and the Golden Fleece and rushed into print in 1596 by Cotton as the first earl's epitaph (first with the claim it came from a "monument" at Castillon, later with the claim it adorned a "tomb" at Rouen), this well-traveled tribute made its way by 1598 into a manuscript kept at Whitchurch, subsequently leading Dugdale to suppose it must have been recorded from "some tablet hanging neere" the hero's English tomb. The process that created John Talbot's "epitaph" is now fully visible: information from a tablet hung at the sixth earl's tomb in 1590 was supplemented by theatrical hyperbole and later by overcredulous misconstruction of Sir William Lucy's rhetorical claim that the Garter was "*worthy* St Michael and the Golden Fleece." It was Shakespeare, or if not Shakespeare, then one of Shakespeare's collaborators in 4.7, who turned a contemporary tribute to the sixth earl of Shrewsbury into the historical John Talbot's unhistorical epitaph.

But when? The first record of the misunderstood tribute is Cotton's publication in 1596. I do not know of any evidence that would connect Gilbert Talbot with the Lord Chamberlain's Men or with their patron in 1596, the date of Talbot's embassy to induct Henri IV into the Order of the Garter, or at any other time. There is a specific date, however, that would connect Talbot very powerfully with *1 Henry VI* and Lord Strange's Men. Gilbert Talbot was inducted into the Order of the Garter on June 20, 1592, within weeks of the March 3 debut of "harey the vj" as a "ne" play at Henslowe's Rose Theatre. And in contrast with the Lord Chamberlain's Men, Lord Strange's Men were a company whose patron had strong personal as well as historical connections with the Shrewsbury earls. That the two Lord Stranges, Stanley and Talbot, shared a common ancestry among the lords Lestrange of Shropshire was but the least of them.

From Polydore Vergil onward, Tudor historians recorded that the earl of Richmond triumphed over Richard III at Bosworth field owing to the support of "Thomas Stanley, William his brother, Gylbert Talbot, and others innumerable."[28] According to Hall, among "the noble men whome" Richard III "most mistrusted these were the principall: Thomas, lorde Stanley, Sir William Stanley his brother," and "Gylbert Talbot," second son of John Talbot, second earl of Shrewsbury (fol. CCiii). "To the right wing of the battell at Bosworth," said Holinshed, Lord Stanley "appointed sir Gilbert Talbot to be the leader" (II, 755). This Gilbert Talbot (d. 1516), who repatriated the bones of his heroic ancestor, was immortalized by mention on the stage as well as in the chronicles. In *The True Tragedie of Richard III* (1594), the supporters of Richmond and the Stanleys include

First, theirs the Lord Talbut, the Earle of Shreuesbury
sonne and heire, with a braue band of his owne.

(sig. G3)

Shakespeare also includes him among the Stanley allies reported to "Darbie" by Sir Christopher Urswick:

Dar. What men of name resort to him.
S. Christ. Sir Walter Herbert, a renowned souldier,
Sir Gilbert Talbot, Sir William Stanlie,
Oxford, reboubted Pembroke, Sir Iames Blunt,
Rice vp Thomas, with a valiant crew,
With many moe of noble fame and worth

(Q1, sig. L)

This Stanley–Talbot alliance, formed at Bosworth, continued during Henry VII's campaign against Lambert Simnel; Hall's claim that the king was supported at Nottingham by "the lorde George Talbot Erle of Shrewsbury, the lorde Straunge [i.e., George Stanley], Sir Iohn Cheyny valeaunt capitaynes" (fol. bbbiiiv) was repeated in Holinshed and Stow. Later, "George Talbot Comte de Sherowsbury" was placed by André Thévet along with "Thomas Stanley Comte d'Orbey" at the siege of Therouënne.[29] Perhaps more significantly, the Stanley-Talbot alliance was commemorated in the manuscript ballads and sagas, devoted to what has recently been called the Stanley Romance, that clearly belonged to the great house culture of the northern counties.[30] "Scotish ffeilde," for example, flashes back from the Lancashire alliance at the Battle of Flodden to the alliance first formed at Bosworth:

Derby that deare earle that doughty hath beene euer,
& the Lord Chamberlaine that was his cheefe brother,
Sauage, his sisters sonne, a sege that was able,
& Gylbert the gentle with a iollye meanye;
All Lancashire, these ladds thé ledden att their will[31]

This same alliance is depicted in "The Song of the Lady Bessie." There, Sir Humphrey Brereton, the Lancashire gentleman who helps Elizabeth of York organize the revolt that will return Henry Tudor to England, watches the Tudor supporters assembling at the suburban London inn where Thomas, Lord Stanley has drawn upon a doorway the heraldic Stanley eagle's foot to mark the secret place of meeting:

Humphrey stood on a high tower then,
  He looked into the West Countrey:
Sir William Stanley and seven in green,

He was aware of the Eagle drawn; . . .
He was aware of the Lord Strange and seven in green,
Come rideing into the city. . . .
He was aware of the Warden and Edward Stanley
Come rideing both in one company. . . .
He was aware of Sir John Savage and Sir Gilbert Talbot,
Come rideing both in one company.[32]

In the heraldic symbolism of "The Rose of England," the Stanley eagle and the Talbot hound combine forces against the Yorkist tyrant:

Then the egle ffollowed fast upon his pray;
    With sore dints he did them smyte.
The Talbott he bit wonderous sore,
    Soe well the unicorne did him quite.

(ll. 109–12, Bullough, 3: 349).

The regional associations behind such imagery, indeed the imagery itself, persisted at the time of "harey the vj." In *The Golden Mirror* (1589), dedicated to Gilbert Talbot in the year before the death of his father George, sixth earl of Shrewsbury, the publisher John Proctor informed Talbot that "those two most noble and loyall men your good honorable Father I meane, and the like right honorable the Earle of Darby, are set as spectacles or looking glasses, wherein all men may see a liuely pourtrayture of right Noble myndes in deede, for the right of their Countreys weale being most vigilant and studious." Accompanied by "certaine Verses penned vpon the name of my Lord Straunge [i.e., Ferdinando Stanley], and sundry others" the opening dream vision in this volume by the poet Richard Robinson depicts a virgin queen beset by a fox and wolf but preserved by the Talbot hound and Stanley eagle:

Upon the sodden presently there came,
A valiant hounde, as white as siluer is:
And did behold this Lady in the face,
As one right ready, to obay her grace.

Streight came an Eagle, soring in the skyes,
With Golden fethers, delighting all mens sight:
Who stooping straight, fell downe vpon his knees.
To doe his duetie, thus he left his flight:
(And sayd) Madame, the Lord preserue thee still,
Thus doe I pray and haue, and euer will.

This Hound and Eagle, with foote and wing so prest,
In sure suruice vnto this excellent Dame:

>   ... the Lyon well may trust,
> That Hound and Eagle, that neuer were vniust.
>
> They both be ready, always for to obey,
> The Prince and Lawes, they truly love in heart:
> No blot of blame, from first vnto this day,
> The banners blanckles, of any euill part:
> Their seruice shows, they sprang of spotless race,
> As at these days, appeareth by their grace.[33]

Proctor, writing in 1589, reports that it was "about two years past" that "I chaunced to haue offered me this present Treatise." The relevance of the alliances depicted in *A Golden Mirrour* to contemporary suspicions about loyalties in the Catholic northern counties should therefore be obvious.[34] As in the past, going back to Bosworth, so on the eve of the Armada, the pairing of Talbot and Stanley, Hound and Eagle, was a patriotic gesture geared to the preservation of local power and interests.

The Talbot papers, now at Lambeth Palace, contain an extensive correspondence with George Talbot's son Gilbert, in which the Stanleys express friendly regards, offer favors, and arrange for mutual support. Henry Stanley, recently returned to New Park in December 1589, sent Talbot the latest court news pertaining to Raleigh and Essex. Exchanging gifts with him in January 1589/90, he enclosed a letter sharing news about ecclesiastical commissions, a sensitive matter to these lords of the northern Catholic counties; a month later he sought a loan of £ 200.[35] Shortly after Talbot became the seventh earl of Shrewsbury in December 1590, the Stanleys began to court his friendship more assiduously. Henry Stanley offered his services at court in April 1591, sent news and documents pertaining to the wars in France in June, with more news twice in July, including plans for the queen's progress; in October he asked after Talbot's plans for the Christmas holidays; in November he promised to support a Talbot client; in December he sent, with his gift of Spanish oranges and lemons, his hopes for peace with Spain.[36] The following February, 1592, he renewed his offer of friendship and service. In September 1592, Talbot enlisted Henry Stanley's support in his escalating quarrel with Sir Thomas Stanhope over the Trent fisheries. In July 1593 Derby sent, from Lathom, a gift of his best falcon from the Isle of Man, together with another offer of his services, and during his final illness, Stanley apologized for his inability to visit.[37] Talbot attended Stanley's funeral, coming, in a procession of hundreds, just second after "Mr. Garter" (William Deticke Garter King of Arms) and Ferdinando Stanley and before Lady Alice, Ferdinando's wife.[38]

Like his father, Ferdinando also cultivated the alliance. In a letter dated from "The Courte" in May 1591, Lord Strange, invoking "your wonted kinde regards," asked "if in this plasse I may in your absence doo you any friendly offis."[39] A lengthy correspondence in January–February 1593/4 shows Talbot mediating in Stanley's dangerous dispute with the Earl of Essex.[40] During his suspicious final illness in April 1594, Ferdinando attempted to settle his debts by entailing his estates to Talbot and three other trustees; following his death, his widow, Lady Alice, sought Talbot's intervention in any dispute with her brother-in-law, William Stanley, sixth earl of Derby, over the property to be inherited by her daughters.[41] Talbot, "Lord Strange of Blackmere," attended the funeral of Ferdinando Stanley, "Lord Strange of Knokyn," and he possessed, endorsed in his own hand, "the maner of the death of the Earl of Derby," a sensational document circulating at the time and detailing the evidence that Stanley had died by poisoning or witchcraft.[42]

This is a set of relationships that, beyond the common Lestrange ancestry and title, might well have inspired a noble patron to ask his players in 1592 to "study a speech of some dozen lines, or sixteen lines, which I would set down and insert in't" (*Hamlet*, 2.2.541–42). I am not suggesting that Lord Strange himself wrote Talbot's "epitaph," a speech that belongs to a much more extensive pattern in *1 Henry VI*'s celebration of the Talbot Shrewsbury earldom and the Order of the Garter. I am, however, invoking Stanley patronage as one of the motives for important features of the Talbot play "harey the vj," and I am offering Sir William Lucy's "epitaph" as evidence for the dating of that portion of the play to 1592.[43] Since nearly all of the disintegrationists who propose multiple authorship and/or possible Shakespearean revision of *1 Henry VI* agree in attributing act 4 scene 7 and the part of Sir William Lucy to the hand of William Shakespeare,[44] I am therefore also offering the "epitaph" as evidence that Shakespeare contributed to the authorship or revision of "harey the vj" in 1592 and as evidence that he therefore did at that time have an association with Lord Strange's Men.

The case I have presented involves the apparent contradiction that a speech intended as a compliment to a nobleman living at the time of the play's debut should apparently inflate the first Talbot's titles while simultaneously undermining the rhetoric of Lucy's tribute in Joan's sarcastic response. A first explanation would be that heraldic exaggeration, in an age characterized by the inflation of honors, might not have been deemed inappropriate or inaccurate praise: the play itself, like Lucy's speech, is not performing archeological recovery but heraldic rhetoric. Not even a herald like Brooke had trouble believing it, and the evidence examined above shows how quickly a mere playhouse epitaph could be seized upon as authentic.[45] A second answer would be that just as Lucy's speech serves more than one purpose or in more than one temporal frame, offering *his* defiance to the princes of France and Burgundy and *the play's* praise of the Garter to the Rose audience, so the play itself—first staged during the final months of the earl of Essex's failed siege of Rouen—shares with the other *Henry IV* plays in taking more than one perspective on the subjects of war, honor, and heraldry. Brockbank, who can be faulted for biting on the subject of Talbot's tomb at Rouen, comments brilliantly on the way that Lucy's tribute and Joan's immediate deflation of it combine to form a kind of *transi* tomb. When Talbot's nemesis Joan replies that "Him that thou magnifi'st with all these titles/Stinking and fly-blowne *lyes heere* at our feete" (4.7.75–76; TLN 2309–10, italics mine), she forms a grim *memento mori* just at the foot of Lucy's glorious "epitaph." The artist who created Talbot's "tomb" at the Rose was perhaps not a Van Dyck but a Velasquez. Yet the grim scenario of defeat evoked by Joan's *memento mori* is in turn answered when Sir William Lucy takes possession of the bodies of the two Talbots with a final, defiant boast:

> Ile beare them hence: but from their ashes shal be reard
> A Phoenix that shall make all France affear'd.
> (4.7.92–93; TLN 2327–28)

Lucy's defiance probably alludes to the English campaign (and siege of Rouen) continuing in France as "harey the vj" was on the boards in the spring of 1592, and perhaps also to the commander of the French expedition, the Earl of Essex, who had been recalled to England in January 1592. But in view of Gilbert Talbot's recent succession to the Shrewsbury earldom and his elevation to the order of the Garter, the Phoenix may also allude, at a time when the old guard at court was passing (Ferdinando Stanley would succeed to the Derby title in September 1593 just as Talbot had succeeded to the Shrewsbury title in November 1590), to the emergence of a younger generation of English nobility, including the two Lords Strange, Talbot and Stanley.

Notes

1. *Henslowe's Diary,* 2d ed. R.A. Foakes (Cambridge: Cambridge University Press, 2002), 16. For Nashe's praise of the Talbot play and Lord Strange in *Pierce Penilesse His Svpplication to the Deuill,* see *The Works of Thomas Nashe,* ed. R. B. McKerrow, 5 vols. (Oxford: Blackwell, 1958), 1:212, 243–45.

2. Michael Hattaway, ed., *The First Part of King Henry VI* (Cambridge: Cambridge University Press, 1990), 36; Michael Taylor, ed., *Henry VI, Part 1* (Oxford: Oxford World's Classics, 2003), 217; Roger Warren, ed., *Henry VI, Part Two* (Oxford: Oxford University Press, 2003), 70; Paul J. Vincent, "Structuring and Revision in *1 Henry VI,*" *Philological Quarterly,* 84 (2005): 379 n. 10; Lawrence Manley, "Motives for Patronage: The Queen's Men at New Park, October 1588," in Helen Ostovich, Holger Schott Syme, and Andrew R. Griffin, eds., *Locating the Queen's Men, 1583–1603: Material Practices and Conditions of Playing* (Ashgate: Farnham & Burlington, 2009), 63.

3. G. E. Cokayne, *The Complete Peerage*, 13 vols. (London: St. Catherine's Press, 1910–59), vol. XII, pt. 1:346, 352, 356.

4. Cokayne, vol. XII, pt. 1:342, 620.

5. It reappears in Thomas Browne's "Additions" to Camden's *Historie of the life and reigne of that famous princesse Elizabeth* (1634), sig. Hhh3v; in Sir Richard Baker's *Chronicle of the Kings of England* (1643), 80; and in Sir William Sanderson's *Compleat history of the lives and reigns of Mary Queen of Scotland, and of her son and successor, James the Sixth, King of Scotland* (1656), 161.

6. "This long list of titles is taken from the epitaph formerly fixed on Lord Talbot's tomb in Rouen in Normandy," *The Plays and Poems of William Shakespeare*, 10 vols. (London, 1790), 6:89 n.6.; "The English associations with the cathedral of [Rouen] are stressed in the references to Coeur-de-lion's heart (3.2.83), Bedford's tomb (3.2.131–33), and Talbot's epitaph (4.7.61–71)," Wilson, *The First Part of King Henry VI*, p. xviii; "Lucy's long intonement of Talbot's titles was taken at first or second hand from the lapidary inscription on Talbot's actual tomb at Rouen, and it retains its lapidary formality," Brockbank, "The Form of Disorder: 'Henry VI,'" in *Stratford-Upon-Avon Studies 3: Early Shakespeare* (London: Edward Arnold, 1961), 76; "the long list of Talbot's titles . . . was apparently taken from Talbot's actual epitaph in Rouen cathedral," Emrys Jones, *The Origins of Shakespeare* (Oxford: Clarendon Press, 1977), 143.

7. "Unless some earlier printed source than is known can be found for Talbot's epitaph, it will be hard to establish a date prior to 1599 for the revised play." *The First Part of King Henry the Sixth* (1918; repr., New Haven, CT: Yale University Press, 1961), 136.

8. *The Origin and Development of 1 Henry VI* (1926; repr., New York: AMS Press, 1971), 128.

9. "An Earlier Talbot Epitaph," *MLN* 59 (1944): 329.

10. Edward Burns, ed., *King Henry VI Part 1* (London: Arden Shakespeare, 2000), 252.

11. *Britannia* (1610), 598.

12. G. Lambin, "Here Lyeth Iohn Talbot," *Études Anglaises*, 24, no. 4 (1971): 361–77. Leland reported that the third earl of Shrewsbury (also the third John Talbot), "had emong his brethren one caullid Gilbert Talbot, after[wards] a knight of fame, the which buried the Erle his grandfathers bones brought out of Fraunce at Whitechurch in a faire chapelle." *The Itinerary of John Leland in or about the Years 1535–1543, Parts IV and V*, ed. Lucy Toulmin Smith (London: George Bell & Sons, 1908), 22. An account of Talbot's tomb at Whitchurch may be found in Hugh Talbot, *The English Achilles: An Account of the Life and Campaigns of John Talbot, 1st Earl of Shrewsbury (1383–1453)* (London: Chatto & Windus, 1981), 172–78.

13. *A tour thro' the whole island of Great Britain*, 3 vols. (London, 1724), 2:112.

14. Alfred H. Burne writes that "a monument was built to [Talbot] by the victorious French generals. It was called Notre Dame de Talbot. The spot came to be known as Le Tombe de Talbot, and it is still marked on the map as Monument de Talbot. The chapel was destroyed during the revolution, but a modern cross has since been erected on the spot. It originally had no inscription on it, but I was told that Talbot's name did appear on the old one." *The Agincourt War* (Fair Lawn, NJ: Essential Books, 1956), 342.

15. "Le Roi en commemoration de ce grand personage, & d'vne victoire si signalee, commands estre bastie vne chapelle au lieu mesme ou auoit esté donnée la bataille, laquelle est encores à present nommée la Chapelle de Talbot. Quant au lieu de sa sepulture ie ne l'ay iamais peu sçauoir asseurement encores que quelques vns ayent voulu dire, que son corps & celuy de son fils furent portez à Bordeaux & enterrez en l'Église des Carmes: toutefois Messieurs de la ville ne m'en ont sçeu assuerer," André Thevet, *Les Vrais Portaits et Vies des Hommes Illustres* (Paris, 1584), fol. 283v.

16. I have consulted the standard chronicles for the period (Monstrelet, Chartier, d'Escouchy) as well as sixteenth-century printed chronicles such as *Le Rozier Historiale de France* (Paris, 1523) and Robert Gaguin, *Rerum Gallicarum Annales* (Frankfurt, 1577).

17. A. J. Pollard, correspondence, January 2011.

18. Lambin, "Here Lyeth Iohn Talbot," 369.

19. *The vnion of the two noble and illustrate famelies of Lancastre [and] Yorke*, fol. Ddvi; cf. Holinshed, *The Third Volume of Chronicles* (1586), 640.

20. On *1 Henry VI* as a "Garter" play, see Giorgio Melchiori, *Shakespeare's Garter Plays: Edward III to Merry Wives of Windsor* (Newark: University of Delaware Press), 114–15.

21. See Giorgio Melchiori, ed., *King Edward III* (Cambridge: Cambridge University Press, 1998), 17–25.

22. Transcribed by William Dugdale in *The Baronage of England* (1675), 1:333–34.

23. Bodleian MS Dodsworth 160, fols. 126v-128v.

24. These include the Bastard Faulconbridge and his brother in *King John* and the Duke of Faulconbridge, whose name appears among the adherents of Charles VI and later among the Agincourt dead in *Henry V*. Longaville in *Love's Labours Lost* is said to have attended the wedding feast "of the beauteous heir/Of Jaques Falconbridge" (2.1.41–42), and "young Falconbridge, the young baron of England" is one of the unseen suitors of Portia in *The Merchant of Venice* (1.2.66–67). The "stern Falconbridge" who "commands the narrows seas" in *3 Henry VI* (1.1.239) is the one historical figure to appear among all of these otherwise fictional Falconbridges, who seem to have been something of a in-joke in Shakespeare's earlier career. J. Madison Davis and A. Daniel Frankforter report that "the baronage of Fauconberg belonged to the Neville family and was claimed by Talbot as the inheritance of his first wife Maud, daughter of Thomas Neville." *The Shakespeare Name Dictionary* (London: Routledge, 2004), 317. This, I believe, is an error. John Talbot claimed through his marriage to Maud, daughter of Thomas Neville, the baronage of Furnivall, not Fauconberg; the Fauconberg title only entered the Neville family with the marriage of William Neville, earl of Kent (d. 1463) to Joan (d. 1490), the heir of Sir John Fauconberg. Neville was father to three daughters and to the notorious Bastard Fauconberg, whose rebellion against Edward IV is recounted in the chronicles, mentioned in *3 Henry VI,* and depicted in Heywood's *Edward IV*. The Fauconberg title did not pass to the Talbots but fell into abeyance after William Neville's death, as his wife, the bearer of the title, was considered *non compos mentis* (see *DNB* s.v. "Neville, William").

25. Joseph Hunter, *Hallamshire: The History and Topography of the Parish of Sheffield* (London, 1819), 150.

26. Ashmolean MS. 854/ 219, cited in J. P. Earwaker, "John Talbot, Earl of Shrewbury," *The Athenaeum*, March 28, 1874, 433–34; Earwaker was writing in response to contemporary reportage on the excavation of Talbot's bones.

27. Cokayne, *The Complete Peerage* 7: 137 n. (f).

28. *Three Books of Polydore Vergil's English History, Comprising the Reigns of Henry VI, Edward IV, and Richard III*, ed. Henry Ellis (London: Camden Society O.S. 29, 1844), 212–26.

29. *Les Vrais Portraits et Vies des Hommes Illvstres* (Paris, 1584), fol. 283v.

30. See Robert W. Barrett, Jr., *Against All England: Regional Identity and Cheshire Writing, 1195–1656* (Notre Dame, IN: University of Notre Dame Press, 2009), esp. chap. 5, "Two Shires Against All England: Celebrating Regional Affinity in the Stanley Family Romances."

31. J. P. Oakden, ed., "Scotish ffeilde" (Manchester: Chetham Society n.s. 94: 1935), ll. 10–18.

32. "The Song of the Lady Bessie," in *The Palatine Anthology: A Collection of Ancient Poems and Ballads Relating to Lancashire and Cheshire*, ed. J. O. Halliwell (London, 1850), 35–36.

33. *A Golden Mirrour* (1589), ed. Thomas Corser (Manchester: Chetham Society, 1851), dedication and 3–4.

34. The author of the poem, the Richard Robinson who identifies himself in his *Reward of Wickedness* (1578) as "seruaunt in housholde to the right Honorable Earle of Shrovvsbury" and a guard serving in Shrewsbury's "watche of the Scottishe Queene" (1569–84), could very possibly have been the author of Shrewsbury's painted epitaph.

35. Catherine Jamison and G. R. Batho, eds., *A Calendar of the Shrewsbury and Talbot Papers in Lambeth Palace and the College of Arms*, 2 vols.(London: H.M.S.O, 1966–71), I 33, I 102.

36. *Calendar of the Shrewsbury and Talbot Papers*, I 112, I 125, H 333, H 357, I 129, I 149, I 131.

37. *Calendar of the Shrewsbury and Talbot Papers*, I 134, H 425, I 174, I 166.

38. *Lancashire Funeral Certificates*, ed. Thomas William King and F. Raines (Manchester: Chetham Society, 1869), 27.

39. Lambeth MS 3200/121.

40. *Calendar of the Shrewsbury and Talbot Papers*, I 661, I 669, I 677, I 681, I 685, I 687, I 709.

41. Barry Coward, *The Stanleys, Lords Stanley and Earls of Derby, 1385–1672* (Manchester: Chetham Society, 1983), 37; *Calendar of the Shrewsbury and Talbot Papers*, M 14.

42. *Calendar of the Shrewsbury and Talbot Papers*, M 14, H 713.

43. There is further evidence for a 1592 dating in Lucy's final lines in the scene: "I'll bear them hence; but from their ashes shall be rear'd/A phoenix that shall make all France afeard" (4.7.92–93).

44. Edmund Malone believed the scenes involving the death of Talbot, which he found "somewhat of a different complexion from the rest of the play," attributed

these scenes to Shakespeare. Malone, *A Dissertation on the Three Parts of* King Henry VI (London, 1787), 46. F. G. Fleay, who attributed combined authorship of the play to Marlowe, Greene or Kyd, Peele, and Lodge, argued that the Bordeaux scenes involving the death of Talbot "did not form part of the original play" but that "Shakespeare's Talbot additions," including 4.7, were made in 1592, *Chronicle History of the Life and Work of William Shakespeare* (London: J. C. Nimmo, 1886), 259–63. Allison Gaw conjectured that all of the Lucy passages (4.3.1–27, 34–36; 4.4, 4.7.51–96) were among Shakespeare's revisions to the play, *The Origin and Development of 1 Henry VI* (1926; repr., New York: AMS Press, 1971), 145. John Dover Wilson, who argued for contribution from Nashe and Greene, believed that Shakespeare "retained the opening speech at 4.7 unchanged, while revising the rest" of the scene; Wilson used this theory as a way of explaining the duplications many have noticed between 4.5 and 4.6 (i.e., he argued that Shakespeare forgot to cancel the version of 4.6 written on the recto of the page whose verso contained the opening speech of 4.7—great thing of Shakespeare to forget!), *The First Part of King Henry VI*, xlvii; cf. 184. Gary Taylor, attributing parts of the play to Nashe and one additional author, attributed 4.2–4.7 to Shakespeare on stylistic grounds but suggested that 4.7.33–96, which includes Lucy's part, "might well be the work of two different authors." "Shakespeare and Others: The Authorship of *Henry the Sixth, Part One*," *Medieval and Renaissance Drama in England,*7 (1995): 171. Hugh Craig, who divided *1 Henry VI* into arbitrary 2,000-word segments and tested for both "Shakespearean" and "non-Shakespearean" function words and "Shakespearean" and "non- Shakespearean" "lexical" words, found that the most "Shakespearean" segment "covers almost all of the actions involving Lord Talbot and his son and their deaths at the siege of Bordeaux," in Hugh Craig and Arthur F. Kinney, *Shakespeare, Computers, and the Mystery of Authorship* (Cambridge" Cambridge University Press, 2009), 51. In this test, the Temple Garden scene (2.4) fell into a longer 2,000-word segment that was statistically "non-Shakespearean" (53), but when 2.4 was tested separately against the rest of this segment, it was "close to the centroid of the Shakespeare cluster" (4.2.56–4.7.40); 4.7 41–96, not tested separately, was included in a segment, extending to 5.3.140, that was assessed statistically as "non-Shakespearean." Craig concludes that "Shakespeare was the author of the Temple Garden Scene and the scenes depicting Talbot's last battle," 68. Among other critics working closely with textual anomalies and stylistic differences who favor the idea of Shakespearean self-revision over multiple authorship are Marco Mincoff, who, while suspecting that the opening scenes were from the hand of another author, attributed "the whole Talbot sequence in Act 4" to Shakespeare and argued for self-revision for "a revival of the play some time about 1594." "The Composition of *Henry VI, Part* I," *Shakespeare Quarterly* 16 (1964): 279–87; E. Pearlman, "Shakespeare at Work: The Two Talbots," *Philological Quarterly* 75 (1996): 1–22; and Paul J. Vincent, "Structuring and Revision in *1 Henry VI*," *Philological Quarterly* 84 (2005): 377–402. Both the disintegrationist Taylor (168) and the self-revisionist Vincent (392) notice that Sir William Lucy of Charlecote, thrice Sheriff of Warwickshire in the reign of Henry VI, was ancestor to the Sir Thomas Lucy of Charlecote, gentleman and sheriff of Warwickshire in the time of Shakespeare, alleged by Nicholas Rowe and other anecdotalists to have arrested Shakespeare for poaching deer in his park. Sir William Lucy did not serve in fifteenth-century France, though he did perish, "striken in the head with an ax," alongside "Iohn Talbot earle of Shrewesburie" and other Lancastrians at the battle of Northampton in 1460; see Holinshed's *Chronicles* (1587), 654. The exceptions among the disintegrationists who deny Shakespeare the creation of Sir William Lucy's tribute to Talbot are (1) H. C. Hart, who said that 4.7 belonged to Shakespeare only "down to the entrance of the Herald (vii.50); the latter forty-five lines seem mongrel." *The Arden Works of Shakespeare. The First Part of King Henry the Sixth* (London: Methuen, 1909), xviii; (2) E. K. Chambers, who, like Hart, thought he could detect two hands in 4.7, but gave only 2.4 and 4.2 unambiguously to Shakespeare. E. K. Chambers, *William Shakespeare: A Study of Facts and Problems,* 2 vols. (Oxford: Clarendon Press, 1930) 1:290.

45. There is a delicious irony in this since it was the same Ralph Brooke who in 1602 challenged the 1596 grant of arms to Shakespeare by the Garter King-of-Arms Sir William Dethick; see Samuel Schoenbaum, *William Shakespeare: A Compact Documentary Life* (Oxford: Oxford University Press, 1977), 231–32.

Richard III's Forelives: Rewriting Elizabeth(s) in Tudor Historiography

Allison Machlis Meyer

ELIZABETH I's paternal grandmother and Henry VII's queen consort, Elizabeth York, provided a fleeting but useful precedent for the reigning queen in 1559. Elizabeth I's pre-coronation procession from the Tower to Westminster Abbey on January 14 included a series of pageants designed to please the new monarch, the first of which emphasized Henry VII and Elizabeth York as the beginning of the Tudor dynasty. An account of the procession printed nine days later parses the pageant as a complimentary comparison of Elizabeth I to her female ancestor:

> This pageant was grounded upon the Queenes maiesties name. For like as the long warre betwene the two houses of Yorke and Lancastre then ended, when Elizabeth doughter to Edward the forth matched in mariage with Henrye the seuenthe heyre to the howse of Lancastre: so since that the Queenes maiesties name was Elizabeth, and forsomuch as she is the onelye heire of Henrye the eight, which came of bothe the howses as the knitting up of concorde, it was deuised that like as Elizabeth was the first occasion of concorde, so she another Elizabeth myght maintaine the same among her subjectes. . . .[1]

Lines delivered by a child appointed to "open the meaning" of the pageant describe Elizabeth York and Henry VII as "two princes that sit under one cloth of state," and the printed text of the procession repeatedly refers to the royal couple as "those two princes."[2] Judith M. Richards argues that the pageant presented Elizabeth York and Henry VII as "coequal monarchs" and linked both Elizabeths together as queens with "shared capacities to end 'all dissention' from dynastic struggle."[3] The pageant emphasizes Elizabeth York's right and ability to rule in order to confirm Elizabeth I's own "eligibility to wear the crown" and to assert the legitimacy of female succession.[4] Thus, Elizabeth York was recursively formed into an appealing precedent for Elizabeth I's female rule through the selective imagining of a princely alliance of co-rulers.

This remaking of a queen consort into a joint monarch was rich with possibilities of flattery or imitation for Elizabethan writers, as it demonstrated an appealing vision of the new queen's familial past as well as support for her current rule. For dramatists taking up this story of union during the vogue of history plays in the 1590s, even stronger precedents for women's political engagement abounded in the Tudor political and chronicle histories that comprised their source materials. In Thomas More's *The History of King Richard the Third* (1543, written c. 1513–18), Polydore Vergil's *Anglica Historia (History of England)* (1534, written c. 1513), and Edward Hall's *The Union of the Two Noble and Illustre Famelies of Lancastre & Yorke* (1548 and 1550), historiographers committed to dynastic politics that afforded women of royal blood important political agency envision key female subjects as model agents and readers of history who inform the authors' own analyses of national events. More, Vergil, and Hall establish the centrality of these women through narrative techniques privileging women's political and maternal responses. These histories were likely to have pleased the future queen in their sympathy for women's participation in politics, though such narratives are often maligned as the source of historical drama's exclusion of women as well as the source of that drama's events.[5] Yet when Shakespeare represented the same female historical figures in *Richard III*, he rejected not only the royal cue of Elizabeth I's coronation pageant but also the precedent of his narrative sources in order to downplay women's authority. The play makes starkly different revisions to record the beginning of the Tudor dynasty by casting Henry Tudor as England's singular savior and eliminating Elizabeth York entirely. The larger exclusion of women from the dramatized political world of the Wars of the Roses, of which Elizabeth York's lack of representation is only one instance, has been adroitly outlined by feminist criticism of Shakespeare's history plays.[6] This essay locates *Richard III*'s much-discussed exclusion of women within this richer context of narrative and dramatic Tudor historiography by reading the play alongside narrative accounts of Elizabeth York's mother, Queen Elizabeth Woodville Grey. Narrative historiography under the Tudors portrayed dynastic models of the state, which allowed women with personal ties to the monarchy, like Elizabeth Woodville Grey, power as political agents. However, Elizabethan history plays drawing on these narratives, such as *Richard III*, dramatized nationalist models that increasingly saw these personal ties as solely familial and separated them from national concerns.

I

Famous for its enduring portrait of a wicked and hunchbacked Richard, More's *History* is often considered a vehicle of Tudor propaganda and the foremost source of Shakespeare's great stage villain.[7] Rarely acknowledged, however, is the *History*'s prominent depiction of women as participants in political and historical change.[8] Through narrative strategies of interjected evaluation, invented dialogue, and interior perspective, Elizabeth is ascribed a privileged knowledge of Richard's aspirations that aligns her character with More's own authorial voice.[9] More likewise calls attention to her central role in historical events and her reflexive awareness of her ability to intervene in dynastic negotiations on overlapping familial and political levels.

More's narrative structure moves directly from Edward IV's death to Richard's attempts to wrestle power from the widowed queen. Dialogue assigned to Richard indicates that he sees Elizabeth as a formidable enemy with the potential to prevent his manipulation of dynastic succession and to turn public opinion against him. Richard accuses her of "womanish forwardness" as well as "great malice toward the king's councillors" and suggests her intent in taking sanctuary is to "bring all the lords in obloquy and murmur of the people."[10] Richard's first task is to stir up antagonism toward Elizabeth in order to challenge her influence and control over the princes. More's villain must work hard to do so, and he is forced to "secretly" use "divers means" to convince her that her sons should travel without escorts, while Hastings and Buckingham, "men of honor" and "great power," "were of themselves ea[sy] to kindle" when Richard set them "afire" against the queen.[11] By juxtaposing a perfunctory account of the ease with which Richard draws in Hastings and Buckingham with a description of his struggle to persuade Elizabeth, More depicts her as both the strongest impediment to Richard and the most wisely skeptical member of Edward IV's former court. The council, further demonstrating how easily Richard can persuade everyone except the queen, affirms Richard's motion to persuade her and her younger son out of sanctuary as "good and reasonable" and shortly agree that the Duke of York can be forcibly removed, "thinking none hurt earthly meant toward the young babe."[12] More thus portrays the king's councilors as dupes who accept Richard's facile gendered arguments against Elizabeth and utterly fail to suspect the threat he poses. Unlike those around her, such as the Archbishop of York, who "trusted the matter was nothing so sore as she took it for," and the councilors who do not question Richard's motives, Elizabeth rightly predicts that Richard "is one of them that laboreth to destroy [her] and [her] blood."[13]

Set apart from other Yorkist figures by her resistance to Richard, More's Elizabeth also demonstrates a belief in her own power to influence the future when she learns Richard has deceived her. Upon hearing of the arrests of her brother and son enabled by her own earlier concessions to Richard, Elizabeth seeks sanctuary for the rest of her family: "in great flight and heaviness, bewailing her child's ruin, her friends' mischance, and her own infortune, damning the time that ever she dissuaded the gathering of power about the king."[14] More gives Elizabeth an interior perspective acutely aware of the efficacy of her individual decisions; the distress that More imagines she feels also shows her awareness of Richard's larger intentions. She astutely assesses her errors and anticipates future danger to her children that others cannot predict, understanding Richard's seizure of the young king as a crucial moment in his accumulation of power. More conceives of her actions as both personal and political: her maternal fear for her sovereign son and other children is also presented as a dynastic fear for Edward's heirs and the ruler of her country.

More devotes about a fifth of his entire text to Elizabeth's debate with the Lord Cardinal over her right to sanctuary and guardianship of her youngest son, highlighting her considerable intellectual skill and her continuing awareness of Richard's intentions. Alan Clarke Shepard argues that Elizabeth's dialogue in sanctuary exhibits an "empowered female voice" that ably mobilizes legal discourses usually reserved for men.[15] Elizabeth's empowered voice in fact uses a hybrid rhetoric that privileges her maternal role and simultaneously positions that maternal role as inextricable from her political defense of Edward V's succession. Elizabeth invokes the laws of nature, God, and English common law to argue for her maternal, legal, and religious prerogative: "man's law serveth the guardian to keep the infant, the law of nature will the mother keep her child, God's law priveilegeth the sanctuary."[16] The core of this debate is familial access to the royal heirs and the implications of that access on the future succession. Elizabeth initially depoliticizes her claim by arguing that motherhood makes her a naturally superior caregiver for her child—a claim that "no man denieth"—but her subsequent insistence that the duke is also her legal ward carries significant political consequences: "He is also my ward; for, as my learned counsel showeth me, sith he hath nothing by descent holden by knight's service, the law maketh his mother his guardian."[17] This legal defense of her guardianship reads as a veiled challenge: applied to her older son, the underage Edward V, such an argument could undermine Richard's right as Lord Protector. Elizabeth's arguments of maternal nature and legal designation emphasize her overlapping political and familial roles of mother and guardian.

Elizabeth's defenses of her guardianship are paired with her distrust of Richard, which she voices to unwilling listeners. Forced to argue with men unwilling to see Richard's ambition, Elizabeth circumspectly veils her knowledge of his intentions to deliver a warning about how those intentions might backfire: "I marvel greatly that my lord protector is so desirous to have [the Duke of York] in his keeping, where if the child in his sickness miscarried by nature, yet might he run into slander and suspicion of fraud."[18] Rather than directly challenge Richard's motives, Elizabeth claims that she fears "no further than the law feareth," citing existing law that forbids custody to men who might gain from the deaths of their wards and raising the question of Richard's fitness as Protector.[19] The debate ends only when the naïve Lord Cardinal, who "neither believed and was also loath to hear" the queen's "biting words against the protector," grows tired and testily tells Elizabeth she must think "that he and all other also, save herself, lacked either wit or truth" to determine whether the Duke of York should be removed from sanctuary.[20] More's characteristic use of irony indicates that in his eyes, Elizabeth is the sole possessor of wit and truth here and in the rest of the narrative.

The privileged insights into Elizabeth's thoughts offered throughout the *History* sanction her political decisions and intellectual arguments, foster readerly sympathy for her choices, and align her with More's own authorial voice. Judith Anderson argues that the *History*'s force and drama comes from its emphasis on an internal, subjective perspective focused on Richard, whereby More "imagines, enters, and inevitably shapes Richard's thoughts and motives, in addition to interpreting or commenting in a variety of less immediate ways on their significance."[21] Certainly More's attention to crafting Richard's thoughts and motives makes his villain a compelling subject. However, More's similar perspective on Elizabeth's awareness of Richard ascribes to her an even more compelling historical forethought similar to the author's point of view. In her discussion with the Cardinal, Elizabeth incredulously asks, "Troweth he that I perceive not whereunto his painted process draweth?" showing More imagines for her a *historical* recognition (shared with More and his readers) of the extent of Richard's goals and his means to achieve them.[22] She also labels Richard's concern for her youngest son the Duke of York a "trifling pretext."[23] Elizabeth makes More's narrative possible by delivering its perspectives and its key subjects: hers is the only voice in the unfinished *History,* besides More's, that expresses the historical Tudor vilification of Richard as a dissembler who uses "painted processes" and "trifling pretexts." By attributing an awareness of Richard's evil to Elizabeth, More acknowledges her as a privileged historical source. Thus, he retrospectively claims her as not only a powerful historical figure, but as a model reader of history who informs his own politicized analysis of the events of the *History*. Given authorial understanding of the *History*'s villain and depicted within the narrative as an active opponent to Richard, Elizabeth shows that women's roles in history and historiography are neither apolitical nor circumscribed, as later drama often stages them to be.

The *History*'s sympathetic representation of Elizabeth's role in history is not an anomaly in early modern historical narrative. Polydore Vergil's 1513 *Anglica Historia,* long considered the origin of the Tudor myth and the greatest example of royally solicited propaganda about the Wars of the Roses, shares with More's *History* a comparable approach that adopts Elizabeth's viewpoints and underscores narrative historiography's willingness to sympathetically represent women's active, political roles in history.[24] When More and Vergil write about the same events in her life—Richard's attempts to convince Elizabeth of his goodwill toward her sons, her retreat to and the removal of her youngest son from sanctuary—they overlap significantly in tone and narrative strategy. For example, Vergil's account of Elizabeth's flight into sanctuary uses interior perspective and ascribes to her privileged suspicions about Richard: "Elyzabeth the quene was much dismayed, and determynyd furthwith to fly; for, suspecting eaven than that ther was no plane dealing, to th intent she might dlyver her other children from the present danger, she convayed hirself with them . . . into the sayntuary at Westmynster."[25] Vergil does not present a long debate and foregoes Elizabeth Woodville Grey's internal struggle; the *Anglica Historia* simply reports that Elizabeth's son is "pullyd owt of his mothers armes" immediately.[26] However, Vergil records her refusal to turn over her son as one founded in accurate concerns about Richard that are shared only with the historiographer himself: "but the woman, foreseing in a sort within hir self the thing that folowyd furthwith after, could not be movid with any perswations to commyt hir self to the credyt of duke Rycherd."[27] This account of Elizabeth foreseeing the "future" "within hirself" privileges an inner narrative within the female subject as a source of history as well as a politically-shrewd observation of events. "The thing that folowyd furthwith after" is the historiographer's version of events, and only Elizabeth is given the ability to see and respond to that future. More's representation of Elizabeth calls attention to women's participation in history; Vergil's significantly shorter but analogous narrative of her likewise shows that historiography often used historical women's perspectives to foreground their own stories.

More and Vergil might be considered unlikely advocates of the voice and influence they both ascribe to Elizabeth Woodville Grey in their narratives of Richard III. Their similar interests in serving successive Tudor governments suggests that their histories needed to satisfy Henry Tudor and his progeny. While stories that emphasized Richard's tyranny fit the bill (and Vergil and More's certainly did), there is little indication that Henry VII's chief goal of legitimizing his Lancastrian claim to the English public and other rulers of Europe would have been well-served by these historiographers' similar portraits of Elizabeth Grey. While Henry welcomed the politically expedient narrative of providential union between himself and Elizabeth York, he had to balance that narrative with calculated suppression of Elizabeth York's better blood claim, lest her popularity and genealogy lead to claims that she could and should rule in her own right, rather than take up the role of queen consort.[28] Both More and Vergil would have been well aware of Henry VII's vexed relationship with his mother-in-law: placed on the throne in part because of her negotiations for his marriage to her daughter, Henry confiscated Elizabeth Woodville Grey's lands and consigned her to a nunnery in 1487. Ostensibly punishing her for relinquishing her daughters to Richard, his delay in doing so led early modern and modern historians alike to speculate that he suspected her political involvement in fostering some of the many pretenders to his throne, who often claimed to be her dead boys, saved from the Tower.[29] By the time Vergil and More began their respective histories, the necessity of the story of union with Elizabeth York was counterweighted by Henry VII's evident distrust of Elizabeth Woodville Grey. Given this context, neither historiographers' representations of Elizabeth Woodville Grey as a privileged authorial voice are directly in service of the particular Tudor myth Henry VII promoted. More and Vergil's dedication to male Tudor monarchs turns out to be somewhat ambivalent; their support of the Tudor succession was most enthusiastic when directed toward Elizabeth and her female offspring, not Henry or his male descendants.

Vergil's book on Henry VII's reign in the *Anglica Historia* reinforces a providential perspective asserting the Tudors as God's chosen rulers of England, but it is also somewhat critical of the first Tudor. Often describing Henry VII as a good prince, Vergil concludes his book on Henry with a final sentence noting that the king's virtues were obscured by avarice: "in a monarch indeed it may be considered the worst vice since it is harmful to everyone, and distorts those qualities of trustfulness, justice and integrity by which the State must be governed."[30] Vergil locates the majority of his praise of the Tudor dynasty not in its male founder but in the symbol of union manifested by the marriage of Henry and Elizabeth, and in its women. He heartily praises Elizabeth York as "a woman intelligent above all others, and equally beautiful," and attributes the true success of Henry's victory to be in the subsequent marriage between rival houses: "It is legitimate to attribute this [marriage] to divine intervention, for plainly by it all things which nourished the two most ruinous factions were utterly removed, by it the two houses of York and Lancaster were united and from the union the true and established royal line emerged which now reigns."[31] When Vergil wrote of other historical female figures of the Tudor family, he did so with praise more ebullient than that of the male monarchs. He calls Henry VII's mother Margaret a "most worthy woman whom no one can extol too much or too often for her sound sense and holiness of life" and a "woman most outstanding both in her pious love of God and charity to all men, and whose countless virtues each one of us may find it easier to admire than analyse."[32] Even in the foreign queen consort Catherine of Aragon he saw a model of gentle benevolence whose deathbed letters professing loyalty to Henry VIII brought out a sympathetic humanity in her erstwhile husband. Vergil's narrative of events after the close of the Wars of the Roses reveals a pattern of positive praise for the female figures wielding influence within the Tudor dynasty.

More's representation of Elizabeth in the *History* is also linked to his complicated political investment in English dynasty. Critical assessments of gender politics in his popular *Utopia*, written in 1516 shortly after the *History*, suggest More is an unlikely figure for an early modern protofeminist.[33] However, his views on women's education and the subjects of some of his lesser-known texts, including his English poetry written in the first decade of the 1500s, suggest that his account of women in the *History* is not an isolated case but a familiar narrative of women's influence well grounded by both his personal interest and his political associations with the Yorkists and the Tudors. More's "A Lamentation of Queen Elizabeth," an elegy written in 1503 upon the death of Elizabeth York, suggests strong parallels to his portrait of her mother in the *History*. The poem, like so many pieces of the *History*, is written from the perspective of its queen. Both Frederic Tromly and Lee Cullen Khanna cite the poem's ability to solicit readers' empathy as well as its emphasis on Elizabeth York's wisdom as part of the poem's unusual contribution to the elegiac form.[34] Khanna notes that the poem's "admiration of virtue" moves beyond description of Elizabeth York as the "traditional ideal of the chaste good wife," because she is portrayed as a "woman of authority and position" who is capable of gaining wisdom through a recognition of her role as God's servant.[35] The poem also suggests a specific evaluation of the Tudor family that helps establish the *History*'s own relationship to the Tudor narrative of restorative union as one that surprisingly imagines alternative royal authority in the figures of Yorkist and Tudor queens. "A Lamentation of Queen Elizabeth" devotes four stanzas to the queen's goodbyes to her children, mother-in-law, and sisters. Her servants and subjects are the focus of the final stanza, and their obedience functions as a model for her own servitude to God. Her son Henry VIII is discussed for only two lines—"Adieu, Lord Henry, my loving son, adieu. / Our Lord increase your honour and estate"—while her daughter-in-law Catherine of Aragon is claimed as her "daughter" and asked by the queen to "Pray for my soul."[36] These goodbyes to her extended kin are women-centered, and they privilege her own position as one of matriarchal authority and imagine the Tudor line as one passed from woman to woman. In her goodbye to her husband, Elizabeth recalls the Tudor legacy as a partnership in which she played a key personal and political role:

> Adieu, mine own dear spouse, my worthy lord.
>   The faithful love that did us both combine
> In marriage and peaceable concord
>   Into your hands here I clean resign
>   To be bestowed upon your children and mine.
>   Erst were you father, and now must ye supply
>   The mother's part also, for lo now here I lie.[37]

Elizabeth describes her marriage and children, as well as the "peaceable concord" created in their home and realm as a combined effort over which she always retained a great measure of control. Resigning her faithful love into Henry's hands, she nevertheless specifies its use: it is meant to be bestowed upon their children, and Henry is instructed to take up the indispensable part of mother that Elizabeth now leaves vacant in order for him to bestow that love properly. Thus, it seems that More's lament imagines Elizabeth York as both the moral *and* practical center of the Tudor dynasty, and the words he writes for her are counsel for his king, instructing Henry VII to take up Elizabeth's part as well as his own. More's belief in Elizabeth York's wisdom and virtue leads him to position her as that best "part" of the Tudor line, a perspective that clearly overlaps with his depiction of her mother as the center of morality, wit, and intellect in the *History*'s account of Yorkist self-destruction. The poem also shares with the *History* a male writer's adaptation of a female perspective occupying both a personal and political realm, further indicating the extent to which some history-writing relied on the voices of its female historical figures as narrators.

"A Lamentation of Queen Elizabeth" is particularly striking in its contrast to More's prose coronation poem, "On the Coronation Day of Henry VIII Most Glorious and Blessed King of the British Isles, and of Catherine his Most Happy Queen, A Poetical Expression of Good Wishes By Thomas More of London," which marks the death of Henry VII and the ascension of Henry VIII in 1509 and was published with his Latin epigrams in 1518. More praises Henry VIII by distinguishing the king from his father, who was in More's eyes, a tyrant: "This day is the limit of our slavery, the beginning of our freedom, the end of sadness, the source of joy."[38] He recalls the unjustness of laws, the severity of taxation, and a climate of fear and oppression created under Henry VII and gloriously removed by Henry VIII. Lastly, he devotes a paragraph of praise to Catherine of Aragon, which includes his assessment of public opinion about the marriage as well as the role of Henry VIII's queen: "It was she, your wife, whom your people were happy to see sharing your power."[39] More characterizes royal marriage under dynastic rule as a power-sharing alliance that affords queen consorts political agency; in his poem the hope the English have for Henry VIII's new reign is grounded in the political benefits of this power-sharing arrangement and predicated upon their approval of Catherine as a co-ruler of sorts. Given More's dislike of Henry VII and the elder More's steadfast Yorkist loyalties, it is perhaps no surprise that More might find the silver lining of the Tudor dynasty in its women, imagining Elizabeth Woodville Grey, Elizabeth York, and even Catherine of Aragon as intelligent and compassionate queen mothers and consorts who might effectively participate in dynastic government through their familial ties to the monarch.[40]

More's poetry and historiography demonstrate a provisional, rather than propagandistic, endorsement of the Tudor family and its history. This endorsement was rooted in female Yorkists, like Elizabeth Woodville Grey, who provided a benevolent model of women's unofficial influence in dynastic politics, and Elizabeth York, whose own blood claim to the throne made her a plausible co-ruler under a dynastic framework that sanctioned queen consorts' political power. Conceived as potential alternative political authorities in More's poetry, Yorkist and Tudor women such as Elizabeth Woodville

Grey function as model authorities on history who inform and authorize his own narration of the past in his historiography. More, of course, was not the only important early modern figure who imagined Elizabeth York as an alternative dynastic authority to her Tudor husband: his foregrounding of Tudor women prefigures the coronation pageant's rewriting of the story of union to position Elizabeth York as a precedent for female rule. More's historiography thus offered early modern playwrights ample source material for dramatic accounts that would have dovetailed with Elizabeth I's recognition and manipulation of the ideological power available in a history of the Wars of the Roses that privileged Tudor women. Mining More's *History* and its chronicle siblings for almost everything *except* this emphasis on women's perspectives, Shakespeare instead rejected early Tudor historiography's view of women within England's dynastic past.

II

Shakespeare, of course, accessed More's *History* through later Tudor chronicles that included and expanded upon More's text, such as Edward Hall's *Union*, posthumously published twice (1548 and 1550) during the reign of the child king Edward VI. The *Union*, like the *History* and *Anglica Historia*, surprisingly depicts Elizabeth Woodville Grey as an active historical agent whose personal and familial relationships enable her positive political involvement in the Tudor succession. However, Hall's portrait of Elizabeth has often served as key evidence in feminist arguments identifying narrative historiography as a genre that negatively evaluates or excludes historical women. Phyllis Rackin, Jean Howard, Nina Levine, and Barbara Hodgdon read Shakespeare's Elizabeth in *Richard III* as a *more* positive rewriting of what they consider a harsh portrayal of her in Hall's *Union*. These critics argue that Shakespeare recuperates Elizabeth's historical character because his queen appropriates and redirects against Richard Hall's charge that she is an inconstant woman who forgets Richard's murder of her sons and delivers her daughters to him like "Lambes" to the "rauenous wolfe."[41] Yet this perspective overlooks the intertextual influence of More's narrative and Hall's own portrayal of Elizabeth in the rest of the *Union*, which shares with its predecessors the use of narrative strategies highlighting women's political and familial agency. Hall incorporated More's *History* in its entirety in all editions of the *Union*, which were, in turn, printed in many other chronicle narratives of the early modern period.[42] The inclusion of the *History* in the *Union* changes the effect of Hall's more critical comments about Elizabeth by establishing the bulk of the historiography (and perspectives) about her accessible to readers. While Hall doesn't reproduce the *Historia*, he uses it to fill in the gaps about Elizabeth's life left by More's unfinished *History* through rewriting and expanding key scenes from Vergil's text featuring Elizabeth. Hall thus takes cues from both historiographers' interest in Elizabeth's active decisions and their assignation of authorial knowledge to her.

Hall begins his account of Elizabeth with positive interjected evaluations, documenting her "beauti^e & fauor," "sober demeanure, louely lokyng, and femynyne smylyng" as well as her "toungue so eloquent, and her wit so pregnant."[43] He details Elizabeth's sexual and intellectual influence over Edward IV as both well-deserved and well-executed: she "wisely" resists the king's desire to make her his mistress, and thus realizes an even more powerful position as his wife. Elizabeth's marriage is "profitable to her bloud," a means for the queen to elevate herself and her family through Edward's preferment, and her recognition and use of that profit is presented as shrewd but not inappropriate.[44]

Even Hall's reputedly negative evaluation of her marriage to the king as a source of great trouble is more ambivalent than critics generally allow. Claiming the common people objected to the preferential treatment given to Elizabeth's relatives after her marriage, Hall speculates that Edward IV's early death and the destruction of the Yorkist dynasty might be punishment for either the marriage or the murder of his brother Clarence. Whereas Vergil simply notes that the people "found muche fault with [Edward] in that marriage," Hall introduces and then evaluates such speculation: "But such cōiectures for ẙ most part, be rather more of mens phātasies, then of diuine reuelacion."[45] Describing with similar uncertainty Elizabeth's possible contribution to Clarence's death, Hall notes that the malice between Edward IV and Clarence might be due to "olde grudges" between the brothers or new resentments "set a fyre by the Quene."[46] As with his account of popular opinion holding Elizabeth responsible for God's punishment of her husband, Hall concludes his provisional indictment against Elizabeth with an even stronger qualification: "the certayntie therof was hyd, and coulde not truely be disclosed, but by coniectures, which as often deceyue the imaginacions of fantastical folke, as declare truth to them in their conclusion."[47] Thus, the statements Hall makes about Elizabeth Woodville Grey frequently understood as entirely unfavorable are actually heavily qualified with reminders that readers should be suspicious of negative information about her. Hall's provisos about Elizabeth show the English public as too quick to incriminate Edward IV's marriage to Elizabeth Woodville Grey as a sign and symptom of corrupt favoritism and familial access. Though Hall's text offers, in general, a defense of Elizabeth's influence through her personal intimacy with the King as a legitimate political mechanism, the public anxiety he consciously refutes is part of what Curtis Perry identifies as an emerging redefinition of "the relationship between the king and the nation" that views favoritism with greater suspicion and concern than ever before.[48] Hall thus uses the public's conjectures to direct his readers to make better evaluations of Elizabeth and her participation in dynastic politics and to speak back to sentiment critical of queenly favoritism.

Hall's text retains and takes cues from More's use of narrative strategies, including interjected evaluation and invented dialogue, and adds to these a somatic form of interior perspective to situate women's perspectives as a legitimate source of history.[49] Included less than a paragraph after the close of More's *History* in the *Union,* Hall's account of Elizabeth's responses to her son's deaths is similar to More's representation of Elizabeth as a sympathetic maternal figure and active agent in history

> But when these newes wer first brought to the infortunate mother of the dead children yet being in sanctuary, no doubte but it strake to her harte, like the sharpe darte of death: for when she was first enformed of the murther of her. ii. sonnes, she was so sodainly amasyd with the greatnes of $\tilde{y}^e$ crueltie that for feare she sounded and fell doune to the ground, and there lay in a great agonye like to a dead corps. And after that she came to her memory and was reuyued agayne, she wept and sobbyd and with pitefull scriches she replenished the hole mancion, her breste she puncted, her fayre here she tare and pulled in peces & being ouercome with sorowe and pensiuenes rather desyred death than life, calling by name diuers times her swete babes, accomptyng her self more then madde that she deluded by wyle and fraudulente promises delyuered her yonger sonne out of the sanctuarie to his enemye to be put to death....[50]

Hall imagines motherly bereavement as a physically painful experience, striking Elizabeth's heart "like the sharp darte of death." Hall's narrative becomes both a spectacular description of performative grief designed to elicit sympathy from his readers and an interior account of emotional response to tragedy. Borrowing Vergil's description of Elizabeth's physical response, which briefly describes her swooning, crying, shrieking, striking her hair and tearing her breast, Hall's account of her grief offers readers access to a historical event through Elizabeth's perspective. While Hall initially proposes—and then refutes—Edward's marriage to Elizabeth Woodville Grey and the favoritism he provides to her family as a possible cause for the king's divine punishment, the *Union*'s depiction and evaluation of Elizabeth's performance of grief further distances her from such blame. The physical description and interior account of her sadness augments Hall's earlier narrative corrections of an overly critical public's judgment, providing readers with a compelling affective appeal that counters accusations against Elizabeth. As both More's and Vergil's do, Hall's interior perspective calls attention to the consequences, and power, of Elizabeth's own individual decisions: paraphrasing Vergil, where Elizabeth "condemn[s] hirself for a mad woman, for that (being dec^{e}avyd by false promyses)," Hall shows Elizabeth lamenting her errors in judgment and holding herself responsible for being "deluded by wyle and fraudulent promises."[51]

The *Union* briefly prefigures *Richard III*'s depiction of appeals to God's vengeance as the only recourse for Richard's female opposition when Hall's Elizabeth identifies God as a necessary vehicle for revenge: she "kne[els] downe and crie[s] on God to take vengeaunce for the disceaytfull periurie" because she "sawe no hope of reuengynge otherwyse, ..."[52] After the deaths of her sons, Elizabeth does not imagine how her own actions might rectify past wrongs or limit future calamity and she self-conciously acknowledges she has lost the ability to influence the future. Yet Elizabeth's pleas of helplessness and acknowledgment of providence have not in fact impeded her desire or ability to enact political change in the larger schema of Hall's narrative, which includes material about Elizabeth's negotiations with the Countess of Richmond for the marriage of Elizabeth York and Henry VII. Dialogue ascribed to Buckingham reveals the unofficial influence Elizabeth retains even after she loses direct access to the court and identifies her and the Countess as the primary dynastic figures capable of defeating Richard:

> if the mothers of bothe parties and especially the erle hym selfe, and the ladye wyll agre, I doubte not but the braggynge bore . . . shall not onely be brought to confusion as he hath deserued but that this empire shall euer be certaine of an vndubitate heyre, and then shall all ciuile and intestyne war cease . . . and this realme shalbe reduced agayne to quietnes renoune and glorie.[53]

While also emphasizing the consent of Richmond and Elizabeth York, Hall indicates that Elizabeth Woodville Grey and the Countess have the most prominent role in establishing the Tudor succession. The Countess's messengers propose the marriage to Elizabeth as a means "to bryng your harte to comforte and gladnes," and "to reuenge ỹ righteous quarel of you and your children" against Richard; if Elizabeth can simply "agree and inuent the meane" to marry her daughter to Richmond, Richard "should be shortly deposed, and Elizabeth's "heire againe to her right restored."[54] The Countess's rhetoric appeals to Elizabeth's twin political and personal desires: to reestablish her connections to the monarchy and to use that influence for revenge against Richard. In this series of invented dialogues, women's motives and interventions characterize dynastic notions of personal monarchy as redemptive for both family *and* country. Hall suggests that only widow-mothers arranging the succession through the marriage of their children can form a new dynastic line and restore peace to England.

Hall also identifies both women's interventions as the result of an accurate "reading" of the past. Hall asserts the appropriateness of Elizabeth's reception of the Countess's proposition by explaining its physical manifestations, which creates proximity between subject, narrator, and reader. He thus endorses her jubilant response and the subsequent political interventions called for by the Countess's suggestion: "When the quene had heard this frendly mocion . . . lorde howe her spirits reuyued, and how her hearte lept in her body for ioye and gladnes."[55] Her somatic reaction to the proposed union of the houses of York and Lancaster is that of a mother rejoicing for the safety and future of her children and that of a Tudor reader of the past who recognizes the positive dynastic consequences of such a marriage. In the moments Hall most strongly aligns Elizabeth's emotions with those of his readers and his own narrative voice, he also shows her to be politically efficacious precisely *because* of her personal and maternal relationships. She promises the Countess the support of "all the frendes and fautoures" of her dead husband Edward IV, and she makes a critical demand: Richard must take "a corporall othe" to marry any of her living daughters.[56] Barbara Hodgdon identifies Hall's account of this demand as a negative critique of Elizabeth's opportunism, but when read in the context of Hall's chosen narrative strategies, intertextual revisions, and larger account of the marriage negotiations, it is represented as a prudent and wise attempt to retain dynastic strength and ensure Richard's defeat.[57] Hall's account, like Vergil's and More's, demonstrates that some historiographers not only looked to women's perspectives for model readers and historical sources, but also valued and emphasized the personal emotions and relationships through which these historical women understood and achieved political action.

Even in the narrative report of Elizabeth Grey's "wolfish" handover of her daughters, so central to critical assumptions that chronicle history indicts and marginalizes its female figures and that Shakespearean drama redeems them as noble victims, Hall still echoes More's emphasis on Elizabeth's active decision making and intelligent resistance. Richard, determined to reconcile with Elizabeth through "faire woordes or liberall promises," sends messengers to excuse his actions and "promes promocions innumerable."[58] According to Hall, Richard is only successful because "men bothe of wit and grauitie so persuaded the quene with great and pregnante reasons, then with fayre large promises, that she began somewhat to relent & to geue to theim no deffe eare."[59] Though he concedes that Elizabeth is ultimately "blynded by auaricious affeccion and seduced by flatterynge wordes," Hall describes Richard's difficulty manipulating her; as it does in More, this suggests Elizabeth's serious opposition to Richard and his perception of her as formidable obstacle. Richard's seduction strategies, including words of praise and promises of preferment, evoke the corrupt processes of royal favoritism addressed by Hall's earlier account of public sentiment toward Elizabeth. Hall's condemnation of Richard's use of these processes and Elizabeth's eventual seduction by them underscore the problems of such alliances under personal monarchy, and his uncertain implication of Elizabeth suggests his concern about the possible abuses of the personal aspects of such politics. Such expressions of anxieties about the reach of monarchal authority and preferment can be briefly contextualized by a consideration of Hall's political investments. As Peter C. Herman notes, "the understanding of Hall's work and its relationship to early Tudor political culture" has changed, and some scholars, most notably Herman himself, have begun to recognize that "far from slavishly endorsing the Tudor myth," Hall's *Union* repeatedly critiques monarchal authority in general and Tudor authority in particular.[60] Herman argues that Hall's narrative valorizes the subtle dissent of the people against Henrician power.[61] However, Hall's earlier defenses of Elizabeth directed at a public he characterizes as overly suspicious of their queen and his representation of her as a privileged historical and authorial voice suggest at least a residual investment in the processes of personal dynastic power, particularly when enacted appropriately by Tudor women. Sympathetic to Elizabeth's historical participation in ending civil dissention through the formation of a dynastic marriage alliance, but wary of dynastic authority, Hall seems fundamentally ambivalent in his authorial evaluations of Elizabeth's personal access to the monarchy and its effects on England. This ambivalence in Hall's narrative, at least as it pertains to Elizabeth Woodville Grey, is generally interpreted as an indication of his—and the historical narrative genre's—exclusion of women from politics, as Hall strongly censures Elizabeth for actions he eventually traces to her gender. Yet this representation of Elizabeth might be better situated in the context of Hall's complicated perspectives about popular dissent and dynastic control, as his sympathy for and indictments of Elizabeth correspond to her ability to successfully use her familial access to the monarchy for the betterment of the nation.

Hall does ultimately characterize Elizabeth's concessions to Richard as the result of her gender, a misogynistic claim that incriminates female influence but also provisionally defends Elizabeth by asserting her own lack of choice: "surely the inconstancie of this woman were muche to be maurueled at, yf all women had bene founde constante, but let men speake, yet wemen of the verie bonde of nature wil folowe their awne kynde."[62] Her inconstancy is unremarkable because it is characteristic, an assumption of typicality that underlies later critiques of women in *Richard III*. When she fails to understand the dynastic consequences of handing over her daughters and cedes to the corrupt promise of personal preferment, Elizabeth is no longer described as an active historical agent or good reader of history, but a woman subject to the determinism of her own gender. Only when her perspective differs from the ideal historical reader she exemplifies elsewhere does Hall condemn her actions as negative, female behavior. Turning to women's nature as an explanation for Elizabeth's political error, Hall ultimately critiques her ability to usefully influence dynastic politics through her personal relationships with royalty. Hall's assessment that Elizabeth is steered by nature rather than agency exists in tension with all three historiographers' descriptions of her astute political interventions and the effect of invented scenes eliciting readers' sympathy and aligning Elizabeth's agency with her narrators' authorial power. The *Union* thus privileges female perspectives, but it also presents an incongruous evaluation of women's nature and critiques the effectiveness of women's familial access under dynasty. In this tension between Hall's inclusive narrative strategies and his expressions of anxieties about female influence, we can see initial signs of history writing's political exclusion of women, which only becomes fully realized on stage.

III

Scholars studying early modern nationhood, including Richard Helgerson, Liah Greenfeld, and Jacqueline Vanhoutte, generally concur that national self-definition gradually shifted throughout the early modern period from the monarch's dynastic realm to the entity of the nation, defined by its citizenry and geographical space.[63] In addition to these ideological changes, England's governance, particularly under the Tudors, developed a more centralized administrative infrastructure, and regional and even religious control came to be located in the monarch and Parliament, rather than in the hereditary dynasty and aristocratic families. Greenfeld argues that the circumstances moving England from dynastic to national identity included transformations in social hierarchy and mobility, whereby nobility became increasingly defined not by descent and blood but by personal deeds, behavior, and learning.[64] The Protestant Reformation disenfranchised Catholic nobles, and changes in Henry VIII's government practices replaced informal, personal relationships of preferment with an "official elite" and a smaller circle of favorites.[65] According to Howard and Rackin, "ironically, the Tudors' relative success at building a more unified and centralized state created conditions in which the centrality of the monarch as the focus of allegiance could diminish."[66] Early modern nationalism as a governmental practice consolidated administrative power around the sovereign; nationhood as an ideological construct consolidated national identity around the country itself as a sovereign entity. Thus, emerging concepts of nationhood were strongly linked to the monarch but could also produce anti-monarchal (and anti-dynastic) sentiment through a newly conceived separation between obedience to the sovereign and loyalty to the nation.

Numerous critics attest to early modern literature's participation in this cultural change: Helgerson finds "traces" of the "never quite complete passage from dynasty to nation" in the self-conscious writing of young Elizabethans such as Shakespeare.[67] Vanhoutte, in an analysis of the trope of the motherland, notes that "[n]ationalist writers had to redefine the country as a sovereign entity where it previously had been viewed as the patrimony of a monarch."[68] Though the change in governmental structures that helped to create this shift began under Henry VII and continued under Henry VIII, many critics claim the rhetoric of national identity solidified under Elizabeth Tudor and understand early modern national consciousness as an Elizabethan phenomenon.[69] Historical narratives written under the male Tudors most often reflect dynastic models of government, where female members of the reigning dynasty retained unofficial influence; history plays written late in Elizabeth's reign often construct national identity as male citizen-centered and critique the reigning female monarch by reducing women's power within dynasty to their reproduction as those plays seek to retell old dynastic stories with a new national understanding of England. Ironically, this compensatory shift toward national identity under a female monarch was perhaps most visible in historical drama through the marginalization of women's political roles.

Richard III first provides characterizations of women's power under dynasty as illegitimate and damaging through Buckingham and Richard. Certainly suspect, as they issue from the play's villain, these challenges to the legitimacy and execution of Elizabeth Woodville Grey's and Mistress Shore's political interventions nevertheless ideologically limit women's influence. Richard presents both women as undeserving beneficiaries of corrupt royal preferment who emasculate the monarchy through unfair access to King Edward IV. He uses gendered stereotypes to deflect suspicion onto Queen Elizabeth and Mistress Shore when he tells Clarence "this it is, when men are rul'd by women: / 'Tis not the King that sends you to the Tower;" (1.1. 62–63) and confides in his brother that "there is no man [is] secure / But the Queen's kindred, and night-walking heralds / That trudge betwixt the King and Mistress Shore" (1.1.71–73). Richard mocks Hastings for "Humbly complaining to her deity" (1.1.76) and sarcastically proposes to Clarence that they "be [Mistress Shore's] men and wear her livery" in order to "keep in favor with the King" (1.1.80, 79). Labeling both women "mighty gossips in our monarchy" (1.1.83) and ascribing their influence to an unmerited boost in status due to Edward IV "dubb[ing] them gentlewomen," (1.1.82) Richard evaluates women's influence as a threat to the realm. While utilizing his blood ties to Edward and Clarence to influence the court, Richard critiques the same interpersonal relationship that benefits his own negotiations when he describes the Yorkist dynasty as an inverted hierarchical order resulting from unfair favoritism toward women. In the misogynistic formulation Richard deploys, Elizabeth and Mistress Shore have undeserved power because Edward has allowed them to unduly affect his rule. Relying on cultural fears about women's witchcraft to make an unlikely case of conspiracy, Richard lumps "Edward's wife, that monstrous witch," and Edward's mistress, "that harlot strumpet Shore," under the aegis of a specifically female threat when he accuses them of deforming his arm (3.4.70–71). This famous manipulation, designed to condemn Hastings, identifies Elizabeth and Mistress

Shore's power as an inversion of gender hierarchy signaling the dysfunction of Edward's dynastic rule.

In *Richard III*, these male indictments of women's access to the monarch challenge the validity of female participation in dynastic politics, while staged representations of Elizabeth Woodville Grey further contrast with prior chronicle histories in their presentation of her place in history and her sphere of influence. The play does follow its narrative predecessors in emphasizing the affective power of Elizabeth's role as a mourning mother and casting women as moral arbiters of Richard's tyranny who elicit readers' sympathy. Feminist critics have read *Richard III*'s depiction of Elizabeth as lacking subversive power but generative of sympathetic evaluation, though they do not see this evocation of sympathy or affect emerging from the play's narrative sources.[70] By diminishing the political dimensions of her maternal role, so clearly important in its narrative predecessors, *Richard III* limits Elizabeth to a strictly personal sphere of sympathetic mourning separate from politics. The play further modifies these sources to make women self-consciously *voice* their own inability to influence history in order to critique women's participation in dynastic politics.[71]

Shakespeare changes More's Elizabeth into a voice of the past who insists on the predetermined nature of future events. Her agency, like that of all the characters in *Richard III*, is circumscribed by the play's providential account of history. Curtis Perry has noted that the play's "historical determinism" is particularly evident in the play's "wailing queens," who "embody the idea . . . of powerlessness vis-à-vis historical determinism in which the future is pre-scripted by the violence of the past."[72] Within this deterministic frame Shakespeare revises Elizabeth so that she identifies her own position within the play's fated history as a particularly limited one. Unlike More's privileged, knowledgeable Elizabeth, whose actions have potent effects on others, Shakespeare's Queen is portrayed as righteous but nevertheless fruitless in her resistance to Richard. Elizabeth responds to the news of her kin's arrests not, as she does in prior historiography, with regrets that highlight the efficacy of her own decisions, but with an assessment of ensuing events as "already" historical:

> Ay me! I see the ruin of my house.
> The tiger now hath seiz'd the gentle hind;
> Insulting tyranny begins to jut
> Upon the innocent and aweless throne.
> Welcome destruction, blood, and massacre!
> I see (as in a map) the end of all.
>
> (2.4. 49–54)

Narrative historiography generally imagines Elizabeth's responses to Richard's actions as struggles to use her political power to change the outcome of events. Shakespeare's Queen speaks prophetically but gives up instantly, "welcom[ing]" certain disaster. Seeing the end of "all" in an already-written map, as one reads recorded history, she seeks sanctuary not as a means of resistance but as an expression of defeat. Elizabeth moves from a political agent and historical scriptor providing later historiographers a privileged source to a reader and interpreter not of history itself but of already-recorded chronicles.

Shakespeare forgoes the rich invented dialogue, ripe for dramatic adaptation, of More's debate over sanctuary, reducing it to a short conversation among men in 3.1. The decision to violate sanctuary is made perfunctorily, as the Lord Cardinal is dismissed to fetch the Duke. Buckingham assesses Elizabeth's claim as an "indirect and peevish course" and it is short work for him to convince the Cardinal that the young Duke of York "hath neither claim'd it nor deserv'd it" (3.1. 31, 51). Richard's authority is already inviolate: as the Cardinal confesses, he is overpowered by will rather than swayed by argument: "My lord, you shall overrule my mind for once" (3.1.57). Snatching the Duke from sanctuary is a foregone conclusion rather than the result of a vividly imagined argument as in the *History,* and Elizabeth is given no place in its negotiation.

Elizabeth is further stripped of power to intervene in ensuing events when the argument More's queen makes in sanctuary is turned into a mangled plea at the Tower gates. Elizabeth questions the lieutenant who denies her visitation to her sons: "I am their mother, who shall bar me from them?" (4.1.21). Reduced to a shorthand that neither intelligibly evokes natural nor common law, Elizabeth's assertion is enlarged by the Duchess of York, "I am their father's mother, I will see them," and Anne: "Their aunt I am in law, in love their mother;"(4.1.22–23). The intellectually viable defense used by More's Elizabeth is transformed in *Richard III* into a means to demonstrate a morally superior but unrealized maternal right to familial access. Denied the contact with male family members lending their maternal roles influence, the women's dialogue emphasizes access to male relatives as the sole source of their power and bemoans the loss of such access. Elizabeth characterizes this loss and its consequences when she instructs her son Dorset to "speak not to me . . . Thy mother's name is ominous to children" (4.1.38, 40). Motherhood and matrimony no longer signal legally protected, powerful unofficial influence; they register either unavoidable, unwished death to offspring or unwelcome power to monstrous children like Richard. The play's women are thus given sympathy only when they position themselves as mourners denied political participation and use their own words to define dynastic familial relationships as impotent, and even destructive, political positions. Thus, the play critiques the efficacy of those dynastic relationships dependent on royal women's diplomacy and political negotiation.

Shakespeare fixes Elizabeth and her female relatives in history as helpless mourners through their represented action and dialogue; they express grief while acknowledging the inability of such expressions to change the past. The cursing of Elizabeth and the Duchess emphasizes female resignation to a vocal but ineffective objection. Elizabeth demonstrates an awareness that this form of truth-telling has no impact beyond the women themselves: "though what they will impart / Help nothing else, yet do they ease the heart" (4.4. 130–31). The duchess implores Elizabeth: "go with me, / And in the breath of bitter words let's smother / My damned son" (4.4.132–34). By their own estimation, their resistance to Richard is measured by their ability to speak about what he has done rather than their ability to limit his power. Richard registers the potential efficacy of their verbal opposition, and he requests noise to drown it out: "Let not the heavens hear these tell-tale women Rail on the Lord's anointed" (4.4.150–51). In spite of this recognition, the represented action afforded to Shakespeare's Queen as a "tell-tale" woman ascribes to her a retelling of history that calls attention to women's limited agency.

In one key scene, often viewed as one of Shakespeare's most positive departures from his narrative sources, the play complicates Hall's account of Elizabeth turning her daughters over to Richard.[73] In a conversation with Richard about his desire to marry Elizabeth York, Elizabeth resists his attempts to swear his love to her daughter on the "time to come" (4.4.387). In doing so, the Queen also reifies her own fixed place in history:

> That thou hast wronged me in the time o'erpast;
> For I myself have many tears to wash
> Hereafter time, for time past wrong'd by thee.
> The children live whose fathers thou hast slaughter'd,
> Ungovern'd youth, to wail it [in] their age;
> The parents live whose children thou hast butcher'd,
> Old barren plants, to wail it with their age.
> Swear not by time to come, for that thou hast
> Misus'd ere us'd, by times ill-us'd [o'erpast].
>
> (4.4.388–396)

Elizabeth's lines remind Richard and the audience of her dead sons as well as Richard's impending fall. However, they also conceive of Elizabeth's future as one of static mourning; she refers to the living left behind after Richard's slaughter, but ascribes to those parents of the dead only wailing. The future itself remains off-limits to Richard's oath because it has already been corrupted by the past—it is "misus'd ere us'd"—and Elizabeth intends to wash the future with tears. Elizabeth's accusations condemn Richard, but they primarily identify her motherhood as a wailing remembrance of the past that forecloses her participation in future political events. Even as she discusses the living child whose marriage to Henry Tudor she orchestrates in prior narrative accounts, Shakespeare's Elizabeth is only given voice to speak of her dead children and to describe herself as a barren parent, thus eliding her historical participation in the formation of the new Tudor dynasty through her daughter.

The account that Shakespeare's Elizabeth gives of her own motherhood as a "barren" position of mourning is suggestive of another metaphorically "barren" Elizabeth: Shakespeare's reigning monarch, Elizabeth I. Katherine Eggert, Leah Marcus, and Nina Levine have all analyzed the first tetralogy's engagement with Elizabethan succession concerns.[74] Reading Richard as the end of a line of succession and a figure of dynastic disruption analogous to Elizabeth I, Eggert sees the "national obsession" with Elizabeth I's childlessness projected onto him.[75] While the play expresses anxiety over the Elizabethan succession, this anxiety is strongest not in a comparison of Elizabeth I's and Richard III's dead ends, as Eggert argues, but through the play's emphasis on Shakespeare's royal analogue, Queen Elizabeth Woodville Grey, as a barren and helpless mother of dead children who is particularly unable to impact the progress of history.[76] *Richard III* ambivalently insists that Elizabeth Woodville Grey's motherhood both matters and matters not. While the play privileges maternity by casting mothers as morally superior witnesses, it also revises its sources to exclude mothers from Henry VII's political victory and makes Elizabeth voice her own ineffectiveness in order to downplay her political involvement in the creation of the Tudor dynasty. By repeatedly figuring Elizabeth Woodville Grey's motherhood as unimportant to securing the succession, *Richard III* denies the political dimensions of royal maternity and points toward a fantasy of masculine restoration only possible through the dynastic disruption created by Elizabeth I's childlessness.

Shakespeare thus refuses the positive queenly allusions available through narrative histories that detail Elizabeth Woodville Grey's active role in securing the Tudor succession. Interestingly, he also rejects Hall's sole anomalous example of Elizabeth's inappropriate interventions into politics, and the moment in the *Union* that most closely approaches the tenor of the play's political exclusions of women: Elizabeth's handover of her daughters, and Hall's attribution of that decision to her inferior female nature. After reminding Richard of his crimes and insisting her daughter cannot love him, Shakespeare's Elizabeth departs, asking, "Shall I go win my daughter to thy will?" (4.4.426). Some critics read this as an acquiescence to Richard's desires, and pair the entire conversation with Richard's wooing of Anne as examples of Richard's rhetorical force, while others see Elizabeth biding time in order to establish an alliance with Richmond.[77] The play recasts Hall's charge of inconstant female behavior as Richard's: he unconvincingly dubs the absent Elizabeth a "Relenting fool, and shallow, changing woman!" (4.4.431). When Shakespeare might easily lift an anecdote from Hall that would preserve the playwright's own emphasis on women's necessary exclusion from politics, he denies explicit precedent, and, rather than stage Elizabeth's error, he reframes Hall's isolated negative judgment of Elizabeth as Richard's misreading. Shakespeare's revisions therefore allude only briefly to Elizabeth's orchestration of her daughter's marriage and gloss over her capitulation to Richard: in the play, she neither endangers nor ensures the Tudor dynasty as she does in Hall. Through this manipulation of available narratives, Shakespeare minimizes Elizabeth Woodville Grey's power to affect the succession in favor of either Richard or Richmond by recasting royal motherhood as apolitical, and hints that Elizabeth I's own failures of motherhood matter little to England's succession.

Richard III's evocation of Elizabeth I through the historical figure of Elizabeth Woodville Grey—and the play's overall attitude toward women's political participation—is part of its expression of a new nationalism marked by the exclusion of women and a revision of sources that have previously recorded English history through the stories of its dynasties. John Watkins sees in another Shakespearean history play, *King John*, a privileging of protonational independence from continental ties through a critique of interdynastic marriage.[78] According to Watkins, this critique "manifests itself in a pervasive distrust of women as the vehicles, and sometimes the negotiating agents of such alliances" and demands the disappearance of female characters, whose prior participation in politics embodies the inadequacies of a dynastic system.[79] Vanhoutte likewise finds in *King John* a challenge to monarchical institutions that allow women access to power, arguing that the play "attributes many of the difficulties associated with the monarchy to its tolerance of female agency."[80] *Richard III* similarly identifies women's diplomacy as failures of a dynastic structure allowing queens and mistresses corrupting influence. From its early censuring of Mistress Shore's and Elizabeth Woodville Grey's political negotiations to its attempts to downplay the importance of Elizabeth's role in the Tudor succession, the play rewrites narrative accounts to situate women's power as a key symptom of dynasty's dysfunction.

The play minimizes the fundamental role of maternal marriage negotiations and the political necessity of Henry's marriage to Elizabeth York, in spite of the fact that alternative histories emphasizing those processes were readily available and historically appealing to Elizabeth I. Moving women to the margins allows praise of Richmond's triumph as a masculine victory and paradoxically dynastic solution to the problem of the Yorkist dynasts that nevertheless conceives of England's future as national and free from female intrusions into politics. The story of union recounted at the play's end finds Richmond characterizing England's civil conflict as analogous to an irrational woman, who "hath long been mad and scarr'd herself" (5.5.23). Yet the fallout of dynasty's female self-mutilation is metaphorized in terms of its cost to men, in spite of the play's memorable string of female mourners: "The brother blindly shed the brother's blood, / The father rashly slaughter'd his own son, / The son, compell'd, been butcher to the sire" (5.5.24–26). Richmond's promise to "unite the White Rose and the Red" (5.5.19) and produce heirs who will "Enrich the time to come with smooth-fac'd peace" (5.5.33) is predicated upon the recuperative power of his masculinity to repair the damage of (female) civil war. As Vanhoutte says, Richmond's closing speech and Elizabeth York's absence "expres[s] a fantasy of generation" without women and "foregroun[d] the primary relationship between Richmond and England, so that their metaphorical marriage and not the dynastic union of the houses of York and Lancaster becomes the source of national redemption."[81] Eggert, however, finds the triumph occasioning such fantasy hollow, since Richmond's success only makes way for the "entirely feminine, dynastically disastrous" Elizabeth I.[82] The play's conspicuous exclusion of women does in fact both look forward to restorative masculine rule and backward to dynastic catastrophe, but not by bankrupting Richmond's victory. Rather, the play betrays an unspeakable desire for its own Elizabethan Richmond, and assuages concerns about the disruption created by Elizabeth's childlessness by bankrupting royal motherhood and seeking continuity through a national England.

While the Gracechurch pageant envisions the stability of the Tudor dynasty emerging from the Yorkists via Elizabeth York and passing to Elizabeth I, *Richard III*'s reframing of the beginning of the Tudor line marks it as a masculine and national break from the dysfunctional dynastic system preceding it. The play paradoxically looks forward to the Tudor dynasty's demise as a masculine redemption, pointing toward James I and a continuity rooted, not in the bloodlines of its ruling family, but in the community of England.[83] When Shakespeare told his story of Tudor genesis, he also created a means to understand the dynasty's end as a new beginning. In the process, he staged a critique of the access and influence possible under an earlier dynastic system, deployed most strongly against women's participation in politics and history. Understanding dramatic exclusions of women as the result of differing conceptions of access to the monarchy under dynastic and national models has many implications, including overturning our placement of the Shakespearean history play at the center of discussions of women in early modern history writing.

Notes

1. *The Quenes Maiesties Passage through the Citie of London to Westminster the Day before her Coronacion,* ed. James M. Osborn (New Haven, CT: Yale University Press, 1960), 33.
2. Ibid., 31, 34.

3. Judith M. Richards, "Love and a Female Monarch: The Case of Elizabeth Tudor," *The Journal of British Studies* 38.2 (1999): 133–60, esp. 148. Helen Hackett also sees in the "description of the spectacle a determined attempt . . . to refute dissent against rule by a woman" in *Virgin Mother, Maiden Queen: Elizabeth I and the Cult of the Virgin Mary* (New York: St. Martin's Press, 1995), 41.

4. Richards, "Love and a Female Monarch," 149.

5. Many feminist critics, including Barbara Hodgdon and Jean Howard, concur with Phyllis Rackin's assessment that "women had no voice" in the historical record of the chronicles and also see in Shakespeare's dramatic adaptations a "legacy of oppression" emerging from historical sources' marginalization of women through "the discursive exclusions of an elitist, patriarchal culture." *Stages of History: Shakespeare's English Chronicles* (Ithaca, NY: Cornell University Press, 1990), 147, xi; See Rackin and Howard, *Engendering a Nation: A Feminist Account of Shakespeare's English Histories* (New York: Routledge, 1997); Barbara Hodgdon, *The End Crowns All: Closure and Contradiction in Shakespeare's History* (Princeton, NJ: Princeton University Press, 1991). Others critics, such as Nina Levine, see Shakespeare's revisions as redemptive, providing political agency for women excluded from the masculine record of his narrative sources. *Women's Matters: Politics, Gender, and Nation in Shakespeare's Early History Plays* (Newark: University of Delaware Press, 1998).

6. For a discussion of Elizabeth York's absence from *Richard III*, see Jacqueline Vanhoutte, *Strange Communion: Motherland and Masculinity in Tudor Plays, Pamphlets, and Politics* (Newark: University of Delaware Press, 2003), 152, and Levine, *Women's Matters*, 117–18.

7. While many scholars note both More's personal and political dislike of the first Tudor king and the *History*'s skeptical attitude toward Tudor rule, the text's vilification of Richard certainly furthered the Tudor dynasty's re-imagining of Richard's reign as Yorkist tyranny. See Richard Marius, *Thomas More: A Biography* (New York: Knopf, 1984), 52, and Peter L. Rudnytsky, "More's *History of King Richard III* as an Uncanny Text," in *Contending Kingdoms: Historical, Psychological, and Feminist Approaches to the Literature of Sixteenth-Century England and France*, ed. Marie-Rose Logan and Rudnytsky (Detroit, MI: Wayne State University Press, 1991), 149–72.

8. The notable exception is Alan Clarke Shepard's "'Female Perversity,' Male Entitlement: The Agency of Gender in More's *The History of Richard III*," *The Sixteenth Century Journal* 26 (1995): 311–28.

9. "Interior perspective" is Judith Anderson's term. *Biographical Truth: The Representation of Historical Persons in Tudor-Stuart Writing* (New Haven, CT: Yale University Press, 1984).

10. Thomas More, *The History of King Richard the Third: A Reading Edition*. ed. George M. Logan (Bloomington: Indiana University Press, 2005), 33, 30.

11. Ibid., 20–21.

12. Ibid., 32, 38.

13. Ibid., 26–27.

14. Ibid., 25.

15. Shepard, "Female Peversity," 326.

16. More, *The History of King Richard the Third*, 45.

17. Ibid., 44–45. The queen argues that her son's landholdings are not by knight's service, so he is not legally independent but her ward. See More, 44 n. 34.
18. More, *The History of King Richard the Third*, 42.
19. Ibid., 46.
20. Ibid.
21. Anderson, *Biographical Truth*, 92.
22. More, *The History of King Richard the Third*, 44.
23. Ibid.
24. Vergil's history of England was commissioned by Henry VII around 1506–7; on its status as the source of the "Tudor myth," see George M. Logan, introduction to *The History of King Richard the Third. A Reading Edition* by Thomas More (Bloomington: Indiana University Press, 2005) xxx and xlv. Logan and Levy assert that More and Vergil were unlikely to have read or borrowed from each other's concurrent histories; the two writers certainly could have discussed them. See Logan, xxx and F. J. Levy, *Tudor Historical Thought*, (Kingsport, TN: Kingsport Press, 1967), 53. Dominique Goy-Blanquet alternatively claims that More did use Vergil as one of his sources. Dominique Goy-Blanquet, *Shakespeare's Early History Plays: From Chronicle to Stage* (Oxford: Oxford University Press, 2003), 210.
25. Polydore Vergil, *Three Books of Polydore Vergil's English History Comprising the Reigns of Henry VI, Edward IV, and Richard III, from an early translation, preserved among the mss. of the old royal library in the British Museum.* ed. Sir Henry Ellis, K.H. (1844. London: Camden Society. Repr., New York: Johnson Reprint Corp., 1968), 175.
26. Ibid., 178.
27. Ibid.
28. See J. L. Laynesmith, *The Last Medieval Queens: English Queenship 1445–1503* (Oxford: Oxford University Press, 2004), 91.
29. See David Loades, *The Tudor Court* (London: Batsford, 1986), 149; Francis Bacon, *The History of the Reign of King Henry the Seventh,* ed. Brian Vickers (Cambridge: Cambridge University Press, 1998), 25.
30. Polydore Vergil, *The Anglica Historia of Polydore Vergil, A.D. 1485–1537.* Translated by Denys Hay (London: Office of the Royal Historical Society, Camden Series, 1950), 147.
31. Vergil, *Anglica Historia*, 7.
32. Ibid., 7, 51.
33. See Janel Mueller, "'The Whole Island like a Single Family': Positioning Women in Utopian Patriarchy," *Rethinking the Henrician Era: Essays on Early Tudor Texts and Contexts,* ed. Peter C. Herman (Urbana: University of Illinois Press, 1994), for an analysis of the highly ambivalent position of women in More's *Utopia;* See Pearl Hogrefe, *Tudor Women: Commoners and Queens* (Ames: Iowa State University Press, 1975), 98–102, for an analysis of More's attitude toward and contributions to women's education in the sixteenth century.
34. Frederic B. Tromly, "'A Royal Lamentation' of Elizabeth: Thomas More's Transformation of Didactic Lament," *Moreana* 53 (1977): 45–56; Lee Cullen Khanna, "Images of Women in Thomas More's Poetry," *Albion: A Quarterly Journal Concerned with British Studies.* Quintessential Essays on St. Thomas More 10 (1978): 78–88.

35. Khanna, "Images of Women," 86.
36. More, "A Lamentation of Queen Elizabeth," *The New Oxford Book of Sixteenth-Century Verse,* ed. Emrys Jones (Oxford: Oxford University Press, 2002) 64–65, 63.
37. Ibid., 43–49.
38. More, "On the Coronation Day of Henry Most Glorious and Blessed King of the British Isles, and of Catherine his Most Happy Queen, A Poetical Expression of Good Wishes, By Thomas More of London" *The Latin Epigrams of Thomas More,* trans. L. Bradner and C. A. Lynch (Chicago: University of Chicago Press, 1953), 138.
39. Ibid., "On the Coronation," 142. The blatant critique of Henry VII offered in this coronation poem did not damage his relationship with Henry VIII; Marius argues this critique might have even endeared More to the later Henry, who was reputed to have had a tense relationship with his father and sovereign, 52. It did, however, attract notice from the French humanist Germanus Brixius, who years later accused More of slandering Henry VII in this poem and advised Henry VIII to banish him for it. See Marius, *Thomas More,* 50–53 and 246–47, for an analysis of More's coronation poems for Henry VIII and his feud with Brixius over his alleged slander of Henry VII.
40. See Elizabeth Story Donno on the elder More's political loyalties, most obviously manifested in his will, which provided money "for masses to be said for the King's soul nearly forty-five years after his death," 408. "Thomas More and *Richard III,*" *Renaissance Quarterly* 35 (1982): 401–47.
41. Edward Hall, *Hall's Chronicle,* original title, *The Union of the Two Noble and Illustre Famelies of Lancaster & Yorke* (1548 and 1550. Repr., London: J. Johnson *et al.,* 1809), 406. Shakespeare gives Elizabeth dialogue reminiscent of Hall twice in the same scene: "Wilt thou, O God, fly from such gentle lambs / And throw them in the entrails of the wolf? . . . No doubt the murd'rous knife was dull and blunt / Till it was whetted on thy stone-hard heart / To revel in the entrails of my lambs" (4.4.22–23, 227–29). According to Rackin and Howard, Shakespeare "appropriates for Elizabeth's use against Richard the very arguments, and even the terms," that Hall uses to describe her, *Engendering a Nation,* 108. All citations of Shakespeare's works are from *The Riverside Shakespeare,* 2nd ed. ed. G. Blackmore Evans (New York: Houghton Mifflin, 1996).
42. Hall's *Union* was reproduced in Holinshed's 1577 *Chronicles of England, Scotland, and Ireland,* Grafton's 1568 *This Chronicle of Britain,* John Stow's 1580 *Chronicle of England,* and John Speed's 1611 *History of Great Britain.* Goy-Blanquet traces Hall's use of More and Vergil, and Holinshed's use of the latter as they pertain to *Richard III, Shakespeare's Early History Plays,* 197–288.
43. Hall, *Union,* 264.
44. Ibid.
45. Vergil, *Anglica Historia,* 117; Hall, *Union,* 265.
46. Hall, *Union,* 326.
47. Ibid.
48. Curtis Perry, *Literature and Favoritism in Early Modern England* (Cambridge: Cambridge University Press, 2006), 17.
49. Hall's rearrangements include adding a heading, "The Tragical Doynges of

Kyng Richard the Thirde," and a subsequent introduction describing Richard's coronation before returning, unacknowledged, to More's text, 374.

50. Hall, *Union*, 379–80.
51. Vergil, *Anglica Historia*, 189; Hall, *Union*, 379.
52. Hall, *Union*, 380.
53. Ibid., 389.
54. Ibid., 391.
55. Ibid.
56. Hall, *Union*, 391; Vergil also mentions the queen's solicitation of Richmond's promise to marry either of her living daughters, *Anglica Historia*, 195–96.
57. Hodgdon, *The End Crowns All*, 109.
58. Hall, *Union*, 406.
59. Ibid.
60. Peter C. Herman, "Hall, Edward," *Oxford Dictionary of National Biography*, (Oxford: Oxford University Press, 2004–9), 4, 6. E. M. W. Tillyard and F. J. Levy argue for Hall's wholehearted endorsement in the Tudor myth, and while their similar claims about other historiographers (and in Tillyard's case, Shakespeare's history plays) have been repeatedly challenged, that has not been the case for Hall's work until recently. See Tillyard, *Shakespeare's History Plays* (1944. Repr., London: Chatto and Windus, 1974), 42–45, and F. J. Levy, *Tuder Historical Thought*, 173–77.
61. Peter C. Herman, "Henrician Historiography and the Voice of the People: The Cases of More and Hall," *Texas Studies in Literature and Language* 39, no. 3 (Fall 1997): 259–75.
62. Hall, *Union*, 406. Vergil's shorter narrative also combines a charge of female inconstancy—"for so mutable is their sex"—with Richard's difficulties in persuading Elizabeth, *Anglica Historia*, 210.
63. The degree to which early modern nationalism resembles modern nationalism has been usefully contested, as has the "dating" of emergent nationalism. See Elizabeth Sauer and Julia M. Wright, *Reading the Nation in English Literature: A Critical Reader* (London: Routledge, 2010) 2–16, and Andrew Escobedo's chapter, "No Early-Modern Nations?: Revising Modern Theories of Nationalism" in that same volume, 203–10, as well as Liah Greenfeld, *Nationalism: Five Roads to Modernity* (Cambridge, MA: Harvard University Press, 1992), 18–47. On the ideological shift from dynasty to nation in the literature of the period, see Rackin, *Stages of History;* 4; Richard Helgerson, *Forms of Nationhood: The Elizabethan Writing of England* (Chicago: University of Chicago Press, 1992); Vanhoutte, *Strange Communion,* and Andrew Escobedo, *Nationalism and Historical Loss in Renaissance England: Foxe, Dee, Spenser, Milton* (Ithaca, NY: Cornell University Press, 2004).
64. Greenfeld, *Nationalism*, 44.
65. Ibid., 47.
66. Howard and Rackin, *Engendering a Nation*, 12.
67. Helgerson, 10.
68. Vanhoutte, *Strange Communion*, 18.
69. On changes in government, see G. R. Elton, *The Tudor Revolution in Government: Administrative Changes in the Reign of Henry VIII* (Cambridge: Cambridge University Press, 1953). On Elizabethan national identity, see Helgerson, *Forms of*

Nationhood, Andrew Hadfield, *Literature, Politics, and National Identity: Reformation to Renaissance* (Cambridge: Cambridge University Press, 1994), and Claire McEachern, *The poetics of English nationhood, 1590–1612* (Cambridge: Cambridge University Press, 1996).

70. Many critics see Shakespeare's Elizabeth as indicative of the history play's typical marginalization of women. Howard and Rackin argue that *Richard III* modifies Shakespeare's earlier representations of women as "dangerous, demonic Others" in the first tetralogy by simultaneously ennobling and disempowering them as "pitiable victims," *Engendering a Nation*, 106. Madonne Miner and Nina Levine argue for a greater degree of theatrical and moral power in these women's positions of maternal authority. Madonne Miner, "'Neither mother, wife, nor England's queen': The Roles of Women in *Richard III*," *The Woman's Part: Feminist Criticism of Shakespeare*, eds. Carolyn Ruth Swift Lenz, Gayle Greene, and Carol Thomas Neely (Urbana: University of Illinois Press, 1980), 48–52. Levine, *Women's Matters*, 24, 102.

71. Rackin and Hodgdon see *Richard III*'s women as voices of, rather than agents in, the past. Rackin, "Women's Roles in the Elizabethan History Plays," *The Cambridge Companion to Shakespeare's History Plays*, ed. Michael Hattaway (Cambridge: Cambridge University Press, 2002), 79; Hodgdon, *The End Crowns All*, 105.

72. Curtis Perry, "Determined to Prove a Villain: *Richard III* and the Historiography of Senecan Drama," unpublished essay, 51.

73. See note 41 above.

74. Katherine Eggert, *Showing Like a Queen: Female Authority and Literary Experiment in Spenser, Shakespeare, and Milton* (Philadelphia: University of Pennsylvania Press, 2000), 57–76; Leah S. Marcus, *Puzzling Shakespeare: Local Reading and Its Discontents* (Berkeley: University of California Press, 1988), 51–96; Levine, *Women's Matters*, 97–122.

75. Eggert, *Showing Like a Queen*, 75.

76. Ibid.

77. See Rackin and Howard, *Engendering a Nation*, 111–12, and Levine, Women's Matters, 104, 107–9.

78. Watkins, "Losing France and Becoming England: Shakespeare's *King John* and the Emergence of State-Based Diplomacy," *Shakespeare and the Middle Ages*, eds. Curtis Perry and John Watkins (Oxford: Oxford University Press, 2009), 87.

79. Ibid., 87–88.

80. Vanhoutte, *Strange Communism*, 150.

81. Ibid., 152.

82. Eggert, *Showing Like a Queen*, 75.

83. Such emerging national identity was not even conditionally separate from the monarch, as Greenfeld notes, but the sovereign under this national schema had greater obligations to a collective nation defined by a public character than to a dynasty defined by blood, *Nationalism*, 74. Kavita Mudan Finn's *The Last Plantagenet Consorts: Gender, Genre, and Historiography, 1440–1627* (New York: Palgrave Macmillan, 2012), published as this essay went to press, redresses critical neglect of Elizabeth Woodville, offering counterpoints to my readings. Finn argues that Vergil undercuts Elizabeth's agency while More recasts her as a "victim of political circumstance" (64, 68). Hall, Finn notes, reads Elizabeth as a "surrogate for Anne Boleyn" and a "successful adversary" in *Richard III* (94, 171).

Heywood's *Silver Age:* A Flight Too Far?

David Mann

ALMOST all statements to do with Elizabethan theater are by their nature suppositions, and none more so than those concerning the performance auspices of Thomas Heywood's *The Silver Age*. Nevertheless, the topic is worth revisiting for the light it may shed on that enduring puzzle in the history of Elizabethan performance: why, if as so many scholars insist every amphitheater was fitted with flying gear, are there so few records of its actual use in performance? The Greeks had their *mechane,* there is plentiful evidence of raising and lowering actors in medieval and Renaissance dramatic activity both civic and courtly, it is not uncommon in Jacobean indoor theater, and very probably suspension gear was installed in the second Globe, but until 1613 evidence of outdoor flying is extremely rare and most of it open to some explanation short of winching from the theater canopy. In a cost-conscious commercial environment it seems very unlikely that after the expense of installing such gear it was not used, *and frequently;* compare the situation with Inigo Jones's introduction of flying at court entertainments where once established and despite the difficulties inherent in being confined to a series of fit-ups for each occasion Jones exploited and developed this facility almost continually. It has generally been supposed that the only clearly documented and apparently unambiguous use of flying outdoors is in *The Silver Age,* where Heywood is widely thought to have used it regularly throughout the play. Closer inspection, however, casts doubt on precisely how much flying, even here, was from the theater canopy.

The Auspices of *The Silver Age*

The Silver Age is the second of five plays drawn together as a sequence by Thomas Heywood some time shortly after 1613. Its predecessor, *The Golden Age,* begins with the birth of Jupiter, his survival against the wishes of Saturn his father, and his various battles with the Titans intermixed with two substantial inserts, the rape of Calisto and the seduction of Danae. The *Silver* and *Brazen Ages* between them tell the story of the birth, triumphs, and death of Hercules, but continue the same episodic admixture of bloodshed, amours, and algolagnia, including the adventures of Bellerophon and Perseus, and Jason and the Argonauts, alongside Jupiter's seductions of Alcmena and of Semele, together with Venus's attempts on Adonis and her affair with Mars, and the rape of Persephone. Each play ends in an elaborate set piece, the first with Hercules' conquest of the three-headed Cerberus and rescue of Persephone, and the second with the madness and self-immolation of the hero. *1 & 2 Iron Age* tell of the Fall of Troy followed by the return home of the Greeks, during which Heywood seems to tire of the story and kills off virtually all his characters. The plays are radically different in tone and in the demands they make on staging. *The Golden Age* makes very few except in its closing moments with the deification of Jupiter and his brothers, which may not have been in the original play. *The Silver Age* was the great flying piece, and *The Brazen Age* has the largest number of original properties, mainly pasteboard monsters. *1&2 Iron Age* are markedly different in subject matter and treatment from the first three, requiring little beyond the Trojan horse and relying on the interplay of humans mostly in battle.

Current scholarship largely assumes that the first three plays were not written until shortly before their publication, *The Golden Age* in 1611 and the other two in 1613. There are, however, substantial reasons to believe that the *Silver* and *Brazen Ages,* at the very least, existed in some form much earlier. Many critics, from Fleay in 1891 onwards, identified them with *1&2 Hercules* performed as "ne" at the Rose in 1595.[1] Ernest Rhodes identifies twenty-five properties and costumes in the Admiral's inventories of 1598, including, he says, "many items that cannot possibly have been used in any known plays except Heywood's trilogy."[2] Some of his suggestions are debatable, and others could have been used in different plays as well, but a substantial group of items, such as the golden fleece, the boar's head, the three-headed Cerberus, and the bull's head make the identification of the *Silver & Bronze Ages* with *1 & 2 Hercules,* revived for Thomas Downton in 1598 just before the inventories were compiled, almost certain.[3] A number of these key properties are also recycled within the same plays. The huge boar's head with which Hercules entertains the centaurs in the *Silver Age* reappears in the *Brazen Age* in the Meleager story; while Cerberus's three heads and the lion's head in the *Silver Age* reappear as trophies in *Brazen Age*. Furthermore, the case is strongly supported by another group of costumes and properties including Neptune's suit, Hercules' "limbs"—whether they be parts of the body or armor, the rainbow, Mercury's wings and caduceus, and Juno's coat, where the association, if not unique, is very strong. At first glance, not all the needs of the plays can be found in the inventories (but that is generally the case). Henslowe does not mention a banquet, for instance, but "marchpanes" might well be his word for it, Pluto may well have used Fayeton's chariot. Vulcan's net, invisible to the eye, could have been mimed, and flying objects like the cloud kept elsewhere together with the star, thunderbolt, and hand. In fact, most of the other items needed could have been improvised from existing stock.

Why should Heywood have changed the name of his plays? To answer this, one needs to look at the treadmill on which he learned his trade as one of Henslowe's writers. Andrew Gurr notes that between June 15, 1594 and November 1597 the Admiral's Men staged eighty-three different plays, fifty-four of them "ne," at a rate of one new play every two or three weeks, and that they gave least 689 performances at the Rose, plus others elsewhere.[4] To supply this huge demand for plays, collaboration was the norm, together with an incredible speed of production. In the preface to *The English Traveler,* Heywood claimed to have had "an entire hand or maine finger" in 220 plays,[5] and Henslowe's *Diary* gives an insight into what Webster called Heywood's "happy and copious industry": in 1598, for instance, after the final payment on *War Without Blows,* it is only fifteen days before he presents a draft of *Joan as Good as my Lady* for an advance, finished apparently, two days later. Again in 1602 within a week of finishing *London Florentine,* he presents a draft of another play (its name not recorded by Henslowe). On September 20, he not only brings in his additions for *Cutting Dick* but also a draft for *Osric,* which he then finishes within ten days. On November 24, the very same day he finishes *Christmas Comes But Once a Year,* he presents a draft for *The Blind Eates Many A Fly.*[6] New plays received a considerable premium in audience receipts, so it was practice to give out revivals as new plays, or at least old plays with additions, as in the case of *Cutting Dick,* and therefore for titles to be changed. The publication of Heywood's plays is a complicated topic outside the scope of the present investigation but sufficient to say that there were many reasons to discourage it. Few got into print, and a delay of fifteen years is not unusual.

In his "Prologue to the Stage" printed with *The Royal King and the Loyal Subject* in 1637, Heywood admits "no History / We have left unrifled,"[7] but he had a special affinity with classical subject matter, which provided him with a ready quarry of sensationalism and erotica, and from early on in his career he translated and adapted almost continually, and, perhaps because of the pace of writing for Henslowe, he became a rampant self-plagiarist. Much of the subject matter of the five *Ages* plays also turns up in a huge poem of about 13,000 lines, *Troia Britannica,* published in 1609 and dedicated to James I, whose lineage he attempts to tack on rather hurriedly to his classical saga. The rapes and seductions from the *Golden* and *Silver Ages* also form the subject matter of the *Escapes of Jupiter,* an undated manuscript probably designed for performance, and its subject matter and treatment consonant with Henslowe and Alleyn's other enterprises that already included animal bating and brothels.

Heywood's self-plagiarism, unfortunately, provided the means for Arthur

Clark to begin the process of denying the association of the *Ages* plays with those written at the Rose in the 1590s by insisting instead that they are based on *Troia Britannica*.[8] Despite the wide acceptance of this argument, closer inspection reveals that the two plays about Hercules cannot be derived from the poem since it does not deal in large areas of their subject matter, except in the briefest outline, including Jupiter's seductions of Alcmena and Semele, and Hercules' birth in *The Silver Age,* the Achelous / Deineira / Nesus story, and Hercules' madness and death, nor the stories of Venus coupling with Adonis and Mars in *The Brazen Age.* In addition, Heywood specifically excludes material associated with Hercules from his poem:

> All these we leaue as tales too often told,
> And rubs that would our running voyage let,
> Not that our thoughts despise them being old,
> (For to antiquity we owe much debt)
> But because Time that hath his acts inrold
> To many a Common sale his deeds hath set,
> Therefore (though no part of his worth to reaue him)
> We now for matters more allide, must leaue him.
>   (Canto 6 Stanza 88)[9]

The most obvious reason for rejecting the Hercules story from the poem is that Heywood himself had already devoted most of two plays to these events, and even if he were not referring to his own work, after this statement Heywood would hardly then go on to write the *Silver* and the *Brazen Ages* which tell Hercules' story anew. Hence for the contents of the second and third to be dismissed in this way, there must be a strong presumption that these plays precede the poem.[10]

Studies such as those of Tatlock and Holaday[11] had broadly supported the identification of *1&2 Hercules* with the *Silver* and *Bronze Ages,* but it was an essay by Ernest Schanzer that seems finally to have settled the modern consensus revoking it.[12] Schanzer puts forward two main arguments: that any Hercules play would have had the same properties as those in the Inventory, and that *1&2 Hercules* were not plays that Heywood had <u>written</u> but ones which he himself had *seen* earlier, long before he sat down to the write his *Ages* plays, and he cites Heywood's *Apology for Actors,* 1612 :

> To see as I have seene, Hercules, in his owne shape, hunting the boare, knocking downe the bull, taming the hart, fighting with Hydra, murdering Geryon, slaughtering Diomed, wounding the Stymphalides, killing the Centaurs, pashing the lion, squeezing the dragon, dragging Cerberus in chaynes, and lastly, on his high pyramides writing *Nil ultra,* Oh, these were sights to make an Alexander! (B4R).[13]

Schanzer's arguments, however, cancel each other out: if he is right in presuming a labor-rich *1&2 Hercules,* then the Inventory could be expected to have contained supporting properties for all of the labors and not just those coincidentally needed in the *Silver* and *Brazen Ages.* One would have expected to have found properties answering to the other labours e.g., the Hydra (the many-headed monster), Geryon (a monster with three bodies and three heads), Diomed (a tyrant who fed his horses human flesh and was punished by Hercules with being fed to his horses), and Stymphalides (carnivorous birds sometimes confused with Harpies). Heywood, of course, had merely chosen the easiest to represent.

It is not clear to what Heywood could be referring when he says he has "seen" the labors. The only other surviving contemporary dramatic material on Hercules appears to be translations of Seneca, his *Hercules Furens* by Jasper Heywood, 1561, reprinted in 1581 in *Ten Tragedies,* together with the "pseudo-Senecan" *Hercules Oetaeus* translated by John Studley from which Queen Elizabeth also translated a Chorus.[14] *Furens* deals with the hero's return from the Underworld, his being sent mad on vengeful Juno's orders, and subsequent slaying of his children. *Oetaeus* concerns the events leading up to Hercules death. In the latter play Hercules does refer to his labors, now all passed; so neither play stages them, nor is there any evidence that the Elizabethan translations were ever performed; Jasper Heywood making it clear that *Furens* was "for the profit of young schollers." However there is no reason to assume the records are complete; Schanzer himself mentions two earlier references to Hercules being performed onstage: Sidney's description in *Arcadia* (1590) of Dametas "leaning his hands vpon his bil, & his chin vpon his hands, with the voice of one that plaieth Hercules in a play," and a declaration of a player in Greene's *Groatsworth of Wit* (1592), "The twelue labours of Hercules haue I terribly thundred on the stage," which is a reminder that description, perhaps with a tableau, was precisely how Heywood himself staged what appears on the face of it to be impossible scenes that his narrative could not avoid. Thus in *The Brazen Age* where one might have thought Jason's exploits with the bulls ploughing and the armed men springing from the dragon's teeth defied representation, Heywood, within his own terms, has a very steady hand and always finds a solution that will appeal to his audience's imagination:

Two fiery Buls are discouered, the Fleece hanging ouer them, and the Dragon sleeping beneath them : Medea *with strange fiery-workes, hangs aboue in the Aire in the strange habite of a Coniuresse.*

G3[15]

Medea then proceeds to tell how Jason tamed the bulls and killed the dragon. Hence Schanzer's standard of ocular proof may be too literal, and either the *Oeteus* or Greene's "thundering" would have enabled Heywood to say he had "seen" the labors. In any event, the context of this quotation from the *Apol-*

ogy makes it clear that Heywood's focus is on the capacity of the stage to represent heroic deeds which will strike emulation in the hearts of modern-day princes. Indeed, Hercules has been mentioned several times already in the book, so it would be natural to enumerate his labors here whether or not Heywood had literally beheld imitations of all of them.

Perhaps the most compelling argument for the *Ages* plays originating at the Rose is the more general one of ethos. The Red Bull in the early seventeenth century had battles and noise aplenty, but special effects and pasteboard monsters, on the other hand, the staple of the Rose of the 1590s, were now a waning taste in any of the theaters.[16] Most especially it is the evident association of *1 Hercules* at its first performance on May 7, 1595 at the Rose with the only known installation of flying equipment, Henslowe's "*throne In the heuenes*" during Lent of that year, which makes further attention to the auspices of *The Silver Age* a matter of considerable interest.

Evidence of Flying Equipment

Where there's a canopy, so most popular academic studies suppose, there must be a winch; its absence offends a sense of the Globe as cosmos; we know there was a trap for evil to come out (although Hell's Mouth was not infrequently "discovered"), and heavens therefore are needed to complement it. Alberti's commentary on Vitruvius, on the other hand, recommends the use of a temporary "Cieling to the Theatre, both to keep off the Weather, and to retain the Voice," and it is likely that the canopy or "shadow" built by the Elizabethans over amphitheater stages had a similar dual function,[17] rather than necessarily involving flying. While the Hope contract in 1613–14, after the building of the Second Globe, calls for "Heavens," that for the Fortune in 1600 refers only to "a shadowe or cover over the saide Stadge."

There still remains a widespread predisposition, inherited from Victorian critics anxious to ameliorate the emphasis De Witt's sketch placed on a bare stage, to interpret every scrap of information that might enrich the visual impact of Elizabethan theater often well behind the limits of probability; hence the amount of attention given to items among Henslowe's properties that might indicate scenic units[18] together with the enduring popularity of C.Walter Hodges's projecting booth,[19] chosen to illustrate an entire generation of New Mermaid editions. Thus it is with flying. Peter Thomson tells his readers that the Swan's stage pillars were "there to satisfy the demands of a theatre more technically advanced than James Burbage could have anticipated in 1576."[20] "The canopy they support," he claims, "was roomy enough to accommodate a throne and any actor who was required to 'fly' down to the platform." John Ronayne, in anticipation of the Bankside replica project, scours medieval and Renaissance handbooks for information on windlasses, counterweights, brakes, crank handles, and much more in preparation for "Reconstructing the flying effect at the Globe."[21] "In most playhouses," says Andrew Gurr, "set on top of the heavens or cover was a 'hut' or huts, within which stage hands operated the machinery for 'flights,' windlass driven descents from the heavens."[22] John Astington concludes, "The *deus ex machina* was popular enough and the essential machinery that drove it cheap enough for it to have been standard equipment in any permanent playhouse";[23] bringing, according to Hodges, "a constant pleasure to Elizabethan audiences."[24]. These critics give little weight to T. J. King's exhaustive analysis of plays first performed between 1599 and 1642, which describes the evidence for flying as "meagre," and finds that in the entirety of the Elizabethan canon "only five plays require actors, or large properties, or both, to ascend or to descend from the acting area above; none of these texts make explicit references to stage machinery";[25] nor are they persuaded by Glynn Wickham's examination of all the documents before 1587, which fails to supply a single reference to flying machinery.[26] Instead, such critics make it an act of faith: "its use," says Hodges, "has to be imagined by little more than commonsense interpretation"; whilst Michael Hattaway suggests 'it was probably used sparingly—on the ground that anything spectacular overdone soon becomes tiresome even to an unsophisticated audience."[27]

To be fair to these critics, the Elizabethan amphitheater as a phenomenon is entirely surrounded by other traditions in which flying is relatively commonplace, in street pageants and mystery plays, in churches, in indoor drama, in the burgeoning court theaters of France and Italy, and, perhaps, in academic drama and in professional drama at the English court.[28] and for some critics a crossover to the public stage is irresistible. "As far as theatre owners and actors were able," says Astington, "they would want to share the spectacular tradition of English civic, academic, and royal entertainments." Three factors, however, may have prevented this. The first is cost (which Astington is determined to minimize), but in all other theater traditions spectacle could be financed by public levy channelled through the privileged in one form or another. Hence the highly competitive professional companies, denied such income, put their energies into developing a form of theater-practice that focused on the performers themselves, often gorgeously dressed, and their capacity to exploit the imaginations of their audiences in daily-varying, briefly prepared,[29] fast-moving dramas careless of locale and largely indifferent to mechanical means–though, as we shall see, not entirely so. The third factor, too often forgotten, is theater configuration. "It is not too difficult," remarks W. F. Rothwell, "to rig up pulleys . . ."[30] Perhaps so, in an indoor context, but the evidence suggests that in outdoor theaters flying was an altogether more hazardous operation.

Wickham terminates his negative survey abruptly in 1587, the year in which the Rose was built and the play *Alphonsus, King of Aragon* thought to have been written. Two of its stage directions are widely interpreted as establishing the existence of flying machinery in the canopies of London amphitheatres by this date: in the Prologue:

> *After you haue sounded thrice, let* Venus *be let downe from the top of the Stage* . . .[31]

and in its Epilogue:

> Exit Venus*: Or, if you can conveniently, let a chaire come downe from the top of the Stage and draw her vp.*

After 1587, according to Hodges, flying gear "had quickly been fitted up in every theatre that could take one."[32] The auspices of *Alphonsus,* however, are nearly as complicated as those of *The Silver Age.* Although there is little doubt that Robert Greene, who died in 1592, is the author, other than this there is little indication of when it was written or where it was performed. Strange's or the Queen's Men may have first performed it and since they were then using not only the Theater and the Curtain, but also the Bel Savage Inn, its original performance may not have been out of doors.[33] Furthermore its crucial place in the conventional history of flying has led scholars to skate over the uncertainties of its relationship to the Rose; for the title does not occur in Henslowe's *Diary,* but is instead only assumed to be *mahomett,* played there eight times between August 14, 1594 and February 5, 1595. The identification with this play is based entirely on the fact that Mahomet, in a minor incident in the play, speaks out of a brazen head and that the Admiral's inventories of 1598 list an "owld Mahemetes head." A brazen head, however, is also required in *Friar Bacon and Friar Bungay,* played at the Rose at the same time, which makes the association at best a slender one. Finally, the references to flying in *Alphonsus* occur in what are essentially appendages unrelated to the story and peopled by characters—Venus and nine Muses— none of whom appear anywhere else in the drama, and could certainly have been added or dispensed with in performance at any time up to the play's publication in 1599.

The author's hesitation, *"if you can conveniently"* relates to raising a performer, seemingly perfectly confident that Venus can be lowered, and this may well give some indication of the particular mechanics anticipated. On both occasions the author uses the phrase *"from the top of the Stage."* This is a term rarely used in Elizabethan theater; Dessen and Thomson give only three other examples from the entire canon 1590–1642.[34] In the first, in *1 Henry VI* III.ii.25, Pucell, after having breached the walls at Rouen, enters *"on the top, thrusting out a torch burning* " and is described by other characters as "*in yonder turret*"; then later in the scene she appears "*on the walls*" with the French generals, which perhaps, Dessen and Thomson suggest, "differentiates the two locations." In *A Double Marriage,* a *"Boy a top"* on a supposed ship's mast cries "a Sail. A Sail," and a similar scene takes place in *Fortune by Land and Sea* (though without the term itself being used). These examples seem to indicate the use of a second gallery above the stage.

Its existence, however, as one might expect, is widely contested. Richard Hosley makes no provision for it in his reconstruction of the Swan,[35] nor does it appear in Hodges's more recent sketches (except of *1 Henry VI,* presumably intended to be at the Rose);[36] nor is it to be found in the present Bankside replica of the Globe. John Cranford Adams, however, makes a strong case for the second gallery as part of the stage facade, pointing out that it existed anyway and that raising the canopy to the roof level improved the sightlines for those on the upper gallery of the auditorium[37] (a point well-demonstrated by the replica which presently leaves the spectators at the sides not only with a restricted view but also, being above the level of the canopy and looking down upon its roof, with a sense of not actually being in the theater but of only looking into it).

John Orrell suggests "The few descents, or possible descents, in early plays could well have been managed with a simple hoist from the highest part of the tiring house: none makes mention of a Heavens trap . . ."[38] Such a "lift" is perhaps assumed in another play with which Greene was associated, *A Looking Glass for London and England:* "*Enters brought by an* Angell Oseas *the Prophet, and set downe ouer the Stage in a Throne.*"[39] It might well serve when a basket containing an unwelcome suitor is suspended halfway between the galleries in *Englishman for My Money,* 1598. As observed above in *The Brazen Age,* "Medea . . . *hangs aboue in the Aire,*" presumably over a discovered tableau of beasts. Later, in the seventeenth century, Inigo Jones made great use of suspension gear guided up and down by slots or grooves in wooden beams, even by this means transporting Henrietta Maria and her ladies when she was in an advance state of pregnancy.[40] It is not suggested that anything as sophisticated as this was available c.1592, but the same opportunities for guiding, steadying, and servicing objects being raised and lowered close to the facade front would obtain.

The excavation of the Rose in 1989 revealed that when first built in 1587 it had no stage posts, and hence presumably no "heavens."[41] In 1592 it was extensively rebuilt and enlarged, this time with stage posts, and in 1595 Henslowe spent a total of £108.9 for "Repracyones" during Lent on improving the Rose, (a very considerable sum, given that building the entire Fortune in 1600 cost only £440) and including "mackinge the throne In the heuenes," before reopening with Heywood's "ne" play *"the firste pte of herculous."*[42]

Thus we have the conjunction on May 7, 1595 of the one piece of evidence for flying equipment (if that is what is meant by "the throne In the heuenes"), and the one play that makes substantial use of it, if *1Hercules* is accepted to be an earlier version of *The Silver Age*. What now needs to be examined is how much use was actually made of the new equipment, given that it does not seem to have been replicated in any other outdoor theatre of the period.

Flying in *The Silver Age*

The first problem concerns the events surrounding the death of Semele, who has been persuaded by jealous Juno in disguise to demand that Jupiter appear to her in all his majesty. Juno with Iris are " *plac'd in a cloud aboue*" to observe the scene that follows:

Enter Semele, drawn out in her bed.

SEMELE: ... Descend, great Jove, in thy full majesty,
And crown my pleasures; here behold me spread,
To taste the sweets of thy immortal bed.

Thunder and lightning. Jupiter descends in his majesty, his thunderbolt burning.

JUPITER: Thus wrapp'd in storms and black tempestuous clouds,
Lightning, and showers, we sit upon the roofs
And trembling terraces of this high house,
That is not able to contain our power ...

SEMELE: What terror's this? Oh thou immortal, speak!
My eyes are for thy majesty too weak.
as he touches the bed, it fires, and all flies up.
Jupiter from thence takes an abortive infant.
JUPITER: Receive thy boon: now take thy free desire,
In thunder, tempest, smoke, and heavenly fire.
JUNO: Ha! ha! ha!
Fair Semele's consum'd; 'twas acted well.
Come; next we'll follow Hercules to hell.
Jupiter, taking up the infant, speaks as he ascends in his cloud. (K)[43]

One can only conjecture how this scene was staged, but, assuming Juno and Iris are watching from one of the galleries, it would seem to require two pieces of lifting gear, since if the newly installed winch in the heavens takes up the flaming bed (minus the actor), it hardly has time to return before Jupiter is required to ascend as well.

Earlier in this extract he had paused in his descent, "upon the roofs ... of this high house," which suggests he may well be a candidate for the "lift" discussed above, attached, or adjacent, to the facade front. This would also allow him to pause on his ascent to deliver his speech of fourteen lines before he exits.

There are therefore two "clouds" involved: one represented by a gallery, decorated or not, and the other by a movable "car" or lift for Jupiter, (though the dialogue earlier had suggested his normal mode of transport was an eagle [I2]).

The burning bed (lit with *aqua vitae*)[44] has to be taken seriously, since Juno earlier anticipates enjoying seeing "Th'adultress sprawl, the palace upward fly" (J3v).

Several other moments, hitherto assumed to be examples of flying, are more likely to have been uses of the gallery, as in the scene where Iris is sent up to the cloud to report on Hercules' slaughter of the Nemæan lion to the waiting Juno below (G-G2), and perhaps again when *Jupiter appears in all his glory vnder a Raine-bow* (a separate property listed in the Inventory) (F2).

A second major problem lies at the end of the play. After Hercules has captured Cerberus and routed Hell in order to rescue Proserpine, Jupiter intervenes to protect the infernal powers and effect a compromise. This concluded:

> *Exeunt three ways* Ceres, Theseus, Philoctetes; *and* Hercules *dragging* Cerberus *one way;* Pluto, *hell's judges, the Fates and Furies, down to hell:* Jupiter, *the gods and planets, ascend to heaven.* [L].

Given that the gods have descended to Hell to arbitrate, it is not altogether clear what the starting point is for these various journeys. Furthermore, Jupiter in his ascent has to be accompanied by Saturn, Juno, Mars, Phoebus, Venus, and Mercury. George Reynolds comments very sensibly: "Except for the end of the play . . . only two come down together and one goes up. This direction may mean only to state their final destination."[45] If so, it makes all other such directions in the play equally problematic—as to whether they refer to practical staging or what is supposed to happen within the narrative. In reality, what amounts to most of the entire company may simply have gone off through the two doors and the central aperture. Alternatively, the gods and planets who come to preside may stay on the first gallery, taking their places, "*as they are in height*" (M3v), and converting the theater to a two-tier Hell; they need only then retire from the gallery. But there is third possibility.

Noting that the infrequency of references to flying in Elizabethan drama scarcely justified the installation of special equipment, T. J. King suggests the possibility of an external staircase to the gallery, pointing to a stage direction in *The Knight of Malta*, a King's Men play c.1616: "*The Scaffold set out and* *the staires."*⁴⁶ He relates this to an item in Henslowe's Inventory: "i payer of stayers for Fayeton," generally glossed as a flight of stairs (*OED* 6b), and points out the convenience this would have for the King's descent from Flint Castle in *Richard II.* In fact it would meet a good many staging problems in venues where there is no other evidence of flying, as with the presiding planets in *Woman in the Moon* who each "*ascend*" to a throne, presumably placed on the gallery, at regular intervals. A portable flight of stairs would certainly be the easiest way of getting seven gods back onto the gallery.

It is important to recognize that there are no magic wands here. As Reynolds's comment suggests, whatever flights of fancy were in Heywood's mind as he wrote, and to be evoked in the imaginations of his spectators, he was an essentially practical dramatist and the means available limited, circumscribed more by time than expense, each play performed only once in the week's sequence, leaving little opportunity for preparation; hence the solutions, despite the rhetoric, would always have been simple ones.

Apart from the burning bed, the only other strong contender for actually using a winch above the canopy is "*Mercury flies from above*" (H). A minor character, and servant, he might well be played by a youth whose lighter weight would be easier to control, like the "Flying Boye" rewarded at Cecil's *Entertainment* of 1608 whose counterparts dominated the flying ballets of later Caroline masques.⁴⁷ If he wore a harness, he would of course have to detach himself from the rope before leaving the stage. Ronane reports on two methods of lowering a performer that would not require even this: "a lightweight saddle-and-stirrup frame made of iron' described by Sabbattini, 'that allowed a dancer to descend to the stage and begin his dance immediately."⁴⁸ "A similar effect," Ronane says, "could be achieved if the actor's foot rested in a loop at the end of a rope."

Significantly Mercury does not return the same way. Earlier, of course Greene had been much more hesitant about the return journey in *Alphonsus.* Nor is there evidence that *2 Hercules/The Brazen Age* made much use of flying performers: Medea hangs in the air over a tableau of beasts discovered within a stage façade aperture, presumably using the earlier lift; and at the end, after Hercules has immolated himself:

> *Iupiter aboue strikes him with a thunder-bolt, his body sinkes, and from the heauens discends a hand in a cloud, that from the place where Hercules was burnt, brings vp a starre, and fixeth it in the firmament.* (L3)

-all of which could be accomplished using the trap and properties, an empty car or perhaps one with a small boy. The only other record of the winch being used in the heavens takes place in *Dr Faustus:*

Musicke while the Throne descends.[49]

Marlowe attempts to provide a pretext for lowering an empty throne:

Good Angel: Hadst thou affected sweet divinitie,
                      . . . *Faustus* behold,
    In what resplendent glory thou hadst set
    In yonder throne . . .

- but it still remains an odd moment in the play, and an indication perhaps of the practical difficulties of flying. Most indicative of such problems, however, is not so much the evidence of flying in *The Silver Age* but of its absence where it might be expected. At the beginning of the play, Perseus arrives to help Bellerophon in his quest against the Chimæra. He has come with his brother and wife on the winged horse Pegasus—which, it would appear from the dialogue, we never see:

Enter Perseus, Andromeda, *and* Danaus.

Perseus: There stay, our swift and winged Pegasus,
And on the flowers of this fair meadow graze.

                                                                   (B3v)

- this presumably spoken through the door as he enters. At the end of the scene he promises Bellerophon a ride to Argos, but they appear to leave the stage again on foot. Subject matter not particularly relevant to the theme of the play but so obviously ripe to exploit the new equipment, one wonders at what point a decision was taken not to do so.

An isolated experiment?

One can only speculate on their reluctance to use the new equipment. Was it to do with outdoor conditions—wind and rain—the cold and damp, making everything slippery and foothold treacherous, or the inevitable tendency to swing? Astington and Ronane, for instance, take many of their winching parallels from mine shafts where, unpleasant though they were, the walls would enable some steadying;[50] while the crane-cum-hoist with which Hodges equips his Second Globe, involving the performer being swung out on "a jib arm some fourteen or fifteen feet long" and then dropped, is dizzying just to contemplate.[51] Was it to do with the height of the drop? Estimates vary from around twenty-two feet, if the heavens were only at the height of the second gallery floor, but perhaps another nine or so if at its ceiling. And then there was the further height of the winch within the canopy/hut.

The conventional theater winch has a hinged piece of metal by way of a brake which inserts itself into a cog wheel with teeth cut at an angle so that it is brushed aside when the hoist rises but automatically locks into the wheel when the hoist comes to rest, so that for lowering it has to be held aside. Raising nowadays is therefore safer than lowering, but the Elizabethans seemed to have been happier with descents, generally leaving their characters to make their own way offstage rather than re-ascending (it is of course a theater of grand entrances and quieter exits). This suggests, however, that they did not have a braking system, and that the issue was either to do with aesthetics—ascents took too long—or with the weights and distances involved. Counterweights were known and used in medieval and Italian theater, and sometimes quite compact, but it is doubtful if they existed in the cramped circumstances of the Rose superstructure. Using a windlass, according to Ronane, depends entirely on the operators, and it would have been a task involving both strength and some finesse, and a lot of trust on the part of the performers. Jonson gibes at the "creaking throne,"[52] and there is plenty of evidence that use of the hoist was often accompanied by music perhaps to cover this.

It would be wrong to assume it was a question of courage: Elizabethan plays regularly have what we would take to be circus feats built into them; as for instance the Lord Admiral's man in 1587, (perhaps playing the Governor of Babylon hanging from the walls in *2 Tamburlaine*), who only just escaped being shot by the missile that killed the spectators,[53] or the simulation of the *strappado* and being hanged in *'A Larum for London*[54] both performed by the same person, as a merchant's factor, probably one of that band of fearless young players in their late teens and early twenties, like Mercury, who took on among their many tasks falling from buildings, setting themselves on fire, with female self-immolation a speciality: Venus, Semele, Olympia, and Dido;[55] not to mention being crushed by rocks or dragged by the hair,[56] and many other tricks and dangerous sleights of hand.[57]. The problems of flying must surely have been logistical.

Whatever the reasons, they created a state of affairs in which convincing evidence of flying before 1613 in the outdoor theatres, apart from the *Ages* plays and Henslowe's throne in the heavens, is more or less non-existent. It may well be that the problems at the Rose discouraged the Chamberlain's Men from installing a throne at the Globe; for the first thirty-three of Shakespeare's plays make no mention of flying at all. Even *Cymbeline,* written after the King's Men took repossession of the indoor theater of Blackfriars, R. B. Graves suggests, may not have acquired its flying eagle until performed at Court.[58]. It is fairly evident from Iris's remark in *The Tempest,*' 'I know her by her gait," in the Folio, that Juno originally walked on; "*descends*" being, like the reference to the Mayor in *3 Henry VI* IV.vii.29, an indication of a descent from the balcony by stairs behind the stage and not proof of flying.

It is not even clear that the First Globe had a canopy. Several critics point to Hamlet's reference to "this most excellent Canopie the ayre; looke you, this braue orehanging firmament, this majesticall roofe fretted with golden fire," (Q2 F2) as evidence that one had newly been installed,[59] but it could be argued to the contrary that it is God's magnificent creation which "delights not" Hamlet, and while he dismisses it in terms of the gaudy, self-assertion of a playhouse "shadow," too close a similarity between his evocation and the immediate playhouse roof could only distract from the point he is making, metadrama sinking into mere confusion.

Richard Hosley offers several possibilities for flying at the Globe,[60] but as both Gabriel Egan and John Orrell point out, none of them seems likely;[61]: simulations of *strappado* and of hanging both require a fixed point on the stage facade with a hook from which the length of rope for the harness can be accurately measured (otherwise the actor is likely to suffer the torments for real); while the old chestnut about the "lifeless" body of Antony needing mechanical assistance to get him into the Monument ignores the probability that Burbage would have surreptitiously aided his own ascent.

In proposing flying equipment at the Swan, Hattaway offers Richard Venner's cod prospectus for *England's Joy* in 1602 which promised Queen Elizabeth "taken up into heaven, when presently appears a throne of blessed souls . . .,"[62] but it also promised performing gentlewomen and much else, and of course, famously was a money-making scam, and not a performance at all. The only reference to a descent at the Fortune is that in *The Whore of Babylon:* "*Time descending,*"[63] but the context makes clear this could only mean either from the gallery or from a throne, and certainly not flying down from heaven, or for that matter going down into a trap. The contract for the Hope demands that a "[h]eavans all over the saide stage" is to be achieved without permanent pillars,[64] which makes flying machinery very unlikely. This leaves only the Red Bull, and in his monograph on that theatre, a model for much that went after, and with the scrupulousness of genuine scholarship, Reynolds acknowledges the weakness of his position in respect of flying equipment:

> The most obvious fact about the use of machinery for ascending and descending . . . is that it occurs in so few plays, even if one includes the doubtful cases. The certain cases at the Red Bull are all in the *Ages*.[65]

Even here, however, flying only occurs in the first three *Ages* plays; it is of a circumspect nature in *The Brazen Age* (as discussed above); in the prefatory material, only that of *The Golden Age* indicates performance at the Red Bull, but the present text appears to have two endings—one terminating with the reconciliation of Jupiter and Ganymede, then a puff for the plays that would eventually succeed it, and then a second ending with Jupiter's deification, which latter requires flying but seems to have been tacked on later; hence it could have been performed on its own without such equipment.[66] As to *The Silver Age,* there is only one seventeenth-century record of performance, that in the *Revels Accounts* of January 12 and 13, 1612:

> By the Queens players and the Kings Men. The Sunday following [Twelfth Night] at grinwidg before the Queen and the Prince was playd the Silver Aiedg: and ye next night following Lucrecia.[67]

This, of course, was an indoor performance, the estranged Queen Anna[68] now holding a separate Court at Greenwich, where facilities could presumably be constructed for flying.[69] Chambers infers it was a joint-company performance and not simply a transfer from the Red Bull, (for John Heminges was the payee), hence perhaps a recognition of the difficult staging demands that it makes, and a special Christmas treat.

Endpiece

This article began with a caveat on the speculative nature of its proposals: a supposition built upon a theory based upon surmise. There is a moment in *Shakespeare in Love* when the engaging if unlikely Henslowe of Geoffrey Rush set amid an evocative little playhouse and its surroundings makes one feel there may be, somehow, direct truth figured here; art might succeed where scholarship has failed . . . But then Ben Affleck appears as Edward Alleyn (Edward *Alleyn?*), the vision fades, the portals close, the light gleams an instant, and it is night once more.

Notes

1. F. G. Fleay, *Biographical Chronicle of English Drama; 1559–1642,* London, 1891,1:283–84; R. A. Foakes, *Henslowe's Diary,* 2nd ed. (Cambridge: Cambridge University Press, 2002), 28–29.

2. Ernest Rhodes, *Henslowe's Rose: The Stage and Staging* (Lexington: University Press of Kentucky, 1976), 201–7.

3. Foakes, *Henslowe's Diary,* 93.

4. Andrew Gurr, *Shakespeare's Opposites: The Admiral's Men 1594–1625* (Cambridge: Cambridge University Press, 2009), 36.

5. Preface to Thomas Heywood, *The English Traveler,* 1633.

6. Foakes, *Henslowe's Diary,* 102, 104, 207–8, 216–17, 219–20; John Webster, "To the Reader," *The White Divel,* 1612.

7. "To the Stage" printed with Thomas Heywood, *The Royal King and the Loyal Subject,* 1637.

8. Arthur M. Clark, *Thomas Heywood, Playwright and Miscellanist* (Oxford: Oxford University Press, 1931), 62–63.

9. Thomas Heywood, *Troia Britannica,* 1609.

10. I suggest that Heywood wrote the poem after the first three plays, and then in the light of the first five cantos (i.e., a third of the poem) very substantially revised the relatively unsuccessful *seleo and olempo* in order to produce the present *Golden Age.* He may have written *Troy* (with its horse), and used its material in the poem, but it is most likely *1&2 Iron Age* in their present form are written after the poem. Possibly Heywood, finding its material too much for one play and not enough for another, completed *Part Two* with material on the Orestes story from another source.

11. John S. P. Tatlock, XXII. "The Siege of Troy in Elizabethan Literature, especially in Shakespeare and Heywood," *PMLA,* 1915, 30, 3, New Series Xxiii, 4, 673–770; Allan Holaday, "Heywood's *Troia Britannica* and the *Ages,*" *JEGP* 14 (1946).

12. Ernest Schanzer, "Heywood's *Ages* and Shakespeare," *Review of English Studies,* n.s.11 (1961): 18–28.

13. Thomas Heywood, *Apology for Actors,* 1612.

14. Jasper Heywood, 1561, reprinted in 1581 in *Ten Tragedies.*

15. Thomas Heywood, *The Brazen Age,* 1613. For a discussion of other difficult scenes to stage see Alan C. Dessen, *Elizabethan Stage Conventions and Modern Interpreters* (Cambridge: Cambridge University Press, 1984) 1–18.

16. One significant exception is the *Birth of Merlin,* with its battling dragons and spirit visions, but a comparison with Rowley's other extant play *A Shoemaker a Gentleman* suggests he may have written only the subplot to *Merlin* in revising another lost Rose play, *Uther Pendragon.*

17. John Orrell, *The Human Stage, English theatre design, 1567–1640* (Cambridge: Cambridge University Press, 1988), 61.

18. Jonathan Gill Harris and Natasha Korda, eds., *Staged Properties in Early Modern English Drama* (2002; repr. Cambridge: Cambridge University Press, 2006), 2, 24–25, 28–29.

19. C. Walter Hodges, *The Globe Restored* (London: E. Benn, 1953), 59, and C. Walter Hodges, *Enter the Whole Army: A Pictorial Study of Shakespeare's Staging* (Cambridge: Cambridge University Press,1999), 1944, 136, illustrated 43, 45, 60, 63, 67, 80, 86, 93, 106, 117, 134, 155, 160, 162–63.

20. Peter Thompson, *Shakespeare's Theatre,* 2d ed. (London: Routledge, 1983), 44.

21. John Ronayne, "Decorative and Mechanical Effects Relevant to the Theatre of Shakespeare," in *The Third Globe,* ed. C. Walter Hodges, S. Schoenbaum, and L. Leone (Detroit, MI: Wayne State University Press, 1981), 207–17.

22. Andrew Gurr, *The Shakespearean Stage 1574–1642,* 4th ed. (Cambridge: Cambridge University Press, 2009), 151.

23. John H. Astington, "Descent Machinery in the Playhouses," *Medieval and Renaissance Drama in England* 2 (1985): 130.

24. Hodges, *Enter the Whole Army,*124.

25. T. J. King, *Shakespearean Staging, 1599–1642* (Cambridge, MA: Harvard University Press, 1971), 148.

26. Glynne Wickham, "Heavens, Machinery, and Pillars in the Theatre and Other

Early Playhouses" in *The First Public Playhouse: The Theatre in Shoreditch 1576–1598,* ed. Herbert Berry (Montreal: McGill-Queen's University Press, 1979), 1–15.

27. Michael Hattaway, *Elizabethan Popular Theatre* (London: Routledge & Kegan Paul, 1982), 32–33.

28. Lilly Campbell, *Scenes and Machines on the English Stage during the Renaissance* (1923; repr. New York: Barnes & Noble, 1960), 59–60, 99–100; R. B. Graves, *Lighting the Shakespearean Stage, 1567–1642* (Carbondale: Southern Illinois University Press, 1999), 40–42; Gordon Kipling, "Richard II's 'Sumptuous Pageants' and the Idea of the Civic Triumph," in *Pageantry in the Shakespearean Theater,* ed. David M. Bergeron (Athens: University of Georgia Press,1985), 86.

29. Tiffany Stern, *Rehearsal from Shakespeare to Sheridan* (Oxford: Oxford University Press, 2000), 52ff, concludes that most productions only had one group rehearsal, and some did not even get that.

30. W. F. Rothwell, "Was there a Typical Elizabethan Stage?", *Shakespeare Survey 12* (Cambridge: Cambridge University Press, 1959), 19.

31. R. G., *The Comicall Historie of Alphonsus King of Aragon,* 1599.

32. Hodges, *Enter the Whole Army,* 126

33. Graves, *Lighting the Shakespearean Stage,* 44.

34. Alan C. Dessen and Leslie Thomson, *A Dictionary of Stage Directions in English Drama 1590–1642* (Cambridge: Cambridge University Press, 1999), 233. The third example is Prospero in *The Tempest.*

35. Richard Hosley, "The Playhouses," in *The Revels History of Drama in English, Vol. III, 1576–1613,* ed. J. Leeds Barroll et al. (London: Methuen, 1975), 136–74.

36. Hodges, *Enter the Whole Army,* 22

37. John Cranford Adams, *The Globe Playhouse: Its Design and Equipment,* 2d ed. (London: Constable, 1961), 298–308.

38. John Orrell, *The Human Stage: English Theatre Design, 1557–1640* (Cambridge: Cambridge: Cambridge University Press, 1988), 65.

39. Thomas Lodge and Robert Green, *A Looking Glass for London and England,* 1594.

40. *Salmacida Spolia,* 1641, in Stephen Orgel and Roy Strong, *Inigo Jones: The Theatre of the Stuart Court* (Berkeley: University of California Press, 1973) 2:730–62. Although the authors talk of a fly gallery, this would seem to have been precluded by the final design which is powered by capstans under the stage.

41. Christine Eccles, *The Rose Theatre* (New York: Routledge, 1990).

42. Foakes, *Henslowe's Diary,* 7 and 28.

43. Thomas Heywood, *The Silver Age,* 1613.

44. Philip Butterworth, *Theatre of Fire: Special Effects in Early English and Scottish Theatre* (London: Society for Theatre Research, 1998), 60–61.

45. G. F. Reynolds, *The Staging of Elizabethan Plays at the Red Bull Theater, 1605–25,* (New York: Modern Language Association of America, 1940), 107.

46. King, *Shakespearean Staging,* 36.

47. "The masquers dance their main dance, which done, and the Queen seated under the state by his majesty . . . Jove, sitting on an eagle, is seen hovering in the air with a glory behind him. And at that instant Cupid from another part of the heaven

comes flying forth, and having passed the scene, turns soaring about like a bird . . ." (*Tempe Restored,* 1632, in Orgel and Strong, *Inigo Jones,* 2:482).

48. Ronane, "Decorative and Mechanical Effects," 216.

49. Christopher Marlowe, *The tragicall History of Dr Faustus,* 1616.

50. Ronane, "Decorative and Mechanical Effects", 214; John H. Astington,"Descent Machinery in the Playhouses," 119–33, and Astington, "Counterweights in Elizabethan Stage Machinery," *Theatre Notebook* 41 (1987): 18–24. Despite the latter's caution, counterweights had long been used in theatrical productions on the Continent, as at Mons in 1501 when the Devil carried Christ to the pinnacle of the Temple "in a trice . . . by means of a counterweight"; see John Wesley Harris, *Medieval Theatre in Context* (London: Routledge, 1992), 141.

51. C. Walter Hodges, *Shakespeare's Second Globe* (Oxford: Oxford University Press, 1973), 84–88.

52. Ben Jonson, Prologue to *Euery Man in His Humour,* in *The Works of Beniamin Jonson,* 1616.

53. *Letters of Sir Philip Gawdy,* Egerton 2804, F35.

54. *Alarum for London, or The Siedge of Antwerpe,* 1602, ll.1007 and 1291.

55. Venus in *The Cobbler's Prophecy,* Semele in *The Silver Age,* Olympia in *2 Tamburlaine,* and the heroine in *Dido and Aeneas.*

56. Omphale in *The Brazen Age* is crushed by rocks, and the Empress in *Alphonsus Emperor of Germany* dragged by the hair (along with many others).

57. Philip Butterworth, *Magic on the Early English Stage* (Cambridge: Cambridge: Cambridge University Press, 2005), 144–45, 164–75.

58. R. B. Graves, *Lighting the Shakespearean Stage,* 49.

59. David Bevington, *Action is Eloquence: Shakespeare's Language of Gesture* (Cambridge, MA: Harvard University Press, 1984), 15; Graves, *Lighting the Shakespearean Stage,* 97.

60. Barroll et al., ed., *Revels History of Drama* III, 192.

61. Orrell, *Human Stage,* 269–70; Gabriel Egan, "Reconstruction of the Globe: a Retrospective," Internet, 1999, 5.

62. Hattaway, *Elizabethan Popular Theatre,*13

63. Dessen and Thomson, *Dictionary of Stage Directions,* 67.

64. E. K.Chambers, *Elizabethan Stage* (1923; repr. Oxford: Oxford University Press, 1974) 2:466–48.

65. Reynolds, *Staging of Elizabethan Plays at the Red Bull,* 106.

66. Their dedicatory matter, however, is confusing in respect of what can be gleaned of their original auspices. The "Epistle to the Reader" in *Golden Age* describes it as "the eldest brother of three Ages" and "accidentally [*sic*] published, but that to *Silver* suggests that in the meantime Heywood had decided the final two plays were to be linked to the other three, (rather than, perhaps, newly written): "Wee begunne with *Gold,* follow with *Siluer,* proceede with *Brasse,* and purpose by God's grace, to end with *Iron."* *1&2 Iron Age* were not published until 1632, and their epistle links them back to the earlier three, but it remains unclear when Heywood says, "these were the playes often (and not with the least applause), Publickely Acted by two Companies, vppon one Stage at once, and haue at sundry times thronged three seuerall Theaters, with numerous and mighty Auditories," as to whether he is refer-

ring merely to these two plays or to all five, especially when in the same sentence he adds, "if the grace they had then in the Actings, take not away the expected luster, hoped for in the Reading, I shall then hold thee well pleased," which obviously refers only to the two final plays.

67. Chambers, *Elizabethan Stage,* 4: 178.

68. Claire McManus, *Women on the Renaissance Stage* (Manchester: Manchester University Press, 2002), 181.

69. The Disguising Theatre at Greenwich, set up by Henry VIII in 1527, appears to have been constructed of ships masts covered with canvas, with a double layer for the roof, the inner one painted with heavens by Holbein. Despite their makeshift construction, such theaters were robust and long-lasting (see Orrell, *Human Stage,* 62). Of the two other productions recorded at Greenwich, "*Cupide cometh downe from heauen,*" in *Gismund of Salerne* in c.1566 may have needed flying facilities, but *Cupid's Banishment,* 1617, did not.

New Conversations on *Othello*

Othello's "Malignant Turk" and George Manwaring's "*A True Discourse*": The Cultural Politics of a Textual Derivation

Imtiaz Habib

I

"*OTHELLO*," declares a modern study, "remains a textual mystery."[1] Although the essay is a useful review of existing scholarly knowledge on the complicated publication history of the play, its characterization of the play as "a textual mystery" resonates with the origins of a particular allusion in it that has remained unacknowledged and ignored. At the end of *Othello,* just before killing himself in remorseful self-punishment for his Iago-induced murder of his wife, to affirm his continuing civic uprightness and integrity as an officer of the Venetian government the title character alludes to an incident in his past that happened in Aleppo:

> And say besides, that in Aleppo once,
> Where a malignant and a turbanned Turk
> Beat a Venetian and traduced the state,
> I took by th' throat the circumcised dog
> And smote him—thus!   *He stabs himself.*
>
> (5.2.350–54)[2]

The source of this allusion has remained unremarked in the play's critical exegeses, and has been regarded silently as an instance of Shakespeare's literary imaginativeness in keeping with the rest of the geographic references (to Arabia and Judea or India) in the lines preceding the passage in the same speech.[3] Yet, just a few years before the staging of the play, there may have circulated in some circles in London a manuscript account of an Englishman's recent journey to Aleppo with the following passage in it:

> At the sixth days end, we came safe to Aleppo, where we were kindly received by one Mr. Colthurst then being consul for the English merchants, and also of the merchants themselves who lodged us in their houses and furnished us with such things as we did want but the Turks did use us somewhat ill for we could not walk

in the streets but they would buffet us and use us very vildly; except we had a Janisary with us; for it is the fashion there that all strangers hath commonly a Janisary in ther house with them for ther safety; one day it was my hap to walk alon in the streets, where to my hard fortune I met with a Turk, a gallant man he seemed to be by his habit, and saluting me in this manner took me fast by one of the ears with his hand, and so did lead me up and down the streets, and if I did chance to look sour upon him, he would give me such a ring that I did think verily, he would have pulled of my ear, and this he continued with me for the space of one hour, with much company following me, some throwing stones at me, and some spitting on me, so at the last he let me go, and because I would not laugh at my departure from him he gave me such a blow with a staff that did strike me to the ground; So returning home to the Consul house the Consul's Janisary seeing me all bloody asked me how I came hurt I told him the manner of it: he presently in a rage did take his staff in his hand, and bade me go with him and shew him the Turk that had used me so; Within a small time we found him sitting with his father and other gentlemen, so I did shew the Janisary which was he; who ran fiercely to him, and threw him on his back giving him twenty blows on his legs and his feet, so that he was not able to go or stand; he was clothed in a cloth of gold undercoat and a crimson velvet gown but his gay clothes could not save him from the fierceness of the Janisary's fury; and in this sort our men were served diverse times.[4]

The account in which the passage appears was written by George Manwaring, a gentleman in the retinue of the notorious Elizabethan aristocratic adventurer, Sir Anthony Sherley, in what is the most well-known of the latter's many dubious political capers: his journey with his brother Robert to Shah Abbas's Persia in 1599 supposedly on the encouragement of the Earl of Essex to forge an Elizabethan alliance with Shah Abbas against Ottoman Turkey.[5] The lives and careers of the Sherley brothers are too well known in historical scholarship to require any further enumeration here.[6] Only one fact needs to be repeated here and that is the extreme displeasure with which Anthony Sherley was regarded by Elizabeth at the time of his journey to Persia, stemming from allegations of Sherley's acceptance of foreign allegiance in the form of a knighthood from the French Henry IV in his earlier mission to France in 1591, allegations for which he was briefly incarcerated. This was a monarchic displeasure that was to last for the rest of Anthony Sherley's life, including with Elizabeth's successor, who while initially relenting also refused to let him return to England. Sherley's penurious death in Spain in the 1630s was the final consequence of the ignominy that surrounded his ill-fated adventuring life.[7] Of the four accounts of the Persian journey that were written by other members of Sherley's group, including that of Anthony Sherley himself,[8] Manwaring's account is by scholarly consensus the fullest and the most interesting. It is also the only account that contains the passage in question. What is curious is that the striking correspondence between the Othello passage and the substance of the incident described by Manwaring has totally escaped critical explanation, partly perhaps because the account did not appear in print until the nineteenth century, and that too, anonymously.[9]

The similarity between the incident described in this account, particularly from the sentence beginning "One day it was my hap to walk along the street" to "he gave me such a blow with a staff, that did strike me to the ground," and Othello's invocation of "a malignant and a turbanned Turk" "beat[ing] a Venetian" and "traduc[ing] the state," in Aleppo "once," is arresting enough to merit critical attention. If to traduce is among other things to " dishonour" according to Thomas Cooper's *Thesaurus Linguae Romanae et Britannicae* dictionary of 1584, or to "defame" according to Robert Cawdrey's *A Table Alphabetical* of 1604, or to "disgrace" according to Randle Cotgrave's *A Dictionary of the French and English Tongue* of 1611, there is a perfect fit in tone and meaning between the political insult (the "traduc[ing]" of the "state") that Othello recounts avenging and the personal and national humiliation that is implied by the speaker of the Manwaring passage ("in this sort our men were served diverse times").[10] Shakespeare himself uses the word "traduce" four other times in his writing in exactly this sense: "A strumpet's boldness, a divulged shame / Traduced by odious ballads: my maiden's name/ Sear'd otherwise;" (Helena, *All's Well That Ends Well* 2.1.781); "He is already / Traduced for levity; and 'tis said in Rome / That Photinus an eunuch and your maids/ Manage this war." (Enobarbus, *Antony and Cleopatra* 3.7.1948); "Rome must know / The value of her own: 'twere a concealment / Worse than a theft, no less than a traducement, / To hide your doings;" (Cominius, *Coriolanus* 1.9.787); "If I am / Traduced by ignorant tongues, which neither know / My faculties nor person, yet will be / The chronicles of my doing, . . ." (Cardinal Wolsey, *Henry VIII* 1.2.398). Among Shakespeare's colleagues, the word appears in their plays in this same sense a total of thirty-three times between 1607 and 1650.[11]

Othello's lines stand out in sharp contrast to the rest of his speech in terms of their spatial, temporal, and tonal character. In them the passage switches from a generalized poetic landscape that sweeps across the Indian Ocean with its fabled "pearl" divers, to Arabia with its mythic "medicinable" gum, suddenly to a particularly identified place, Aleppo. The abrupt shift from an imaginative landscape to a real geographic location is accompanied by a sharp narrowing of the fluid memorial time of his speech up to that moment to the precision of a specific day, the immediacy of the contraction imposed by a new imperative tone of "Set you down this," in itself another instantaneous substitution of the soft tonal supplication of his dialog's beginning: "Soft you, a word or two before you go." These textural disjunctions profile the distinctiveness of Othello's reference to the malignant Aleppine Turk, who also appears in Manwaring's text with the same specificity if not singularity.

Although the precise reason for the Turk's assault of Manwaring is not detailed, the rest of Manwaring's travel account as a whole, as well as other contemporary texts of this class, make it quite clear that the Turk's behavior is typical of the violence singled out for Christians by the Turks. If national identity in this historical moment is still based in part at least on religious affiliation as it was in the Middle Ages, and as it is at this moment particularly for the Turks (for whom all of Europe is simply the land of the Christians),[12] the Turk's battering of Manwaring in his text is a stateist rather than a local community gesture, precisely what is the nature of Othello's retaliatory violence against the Turk who has traduced the "state" of Venice that Othello has loyally served. The two Turk figures in Manwaring's text are reflected in their single counterpart in Othello's lines in a creative transformation that bears the traces of its operation, in the correspondences of the "malignant" Turk to the "traduc[ing]" civilian Turk in Manwaring and the neutral exoticism of the "turbanned" one to the janissary who punishes him. Furthermore, the particular identities of Manwaring's two Turks, as miscreant and as officer of the law, are fused in the next line in the similar actions of "beat[ing] a Venetian" and "traduc[ing] the state" for *both,* their plurality finally transformed into the single figure of the last line's "circumcised dog." As this essay will show, buried in these dynamics of the transformative operation are the cultural politics of the derivation of Shakespeare's lines from Manwaring.

II

The question of how Manwaring's account got to England, and more importantly, to Shakespeare, is a difficult but not impossible question to answer. All that Hans Sloane, in whose collection the manuscript of Manwaring's account turned up before permanently ending up in the British Museum, himself said about its origins, is that he got it in 1693 for one shilling.[13] Even who George Manwaring was, and how and when he got back to England, are uncertain. As one scholarly source on Anthony Sherley's Persian trip, Denison Ross, put it, after the Persian trip "he [George Manwaring] is never heard of again"[14] He may, however, have been from Edstaston in Shropshire, where according to Shropshire local historians, in 1561 resided the Manwarings, a younger branch of the Manwarings of Ightfield. Since the time of Henry VIII, when "T. Manwaring esq." purchased "two copyhold estates," the family's home was in Edstaston Hall in the manor of Wem, "a large timber house" which a "George Manwaring" inherited on April 29, 1591, together with "the estate above the Chettal Wood."[15] This may be a likely identification, since Anthony Sherley's wife, Frances Vernon, the Earl of Essex's cousin, was also from Shropshire, from the parish of Hodnet, which is only seven miles from Wem, and George Manwaring was her kinsman.[16] He may thus have been her appointee in her husband's staff.

The title of the anonymous *True Report* detailing Sir Anthony's government credentials, that was published illegally in 1600 / 1601 and quickly suppressed, mentions "two gentlemen" as its source for the information it presents. So, could the other gentleman have been Manwaring, i.e., could Manwaring also have returned to England with Parry in 1601? Given the dangerous government displeasure with which Anthony Sherley was held, and given the fact that the entire Persian enterprise was one of the many clandestine and often dangerous projects that the Earl of Essex frequently initiated throughout his public career to leverage influence with Elizabeth, and considering the extreme political sensitivity of the Sherley mission, namely to forge for England an expedient political alliance against the Turk with another Muslim country, it is very possible that George Manwaring and his account were both under an extreme pressure of silence minimally from Essex himself, when either he or the document itself reached England.

Alternatively, because Essex himself was in serious trouble with Elizabeth by 1600,[17] Manwaring may have been under a double fear of persecution from the authorities, for having been involved in Sherley's politically dangerous mission, and for being a client of Essex.[18] So, upon returning to England or while in transit to it, he may have decided to enter surreptitiously, after entering England may have laid low, and then may have disappeared into obscurity in Shropshire, taking his manuscript and his memories of the Persian trip with him. While this does not explain how and why the other accounts of the Persian trip, such as that of William Parry in 1601 could nevertheless find normal publication, it does offer a plausible scenario for the strange total invisibility of the Manwaring account in its own historical moment. As the fullest, i.e., the most unexpurgated of all the accounts, it may have been deemed by the trip's principal backer to be a document unfit for public release. Ultimately, the document's suppression may also have been a personal choice of its author, who may have had personal reasons to feel his own vulnerability in that dangerous moment far more than did Parry. There is a distinct possibility that for his personal security and to ensure the safekeeping of the document, he may have turned it over to members of the Sherley family, still resident at the family home in Wiston, Sussex, and elsewhere.[19]

All of the above could explain how the Manwaring account could have been secretly available in London in 1600 / 1601 despite not actually being published before 1820 in the *Retrospective Review* and in the anonymous *Three Brothers* in 1825, neither of which explain the history of the manuscript. That the document did reach England is suggested by the fact that it became a part of the state papers, since it is listed without comment in in the *Calendar of State Papers* for 1599.[20] The document may have been returned to the Sherley family afterwards, in the process of which Hans Sloane may have acquired a copy which then ended up as part of the Sloane collections in the British Museum. Two centuries later, the Sherley family may have released the Manwaring manuscript cautiously for anonymous publication, in the interests of publicizing the family's adventurous history. This is to say that enroute to his deliberate disappearance others may nonetheless have had private contact with Manwaring, and hence access to the contents of his manuscript.

The various ways by which hack writers and printers could acquire manuscripts in popular or surreptitious circulation has long been well known. News, in and of manuscripts, traveled invisibly in a variety of informal and instantaneous ways, so that the "simultaneous existence of regional, familial, and wider-ranging interest-based networks of exchange, all frequently overlapping with one another, meant that texts could travel with astonishing speed throughout the country."[21] One such way was through the congregation of carriers at busy inns, such as the Rochester Inn, the Bell Inn in Carter Lane, and the Bosome's Inn in Lawrence Lane. The Bosomes, which was the inn for carriers from Chester in Cheshire immediately adjoining Shropshire, is of particular interest here as it would have been the transit point for the Manwaring material, if not for Manwaring himself, enroute to Shropshire and Cheshire.[22] As Mark Shaaber put it, in an important detailed study of the procurement practices of Elizabethan media more than seven decades back, "There is no doubt that some news were taken out of the mouths of witnesses (possibly of others too, such as travelers, who were merely telling what they had heard) willing to narrate their experiences, but unwilling or unable to write them out." In direct confirmation as it were is the statement on the title page of Richard Hasleton's 1595 travel account that Shaaber cited, declaring *"Penned as he delivered it from his own mouth."*[23] There were manuscript brokers, what a past scholar called "an embryonic version of the literary agent,"[24] such as Ferdinado Ely and John Sherley in Little Britain, and Christopher Barker and John Walley in St. Paul's churchyard, some of whom, as H. R. Woudhuysen has shown, were also booksellers, and generally dealers in both kinds of materials.[25]

As Harold Love and Arthur Marotti have observed, the manuscript text afforded authorial anonymity and protection.[26] Since manuscript culture could both "preserve and imperil texts,"[27] a now-lost anonymous copy of the Manwaring manuscript in surreptitious circulation is a feasible possibility because it would not be intrinsically objectionable to Manwaring himself. Anonymous manuscripts would allow the author's work to circulate, while preserving what Brian Vickers describes as his "freedom to disclaim authorship should it prove contentious."[28] Ephemeral things such as manuscripts would then, and in subsequent times, be very hard if not impossible to track, since in the culture of manuscripts texts, readers were a closed circle of initiates, i.e., a coterie circle, for which the lower or rougher the social level of the clients the more obscure and intangible would be their circle of participation. Furthermore, despite official hostility to it, such as Treasurer Buckhurst's fulmination against it in 1599, there was no effective way to prevent illicit manuscript text transmission.[29] The pervasiveness of the culture of informal, or illicit, or surreptitious, manuscript circulation is evident in the fact that even notables like Francis Bacon were immersed in it, and Shakespeare himself was closely connected to the carriers' system.[30] Even though Love and Marotti focus on literary manuscripts, their findings are even more applicable to non-classifiable texts such as Manwaring's.

In this murky landscape, two figures are of particular interest in terms of the connections they have to Shakespeare. The first is Thomas Thorpe, publisher of Shakespeare's *Sonnets* in 1609, and regarded until recently as one of the most unsavory traffickers of news and manuscripts,[31] Thorpe likely was in contact with Francis Bacon, who was "the lifelong friend" of the most probable dedicatee of the *Sonnets,* William Herbert.[32] The second is John Jaggard, illegal publisher of the *A True Report.* John Jaggard was not only the brother of William Jaggard, and uncle of Isaac Jagard, both publishers of Shakespeare, but he was also a central figure in Francis Bacon's publishing arrangements, and Bacon had connections to Anthony Sherley through Essex, who was a patron of both the Bacons and the Sherleys, and who was one of Essex's closest confidantes and counselors in the late 1580s and the 1590s, even if he became the chief legal counsel for the prosecution of Essex in the trials of 1600 and 1601.[33] If anyone would be automatically privy to any secret reports or papers of Sherley, including an illicit copy of Manwaring's account, it would be Bacon. Indeed, Bacon's own Persian allusions in his *New Atlantis* may have come from his perusal of one of the many accounts of the Sherleys' Persian enterprise, or from the letters Anthony Sherley wrote to Francis and Anthony Bacon, or as one study of Francis Bacon has suggested, even from his personal conversations with members of the Sherley family in England.[34] At the same time, the menacing impress of Essex, behind Manwaring's silence, or his dangerous notoriety after 1600, would have effectively killed in both Thorpe and John Jaggard any thoughts of their illegal publication of the Manwaring manuscript or of its contents that they might have acquired access to and/or retained from memory. This situation could have afforded Shakespeare access to the contents of the Manwaring account, since he was already involved with the Jaggards in the publication of his works and he must have had by this time connections to Thorpe if Thorpe was to publish his sonnets a few years later.

In addition, Shakespeare himself had links to the Sherley family's older branch in Warwickshire via the Underhills in Stratford. The Underhills had leased the property of the Sherleys in Stratford, including New Place, in 1509, after the head of the Sherley family had married into the Staunton family of Staunton Harold in Leicestershire and relocated there permanently.[35] Since it is this branch of the family that starts the compilation of the family's history, initially by Thomas Shirley in the seventeenth century and continued by Evelyn Philip Sherley in the nineteenth century, including memoirs of the Persian adventures of Anthony Sherley and his two brothers, clearly the Warwickshire Sherleys were fully informed of the careers of the Sussex branch at the time, and to which the Underhills through their presumable closeness to the former were also privy. The Underhills sold the property to Shakespeare for £60 in 1597 when they were facing financial difficulties.[36] Shakespeare's purchase of New Place from the Underhills was the result of the close relations of his in-laws, the Ardens, who were located in Wilmcote, a few miles outside Stratford, to the Underhills. The Underhills had property in Wilmcote, and like the Ardens were recusant Catholics.[37] The Underhills were also known to Francis Bacon through William Underhill's father who had been an Inner Temple lawyer.[38] Thus, a double—rather than a single—web of relations extended between the Sherleys, the Underhills, the Ardens, and Shakespeare, and between Bacon, Anthony Sherley, Underhill, the Jaggards and Shakespeare. Through either network or both, Shakespeare would very probably have been aware of the activities of the Sherleys, at home and abroad, and would have been within a very likely circle of accessibility specifically to Manwaring's manuscript and/or its contents however and whenever it reached London.

There is the further possibility that Manwaring's account could have reached Shakespeare through one of his most famous theatrical colleagues, Will Kempe, even if Manwaring never returned to England and instead had remained in Spain with Anthony Sherley until his death. Since Will Kempe met Anthony Sherley in Rome in 1601[39]—he could have talked to Manwaring if the latter was still with Anthony Sherley then. In a letter of Sherley to Robert Cecil written in March 1602, Anthony Sherley mentioned that he had sent back to England with Henry Wotton, whom he called his cousin, and whose paternal aunt, the editor of Wotton's *Letters* explains, was Sherley's maternal aunt, an "account" of his "proceedings," which he fears is "lost" since Wotton has disappeared.[40] These "proceedings" could have contained the Manwaring manuscript, and Kempe—not Wotton—may have been the carrier. Unknown to Sherley Wotton had to conduct a secret trip to the Stuart court in Scotland on behalf of Ferdinand the Grand Duke of Tuscany,[41] and when after his visit with Sherley he embarked on this assignment, he may have expediently handed over to Kempe what Sherley had given him to carry back to London. If Sherley's purpose in giving the "proceedings," including the Manwaring account, to Wotton to take back to London, was part of his many desperate attempts to win back favor from the English government, and permission to return to England, by offering as proof of his service to England a more detailed and authentic account of his work in Persia than what he felt may have reached the government's ears otherwise, that purpose would be compatible with a general instinct on his part to also publicize his enterprise in London by other means as well, such as the popular stage, given that the stage was also an effective platform for broadcasting sensational "news of the world." This, in fact, was precisely what Sherley asked Anthony Nixon to do some years later in 1607. According to E. K. Chambers, Kempe regularly carried documents for the government from the Low Countries from as far back as 1585, and Kempe was desperate for money from 1599 onwards, including when he met Anthony Sherley in Rome in 1601.[42] Thus, in more ways than one, Kempe would have been a perfectly appropriate expedience for Wotton, for transmitting the Sherley papers to London.

Shakespeare may then have accessed the manuscript from Kempe, who was one of the most trusted actors of his plays when both were in Strange's Men and in the Lord Chamberlain's Men throughout the 1590s. Kempe may have left the latter company, not in the traditionally assumed date of 1599, but after 1600 and as late as 1602–3, as some scholars are now arguing.[43] That he appears in *The Return from Parnassus* with Richard Burbage would point to the fact that the authors of that work still associated Kempe with Shakespeare's company in 1602–3, as James Nielson has pointed out.[44] In any case, Kempe was still active on the stage, appearing in performances by Worcester's Men in 1602–3, according to E. K. Chambers, who asserted from entries of payments to Kempe in Phillip Henslowe's *Diary* that "during the winter of 1602–3 he [Kempe] was certainly one of Worcester's Men."[45] Even if Kempe left Shakespeare's playing company in 1599, there surely would have been continuing communication between them after that date, given their close professional association in the past. It is plausible, then, that Shakespeare, on receiving the Manwaring material and deciding to use it carefully, given the dangerous reputation of Sherley, would only have cannibalized from it. It must be significant that of the few people who met Sherley and possibly Manwaring immediately after their Persian trip, one was a prominent figure of the popular English theater industry, and one of Shakespeare's closest professional colleagues, Will Kempe. That he returned to London immediately afterwards in 1601 or 1602, that is, in time for whatever news and reports he was carrying to be disseminated in the theater industry, possibly clandestinely and for profit, is equally worth noting. If Kempe did bring back Manwaring's manuscript, it may have been as an illicit item, and it may have become one of the many illicit manuscripts circulating in early modern London discussed earlier. That Shakespeare received news of Sherley's trip from Kempe and incorporated it into *Twelfth Night* is a frequent modern scholarly assumption. Perhaps, to this needs to be added the possibility he also used a part of it some years later when he started to write *Othello*.

The multiplicity of the highly probable circuits of transmission sketched above makes unnecessary the exact identification of how Shakespeare could have known Manwaring's manuscript and the episode about the "traducing" Turk in particular. But that he must have, is mandated by the strong fit between the episode in Manwaring and the "malignant" Turk incident that otherwise appears suddenly and mysteriously in the closing lines of *Othello*. Furthermore, given the surprising absence of *any* explanations so far in the history of the play's commentary about the source of the lines, Manwaring's manuscript deserves serious consideration. There are also considerable scholarly dividends in connecting Manwaring's manuscript to the lines in Shakespeare's play.

III

An interesting difference between the Manwaring account and the passage in *Othello* is that the person who *helps* Manwaring in his account becomes in Shakespeare the violent individual who Othello kills in a self-identifying act of retributive justice. In fact, Manwaring's account may have been blocked by Essex from public release specifically because the passage in question contained two elements that were contrary to the prevailing political opinion in England regarding the Ottoman regime. The first was the account's favorable descriptions of civic arrangements in the Ottoman regime, such as the scrupulous punishment of the Turk in question by one of the Ottoman regime's most typical law enforcement figures, the Janissary officer. Janissaries, who were the Turks most feared military officer corps, were also in effect Ottoman policemen or law enforcement officers performing a wide range of civic functions at the behest of the state. They were frequently attached to foreign delegations as a measure of the state's guarantee of their security, as other contemporary English accounts of Ottoman Syria and Aleppo also reported:

> one Janizarye of the least, is sufficient to guard a man against a thousand Mores, or Arabians or Plebean Turkes in respect of his awfull authority ouer them, as also against all other Soldiers or Janizaries in respect of their brotherly agreement, and feare to breake their law by fighting or quarrelling among themselues. Therefore the Christian Ambassadors at Constantinople haue assigned to each of them, fower or six Janizaries, and the Consulls of Christian nations lying in other Citties and Townes, haue one or two of them to guard their houses and persons from all Wrongs, neither will any Christian having meanes to spend, goe abroad in Cittyes and Townes or take a iourney without a Janizarie to guard him . . . myself haue by experience found them faithfull, courteous and faire Companions
> (*Fynes Moryson's Itinerary,* 54–55)[46]

> At our return from Tarsus, Edward Rose our factor Marine, provided us horses to ride to Aleppo, and a Jenesary called Paravan Pasha to guard us
> (William Biddulph, *Travels of Certain Englishmen in Africa, Asia,. . . .*, 38–39)[47]

As modern historians have explained it, by the end of the sixteenth century, "Some *orta* (regiments) [of the janissary corps] had won the right to certain traditional duties, such as guarding foreign embassies, policing Istanbul harbor and custom houses, and acting as a fire brigade," and that generally "They provided security, law and order, or similar municipal duties."[48] All of this is exactly confirmed by Manwaring's directly observed explanation that "all strangers have commonly a Janisary in the house with them for their safety."

The presence of the Janissary in Manwaring's account and his prompt and strong intervention in the violent harassment by a Turkish civilian of a member of the visiting foreign party that was his official responsibility to protect, reflected the strictly maintained security of life and property in the Ottoman domains for all people, including its tolerance and scrupulous protection of people of all faiths who submitted to them. Indeed, as one of the most respected historians of Ottoman history, Daniel Goffman, has observed, "The insertion of the janissary corps into the body politic [in the 1590s] . . . encouraged the development of a sophisticated civil society."[49] The point here is not that the Ottoman state was a perfect one. It was violent, and Christians were harassed in it, as reports like Moryson's and Biddulph's frequently describe, and that is Manwaring's overall point in his narration of his harassment. But what such indictments are unable to conceal is that the Ottomans weren't simply a barbaric regime either, and that they had elaborate mechanisms of providing security in civil life, of which the janissaries were a prominent example, irrespective of how well or completely such arrangements worked, and which would probably compare favorably to the law and order protocols of early modern Europe as a whole. In fact, the elaborate structures of stability and protection in Ottoman civic life were much valued commonly (if not officially) across Europe, and that reputation was what made the Ottoman regions in general, and Constantinople in particular, the dreamt-of haven of refuge for all persecuted European religious minorities, including Jews.[50] The attractiveness of migrating to Ottoman lands and to Constantinople, even for Anglo-European Christians, was the reason for the steadily increasing exodus of ordinary Europeans to Ottoman urban regions throughout the sixteenth century, especially in England in the late Tudor and early Stuart regimes, including even for their willing conversion to Islam (for tax benefits). That act of betrayal for Christian thinking coined the popular phrase "turning Turk," as well as a word that was the origin of the modern word renegade: "renegado."[51]

This feared, and what was to some, apocalyptic, trend, inspired many popular English plays, notably Robert Daborne's *A Christian Turned Turk* and Phillip Massinger's *The Renegado*. Even if for a struggling Protestant England, the Ottomans' power and influence made it a useful if secret ally against Catholic Europe,[52] and which may have made possible, according to one scholar, the very survival of England (because of the relentless military pressure against the Catholic regimes that the Ottomans kept up from the southeast that sapped the former's resources and strength),[53] that was a nervous, expedient, and secret, alliance that did not visibly permeate the overall public status of the Ottomans in Elizabethan England as a menacing presence looming over all of Europe. A positive public depiction of the Ottomans and their civic life as is obliquely visible in Manwaring's account was thus directly contrary to the compulsive *official* English stereotype of the Ottoman regime as a barbaric and savage Islamic empire oppressing Christendom.

The second unacceptable element in Manwring's narrative was its graphic portrayal of the humiliation of an Englishman by a Turk. Such a portrayal would not only be hurtful to the national psyche, it would also embarrass Essex in an enterprise he had supported. It is therefore a probable inference that Essex, as one of the "hawks" in Elizabeth's cabinet (compared to the Cecils),[54] would have suppressed the publication of Manwaring's narrative on both counts, even if and perhaps especially because he was already in trouble with the government himself at the time. If James in 1601, before he had become King, could in a letter cited by Evelyn Phillips, advise Sherley to "remain quiet" in view of the fallout from Essex's failed rebellion and execution,[55] that must have been an even more urgent if secret effort on Essex's part in the months preceding his death, through however much of his personal network that remained available to him, to discourage any further dissemination in London of news of Sherley's trip such as that of Manwaring, irrespective of whether such a suppression would have been in Sherley's own interests in trying to create a favorable enough atmosphere with the English authorities to enable his return.[56]

Generally, it is also worth noting the status of Aleppo as the principal site in the popular English imagination for the enactment of the victimization of the innocent Englishman at the hands of the malignant Turk, that Manwaring's account represents and that Othello's lines replicate. As is well established in modern scholarship, Aleppo's ancient history, as a natural trading crossroads between Europe and Asia, located as it was on a route that provided a short land transit for Mediterranean commercial traffic to the Euphrates valley and points farther East, ensured its importance to the political regimes of the regions through the ages, down to the Islamic Arab Mamluks of Egypt and the Ottomans who succeeded them in West Asia in the early sixteenth century.[57] Thus, as Peter Stallybrass has recently shown, Aleppo in the early modern moment was known as a city of traffic and commerce, and of diversity and multiethnic coexistence. The reputation stemmed perhaps from the coexistence in Aleppo of the older Egyptian Arab civil population derived from late Mamluk times and professing the new strict Islamic culture of the early medieval philosopher Al-Ghazali, on the one hand, and the Turkic Ottoman administrators with their history of a necessarily inclusive multiethnic cultural and political life who ran the city, on the other (and which two groups of Aleppines are reflected, as it so happens, by the aggressive civilian Turk and the avenging Janissary respectively, in Manwaring).[58]

The commercial attractiveness of Aleppo for England is manifest in the stationing of a line of English consuls and trade representatives in the city between the sixteenth and seventeenth centuries. One testimony of that attractiveness is that of the English traveler to Aleppo, shortly after Manwaring, John Cartwright, who according to Stallybrass, not only observed that, "Aleppo is now become the third capital of the Turkish empire. And well may it be so accounted, since it is the greatest place of traffic . . . for hither resort Jews, Tartarians, Persians, Armenians, Egyptians, Indians, and many sorts of Christians, all enjoying freedom of conscience, and bringing together all kinds of rich merchant life . . . ," but who concluded his observation drily with the remark that "the trade and trafficke of which place, because it is so well known to most of our nation, I omit to write thereof."[59] It is precisely this cosmopolitan diversity, albeit commercially necessitated in part perhaps, that Stallybrass says surprised English travelers, because there was little in their home life that compared: "The shock that Renaissance English travelers registered in Aleppo was the shock of the toleration of such diversity . . . that had only the remotest echo in England in the stranger churches—of the Huguenots and other Protestant exiles." Cartwright's view was untypical however, not just of the European or Venetian views of Aleppo that Stallybrass cites, but also of the English media of the moment, published as it was a decade later in 1611.[60] Consequently, it is precisely this reputation of Aleppo that was inadvertently visible in Manwaring's account that would have made it unsuitable for public consumption in the eyes of a Tudor government nervous like the rest of Europe about the rising tide of the Ottoman empire's military and cultural renown, and especially dangerous for Manwaring's already beleaguered principal backer, Essex. It would have been another element in need of suppression or modification, if the document was to be used at all, most expediently as a site for staging the harassment of Christian English strangers instead of as a well-known locale of their profitable business endeavors, that is, to be used to blacken the image of Ottoman urban life, and not broadcast its cosmopolitan allures.

The re-shaping of news or information about Protestant England's adversaries, Catholic or Ottoman, or to appropriate a prevailing English term for such phenomena, the "turning" of such material, into conformity with the official hostile view of such parties was a principal characteristic of late Tudor and early Stuart media. As Nabil Matar has shown, one of the most convenient platforms for the inimical public projection of the Ottoman was more often than not the popular theater.[61] If, as one of the most well-known foreign observers of Elizabethan drama reported in 1599, the Elizabethans received their news of the world from what they saw on the popular stage, such "news," then as now, would be subject to direct or discreet control and manipulation by the authorities.[62] Thus, if Manwaring's account was to be salvaged at all for popular consumption—and news about foreign lands and people was a highly saleable commodity for the popular theater—that could only happen with its selective transformation.

Shakespeare himself was inevitably a part of the overall hostile, even if at points complex, English political climate regarding the Ottoman Turk, in the conflicted ways he alludes to the Turk throughout his works. As has been demonstrated elsewhere, in the steady stream of references running throughout the Shakespearean *oeuvre,* the Turk is a persistent spectral figure, a presence that can neither be accepted (represented on stage as a character) nor denied (completely excluded from the framework of political and historical references required by the topical, popular nature of the plays), and whose associated attributes change and grow across the two decades of the playwright's career in a rough parallel to the fluctuating fortunes of Anglo-Ottoman relations at the end of the sixteenth and the beginning of the seventeenth centuries. One of the climactic points in this line of spectral but ubiquitous representations is the sudden but catastrophic emergence of the Turk in Othello's self-avenging suicide.[63]

The Manwaring material may have reached Shakespeare through any of the routes suggested earlier, including most likely through Will Kempe and the hands of one of the Jaggards, and because Sherley was a politically sensitive topic, all that was used from the Manwaring account was the figure of the "traduc[ing]" Turk, but not his instant and severe punishment by the Ottoman law officer. Jonathan Burton has suggested that "If English texts of the early modem period develop an imperial rhetoric, the defining mode of that rhetoric is appropriation . . . where the foreign is grasped, translated, and puffed up beyond its original consequence"[64] If this is correct, then what could have happened to the Manwaring account in the text of *Othello,* may not only be a perfect confirmation of that process, but also an extension of what Burton describes: what is inconvenient in the "foreign," especially in an inimical foreign power, is silently expunged, and the invocation of the inimical foreign is reshaped to accentuate its negative contours. If the text of *Othello* was in process as early as 1601–2,[65] that would make it contemporary to the moment of the arrival in London of the news of Sherley's Persian adventure, since that is when Parry returns to London and his account, as well as the illegal, anonymous, and quickly suppressed *True Report,* are published. This is also the moment when Ottoman Turkey is a particularly prominent subject in the popular imagination, as is witnessed by the appearance in print of Robert Carr's *The Mahumetane or Turkish Historie* in 1600, Richard Knolles's *History of the Turks* in 1603, and the republication of a poem by King James titled *Lepanto* in 1603 to proclaim the new king's interest in Anglo-Turkish relations.[66] As the Turkish scholar Salih Ozbaran has found, in London between 1590 and 1609, books on the Turk, which were published intermittently over the previous two decades, rose to a frequency of one book on the subject each year.[67] This phenomenon represents the intensity of a mixed English *angst* about the Turk at this moment, it should be understood, rather than any simple public admiration of that regime.

IV

In a stimulating recent study Jonathan Sell has sketched the possible outlines of the process by which the contents of illicit manuscripts were molded by several anonymous editorial interventions for commercially successful public dissemination, where one of the determinants of commercial success is the perceived political or cultural imaginary of the community, projected by its authorities and absorbed by its members. The manuscript in question is William Biddulph's account of Ottoman Syria and Aleppo, cited earlier:

> Over a period of time, Biddulph writes a series of letters in Aleppo. The letters are delivered to a relative Belaziel Biddulph in England. Belaziel dies and the letters are discovered by some third parties, read by them, and passed on to the editor. The editor knocks them into shape and publishes them. Finally a reader reads them. By the time the first page of this *wonder text* is turned by the reader's thumb, it has already passed through four other pairs of hands and bears the marks of a by-now familiar piece of consensual reality. How much of this metatextual apparatus is true is beside the point. What is clear is that, together with the 'travail' and the 'reluctant travel writer' topics, the text is being generically situated and the reader's expectation cued: the genus of the works . . . is the *admirabile genus,* this particular species of which is the travel account. Our editor, this small-scale compiler, is quite consciously and deliberately working within a tradition to which he further nods when counters the common charge that 'travellers may lie by authority' by appealing to the traveller's god fearing nature. . . .[68]

What makes Sell's outlining of the process particularly relevant here is that he works with a text that is of the same class of writing as Manwaring's, the travel account, notwithstanding the difference between Biddulph's background as an English preacher assigned by the Levant company to its factor in Aleppo and Manwaring's as an aristocrat's secretary on a secret diplomatic mission abroad. An authorial reluctance comparable to Manwaring's authorial absence also surrounds the publication of Biddulph's work, comprising as it does the compilation by several nameless editors of a series of private letters he wrote from Syria to his brother in England in 1600, and to the publishing of which he was initially opposed. Arguably, Sell's hypothetical outline of the "metatextual apparatus" of the publication history of Biddulph's work could be said to speak generally to the degrees of manipulation involved in the textual derivations and assemblages of all popular English printed material of the time.[69] The editorial insistence of the "truthfulness" of Biddulph's descriptions that prefaces the work, which Sell says identifies its travel-writing genre, could also indicate an earlier cultural convention of the truthfulness of works presented to the public, by which the contents of such works were held to be true precisely because they had been shaped (perhaps as in checked, or filtered, or amplified), by many hands, not one. If so, that also points valuably to the coexistence of the earlier technology of manuscript production with the newer one of book production, as well as to the synchronicity of the medieval tradition of collective authoring with the emerging fashion of individual authorship at the end of the sixteenth century in England.[70] As such, the process by which Biddulph's writing appeared in print points feasibly to the same process by which the details of the Turk episode in Manwaring's were modified and put into *Othello,* in a lingering cultural practice that was normative rather than fraudulent.

Sell's delineation of a hypothetical process of transformation of textual content during a Tudor or Stuart work's publication invites a consideration of the specific points of divergence between the details of the malignant Turk episode in the Manwaring account and in *Othello.* Such a consideration helps to reveal a protocol of conversion that matches the late Tudor agenda of reshaping for domestic consumption an inimical view of the Ottomans sketched earlier, and is valuable because, uniquely perhaps for the popular English stage, it clearly profiles such a practice at work, and in doing so makes further credible a directly derivative connection between *A True Discourse* and *Othello*'s lines about the malignant Turk.

Drawing on a frequently invoked critical context for Othello's lines about the malignant Turk, it can be said that at the play's end the Turk lives in Othello—that's what the latter is trying to exorcise in his last speech, in a terminal gesture of expiation before the Venice that he has served. So too, the Manwaring text lives in the text's closing lines, the latter's garbling of the incident in Manwaring being *its* exorcism of the corrupting presence of the law enforcing Turk in the Manwaring text—the deliberate or inadvertent positive picture of the strictly upheld justice of Ottoman civil life. The act of textual exorcism occurs specifically in the shift between lines 350 and 353, as the visibly double Turk identities of "*A* malignant" and "*a* turbanned Turk" (emphases added) of the earlier line corresponding to the two Turks in Manwaring as was noted before, coalesce in the single figure of "the circumcised dog" of the latter line, via the intervening line's silent transformation of the opposed actions of the civilian Turk's misdemeanor and the janissary's retributive intervention in Manwaring into the commonly punishable offenses of "beat[ing] a Venetian" and "trad[ucing] the state" for both in Shakespeare.[71] As perpetrator and punisher are folded into each other in a syntactical homology wherein *both* become offenders, the possibility of law and order and civic life in the Ottoman world is dismissed and a strongly functioning civil order is painted over as a lawless barbaric one.

As "turning" functions in the English lexicon of the moment to connote transformation, change, seduction, betrayal, these valencies may be tracked metaphorically in the changes cohering between the Turks in Manwaring's account and in *Othello,* including in the title character's closing lines. Generally, over the course of the play the Ottoman is "turned" from menacing to fragile (blown away in an offstage storm), from being overwhelming to something that is simply put away, "smote him thus," where "smote" connotes in sixteenth- and seventeenth-century usage the deadly finality of a terminal act of violence of Biblical character.[72] Likewise, Othello is "re-turned" to both Venice and the Asiatic-African other, the former posthumously in the penitently self-exorcised figure of the dead Othello that is the stage's final offering to its historical audience, and the latter in the dismissal of the inimical exotopy that has lain in his being that Othello acknowledges and to which he implicitly surrenders in his invocation and execution of the malignant Turk in himself.

All this together might constitute the Shakespeare play text's "turning" of the Manwaring account, and in that signal Shakespeare's "re-turning" of the Turk that is "turning" his Christian Anglo-European world.[73] That, in turn, might reflect the lines' symbolic "re-turning" of the residue of its historical origin in Manwaring, its creative masking of its formal source, otherwise the surreptitious cooptation that is the general practice of early modern English illicit manuscript culture and that is the specific necessity mandated by the dangerous political content of the passage in the manuscript's moment of availability in London. There is also the turning or conversion of Ottoman Aleppo (the city of flourishing trade, international commerce, and ethnic coexistence) into Christian Venice, even if this is a double conversion—that of Aleppo into Venice, and of Catholic Venice (i.e., Cesare Vecellio's Venice, for instance, which admires and emulates Ottoman material life)[74]—into a Protestant London inimical to the Turk.

Such fluid "turnings" confirm, not contradict, the instability of identity and identification that Lawrence Danson has found binding expediently Protestant English and Ottoman Moor against the idolatrous Catholic and infidel Turk in the travel-writing imagination, and that by implication underlies the deployment of Othello the Moor to strike down the "circumcised dog" in Shakespeare's play. If the historical cultural politics of Othello's last lines, and the critical poetics of our times (in Danson), can flexibly "accommodate" a view of the Turk as both "fix[edly]" barbaric *and* not "absolute[ly]" so, that is if they can articulate an animosity simultaneously of Christian towards Turk *and* of English Christian towards fellow European Christians, if they can make legible a heuristic for the play as hostile to the other and as hostile to oneself, that reversibility can point back to a practice of popular writing in which an allusion is both of the text and outside it, in which Manwaring's clumsily split Turks can live in Shakespeare's smoothly unified malignant figure without remembering or evoking their origins.

To track these "turnings" is therefore also to locate *Othello* in the "turns" of its critical history, to "re-turn" the play from its historically antiseptic readings divorced from history, or from the anxious defenses of its awkward ethnic hostilities,[75] to its situation in the political moments of its time and ours, to in effect "re-turn" Shakespeare's "re-turning" of the Turk—from civil and helpful to lawless and barbaric—back to the urgent exigencies of a historical writing moment in which not to be Christian is compulsively, necessarily not to be civilized, to in fact "re-turn" literature to material history.

V

The murky circumstantial relationship between Manwaring's account of the malignant Turk and Othello's allusion of such an episode that this essay has tried to suggest may be the textual archeology of Shakespeare's lines, falls within the purview of David Scott Kastan's recommendation of a return to material history in Shakespeare studies, in a work tellingly titled *Shakespeare After Theory*. As James Knapp puts it, in his citation of Kastan, "He [Kastan] seeks to incorporate . . . [the] values [of a "material," empirical method] into a historicism made all the more confident by its having learned the lessons of theory once and for all:

> If theory has convincingly demonstrated that meaning is not immanent but rather situational, or, put differently, that both reading and writing are not unmediated activities but take place only and always in context and action, the specific situations, contexts and actions—that is, the actual historical circumstances of literary production and reception—cannot be merely gestured at but must be recovered and analyzed.[76]

In the fractious disputes, however, that have attended the turn to material history in contemporary critical practice, over the double bind of the "constructedness" of *both* the "facts" of history and its fictions,[77] what may be partly overlooked is that in a post-Kantian millennia a return to the autonomously accessible objecthood of facts, to an uncontaminated, directly available facticity, cannot be a tenable proposition. This is why, in the view of a recent scholar of the cultural history of archives, "Distinguishing fiction from fact has given way to efforts to track the production of and consumption of facticities as the contingent coordinates of particular times and temperaments, places and purposes."[78] Material history can thus only be a constructed modality that aims to destabilize and expose the fashioning of master histories by appropriating the latter's high ground of facticity with competing verities, to reveal as it were the back life of "facts," their always-already-contaminated phenomenology. In thus implicitly extending the claim of constructedness across the phenomenological level material history aims at a new, more equitable, historicity where "high" truths can exist coequally with "low" ones, and the meaning of the past is forever a discourse of competing values. This is not to say that material history is a judgment-neutral heuristic, or that it is not. On the contrary, the substance and interest of material history is the occluded excess, the supplement, of the phenomenology of time that the fiction of history or its literary re-telling, its narrativization, leaves out, and that is always the contestatory alterity of its narrative life, its silent other, and the destabilizer of its facticity. Put slightly differently, these "are the 'arrested histories'—histories suspended from received historiography—that are its effects."[79]

Thus, the supplement of early modern English defensiveness against the Turk's unstoppable ingress into Europe (or Spain's aggressive world presence), is the reflex of English assertion in world trading projects (transoceanic and transcontinental trading ventures as in the enterprises of the Virginia, the Levant, and the East India companies and the military accoutrements that they bred), and which impels English history in the late sixteenth century toward an emerging protocoloniality, what, following Etienne Balibar, has been described as colonialism without or before colonization.[80] In this view the effect of the Ottoman empire, and Spain, on England is to turn it to dreams of dominion to thoughts of world presence and penetration, to what will materialize eventually as the idea of empire. The "turning" of the Turk in *Othello* also marks, then, the "turning" of England in its early modern history, the birthing of a rhetorical style that is the outrider of a political stance that will become colonialism.

If the Turk is seen in the Tudor-Stuart political imagination as something that must be matched and exceeded in his re-enactment, that is, overturned *rhetorically* on the popular stage, if the Turk is seen as a rhetorical style, that is precisely what is manifest in the divergences between Manwaring's account of the Turk in Aleppo and Shakespeare's representation of the malignant Turk who must be, and is, struck down terminally, "smoted, thus." The finalistic "smot[ing]" of the Turk, in Othello's closing words, is the culmination of the rhetorical reduction of the Turk in Shakespeare over his oeuvre, beginning with his first reference to him as an example of a rhetorical style worth emulating in *1 Henry IV,* in Joan Pucelle's (Joan of Arc's) sharp reprimand of William Lucy's expansive eulogy of the English commander John Talbot whom her forces have slain "The Turk that two and fifty kingdoms hath, / Writes not so tedious a style as this" (4.7.75–76).[81] This trajectory articulates not just the growth of a steadily hostile attitude towards the Turk in Shakespeare, as suggested earlier, but also the very semiosis of political rhetoric and national intention. For between the first invocation of the Turk in *1 Henry IV* in 1591 and the last in *Macbeth* in 1606, England has moved from Elizabeth's cautious defensive posture and discreet diplomacy to James's international ambitions for England to be a major European power, which is the distance between the careful detachment of Elizabeth's *semper eadem* outlook and the grand interventionism of James's *rex pacificus* mentality. To invoke Jonathan Goldberg's precise description of this phenomenon, from his masterful study of the style of James I's monarchy, "language and politics . . . are mutually constitutive, [and] society shapes and is shaped by the possibilities of its language and discursive practices . . . [because] the real requires realization; representation, understood in its full complexity—both as restatement and as recasting, replacing representation—realizes power." These connections are especially valid for James's accession and reign, in which "the links between the state and the theater were particularly strong . . . not only because the theaters had come under direct royal patronage . . . [but also because] the theater was the public forum in which [James's] royal style could be most fully displayed."[82]

If, as Neill has suggested, the performance of *Othello* in 1604 bears the impress of the new Jacobean regime's cultural tastes,[83] a part of that impress would include complimentary adherence to that regime's political ideology. Such adherence would underwrite Shakespeare's quick importation, modification, and deployment of the Manwaring material at least by the play's end (especially into what some scholars have hypothesized was the text of the play that was in process in 1601–2 that was mentioned earlier)[84], to express a national stance matching that ideology, one in which an English-ed Venetian empire triumphs over the imperial Turk. This verbal outreach is perfectly congruent with the replacement of Elizabeth's uneasy and conditional support of English sea ventures by James's sweeping royal cooptation of all the trading companies on land and sea, and by his adoption in October 1604 of the title of Great Britain for England, less than a fortnight before *Othello* is performed before him at court.[85] Both, James's initial refusal to sign any trade agreements with the Ottoman regime in 1603 because it would be unbecoming of a Christian prince, as well as his subsequent acquiescence to such an initiative in his new charter to the Levant company in 1605 on the grounds that it would yield expedient profit to England that Daniel Vitkus has detailed,[86] exude the same assertive national stance that Shakespeare's reshaping of the Manwaring material projects. *Othello*'s performance in 1604 is followed by the establishment of the first English colony in America in 1607, and by the start of the first English trading activity in India in 1608 that will culminate in the British Indian empire two centuries later, even as the vanquishing of the menacing Turk continues to be staged before the monarch and his court, as in the spectacle of a sea fight in 1610 on the Thames to celebrate Prince Henry's investiture as the Prince of Wales, and then again in 1612–13 to celebrate Princess Elizabeth's marriage to Frederick, Elector Palatine of Germany, the latter according to an eyewitness account moving the king to "delight."[87] The unverifiabilty of the relations of the Manwaring account to *Othello* are precisely what make the former a supplement of the latter, and a part of the supplementarity of material history to literature, with the widening ripples of effluences binding them, such as those just sketched, serving to authenticate the Manwaring passage's signature in Othello's lines as a pointillist presence and not an apodictic one.

Othello's last speech has itself been described recently as a supplement,[88] and as a teleological afterthought of the text, a kind of interruptive textual stepping forward in the plot's closing operations,[89] to control and correct its final thematic legacy as it were, and which is an effect of the cumulative body of the play's action, where effect is understood not just as a natural progression but as an antithetical consequence. If this exemplifies what Michael Neill has described as the deliberate "designs" of the play's ending,[90] it would be as an altered design, signaling Shakespeare's working into the play he was writing the material from Manwaring that he had come across. As the speech as a whole "inscribes," in Maurizio Calbi's words, "what Jacques Derrida would call the *sur-vie* 'an after life,' 'life after life,' . . . some kind of 'living on,' that effectively problematizes textual boundaries,"[91] the malignant Turk lines in particular can be seen as embodying that "living on." In them, at the very moment of the vindication of a Londonized Christian Venice that Othello's self-punishment aims to achieve, the ongoing history of the Turk's domination which that vindication necessarily has to suppress springs up to mock it with the threat of its survival in the future. Correspondingly, at the very instant of the domestication of the Manwaring allusion into Shakespeare's play, the allusion floats away into the text's future life, into its imaginative critical paratext, as a ghostly reminder of the mystery of its origins.

The supplementarity of literature and history is also at once a complementarity, their relationship projecting both a convergence as well as a divergence, a confirmation and a refutation, a validation and a denial, an antithesis as well as a synthesis, asynchronously of the one by the other. Thus, material history as literature supplement is simultaneously literature as the supplement of material history, their cohabitation being a symbiosis rather than causality. That symbiosis can serve in Shakespeare's early modern moment to underline the ambiguity of relations between history and literature, the one not yet fully understood as a specific discipline of learning and the other unrecognized still as a master instrument of culture. The fluidity of writing practices, of literature and history, that is, their mutual permeability, may afford some insights into the nature of the relationship between the account of the "malignant" Turk in Manwaring and in *Othello,* and the meaning of the differences between them.

Appendix: The manuscript of George Manwaring's *A True Discourse*
(BL Sloane ms. 105 f.8. 35)

[Reproduced with the kind permission of the British Library.]

Extract of the Turk episode, 1 (beginning indicated by square bracket)

him and shew him the turke that had vsd me so, who
in smale time we found him sittinge wth his father
and other gentle men, soe I did shew ye Ianisare
wch was he, who ran fercly to him and threw him on
his bake givinge him twentie blowes one his leges and his
feete so yt he was not able to goe or stand; he was clothed
in a cloth of goule vnder cote and a chimson velvett gown
but his gay clothes could not save him fro ye tershes of
the Ianisares fury; and in this sort our men weare served
divers times] I will wright somthinge of ye fashion of
ye turkes although it be knowne vsually to our marchants
yet is it not comonly knowne to all men; first conserning
the libertie and freedome the great turke doth give to
his souldiers caled Ianisaries, wch is they have ye libertie to take vituales for them selves or ther horses wth
out paynge ever a penie for it; in what towne soe ever
they come into vnder the turkish gouerment; and if
they will not earue them to ther content they will beat
them like dogs. wch if they chance to resist, then doe they
forfet all ther goods to the Great turke; in my beinge in turkey
I will shewe you of a pittiefull example comited by ye Ianesa~
wch was thus 6 of them travilinge through the countrey
came to a towne, and did vse them selves in most vilde
fashion wth the weemen, ye men of ye towne beinge ther
abuses, did wthstand them; so yt in the eand one of the
Ianesaries weare slaine, the other 5 left ye towne presently
and came to Alepo beinge but 20 miles fro the place; and
tould ye Ianesaries of the castle what had happened; ther
linge all wayes in the castle 300 the next day ther went
forth of ye last 200 of them to ye towne where as the
Ianesarie was slaine; and cominge thether they did kille
man woman and child, pullinge downe ther howses and
caringe away the spoyle of all ther goodes; this towne
I my self wth in 8 dayes after this happened whee I did

Extract of the text of the Turk episode, 2 (end indicated by square bracket)

Notes

1. Scott McMillin, "The Othello Quarto and the 'Foul Pape' Hypothesis," *Shakespeare Quarterly* 51, no. 1 (2000): 67–85, esp. 67.

2. *Othello,* ed. E. A. J. Honigmann, The Arden Shakespeare, 3rd. ed. General ed. Richard Proudfoot, Ann Thompson, and David Scott Kastan (Surrey, UK: Thomas Nelson & Sons, 1997).

3. For some typical current instances of this lack, see the commentary on Othello's last speech, in addition to the Honigmann edited *Othello,* in *The Tragedy of Othello the Moor of Venice,* ed. Russ McDonald, The Pelican Shakespeare, Series Editors Stephen Orgel and A. R. Braunmiller (New York: Penguin books, 2001); *The Tragedy of Othello,* The Norton Shakespeare, 2nd. ed., ed. Walter Cohen, Jean E. Howard, and Katharine Eisaman Maus (New York: W.W. Norton & Co. Ltd., 2008); *Othello, the Moor of Venice,* ed. Michael Neill, The Oxford Shakespeare, Series Editor Stanley Wells (Oxford : Clarendon Press, 2006); *Othello, the Moor of Venice,* ed. Kim Hall, The Bedford Shakespeare Series, series editor Jean Howard (New York: Bedford/ St. Martin's, 2007); *Othello and The Tragedy of Mariam,* ed. Claire Carroll, A Longman Cultural Edition, General Editor Susan Wolfson (New York: Longman, 2003). Two recent critical discussions, specifically of the Turk passage in Othello's speech, but without interest in its possible allusion, are those of Lawrence Danson, "England, Islam, and the Mediterranean Drama: Othello and Others," *Journal of Early Modern Culture* 2, no. 2 (2002): 1–25; and Peter Stallybrass, "Marginal England: The View from Aleppo," in *Center or Margin: Revisions of the English Renaissance in Honor of Leeds Barroll,* ed. Lena Cowen Orlin, and J. Leeds Barroll (Selinsgrove, PA: Susquehanna University Press, 2006), 27–39.

4. Transcription of a section of George Manwaring, A True Disourse of Sir Anthony Sherley's Travel to Persia, British Museum Sloane Ms. 105 f.8. 35 (spellings partly modernized). See photocopy of of the original text of the Turk episode in the Appendix.

5. E. Denison Ross, *Sir Anthony Shirley and His Persian Adventure* (London: Routledge, 1933), 7; Evelyn Philip Shirley, *The Sherley Brothers; An Historical Memoir of the Lives of Sir Thomas Sherley, Sir Anthony Sherley, and Sir Robert Sherley, Knights* (New York: B. Franklin, 1972), 15–16.

6. The fullest account is still that of Ross. Others include Boies Penrose, *The Sherleian Odyssey* (Taunton: The Wessex Press, 1938), and that of Evelyn Philip Shirley. Victorian accounts include Major General.Briggs, "A Short Account of the Sherley Family," *Journal of the Royal Asiatic Society of Great Britain and Ireland* 6 (1840): 77–104; "The Three Sherleys," *The Gentleman's Magazine,* 22 n.s.177 (1844): 473–83; and "The Sherleys," *The Calcutta Review* 26 (1856): 285–312. Modern studies include David William Davies, *Elizabethan Errant: The Strange Fortunes of Sir Thomas Sherley and his Three Sons* (Ithaca, NY: Cornell University Press, 1967); and N. I. Matar, *Turks, Moors and Englishmen in the Age of Discovery* (New York: Columbia University Press, 1999), 52–67. The family name was spelled variously. The Sussex branch preferred the spelling Sherley, whereas the older branch of the family in Stratford, Warwickshire, used the spelling Shirley. To avoid confusion, it is the former spelling that will be used throughout this essay, with each branch identified by its regional location.

7. For a detailed discussion of the downturn of Sherley's life in the closing decades of Elizabeth's reign see Ross *Sir Anthony Shirley*, 32–45, Evelyn Philip Shirley's *The Sherley Brothers*, 32–40, and Scott Frederick Surtees, *William Shakespeare of Stratford Upon Avon: His Epitaph Unearthed* (London: Henry Gray, 1888), 18, 21, 34–35 (containing extracts of Anthony Sherley's letter to Robert Cecil in 1600 pleading for permission to return to England, and notations in the *State Papers* of the Queen's refusal to relent, taken from *The Sherley Brothers*).

8. William Parry, *A New and Large Discourse of the Travels of Sir Anthony Sherley Knight, by Sea and Overland, to the Persian Empire* (London: Valentine Simmes for Felix Norton, 1601); Anthony Nixon, *The Three English Brothers* (London: J. Hodgetts, 1607); John Cartwright, *The Preachers Travels* (London: Thomas Thorpe, 1611); *Sir Anthony Sherley, His Relation of his travels into Persia* (London: Nathaniel Butter for Joseph Bagfet, 1613); Abel Pincon, *"Relation D'un Voyage De Perse Faict Es Anees 1598 Et 1599,"* ed. Claude-Barthélemy Courbé Augustin Morisot (Paris: Augustin Courbé, 1651). Nixon's account is generally regarded as unreliable. The earliest account, however, which was illegally and anonymously published and quickly suppressed, and which contained only Sherley's letters of credentials for his journey, was *A True Report of Sir Anthony Sherley's Journey overland to Venice, fro thence by sea to Antioch, Aleppo, and Babilon, and soe to Casbine in Persia* (London: R. B[lore] for J. J[aggard], 1600).

9. First in *The Retrospective Review* vol. 2 (London: Charles and Henry Baldwin, 1820), 351–81; and then in the *The Three Brothers or the Travels and Adventures of Sir Anthony, Sir Robert, and Sir Thomas Sherley, in Persia, Russia, Turkey, Spain* (London: Hurst, Robinson and co., 1825), 34–35; the incident appears only in the latter version, which according the volume's anonymous editors, is the most complete one, containing material "that is now for the first time made public" (23). Subsequently, the incident was also extracted in Major General Briggs's "A Short Account of the Sherley Family," *Journal of the Royal Asiatic Society of Great Britain and Ireland* 6 (1840): 77–104, on 84–85. It is only modern Iranian and Turkish scholars who have consistently pointed to the usefulness of the Manwaring account for Shakespearean and early modern English literary and cultural studies. See, for instance, the electronic essay of Gonul Bakay, "The Turk in English Renaissance Literature," (2003), 11.20.2011 <http://www.opendemocracy.net/faith-turkey/article_982.jsp>. The most recent Western discussion of the account is Jonathan Burton's essay, "The Shah's Two Ambassadors," in *Emissaries in Early Modern Literature and Culture,* ed. Brinda Charry and Gitanjali Shahani (Burlington, VT: Ashgate Publishing co., 2009), 23–40, which, however, is curiously silent about the parallels between the account's text of the episode of the Turk's manhandling of George Manwaring in Aleppo and Othello's lines about the "malignant Turk" in Aleppo in *Othello.*

10. See the head words for "traduce" in Thomas Cooper, *Thesaurus Linguae Romanae & Britannicae Tam Accurate Congestus* . . . 1584; Randle Cotgrave, *A Dictionarie of the French and English Tongues* (1611); Robert Cawdrey, *A Table Alphabeticall, Conteyning and Teaching the True Writing, and Vnderstanding of Hard Vsuall English Wordes, (1604), all in Lexicon of Early Modern English* (LEME) at http://leme.library.utoronto.ca/search/results.cfm.

11. Number derived from a search of the electronic full text data base of English

Verse Drama at the University of Virginia, Charlottesville, library at <http://lib.vir ginia.edu.proxy.lib.odu.edu/digital/collections/text/ch_eng_verse_drama.html>1.12 .2010.

12. For most Ottoman and non-Ottoman Muslims, Europeans were Christians and Europe was the simply "Lands of the Christians," or the *bilad al-nasara;* for some discussion of the primary sources on this topic see Nabil Matar, *In the Land of the Christians: Arabic Travel Writing in the Seventeenth Century* (New York: Routledge, 2003), xvi–xviii, xxx. Some related primary sources on this would include: Sidi Ali Reis, *Miral Ul Memalik or The Mirror of Countries* (Dersaadet, Istanbul: Ikdam Matbaasi, 1895), and Eveliya Celebi, *Seyahetnama or Narrative of Travels in Europe, Asia, and Africa in the Seventeenth Century,* trans. Joseph von Freiherr Hammer-Purgstall (London: Translation Fund of Great Britain and Ireland, 1834).

13. M. E.Nickson, "Hans Sloane, Book Collector and Cataloger 1682–98," *The British Library Journal* 14.1 (1988): 52–89, esp. 70.

14. *Anthony Sherley,* xix.

15. Samuel Garbet, *The history of Wem, and [other] . . . townships [in Shropshire]* (Wem: Franklin, 1818), 267–68. For an online extract, see Samuel Garbet, *The History of Wem: Edstastson,* 2008, Shropshire County Council, available at: http:/www3 .shropshire-cc.gov.uk/roots/places/wem/garbet/wem47.htm, 12.22.2010.

16. Francis Gastrell and Francis Robert Raines, *Notitia Cestriensis Or Remains Historical and Literary Connected with the Palatine Counties of Lancaster and Chester,* vol. VIII: V.1 (Manchester: Chetham Society, 1845), 209n201. The note says:

> The Vernons were Lords Paramount of Baddiley (Bedilei in Domesday) in the 16th Edward I., and the mesne Lords were the family of Praers of Barthomley, whose descendent and co-heiress, Joan Praers, about the time of Richard II married Willian Mainwaring of Peover, and conveyed a moiety of the manor to this family, . . .
> After the death of Sir Henry Mainwaring of Peover Bart in 1797, this Manor was sold by his executors.

Peover is in Cheshire, which adjoins Shropshire on its northern border.

17. For a recent detailed, if at times defensive, account of Essex's increasing troubles with Elizabeth by the turn of the century, see Paul Hammer, "Shakespeare's *Richard II,* the Play of 7 December 1601, and the Essex Uprising," *Shakespeare Quarterly* 59, no. 1 (2008): 1–35.

18. See the letter of the Venetian ambassador of May 22, 1603 about this in the *Calendar of State Papers Relating to English Affairs in the Archives of Venice,* Vol. 10: 1603–1607 (1900): 35, "Venice: May 1603, 16–31."

19. For a history of the Sherley family home see the electronic book, *"Wiston," A History of the County of Sussex Volume 6 Part 1 (Bramber Rape Southern Part),* 259–68, ed. T. Hudson, et al (British History Online, 1980), <http://www.british-history .ac.uk/report.aspx?compid=18265 January 13, 2009>. ; and the web page, The Wiston Archives [Wiston/1-Wiston 2106], 2009, West Sussex Record Office and National Archives, Available: http://www.nationalarchives.gov.uk/A2A/records.aspx?cat=182 -wiston_1-1_1&cid=-1&Gsm=2008-06-18#-1 January 14, 2010.

20. *Calendar of State Papers: Colonial Series East Indies, China, and Japan*

1513–1616, ed. W. Noel Sainsbury (London: Longman, Green, & Roberts, 1862), 99, Item 255.

21. Harold Love and Arthur F. Marotti, "Manuscript Transmission and Circulation," *The Cambridge History of Early Modern English Literature,* ed. David Lowenstein and Janel Mueller (Cambridge: Cambridge University Press, 2002), 77–78.

22. John Taylor, *The Carriers Cosmographie: Or a Briefe Relation, of the Innes, Ordinaries, Hosteries, and Other Lodgings in, and Neere London, Where the Carriers, Waggons, Foote-Posts and Higglers, Doe Usually Come, from Any Parts, Townes, Shires and Countries, of the Kingdomes of England, Principality of Wales, as Also from the Kingdomes of Scotland and Ireland with Nomination of What Daies of the Weeke They Doe Come to London, and on What Daies They Returne.* (London : Printed by A[nne] G[riffin], 1637), section "C."

23. *Some Forerunners of the Newspaper in England 1476–1622* (Philadelphia: University of Pennsylvania Press, 1929), 234–35.

24. Lambert Ennis, "Anthony Nixon: Jacobean Plagiarist and Hack," *Huntington Library Quarterly* 3, no. 4 (1940): 377–401; see 382–83.

25. H. R. Woudhuysen, *Sir Philip Sidney and the Circulation of Manuscripts, 1558–1640* (Oxford: Oxford University Press, 1996), 48–49.

26. Love and Maretti, "Manuscript Transmission and Circulation," 58–59.

27. Ibid., 70.

28. Brian Vickers, "Authenticity of Francis Bacon's Early Writing," *Studies in Philology* 94, no. 2 (1997): 248–96; see 248.

29. Love and Maretti, "Manuscript Transmission and Circulation," 74.

30. For Bacon, see Vickers, "Authenticity" 248–50; for Shakespeare see Alan Stewart, "Shakespeare and the Carriers," *Shakespeare Quarterly* 58, no. 4 (2007): 431–64, esp. 440–41.

31. Sidney Lee, in his *Shakespeare's Life and Work* (New York: Macmillan, 1900), 72–73, and in the *Dictionary of National Biography* (New York: Macmillan, 1898), 56: 323–24, was the chief proponent of Thorpe's reputation as a predatory dealer of manuscripts, and held that the sonnets were a ms illicitly acquired by Thorpe's assistant William Hall (reading the dedication's "begetter" as procurer) and that he is the dedicatee, not William Herbert, and Katherine Duncan Jones in "Was the 1609 Shakespeare Sonnets Really Unauthorized?" in Stephen Orgel, ed., *Shakespeare's Poems* (New York: Garland, 1999), 111–46, argues the manuscript was a straight purchase offered by Shakespeare to Thorpe in 1609 and that Thorpe was not an unsavory dealer but a perfectly respectable publisher; for a good survey of the history of the scholarly debates on the meaning of the dedication of the Shakespeare Sonnets, and including on Thomas Thorpe's reputation, see Donald W. Foster, "Master W. H., R. I.," *PMLA* 102, no. 1 (1987): 42–54). Thorpe remains a figure whose business reputation is difficult to satisfactorily ascertain.

32. *Baconiana* (London: R. Banks, 1895), 192.

33. For a detailed documentary study of Bacon's relationship with Essex, based on their letters, and including of Bacon's complicated divergence from Essex by the end of the decade, see Andrew Gordon, "'A Fortune of Paper Walls': The Letters of Francis Bacon and the Earl of Essex," *English Literary Renaissance* 37, no. 3 (2007):

319–36. Also see Thomas Birch, *Memoirs of the Reign of Queen Elizabeth From the year 1581 till her death* . . . : *From the Original Papers of his Intimate friend Anthony Bacon, Esq.* . . . (London: A. Millar, 1754), 2: 432–61.

34. Howard White, *Peace Among the Willows: The Political Philosophy of Francis Bacon* (The Hague: Martinus Nijhoff, 1968), 137n4.

35. Alice Dryden, *Memorials of Old Warwickshire* (London: Bemrose and Sons Ltd., 1908), 60–61. Dryden cites the Sherley family memoir by Evelyn Philip Sherley as her source. See 62 for the relationship of the Wiston, Sussex branch of the Shirleys (to which Anthony and his brothers belonged) to the Warwickshire Sherleys.

36. René Weis, *Shakespeare Unbound: Decoding a Hidden Life* (New York: Henry Holt, 2007), 211.

37. Michael Wood, *Shakespeare* (New York: Basic Books, 2003), 89.

38. Peter Dawkins, *The Shakespeare Enigma* (Polair Publishing, 2004), 258.

39. *Twelfth Night,* ed. M. M. Mahood (New York: Penguin, 1968), 22; G. R. Hibbard, Stanley Wells, ed., *William Shakespeare: Four Comedies* (London: New Penguin Books, 1996), 530.

40. Logan Pearsall Smith, ed., *The Life and Letters of Sir Henry Wotton,* 2 vols. (Oxford: The Clarendon Press, 1907), 1:37, and 1:38n2.

41. *The Life and Letters of Sir Henry Wotton,* 1: 40.

42. E. K. Chambers, "William Kempe," *The Modern Language Review,* 4, no. 1 (1908): 88; Robert Forse, *Art Imitates Business: Commercial and Political Influences in Elizabethan Theatre* (Bowling Green, OH: Bowling Green State University Popular Press, 1993), 128–29.

43. Juliet Dusinberre, "Pancakes and a Date for *As You Like It,*" *Shakespeare Quarterly* 44, no. 44 (1993): 371–405; see 380 n35.

44. James Nielson, "Will Kemp at the Globe," *Shakespeare Quarterly* 44, no. 4 (1993): 466–68; see 468n9.

45. Qtd. in Nielson, 467.

46. Charles Hughes, ed., *Unpublished Chapters of Fynes Morrison's Itinerary: Being a Survey of the Condition of Europe at the end of the 16th Century* (London: Sherratt and Hughes, 1903), 54–55.

47. William Biddulph, *The Travels of Certain Englishman in Africa, Asia, Troy, Bythinia, Thracia, and the Black Sea.* . . . (London: William Aspley, 1609), 38–39.

48. David Nicolle and Angus McBride, *Armies of the Ottoman Empire 1775–1820* (Oxford: Osprey Publishing, 1998), 12; Mehrdad Kia, *Daily Life in the Ottoman Empire* (Santa Barbara, Calif.: Greenwood, 2011), 64. For studies of the origins, organization, and functions of the janissary corps, see David Nicolle and Christa Hook, *The Janissaries* (Oxford: Osprey, 1995), 3–7; Nigel Crawthorne, *The Immortals: History's Fighting Elites* (London: Quercus, 2010), 44–47; Ahmet Akgündüz and Said Ozturk, *Ottoman History. Misperceptions and Truths* (Rotterdam: IUR, 2011), 57–59.

49. Daniel Goffman, *The Ottoman Empire and Early Modern Europe* (Cambridge: Cambridge University Press, 2002), 121.

50. Stallybrass, "Marginal England," 28. For historical sources, see for instance, Moryson's and Biddulph's references to the thriving multiethnicity of Ottoman Aleppo and Constantinople.

51. For sixteenth century notations of this etymology see the entries for the word

in John Florio, *A World of Words* (1598), and Randle Cotgrave, *A Dictionary of the French and English Tongues,* 1611, both in LEME; for a discussion of the history and impact of the "renegado" phenomenon, see N. I. Matar, "The Renegade in English Seventeenth-Century Imagination," *Studies in English Literature, 1500–1900,* 33, no. 3 (1993): 489–505.

52. As Burton has shown in "Anglo-Ottoman Relations and the Image of the Turk in *Tamburlaine,*" *Medieval and Early Modern Studies,* 30, no. 1 (2000): 125–56, esp. 128–38.

53. G. J. Meyer, *The Tudors* (New York: Random House, 2010), 484.

54. For an estimate of Essex as part of the militant hawkish group of Elizabeth's advisors in the line of Leicester, Walsingham, and the Sidneys, see John Guy, *Tudor England* (Oxford: Oxford University Press, 1988), 439–43., esp. 440, 443; Paul Hammer, *The Polarisation of Elizabethan Politics: The Political Career of Robert Devereaux, 2nd Earl of Essex, 1585–1597,* Cambridge Studies in Early Modern British History, ed. John Guy, Anthony Fletcher, and John Morrill (Cambridge: Cambridge University Press, 1999), 112–26.

55. Evelyn Philip Shirley, *The Sherley Brothers,* 36–37.

56. See for example his letter to Robert Cecil of March 5, 1604, where he cites the successes of his Persian adventure for England, cited by Evelyn Philip Shirley, *The Sherley Brothers,* 48–49.

57. See for instance, Edhem Eldem, Daniel Goffman and Bruce Masters, *The Ottoman City between East and West: Aleppo, Izmir, and Istanbul* (Cambridge: Cambridge University Press, 1999), 19.

58. Stallybrass, "Marginal England," 27–39; Eldem et al., *The Ottoman City,* 23–25. Abu Hamid Muhammad Al Ghazali was a highly influential 11th century Islamic philosopher whose brilliant demonstration, in his *Tahafut al Falasifa (*The Incoherence of Philosophy), of the inadequacy of (western) rationalism for understanding revelation, and his concomitant advocacy of faith as the exclusive instrument of understanding the ultimate truth of creation, led unfortunately in subsequent centuries to a rigid, intolerant, and literalist Islam, including in modern times to fundamentalism, even though, ironically, Ghazali himself was a rationalist sufi mystical thinker, discernibly influenced by Platonic thought and opposed to the literalist bookish Islamic theology of his times. See Roy Jackson, *Fifty Key Figures in Islam* (New York: Routledge, 2006), 89, and Anthony Black, *The History of Islamic Political Thought: From the Prophet to the Present* (New York: Routledge, 2001), 106.

59. John Cartwright, *The Preachers Travels* (London: Thomas Thorpe, 1611), 8.

60. Stallybrass, "Marginal England," 29. Stallybrass points out on the same page, citing another English account of Aleppo, a *negative* one from more than a decade earlier, that of John Eldred, who on arrival in the city was imprisoned as a spy, on the instigation of Portuguese and Venetian merchants angered by English piracy of Catholic ships on the high seas, that if the English had reasons to fear for their safety it was from Catholics and not the Turks. That the Turks entertained the Venetian and Portuguese view of the wrongness of English piracy also points, though, to the Ottomans' valuation of legality in the conduct of international trade.

61. Matar, "The Renegade in English Seventeenth-Century Imaginations," 495. For a brief acknowledgments of this phenomenon, see Lisa Hopkins and Matthew

Steggle, *Renaissance Literature and Culture* (New York: Continuum International Publishing Group, 2006), 19, and for a complex discussion see, Jacques Lezra, "Translated Turks on the Early Modern Stage," in Robert Henke and Eric Nicholson, *Transnational Exchange in Early Modern Theater* (Burlington,VT: Ashgate Publishing, 2008), 159–80. Also see Daniel Vitkus, *Turning Turk,* 29–37; Richmond Barbour, *Before Orientalism: England's Theatre of the East* (Cambridge: Cambridge University Press, 2003), 26–29, 37–57; Matthew Dimmock, *New Turkes: Dramatizing Islam and the Ottomans in Early Modern England* (Burlington, VT: Ashgate, 2005), 95–108; Jonathan Burton, *Traffic and Turning: Islam and English Drama, 1579–1624* (Newark: University of Delaware Press, 2005), 55–65. Although, this latter group of scholars do not see the popular stage's representation of the Turk as uniformly hostile, they all show the stage Turk as an expedient if variable construction.

62. *Thomas Platter's Travels in England 1599,* trans. and ed. Clare Willliams (London: Jonathan Cape , 1937), 170.

63. Imtiaz Habib, "Shakespeare's Spectral Turks: The Postcolonial Mimetics of a Spectral Narrative," *Shakespeare Yearbook* 14 (2004): 237–70.

64. Charry and Shahoni, *Emissaries in Early Modern Literature,* 39–40.

65. E.A. J. Honigmann, "The First Quarto of Hamlet and the Date of Othello," *The Review of English Studies* 44, no. 174 (1993): 211–19, and *Othello,* ed. E.A.J. Honigmann, 2: 344–50; Neill, *Othello,* 401–3; McMillin, "The Othello Quarto," 72, 82.

66. Honigmann, "Date of Othello," 216–19; Neill, *Othello,* 399, and Emrys Jones, "*Othello, Lepanto,* and the Cyprus Wars," *Shakespeare Survey* 21 (1968): 47–58 (cited by Neill); Vernon. J. Parry, *Richard Knolles' History of the Turks,* ed. Salih Ozbaran, (Istanbul: The Economic and Social History Foundation of Turkey, 2003), 34. Honigmann cites some other factors as well. Neill also suggests the interesting possibility that "a passing fascination for blackface exoticism among the Queen [Anne's] circle" may have propelled Shakespeare's "choice of a Moorish protagonist," 400.

67. Vernon J. Parry, Appendix 1, 95–104.

68. Jonathan Sell, *Rhetoric and Wonder in English Travel Writing, 1560–1613* (Burlington, VT: Ashgate Publishing Co., 2006), 73.

69. As described, for instance, by David Scott Kastan: "Plays were not autonomous and self-contained literary objects . . . [they were] inevitably subjected to the multiple collaborations of production . . . where of course, actors, prompters, collaborators, annotators, revisers, copyists, compositors, printers and proofreaders all would have a hand in shaping the play-text" *Shakespeare after Theory* (New York: Routledge, 1999), 33.

70. For discussions of both these historical phenomena see, David Scott Kastan, "Print, Literary Culture and the Book Trade," in *The Cambridge History of Early Modern English Literature,* ed. David Lowenstein, and Janel Mueller, (Cambridge: Cambridge University Press, 2002), 55–80, esp. 81; Marotti and Love, "Manuscript Transmission and Circulation," 55–56; Heidi Brayman Hackel, *Reading Material in Early Modern England: Print, Gender, and Literacy* (Cambridge: Cambridge University Press, 2059), 29–30; George Justice and Nathan Tinker, *Women's Writing and the Circulation of Ideas: Manuscript Publication in England 1550–1800* (Cambridge:

Cambridge University Press, 2002), 8. See also Neill, who in deliberating on the play's textual archeology quotes Paul Werstine thus:

> These [early modern] texts were open to penetration and alteration not only by Shakespeare himself and his fellow actors but also by multiple theatrical and extra theatrical scriveners, by theatrical annotators, adapters and revisers (who might cut and add), by censors, and by compositors and proof readers. (431)

71. Even on a syntactical level it may be possible to read "A malignant and a Turbanned Turk" as two figures, since Shakespeare's linguistic practice includes the deployment of separate articles to denote a single figure as well as two separate figures or entities, at least two instances of the latter of which include the following: "let/ A Roman and a British ensign wave/ Friendly together;" Cymbeline in *Cymbeline,* V.v. 480–82; "*Enter a* King *and a* Queen, *the Queen embracing him and he her,*" Stage directions for the Dumb Show, *Hamlet,* 3.2.

72. For some instances of this association, see *Bible* (Coverdale), 1535, Job xiv. 2; J. Sylvester tr. G. de S. Du Bartas *Deuine Weekes & Wks.* (new ed. 1606), ii. iii. 78, both cited under the head words for "smote" in the *Oxford English Dictionary* online edition at http://www.oed.com; and Thomas Wilson's *A Christian Dictionary* (1612) in LEME.

73. For a slightly different deployment of the critical metaphor of "re-turning" in *Othello,* see the recent essay by Dennis Austin Britton, "Re-'turning' *Othello:* Transformative and Restorative Romance," *English Literary History* 78, no. 1 (2011): 27–44.

74. Stallybrass, "Marginal England," 30.

75. See the last group of scholars named above in n. 57.

76. James Knapp, "Between Thing and Theory," *Poetics Today* 24, no. 4 (2003): 641–71, esp. 635; the Kastan citation is from *Shakespeare after Theory,* 31.

77. This is a debate aptly summed up by the title of Knapp's essay, although Knapp's point about the problem with Kastan's ignoring the always-already theorized nature of the "actual historical circumstances of literary production and reception" that the latter calls for (in his quotation from Kastan cited above), may be in itself problematic, as I point out here.

78. Ann Laura Stoler, *Along the Archival Grain: Epistemic Anxieties and Colonial Common Sense* (Princeton, NJ: Princeton University Press, 2009), 33.

79. Ibid.

80. Habib, "Shakespeare's Spectral Turks," 238–39.

81. *The First Part of King Henry VI,* ed. Andrew Cairncross, The Arden Shakespeare (London: Methuen, 1969).

82. Jonathan Goldberg, *James I and the Politics of Literature* (Baltimore: Johns Hopkins University Press, 1983), xi–xiii. For studies of James's imperial style, often described by scholars as a Caesarist Roman one, see Tristan Marshall, *Theatre and Empire: Great Britain on the London Stages under James VI and I* (Manchester: Manchester University Press, 2000), 31–39; Ralph Anthony Houlbrooke, *James VI and I: Ideas, Authority, and Government* (Burlington, VT: Ashgate, 2006), 53–58; Simon Wortham, " 'Pairte of My Taill is Yet Untolde': James VI and I, The *Phoenix,* and the Royal Gift," in Daniel Fischlin and Mark Fortier ed., *Royal Subjects: Essays on the*

Writings of James VI and I (Detroit, MI: Wayne State University Press, 2002), 182–204, esp. 186–93. Revisionist views include Jenny Wormold, "James VI and I: Two Kings or One?," *History* 68 (1983): 187–209; John Cramsie, *Kingship and Crown Finance under James VI and I, 1603–1625* (London: Boydell and Brower, 2002), 40–67; Diana Newton, *The Making of the Jacobean Regime: James VI and I and the Government of England 1603–1605* (London: Boydell and Brower, 2005), 25–27. The long-held scholarly view of James's imperial style of kingship has not been much affected by recent studies of James's reign that have sought to rehabilitate his reputation, such as the last three studies named here, as a politically shrewd and experienced rather than an inept king, with scholars explaining his ambitious monarchic stance as the result of conflicts in the evolving history of English monarchy over the necessity of absolute governance from Yorkist times and especially from the Reformation onwards, and as the result of James's anxieties about challenges to his right to the English throne in general and to the unified throne of Britain in particular.

83. Neill, *Othello*, 399–400, 403.

84. See note 61.

85. The event of James's self-titling is obliquely recorded in the diary entry of the religious squire, Adam Winthrop for October 24, 1603: "it was proclaimed that England and Scotland should be called Great Britain,": cited by Nicholas Canny in "The Origins of Empire: An Introduction," in William Roger Louis, Alaine M. Low, Nicholas Canny, *The Oxford History of the British Empire* vol. 1 (Oxford (UK): Oxford University Press, 1998), 5. Winthrop's date is wrong. The year should be 1604. See the *Calendar of State Papers: Domestic Series The Reign of James I 1603–1610,* ed. Mary Anne Everett Green (London: Longman, Brown, Green, Longmans and Roberts, 1857), 159, and James Larkin and Paul F. Hughes, ed., *Stuart Royal Proclamations: Royal Proclamations of James I 1603–25* (Oxford: Clarendon Press, 1973), 94. Louis et al., however, argue defensively *against* the notion that the title represented English expansionism. For more recent and less defensive views see, Kevin Curran, *Marriage, Performance, and Politics at the Jacobean Court* (Burlington VT: Ashgate Publishing, Ltd., 2009), who shows that James's interventions in the way the kingdom was represented was rhetorical and administrative (22), and W. B. Patterson, *King James VI and I and the Reunion of Christendom* (Cambridge: Cambridge University Press, 2000), who points out that James's appropriation of the title of "King of Great Britain" was connected to what the monarch saw as "exciting opportunities of peace for Europe." (31). For the date of Othello's performance at court before James on November 1, 1604, see *Othello* in *The Arden Shakespeare Complete Works,* ed. Richard Proudfoot and Ann Thompson (London: Thompson Learning, 2001), 941; Honigmann, ed., *Othello,* 344, and McMillin, "The Othello Quarto," 72.

86. Daniel Vitkus, *Turning Turk: English Theater and the Multicultural Mediterranean, 1570–1630* (New York: Palgrave Macmillan, 2003), 32.

87. In the *firman* (decree) that the London merchant John Mildenhall seeks and gets from the Mughal emperor Jahangir for trading in Gujarat, on the west coast of India. See John Stewart Bowman, *Columbia Chronologies of Asian History and Culture* (New York: Columbia University Press, 2000), 280; and Thomas Goddard Bergin and Jennifer Speake, *Encyclopedia of the Renaissance and the Reformation* (New York: Facts on File, 2004), 154. For the staging of the sea fights before James, show-

ing the vanquishing of the Turk, see David M. Bergeron, "Are we turned Turks?: English Pageants and the Stuart Court," *Comparative Drama* 44, no. 3 (2010): 255–75, esp. 262–63, and 267–69.

88. Maurizio Calbi, "*Othello's* Ghostly Reminders: Trauma and Postcolonial 'Dis-Ease' in Tayeb Salih's *Season of Migration to the North,*" in *Shakespeare's World/World Shakespeare's: Selected Proceedings of the International Shakespeare Association World Congress, Brisbane 2006,* ed. Richard Fotheringham, Christa Jansohn, and R. S. White (Newark: University of Delaware Press, 2008), 432–57; see 342–43.

89. Imtiaz Habib, *Shakespeare and Race: Postcolonial Praxis in the Early Modern Period* (Lanham, MD: University Press of America, 2000), 144–45.

90. Neill, *Othello*, 130–31, 134–35.

91. Calbi, "*Othello's* Ghostly Reminders," 342.

"O blood, blood, blood": Violence and Identity in Shakespeare's *Othello*

Jennifer Feather

AT the moment when Othello finally becomes fully convinced of Desdemona's infidelity, he cries out "O blood, blood, blood."[1] Because early modern writers participate in a collective cultural attempt to stabilize existing categories of difference by attaching them to fixed biological characteristics, one might be tempted to understand the visceral and seemingly unsophisticated nature of this utterance as a sign of Othello's atavistic descent into murderous rage, his barbarous nature emerging from beneath his heroic self-presentation.[2] Understanding the word "blood" in this light evokes the entire apparatus of biological determinism that develops over the course of the early modern period in which "blood" dictates rank, culture, and identity itself.[3] However, focusing on the burgeoning language of biological determinism obscures the persistent centrality of violence, also implicit in the word "blood," in early modern constructions of self that continue to rely on humoral ideas of bodily fluidity.[4] This single word encapsulates the tensions between these two modes of self-understanding—one that sees blood as stable and another that understands it as constantly in flux. Not simply a marker of barbarism, blood and the violence it connotes is a flexible form of self-fashioning that Othello uses to repair his understanding of the world shattered by Desdemona's purported infidelity and to negotiate this tension between stability and fluidity.

Recent critics have persuasively shown the implication of the play in a burgeoning racialism that focuses on skin color as a measure of moral worth.[5] However, this system of difference is not yet fully instantiated and competes with a much different understand of biology that threatens the biological stability often associated with the notion of blood. As Jean Feerick explains, while the early modern understanding of the word "race" relies primarily on notions of bloodlines, the physiological fluid itself is seen as in constant flux and danger of degeneration. Thus, "Early modern racial ideologies ... articulate with compelling force what modern racial ideologies seek to bury: the ever-present prospect of racial reversibility."[6] Ian Smith similarly notes the instability present in early modern racial ideologies and understands skin color as a means of stabilizing categories of difference, encapsulated in the notion of barbarism, that are based on varying degrees of linguistic facility. To be a barbarian is by definition to be one who is lacking the ability to use language and is hence, bestial. Smith attributes focus on the "apparent biophysical fixity of color" as a means to buttress classical tropes of barbarism "whose inherent weakness is linguistic adaptation."[7] Othello, whose linguistic facility wins over Desdemona and secures his defense before the Duke, is a prime example of the sort of linguistic adaptation that makes barbarism an unstable category of difference. In this reading, Othello returns to a barbarous state under pressure: lacking other means of persuasion he resorts to wanton violence and savage cruelty. Smith's reading, by opposing civilized rhetoric and barbarous violence, presumes that the play and Elizabethan culture more broadly work ultimately to stabilize modes of ascribing difference and the identities on which they are based. This fixity in turn serves as the foundation for humanist ideas of selfhood as individual and autonomous. Shakespeare's play, however, dramatizes the tension between a social system that values stability and one that relies on flexibility, valorizing one as much as the other.

Because "blood" is implicated equally but distinctly in both the stabilizing force of biological determinism and the fluid nature of humoral physiology, this single word both highlights and embodies the tension between these two systems of difference—one that sees flexibility as dangerous and another that acknowledges and negotiates fluidity. Surely, Othello's cry is one of anguish that signals the breakdown of the previously firm foundations of his sense of himself, assiduously constructed through linguistic performance. However, even as this cry is a recognition of Desdemona's infidelity and the extreme cognitive dissonance it causes, understood in terms of chivalric violence, it is also solution to the very set of problems posed by Desdemona's infidelity. In fact, precisely because blood is implicated in multiple overlapping and competing understandings of corporeal and social order, chivalric violence serves a reparative function at the heart of the play. Rather than understanding the play as ultimately marginalizing chivalric virtue at the expense of a burgeoning valorization of mercantile skills, this article demonstrates how Othello deftly uses the chivalric codes of combat to repair the damage done by Iago.

Many readers have refuted the racial essentialism of the play but fail to account for the importance of violence in these constructions of difference and the consequent understanding of self in the play. For modern readers, embedded in a culture that easily, almost instinctually, understands "blood" as the bearer of both inherited difference and racial essence, the violent connotations of the word all but disappear. However, I would argue that Othello's anguished cry suffers from a surfeit rather than a dearth of meaning, bringing to the surface not Othello's essential savagery but the centrality of violence in early modern structures of meaning. If modern readers have difficulty separating "blood" as a signifier of lineage from "blood" as a signifier of race, in an early modern context separating lineal claims and bloodshed poses as many if not more difficulties. Whereas in modern understandings of the term "blood" automatically signifies inheritance in both a familial and racial sense, the echo of "blood" as "bloodshed" is almost inescapable in these texts. Othello's attempts to restore the integrity of social identity and corporeal person implied by his notion of "blood" draw on chivalric notions of combat, and thus make manifest the violent connection between word and deed absolutely central to the Venetian social order. Othello's cry, then, is not primarily an expression of his essential savagery but of the way that he intends to utilize bodily damage to restore his own and Desdemona's integrity.

Not only do early modern medical texts, including Robert Burton's *Anatomy of Melancholy* and Thomas Geminus's reproduction of Vesalius's *Epitome* present blood as central to the healthy functioning of both body and state, they emphasize both its unifying properties and its ability to connect body and soul as sources of identity. These unifying properties reveal how the multiple meanings of the term connect to one another. "Blood," whether it is understood as "vital spirit," "bloodshed," "the seat of emotion," or "lineage," represents the physical grounding of social identity. This physical grounding relies not, as modern notions of race do, on a sense of biological fixity, but on relationships between word and deed created through violence.

The term "blood" bears the weight of these multiple meanings throughout the play.[8] Desdemona's supposed infidelity questions the collocation of nature, will, and social status implicit in the early modern understanding of blood, disturbing the relationship between these terms that is created through constitutive forms of bodily damage. Though "blood" as it is used to describe Desdemona's betrayal is the source of unbearable psychic dissonance for Othello, blood in the sense of "bloodshed" is also the solution to that problem. In response to her purported betrayal, Othello re-imagines his sense of integrity, basing it on the ability of violent acts to connect word and deed. Examining the use of the word "blood" throughout the play, as I propose to do here, reveals that the play's central issues—namely race, sexuality, and violence—are encapsulated in this one polysemous utterance that reveals a conception of identity rooted in violent action rather than fixed bodily essence. What Othello makes manifest in murdering Desdemona is not the fundamental racialism of Elizabethan society that assumes he must be savage and thus, prone to impulsive violence, but its reliance on violence to connect word and deed, meaning and reality. His resort to violence is neither a repressed racial essence surfacing nor a simple reversion to chivalric values. Rather, it is a compromise between two social systems. By exploring how Othello's conception of the body informs our understanding of the violent action in the play, I will begin to elucidate the delicate balance early modern thinkers negotiate between these social systems and its relationship to a contemporary discourse of the body.

I

The conception of the body with which Othello begins, and which he attempts to repair in the final acts of the play, bears upon his conception of self. Over the course of the play, Iago introduces a new epistemology that fundamentally relies on a fixed corporeality to determine individual identity and bears much in common with modern conceptions of race that figure race as a biological essence expressed in behavior, rather than as an essence created by that behavior.[9] It is this conception of self that enables Iago infamously to claim "I am not what I am" (1.1.64), invoking an individual essence from which his outward performance deviates. Many critics see the play as participating in the emergence of such an idea of self and difference in which biological essence is relatively fixed, limiting the control that an individual has over her self-presentation.[10] Readings of the play that see *Othello* as participating in the increasing resort to biological fixity as dictating racial difference see Othello's bloody acts as sign of his barbaric essence emerging. However, this narrative elides the type of thinking with which Othello begins that relies on combat to unify corporeal and social ideas of self.

Othello begins with a conception of self rooted equally in chivalric combat and humoral ideas of the body. These ideas see the body, self, and environment as consisting of a fluid set of humors that mutually influence one another. In such a conception, violence is not the mere violation of an inviolable individuality but a means of ensuring harmony between body, self, and social position. Othello sees his heroic acts as creating this sort of integrity, invoking an idea of body and self that bears much in common with early modern ideas of race that critics such as Mary Floyd Wilson and Daniel Vitkus, using geo-humoral theory and narratives of conversion respectively, argue was not nearly as stable as modern ideas of biological fixity would suggest.[11] However, once he has been confronted with blood's instability in the form of Desdemona's infidelity, he resorts to racialist thinking that relies on biological stability in his search for "ocular proof." His fundamentally violent response is simultaneously a product of his desire for essence and appearance to be in line and also for essence to be visible in performed acts, rather than hidden deep in a man's physical being, demonstrating the uneasy coexistence of these two competing ideas of self.

Having been confronted with an epistemology that sees selfhood as dictated by an internal essence, an epistemology that critics, such as Kim Hall, see in the kind of racialist thinking operating throughout the play, Othello attempts to restore his conception of self, which sees acts rather than essence as determinative. He does not simply wish to make interior essence visible but to create his idea of himself in unifying acts of prowess. This response, then, is not violent simply because he only knows how to act in a violent fashion, either because of his race or because of his chivalric identity, but rather because of the ways that violence specifically is able to restore wholeness to his fractured identity. His identity as a warrior, like his identity as a Moor, is not significant because of its predisposition to violence but because of its insistence on both physical and mental integrity. Thus, rather than seeing Othello's violence as a consequence of his essential biology, either because he is a soldier or a black man, I see his use of violence as stemming from its unique ability to make essence and performance one and the same, as they were for Othello prior to Iago's manipulations.[12]

Othello relies on violence to repair his fractured sense of self, just as he relies on martial prowess to unify his own identity when he is questioned before the Duke, conceiving of blood as unifying social and individual identity. If his uttering of the word "blood" prefigures the violence against Desdemona, it also represents the restoration of her integrity in those acts. To reduce this conception to simple biological determinism, as the reading that sees Othello's acts as atavism does, collapses the rich set of early modern associations with the term "blood," obscuring the idea of identity at work in the play. In fact, racialism—the notion that Othello possesses a racial essence that might conflict with his social performance—is precisely the problem. His use of violence, rather than being a regression into barbarism, is a reparative measure intended to restore the unified conception of identity imagined in the early modern understanding of "blood."

II

Starting with Desdemona's betrayal of her father, which undermines the stability of "blood" as a source of identity, the characters in the play consistently struggle with competing conceptions of identity and difference. Othello's anguished cry encapsulates these struggles in a single repeated word, "blood." The twenty-one other uses of the word "blood" in the play make manifest the stakes implicit in how one understands this one term. Brabantio initially calls upon the multifaceted notion of blood in the first scenes of the play to describe Desdemona's marriage to "the Moor" as a disruption of her corporeal and spiritual integrity. He presents Desdemona's chastity as a form of integrity that cannot be shattered except by force. This force is conceived of in terms of "some mixtures powerful o'er the blood / . . . / that [Othello] wrought upon her" (1.3.105–7). Taking her physical and spiritual integrity as a fact, Brabantio uses it as incontrovertible evidence that a crime has been committed, that coercion was necessary to get Desdemona to concede to marry Othello. He pleads before the Duke that "It is a judgment maimed and most imperfect / That will confess perfection so could err / Against all rules of nature" (ll. 99–101). Because her perfection is a certainty, her actions must have been coerced to have deviated so far from the rules of nature. Her integrity should be inviolable and can only have been breached by force. This integrity encompasses her entire individual and social being. Brabantio wonders that,

> A maiden never bold
> Of Spirit so still and quiet that her motion
> Blushed at herself; and she, in spite of nature,
> Of years, of country, credit, everything,
> To fall in love with what she feared to look on?
>
> (ll. 95–99)

He understands her nature, age, national origin, and reputation—in short everything about her—as functioning in complete harmony. In presenting her abduction as an assault against her blood, Brabantio suggests that her blood is the seat of this unified identity.

This notion of subjective harmony is in line with one of the most prominent early modern conceptions of the way that blood functions, represented by the works of Thomas Geminus and Robert Burton, among others.[13] According to Thomas Geminus's English version of Andreas Vesalius's anatomy, the blood as it is decocted in the heart is "spirite, more clearer, bryghter, and subtyller, then is any corporall thynge, compounded of the foure Elementes, for it is a thynge that is a meane betwene the bodye and the soule, and therefore the Philosophers lyken it rather to a heauenlye thynge then to a bodelye thynge."[14] In this context, blood is that which unites the body and conveys the identity of the soul. This conception persists into the seventeenth century when the physician George Thomson described blood as "the immediate instrument of the soul . . . sweetly uniting all the parts of the Body for the conspiration of the good of the whole."[15] He, thus, conceives of the blood as the basis for both a psychological and a corporeal identity that unifies and pervades the entire individual. He sees no distinction between what later thinkers would understand as the psychological, what he calls the soul, and what will become the physiological. The blood is an "immediate" instrument, admitting little distinction between its material and immaterial qualities. In his *Anatomy of Melancholy,* Robert Burton describes blood, saying that is "a hot, sweet, temperate, red humour . . . whose office is to nourish the whole body, giving it strength and colour. . . . And from it *spirits* are first begotten in the heart, which afterwards by the *arteries* are communicated to other parts."[16] As in Thomson's description, Burton conceives of blood as dispersed throughout the body, a conception all the more powerful for its inclusion in a work directed not at trained anatomists but at those who might be unfamiliar with certain physiological terms.[17] Furthermore, Burton describes the blood as the source of "Spirit . . . a most subtle vapour, which is expressed from the *blood,* and the instrument of the soul, to perform all his actions; a common tie or *medium* betwixt body and soul."[18] As Burton describes it, the blood offers a physiological basis for the soul and all its actions, unifying psychological and physiological sources of identity that later writers understand as distinct.[19]

Brabantio understands the violation of Desdemona as perpetrated against her "blood" in this comprehensive sense. The "mixtures powerful" act specifically not only against her physical body but against her blood. Othello, then, has attacked her entire identity, both social and physical, conceived of corporeally as her blood. This conception of the crime simultaneously figures it as a violent assault against her person—Othello has wrought something upon her—and as a property crime that violates the "natural," patriarchal economy—the rules of nature have been transgressed. Bringing into relief the almost imperceptible slippage between these two crimes, Brabantio argues before the Duke that he has been the victim of theft. When a senator asks Brabantio if his daughter is dead, Brabantio responds:

> Ay, to me:
> She is abused, stolen from me and corrupted
> By spells and medicines bought of mountebanks,
> for nature so preposterously to err.
>
> (ll. 60–63)

He not only responds to the senator's question affirmatively, claiming that she is dead, but goes further to say she has been stolen and abused, envisioning the crime simultaneously as a physical assault and as a theft. In fact, the slide from assault, a violation of Desdemona's bodily person, and theft, a violation of patriarchal order, naturalizes the patriarchal order, connecting it to a physical reality. Thus, "blood" for Brabantio unifies identity situating Desdemona's gender, rank, and person in biological fixity. The resort to the unifying of properties of blood offers to Brabantio a possible explanation for what otherwise would appear inexiplicable—the unstable erring of "nature" presumed in Desdemona's marriage to Othello.

Only if the abuse Desdemona suffers is clearly psychological as well as physical can Brabantio restore his conception of the relationship between Desdemona's character and her behavior. This idea is consistent with the same medical texts that understand blood as uniting body and soul in one undifferentiated whole. These texts also conceive of medicines as having both physiological and psychological functions. For instance, Burton proposes a long series of remedies for melancholy that include not only "Philosophical and Divine precepts, [and] other men's examples" but also, though he warns against their improper use, medicines and simples.[20] Thus, the crime in Brabantio's mind must be perpetrated against Desdemona's otherwise stable blood as representative of her bodily but also her spiritual identity. Furthermore, in representing the crime as a theft, Brabantio figures it as an attack against Desdemona's social identity and the communal order to which it belongs. The theft is a transgression of the patriarchal order that is naturalized by treating it as an assault that attacks her person and her social position embodied in her blood.

Whether Brabantio presents the case as a physical assault or a social and psychological attack, the crime remains a sexual one. Infamously, Iago's call to arms warns Brabantio that "an old black ram / Is tupping your white ewe!" (1.1.87–98). In Iago's crass admonition, the crime is understood as a problem of miscegenation, of a mixing of bloodlines.[21] Characters repeatedly associate blood with sexual passion, as when Iago suggest that Desdemona's feelings for Othello will fade when "the blood is made dull with the act of sport" (2.1.225). Brabantio makes no distinction between theft, assault, and miscegenation. Invoking the supple language of early modern physiology, he instinctually calls the crime "a treason of the blood" (1.1.167)—a phrase that draws together these multiple perceptions of the crime. He imagines Othello's action as an assault perpetrated against both the physical and social person of Desdemona located in her blood. It is both a violent attack and a theft. Moreover, it encompasses the sexual violation of Desdemona and the purported conjuring that enabled it. Sexual violation involves miscegenation and hence a distortion of nature just as the "mixtures powerful o'er the blood" changed Desdemona's fundamental identity causing her "perfection so to err against all rules of nature." Both are treasonous in an early modern sense—that is, they transgress the natural order in which Desdemona would fear to look upon so spirited an individual as Othello. Brabantio resorts to this formulation of a crime perpetrated against her blood, treating theft, assault, and sexual congress as one crime, and thereby naturalizes the relationship between Desdemona's body, behavior, and social identity.

However, the phrase "treason of the blood" also tempts one to a more sinister reading. Though Brabantio suggests that in fact treason has been committed against Desdemona's blood—that is against her social and physical person—one could just as easily read the phrase as suggesting that *her blood* has committed treason, usurping the governing power of her otherwise stable perfection. Early modern treatments of the blood as often usurping reason would tend to support this reading. In certain respects, Brabantio's focus on the supposed "mixtures powerful" that have tainted her blood subtly suggests this reading, but subsequent uses of the term "blood," notably by Iago, offer an even more persuasive context for it. Iago suggests that love is "a lust of the blood and a permission of the will" (1.3.335–36), envisioning blood and the identity it conveys as subservient to the will. In the context of such a formulation, Desdemona's blood has behaved treasonously, usurping the governing power of the will.

This understanding of treason is readily available in the early modern imaginary that saw an analogy between the king's rule over the commonwealth, a man's governance of his household, and the governing function of reason over the individual.[22] Again, texts such as Burton's support such a reading. In his preface "Democritus to the Reader," Burton writes:

> *As in human bodies* (saith [Boterus]) *there be divers alterations proceeding from humours, so there be many diseases in a commonwealth, which do as diversely happen from several distempers,* as you may easily perceive by their particular symptoms. . . . But whereas you shall see many discontents . . . rebellions, seditions, mutinies, contentions, idleness, riot, epicurism . . . that kingdom, that country, must needs be discontent, melancholy, hath a sick body.[23]

Following Boterus, Burton directly compares the physiological sickness of melancholy, with its imbalanced humors, to a seditious nation. Thus, Desdemona's body is both a kingdom suffering under a treasonous usurpation and physically ill, having its humors out of balance. The phrase "treason of the blood" encapsulates not only the perception of the crime as both a physical assault and a theft but also the perception of it as a violent overthrow of the governing power of reason and hence, of the social order. Thus, "blood" comes to imply not just individual identity but social order. Brabantio's invocation of the "mixtures powerful o'er the blood" restores his shattered sense of the social order by relocating Desdemona's identity in her corporeal person, naturalizing the ideas of culture and rank that her transgression disturbs.

III

This multiplicity of meanings that hovers around every use of the term relies as much on the naturalizing power of violence that connects theft and assault as it does on biological determinism. Understood in this context, Othello's cry "O, blood, blood, blood" is far more than a desperate and inarticulate expression of pain. Rather, it is an astute encapsulation of the full import of Desdemona's supposed betrayal as well as its solution. As such, it suggests the important role that violence rather than biological determinism in terms of either lineage or race plays in securing both individual identity and social order. Othello is as invested in patriarchy as Brabantio is but sees that patriarchy as relying on valorous acts of combat rather than on sexual purity and emerging ideas of biological difference. "Blood" for Othello does not merely connote biological determinisim but rather implies the process by which matter, or in modern terms biology, becomes identity through combat. Desdemona's supposed infidelity disturbs the notion of identity fixed in violent acts that her father and Othello espouse. Having used Desdemona's infidelity to unravel Othello's sense of himself, Iago offers an essentialist epistemology much like the one to which Brabantio resorts, as the solution to the disruption her infidelity poses. However, Othello ultimately rejects this solution to corporeal instability and returns to acts of bodily damage to stabilize his sense of himself.

The language of blood as "wrought upon" tends to highlight the instability that Desdemona's sexuality makes manifest. Such language disrupts essentialist notions of identity within the play by making blood a changeable object of action rather than a stable source of identity. Whereas Brabantio's use of the phrase is meant to evoke an image of integrity breached, two other uses aim at describing or, what is more, effecting a psychological change, conceived of corporeally. Upon his arrival in Cyprus, Lodovico wonders at Othello's treatment of Desdemona saying "Is it his use? / Or did the letters work upon his blood, / And new create this fault" (4.1.274–765). As Brabantio did with respect to Desdemona's behavior, Lodovico assumes that a change in blood can effect a fundamental change in personality. The letters work on the blood to change Othello's expected bearing. Similarly, Iago describes his actions against Othello as "Dangerous conceits [that] . . . with a little act upon the blood" (3.3.329–31). Tellingly, both instances figure words—the tool that Othello admits to using to woo Desdemona—as wreaking the kind of havoc on the blood that Brabantio sees in Desdemona's changed behavior. All three characters—Iago, Brabantio, and Lodovico—recognize actions against the blood as causing a change in personality at once physical and psychological. Blood in these instances is not a fixed essence but a changeable fluid.

Desdemona's marriage ultimately brings Brabantio to the horrible realization not that blood incontrovertibly dictates her identity but, quite the opposite, that her blood is not a stable marker of identity, that it can in fact be wrought upon by mere words. His language moves from the violent overthrow of her person to a recognition of her betrayal. She is no longer merely stolen but has willfully and deceitfully made her "escape" (1.3.198). As Brabantio famously predicts saying, "Look to her, Moor, if thou hast eyes to see: / She has deceived her father, and may thee" (1.3.2921-13), Desdemona's purported infidelity brings Othello to the same unbearable realization that social position does not secure behavior. Othello's disquiet is clearly caused by the instability that her infidelity implies. He vacillates in doubt, saying "I think my wife be honest, and think she is not" (3.3.387), unequivocally disturbed by his inability to fix his sense of her. In fact this inability threatens the basis both of Othello's previous conception of Desdemona and of his own masculinity. In his description of jealousy, Richard Burton writes that " 'Tis full of fear, anxiety, doubt, care, peevishness, suspicion, it turns a man into a woman."[24] The suspicion that Iago engenders in Othello effeminates him, disrupting the stability of his identity.

This instability undermines his insistence on presenting an unified identity, ensured by violent acts that bring together social position and physical reality. Much as Brabantio represents Desdemona as possessing a comprehensive integrity, Othello originally presents himself as an integral whole. Rather than understanding himself as having an interiorized identity which could conflict with his behavior, he sees his identity as pervasive and undifferentiated. When discovered on his wedding night, he refuses to hide, insisting, "Not I, I must be found. My parts, my title and my perfect soul shall manifest me rightly" (1.2.30–32). Just as Desdemona's nature, years, country, and credit all dictate a single action that Brabantio cannot believe she did not take, Othello insists that his parts, title, and perfect soul must show his true nature. Even when invoking the term "blood," Othello presents his identity as both stable and outwardly manifest. He insists upon confessing "the vices of his blood" (1.3.125), bringing into line his identity and its corporeal source. This sense of integrity, implied in the early modern conception of blood, is precisely what begins to unravel because of Iago's treachery, pointing not to the stability of blood but to its variability.

Initially, Iago disturbs the stability of "blood" as the basis of identity, but more importantly, he offers biological determinism as a means of repairing that identity. By questioning Desdemona's fidelity, presenting her essential identity as hidden rather than visible in her public acts, Iago creates a fissure between social and personal identity, between what Iago calls in his criticism of Cassio's martial prowess "prattle" and "practice" (1.1.25–29). The very language of the exchange between Iago and Othello creates the kind of doubt Iago claims Othello should have. Iago's repetition of Othello's word, "honest," obscures Othello's view of Iago's interior thoughts (3.3.100–109). Rhetorically, he creates a question out of precisely what Othello felt was unquestionable, Cassio's honesty and Desdemona's fidelity.

Othello responds to this threat by attempting to stabilize both his own and Iago's identity within this new system. He demands of Iago "Show me thy thought" (l.3.3.119), seeking Iago's disclosure of his essential self as a way to stabilize Iago's identity. As he explains,

> For I know thou'rt full of love and honesty
> And weigh'st thy words before thou giv'st them breath
> Therefore these stops of thine fright me the more.
> For such things in a false disloyal knave
> Are tricks of custom, but in a man that's just

> They're close delations, working from the heart
> That passion cannot rule.
>
> (3.3.121–27)

At this moment, he pictures true meaning as interior and stable. Meaning, no longer externally visible in acts, must be discovered and uncovered. This quest to locate interior meaning produces the idea that a stable essence exists. Unless one is a false, disloyal knave, whose meaning and identity are never stable, one's essence lies in "close delations . . . that passion cannot rule." Othello fantasizes here about the stable essence hidden deep within a "just" man that is not at the whim of the fickle passions. To know this hidden essence, another man must be "shown" this man's thought. In this moment, the epistemology, which will drive Othello through much of the play, crystallizes in his mind. Not only does Othello proceed to search for hidden secrets inside the body of Desdemona, from this point forward he also shows Iago his thought, constructing himself as just the kind of just man he believes Iago to be. Like an anatomist, he attempts to locate the truth about Desdemona in her physical being and his repetition of the word "blood" in one sense suggests this strategy. "Blood," as ideas of biological determinism, would suggest, is a stable, interior essence—a physical guarantor of behavior. However, as we have seen, the notion of blood operating in the early modern period cautions us against a solitary reading of Othello's approach, urging us to explore the equally prevalent notion of "blood" as a unifying principle associated as much with the power of bloodshed as with biological essence.

IV

Rather than wholly accepting Iago's introduction of essentialism as a solution to the unstable meaning of Desdemona's identity, Othello uses violence not to uncover Desdemona's essential identity but in fact, to stabilize her identity. Drawing on his sense of "blood" as capable of unifying psychology and corporeality, he reconstructs Desdemona's integrity just as he constructs his own. Othello's consistent presentation of pervasive integrity is fundamentally grounded in physical acts of violence. Rather than these acts of violence being the performance which manifests some stable interior, as Iago would have it, Othello sees action and essence as one in the same. What the undoing of Othello reveals is that this integrity is produced for Othello not by "blood" in the sense of heredity but by "blood" in the sense of heroic, violent action.

Many scholars have noted the anatomical epistemology that Iago introduces, which seeks truth in fixed and interior physical evidence, understanding Othello's descent into murderous rage as a failure of Othello's interpretive capabilities, as I do above. This confrontation with a new epistemology grounds Othello's introduction to an individualized and interiorized notion of self.[25] For instance, Mark Rose argues that Othello is caught between mercantile values and the absolute world of chivalry, Iago representing the former. As he explains it, "In the transitional culture of the early modern period the concept of the soul is also affected by the hegemonic principle of property. Now a soul is something a person *has* as well as something a person *is*."[26] Identity thus becomes a possession as well as an all-encompassing being. Though I agree that Othello finds himself poised between two worlds, one based on martial might and the other based on securing private property, Rose's characterization of that previous world as superstitiously supernatural and one in which "the cosmos is a single vast text and [in which] knowledge is a form of interpretation, a matter of reading mystic signatures written in things" misunderstands the relationship between matter and meaning in the period, seeing the two as entirely separate. Rose continues claiming that "There is finally no difference between language and nature, authority and observation."[27] Even as Rose sees no difference between language and nature, he also suggests a hidden meaning separate and apart from physical reality that must be uncovered. At the same time that Rose's notion of "reading" implies an analogy between word and deed, or "language and nature," it also implies a disjunction between the two. "Blood" in its multiplicity of meaning provides a far more fertile analogy for this relationship. In fact, in the period, it serves not as a mere analogy but as the mechanism whereby the relationship between things and ideas, identity and bodies, occurs and is perceived.[28]

In his self-assured defense before the Duke, Othello explicitly refuses the kind of interpretive process Rose claims marks his chivalric identity. Othello constructs his identity by valorizing the very interpretive lack characteristic of his martial identity, promising that because he is rude in his "speech, and little blest with the soft phrase of peace, . . . [he will] a round unvarnished tale deliver of [his] whole course of love" (1.3.82–91). He connects his "rude speech" both with his heroic identity and with the honesty of his "round unvarnished tale." His heroic identity, his martial prowess, is in direct opposition to perfidious speech, and his heroic actions make him incapable of uttering "the soft phrase of peace." Martial prowess, as much as barbarism, is associated with a lack of linguistic sophistication. He can only present a "round, unvarnished tale" that admits no distinction between surface and essence. By pointing to his martial identity, Othello authenticates the claim of individual and social integrity he made in insisting on being found, insisting on the integrity of his "parts," "titles," and "perfect soul." His social presentation and his individual identity must be one and the same, just as Desdemona's were. As a solider he has little eloquence, and therefore, his tale must necessarily be without deception or inconsistency. His martial acts are necessary to maintain his integrity.

Moreover, he argues that he has no identity beyond that of a soldier, that nothing is hidden from view. His words cannot and do not require interpretation, though they do rely on physical acts for their significance. He presents Desdemona's love for him as based on his soldierly qualities. As he says before the Duke, "She loved me for the dangers I had passed" (1.3.168). He claims not that his eloquence wooed her but that the history itself did. Though Othello is actually quite linguistically sophisticated and gains access to Brabantio's house through his words, he insists upon a lack of verbal skill that implies plainness much as Henry V does in Shakespeare's depiction of his wooing of Katharine of Valois.[29] Others agree with his self-perception. As Iago muses, "The Moor is of a free and open nature / That thinks men honest that but seem so" (1.3.398–99). Iago believes that Othello lacks the guile to suspect other men, precisely because he lacks the guile to be deceptive himself. His very guilelessness indicates his understanding of himself as an integrated whole.

The opposition between Othello's method of securing identity through martial violence and the biological determinism Iago propounds is perhaps best articulated in Iago's description of Cassio to Roderigo. He says:

> Forsooth a great arithmetician,
> One Michael Cassio, a Florentine
> A fellow almost damned in a fair wife,
> That never set a squadron in the field
> Nor the division of battle knows
> More than a spinster—unless the bookish theoric,
> Wherein the togaed consuls can propose
> As masterly as he. Mere prattle without practice
> Is all his soldiership; but he, sir, had th'election,
> And I of whom his eyes had seen the proof
> At Rhodes, at Cyprus, and on other grounds
> Christened and heathen—must be be lee'd and calmed.
>
> (1.1.18–29)

Here Iago makes a distinction between practice and performance, essence and appearance, that defines early modern gender identity. Heroic deeds are set against theory that is no more related to military reality than the female work of the spinster. Martial action, which Iago calls "proof," is set against "bookish theoric," as Iago makes a gendered distinction between representation and actual practice. Practice, as the basis for identity, consists of deeds whose reality is unquestionable because of their bloodiness. Not only does Iago question Cassio's masculinity, comparing him to a spinster whose work is not only feminine but discontinuous, he implies that no substance underlies his military title. He is "mere prattle without practice" just as a spinster is dismissed as both female and lacking steady work.[30] Soldiership, then, serves as the ultimate basis of masculinity because it is a practice that unifies identity, connecting titles to prowess through corporeal acts of bodily damage.

Othello's defense before the Duke does not acknowledge a distinction between his tales and the trials themselves. What Othello, then, represents is practice as essence. He does not allow the kind of difference Iago creates between "prattle" as a false performance, and "practice" as a true essence. As evident in Iago's slander of Cassio, this kind of bounded integrity is central to masculine identity.[31] As Robert Burton explains, love melancholy, of which jealousy is a type, effeminates because it is "immoderate, inordinate, and not to be comprehended in any bounds."[32] Having a bounded identity created by military feats is central to masculine identity. Othello's acts of martial prowess fundamentally unify his identity by realizing his self-presentation, grounding his identity in physical reality—the physical reality of prowess rather than the physical reality of lineage or race.

V

Othello ultimately resorts to bloodshed because of the ability of blood to unify his fractured sense of himself in visible acts of prowess. Othello's violent response to Desdemona's purported infidelity is a strategy that partakes of both the recently accessible anatomical literature and the more pervasive fluid conception of the body, bolstering the faltering connection between self and self-presentation. Understood in the context of the polysemous utterance that marks Othello's realization of betrayal, his ultimate actions restore the social significance of blood. Throughout the initial scenes of the play, "blood" comes to signify the coherence of physiology, action, and social position. In separating blood from will, Iago made manifest to Othello the possibility that these forms of selfhood might be at odds and that blood might not stably signify identity. However, rather than resorting to Iago's essentialist model, seeking merely to uncover Desdemona's lascivious nature, Othello ultimately embraces the unifying power of bloody action.

The solution Iago offers to blood's instability is a notion of blood as conveying a physiological essence apart from will, an idea that becomes increasingly common in the seventeenth century as evidenced in early modern medical texts.[33] Iago creates for Othello the necessity for firsthand knowledge as Othello searches for and demands "ocular proof" of Desdemona's infidelity, indoctrinating Othello in an anatomical epistemology. The impact of this epistemology extends beyond inciting in Othello a need for visible evidence, however. It introduces an entire new conception of the body and its relationship to identity. Anatomical literature of the period, as Jonathan Sawday has explained, begins a process whereby "the body became objectified; a focus of intense curiosity but entirely divorced from the world of the speaking and thinking subject. The division between the Cartesian subject and corporeal object, between an 'I' that thinks and an 'it' in which 'we' reside, had become absolute."[34] Though I question the absolute nature of this split, certainly before and even after Descartes, it is precisely the split that Iago introduces to Othello. The subject, once evenly dispersed throughout the body in the blood is now isolated in its interior, or better yet in the will as Iago would have it. Again, Iago calls love "merely a lust of the blood and a permission of the will," invoking a guiding consciousness absolutely in control of the animal nature contained in the blood. Iago here anticipates William Harvey's discovery of the circulation of the blood, which understood blood, not as the seat of identity or as the source of "animal spirits . . . brought up to the brain, and diffused by the nerves, to the subordinate members, giv[ing] sense and motion to them all" as Burton had, but as simply another part of the mechanical body.[35]

This fundamentally different sense of the body creates an understanding of identity as hidden and in need of discovery and, according to many, is responsible for Othello's tragic end. Both Michael Neill and Patricia Parker have noted the similarity of the epistemology Iago presents here to the project of anatomical texts of the period.[36] However, the compromise that Othello develops between this system of meaning making and the chivalric one is more subtle than either these authors or Mark Rose would suggest, combining elements of both systems in a way similar to the one presented in early modern anatomies. Rose is representative of scholars who see Othello as tragically overtaken by a new system of meaning. Othello's tragic demise, then, is a result of his inability to adapt to the development of a new form of heroism. As Rose explains, "The arts of the modern hero must be to govern and give laws . . ." not to engage in violent action.[37] Ultimately, Rose feels that Othello's death partakes of a chivalric nostalgia typical of Elizabethan tilts and that the play explores the playwright's role in the demise of the chivalric world. Thus, Othello and Desdemona become the tragic victims of a shifting notion of the place of the body.

However, I would argue that Othello more or less successfully negotiates this shifting scenario, despite his death, by restoring the social significance of blood and providing a workable model for his Venetian comrades. This model uses violence to authenticate self-representation, actually repairing the split Iago has suggested to him between behavior and identity. Though Othello and Desdemona are indeed victims of the tensions the play invokes, we have every reason to believe that Othello's compromise is adopted by the society around him, suggesting the ultimate triumph of his model even in the face of his death. Othello begs of Lodovico, "Speak of me as I am. / Nothing extenuate nor set down aught in malice" (5.2.340–41). Tellingly, his greatest concern is how he will be presented, betraying his preoccupation with unifying his body and his social identity. He authenticates the narrative that he suggests—that he was one who loved "not wisely but too well" (5.2.342)—by stabbing himself to which Lodovico responds "O bloody period" (5.2.354) and Gratiano replies "All that's spoke is marred" (5.2.355). One could understand Gratiano as exclaiming that the deaths of Desdemona and Othello mar all the power of Othello's speech, but it seems at least as likely that Gratiano indicts speech in general here, especially given Othello's worries about the distortion of his story. The "bloody period" ensures that Othello's identity is fixed in his actions. He uses a bloody deed to tie the narrative of his identity to his physical person, just as he initially "confesses the vices of his blood" bringing action and identity in line through blood.

He demonstrates this notion of identity construction early on when he arbitrates the conflict between Montano and Cassio. Upon seeing the uproar, he admonishes Montano that, "My blood begins my safer guides to rule / And passion, having my best judgment collied, / Assays to lead the way" (2.3.201–3), suggesting precisely the split that Iago does between "blood" and will. However, his identity does not reside in these passions but in the ability to rule them. This ability, not an essentialized notion of the passions, separates Christians from barbarians. A hundred lines earlier he demands:

> Are we turned Turks? And to ourselves do that
> Which heaven hath forbid the Ottomites?
> For Christian shame, put by this barbarous brawl;
> He that stirs next, to carve his own rage,
> Holds his soul light: he dies upon his motion.
>
> (2.3.166–70)

What separates the Turk from the Christian is not racial essence but a lack of heroic values—allowing personal rage to interfere with social order. Moreover, in behaving like Turks, Cassio and Montano not only draw Othello's wrath jeopardizing their physical life, they place their souls in jeopardy. Again, Othello uses violence to make psychological truth—they will lose themselves in behaving like barbarians—into physical reality—they will lose their actual lives. His masculinity resides in his ability to govern the "blood" that attempts to behave treasonously and rule his "safer guides." Othello not only articulates his sense of identity but secures it by using violence to bring physical and psychological realities together.

His murder of Desdemona too speaks of the unifying properties of bloody action. Just before strangling Desdemona, Othello explains to himself the urgency and inevitability of what he must do saying,

> It is the cause, it is the cause, my soul!
> Let me not name it to you, you chaste stars,
> It is the cause. Yet I'll not shed her blood
> Nor scar that whiter skin of hers than snow

> And smooth as monumental alabaster:
> Yet she must die, else she'll betray more men.
>
> (5.2.1–6)

Here Othello refuses to cause a breach of Desdemona's corporeal integrity, insisting on keeping her "blood" intact, yet the possibility of her betraying more men demands her death. He wants to freeze her in a state of corporeal integrity to prevent the unbearable fragmentation of identity implicit in her supposed sexual perfidy.

This sexual perfidy is intimately connected to the notion of blood. The blood that should serve as the basis of a coherent social identity, one in which Desdemona would never commit such an infidelity, has actually caused Desdemona, according to the fantasy that Iago creates, to behave in direct opposition to her essential nature as defined by her social position. In fact, it has been treasonous. The blood, then, rather than being the stable basis for social position, is the uncontrollable essence of nature, making nature and social structure unbearably incongruent and fractured. By keeping her blood contained, he does not, like the anatomist, search for a stable essence but keeps her body both intact and filled with unifying blood. Rather than choosing to reveal her essence, he uses her murder as a means of stabilizing her blood, containing it within her corporeal integrity.

Though Iago's understanding may be more and more visible in seventeenth-century texts, the older conceptions persist, and early modern anatomists work out a compromise similar to the one Othello does. Perhaps no better example exists than Andreas Vesalius and his English "borrowers." While little original anatomical work is published in England before the sixteenth century,[38] several versions of Vesalius overseen by a Flemish engraver named Thomas Lambrit (who used the pseudonym Thomas Geminus) appear in 1544, 1553, and 1559 respectively. The text, when it is in English, is drawn not from Vesalius but from a fourteenth-century manuscript, itself a compilation of several medieval anatomists. These works and the works of English anatomists, such as Thomas Vicary whose *Anatomy of the Bodie of Man* draws from the same fourteenth-century manuscript, present a conception of the body and identity much like Othello's. Geminus's version of Vesalius describes blood in much the same way Burton did, saying, "And by hyt [the blood from the heart] are refreshed and quickened all the membres of the bodye syth the spirite that is receyued in them is the instrument and treasure of the virtue of the soule."[39] Again, the blood is the source of the spirit which not only nourishes the body but is "virtue of the soule" and thus, determines identity. As in both Burton and Othello's conception, blood is responsible for keeping the different parts of identity in harmony.

Othello's murder of Desdemona and his eventual suicide show blood serving a similar function, connecting the narrative of identity Othello produces specifically to the body. Cassio immediately exclaims that but for the fact that he believed Othello to be weaponless he would have expected such a bloody end "For [Othello] was great of heart" (5.2.359). Cassio's expectations construct Othello as a heroic figure, reinstating the integrity which is central to his masculine identity. Because Othello is "great of heart," he prefers to proclaim his integrity through his suicide than to preserve his physical life. Cassio locates Othello's heroism in his heart, situating his identity in the organ that purifies the blood with its unifying properties.[40] Thus, Cassio extols Othello's blood and remarks upon it as the source of a unified identity. Violence connects Othello's narrative to his physical body, defining him as the proud and honorable individual he is. However, this body is neither the mechanistic body that Sawday locates in the work of William Harvey nor the essentialized racial body that Iago suggests but the body permeated by blood and the spirits it produces. As we have seen time and again, Othello uses violence to create an identity at once rooted in the body and nonessentialized. This conception of identity provides a sense of pervasive integrity but only through acts of violence.

Othello's actions in the end of the play unify word, deed, and social status, knitting together the discrepancies which Iago revealed to him. They are neither, as some suggest, the last gasp of a romantic heroism soon to be replaced by a mercenary mercantilism, nor are they the projections of a racialist epistemology but a subtle negotiation between the two. Employing the early modern conception of blood, Othello uses action to cement his and Desdemona's identities, repairing the integrity breached in Desdemona's supposed actions, in her "treason of the blood." Othello specifically describes Desdemona's murder as a sacrifice (5.2.65), and I would suggest that his own suicide is a sacrifice as well. His death, as he suggests of Desdemona's, will make the crucial and violent connection between body and identity. After Cassio's encomium, Lodovico reorders the scattered Venetian state by proclaiming the social meaning of the dead bodies. He demands that Iago "Look on the tragic loading of this bed: / This is thy work" (5.2.361–62). unmistakably joining Iago's deeds to the bodies themselves. He begs Gratiano to enforce justice against Iago, explicitly associating the bodies with Gratiano's governing actions. The social order, disturbed by Desdemona's "treason," is restored using the model Othello enacts. In this model, violence connects social identity and the body. Unlike an essentialist model that understands the body as innately determining identity, Othello's understanding connects social identity and the body through bloody action. Thus, Othello's final actions, rather than revealing his innate barbarism and the play's racialism, manifest one solution to the tension between a mechanistic and a fluid identity. In fact, these actions like the utterance that prefigures them are not atavistic but the basis for restoring social order. Othello's anguished cry explains the necessity of the violent actions of the end of the play. Rather than following Iago's instruction, Othello uses martial violence and his polyvalent understanding of blood to unify physical, social, and psychological bases for identity.

Notes

Previous versions of this article were presented at the October 2006 Ohio Valley Shakespeare Conference (Marietta, OH) and at the April 2002 Symposium on Violence, Politics, and Culture in Early Modern Europe at the University of Mississippi (Oxford, MS). I would like to thank the participants at each for their comments and suggestions. I would also like to thank the members of the Mellon Workshop on issues of embodiment at Brown University (2005–6) and the members of the Folger Shakespeare Library Seminar on Early Modern Embodiment led by Valerie Traub for helping develop the project. Finally, I would like to thank Coppélia Kahn and Michelle Dowd for their careful reading of the many drafts of this article.

1. 3.3.454. All citations are taken from William Shakespeare, *Othello,* ed. E. A. J. Honigmann (New York: Arden, 2001).

2. For a discussion of various iterations of this argument, see Virginia Vaughn, *Othello: A Contextual History* (New York: Cambridge University Press, 1994), esp. 68.

3. This reading contends that the pressures of living as a cultural and social minority in Venetian society drive Othello to revert to the stereotypical behavior to which the Elizabethan mind thought he was predisposed. In other words, the strain of Desdemona's infidelity causes his racial essence violently and visibly to emerge from underneath his composed exterior. Michael Neill has suggested that this type of reading is, indeed, the "most common twentieth-century strategy" to deal with the issue of race. Michael Neill, "Unproper Beds: Race, Adultery, and the Hideous in *Othello,*" in *Critical Essays on Shakespeare's Othello,* ed. Anthony Gerard Barthelemy (New York: Macmillan, 1994), 216–38, esp. 191 first printed in *Shakespeare Quarterly* 40 (1989): 383–412, esp. 393. In rejecting this narrative, I follow the work of Natasha Korda who argues that such a conception "define[s] him as irremediably other." Korda, "The Tragedy of the Handkerchief: Female Paraphernalia and the Properties of Jealousy in *Othello,*" in *Shakespeare's Domestic Economies* (Philadelphia: University of Pennsylvania, 2002), 129.

4. For the reliance of ideas of difference on humoral distinctions and the flexibility implicit in this system see Mary Floyd-Wilson, *English Ethnicity and Race in Early Modern Drama* (New York: Cambridge University Press, 2003) and Daniel Vitkus, *Turning Turk: English Theater and the Multicultural Mediterranean 1570–1630* (New York: Palgrave Macmillan, 2003). Ania Loomba suggest that it was in fact the problem of conversion that "catalysed the development of 'biological' ideas of race," suggesting that new, racialist discourses were created in response to the inadequacy and instability of existing racial discourse *Shakespeare, Race, and Colonialism* (New York: Oxford University Press, 2002), 26. For further evidence of a "climatological but non-essentializing discourse" of difference, see Carol Thomas Neely, "Hot Blood: Estranging Mediterranean Bodies in Early Modern Medical and Dramatic

Texts" in *Disease, Diagnosis, and Cure on the Early Modern Stage,* eds. Stephanie Moss and Kaara L. Peterson (Burlington, VT: Ashgate, 2004), 55–68, esp. 58.

5. See, for example, Lara Bovilsky, *Barbarous Play: Race on the English Renaissance Stage* (Minneapolis: University of Minnesota Press, 2008) and Sujata Iyengar, *Shades of Difference* (Philadelphia: University of Pennsylvania Press, 2005). While Bovilsky insists that an idea that we can understand as racialization that later becomes embedded in scientific racialism operates in the early modern period, Iyengar, following Raymond Williams, helpfully distinguishes between the residual, dominant, and emergent structures of feeling, arguing that a residual mythology of color competes with an emergent mythology of race over the course of the sixteenth and seventeenth centuries.

6. Jean Feerick, *Strangers in Blood: Relocating Race in the Renaissance* (Buffalo, NY: University of Toronto Press, 2010), esp. 31.

7. Ian Smith, *Race and Rhetoric in the Renaissance: Barbarian Errors* (New York: Palgrave, 2009), esp. 130.

8. The *Oxford English Dictionary* cites multiple meanings of the word "blood" operating in the seventeenth century. Particularly frequent are references to blood as "taking of life, manslaughter, murder, death" (Def. 3a), "The vital fluid; *hence,* the vital principle, that upon which life depends; life" (Def. 4a), and "The supposed seat of emotion, passion;. . . Passion, temper, mood, disposition; *emphatically,* high temper, mettle; anger" (Def. 5). In addition, it bears the sense of familial kinship. However, the *Oxford English Dictionary* distinguishes between the definition of blood that is "popularly treated as the typical part of the body which children inherit from their parents and ancestors; hence that of parents and children, and of the members of a family or race, is spoken of as identical, and as being distinct from that of other families or races" (Def. 8) most popular in the nineteenth century and the notion of blood as "Blood-relationship, and *esp.* parentage, lineage, descent" (Def. 9a) more prevalent in the seventeenth century.

9. Both Emily Bartels and Michael Neill suggest that Iago is responsible for instituting a racialist epistemology. As Bartels explains, "It is Iago and not the play itself that attempts to fix the terms of difference, and Iago's terms not Othello's difference that come under fire." Bartels, "Making More of the Moor: Aaron, Othello, and Renaissance Refashionings of Race," *Shakespeare Quarterly* 41, no. 4 (Winter 1990): 433–54, esp. 448. Michael Neill, "'Mulattos,' 'Blacks,' and 'Indian Moors': *Othello* and Early Modern Constructions of Human Difference," *Shakespeare Quarterly* 49, no. 4 (Winter 1998), 361–74, esp. 362.

10. What follows is by no means an exhaustive list of discussions of race as calling on an increasingly fixed idea of biology in *Othello.* However, it should serve to offer some exemplary instances. Arthur A. Little, Jr., for instance, argues that "Blackness. . . is an individual body or soul that creates and gives meaning to already present cultural meanings." He points back to the stability of the body as a foundation for cementing cultural meanings. Little, "'An Essence that's Not Seen': The Primal Scene of Racism in *Othello,*" *Shakespeare Quarterly* 44, no. 3 (Autumn 1993): 304–24, esp. 322. Similarly, Karen Newman invokes the notion of "stock prejudices against blacks" implying the existence of a relatively stable racial discourse. Newman, "'And wash the Ethiop white': Femininity and the Monstrous in *Othello,*" *Criti-*

cal Essays in Shakespeare's Othello, ed. Gerard Anthony Barthelemy (New York : G. K. Hall, 1994), 124–43, esp. 128. This discourse, which figures black men as overly preoccupied with sex, is one that Anthony Barthelemy argues even representations of non-villainous Moors confirms. Barthelemy, "Ethiops Washed White: Moors of the Nonvillainous Type," *Critical Essays in Shakespeare's* Othello, ed. Gerard Anthony Barthelemy, (New York : G. K. Hall, 1994), 92–104. Kim Hall argues that the use of the terminology of black and fair cannot be ignored as evidence of a racialized discourse. As Hall puts it, "The language of fairness and darkness is always potentially racialized." Hall, *Things of Darkness: Economies of Race and Gender in Early Modern England,* (Ithaca, NY: Cornell University Press, 1995), 261. In a similar vein, Dympna Callaghan argues that "black skin is at once immutable and superficial," expressing a sense of racial essence, even if that essence is on the surface. Though these critics are right to point out the burgeoning racial discourse, to impute this sense to Othello himself or even to the broader Venetian community seems problematic.

11. See note 4.

12. For examples of the idea that Othello's occupation drives him violently to restore a world of absolutes, see Vaughn, *Othello,* 50 and C.F. Burgess, *Shakespeare Quarterly* 26, no. 2 (Spring, 1975): 208–13.

13. Not all early modern medical texts operate with the same conception of the body. In addition to a burgeoning discourse of the mechanistic body, both Galenic and Paracelsan model compete in these texts. See Stephanie Moss, "Transformation and Degeneration: The Paracelsan/Galenic Body in *Othello,*" in *Disease, Diagnosis, and Cure on the Early Modern Stage,* eds. Stephanie Moss and Kaara L. Peterson (Burlington, VT: Ashgate, 2004), 55–68, esp. 58.

14. Andreas Vesalius, *Compendios a totius anatomie delineatio, aere exarata: per Thomam Geminum* (London: 1553), 15r. The ascription of this text to Vesalius is somewhat misleading. Geminus copied plates from Vesalius's *De Humani Corporis Fabrica* but appended a Fourteenth-century manuscript. See also page twenty six above.

15. Quoted in Gail Kern Paster, *The Body Embarrassed* (Ithaca, NY: Cornell University Press, 1993), 65.

16. Robert Burton, *The Anatomy of Melancholy,* ed. and trans. Floyd Dell and Paul Jordan-Smith (New York: Tudor Publishing Co., 1927), 128–29.

17. Burton, *Anatomy of Melancholy*, 127.

18. Ibid., 129.

19. For further discussion of this distinction, see John Sutton, *Philosophy and Memory Traces: Descartes to Connectionism* (New York: Cambridge University Press, 1998), esp. 57.

20. Burton, *Anatomy of Melancholy*, 540. In early modern medicine, a "simple" is any medicine that is formed of a single constituent. See *Oxford English Dictionary,* "Simple" (Def. 6).

21. For a further discussion of the importance of miscegenation in the play see Newman, "And wash the Ethiop white."

22. For further explication of the analogy between commonwealth, individual household, and individual health see Susan Dwyer Amussen, *An Ordered Society: Gender and Class in Early Modern England* (New York: Blackwell, 1988) and

Frances Dolan, *Dangerous Familiars : Representations of Domestic Crime in England, 1550–1700* (Ithaca, NY: Cornell University Press, 1994).

23. Burton, *Anatomy of Melancholy*, 65.

24. Ibid., 728.

25. For examples of this reading see Stanley Cavell, *Disowning Knowledge in Six Plays of Shakespeare* (New York: Cambridge University Press, 1987), Mark Breitenberg, *Anxious Masculinities in Early Modern England* (New York: Cambridge University Press, 1996), and David Hillman, *Shakespeare's Entrails: Belief, Scepticism and the Interior of the Body* (New York: Palgrave, 2007), esp. 1–57. For its relationship to Othello's interiorized sense of self see also, Katharine Eisaman Maus, *Inwardness and Theater in the English Renaissance* (Chicago: University of Chicago Press, 1995) and Howard Marchitello, *Narrative and Meaning in Early Modern England: Browne's Skull and Other Histories* (Cambridge: Cambridge University Press, 1997).

26. Mark Rose, "Othello's Occupation: Shakespeare and the Romance of Chivalry," *English Literary Renaissance* (Autumn 1985): 15, no. 3 293–311, esp. 305.

27. Ibid., 305.

28. Richard Sugg argues that anatomy, at least in its early forms, tends to make the connection between body and soul literal rather than one of mere analogy. Richard Sugg, *Murder after Death: Literature and Anatmoy in Early Modern England* (Ithaca, NY: Cornell University Press, 2007), 89.

29. For more on Othello's verbal acumen in relation to race see Ania Loomba, "Shakespeare and Cultural Difference," *Alternative Shakespeares, Vol. 2* (New York: Routledge, 1996) 164–91, esp. 174.

30. "Spinster," like blood, is a polyvalent term in early modern England, denoting alternately an occupation, a criminal category, or a sexual category. As an occupation, spinning could not be the sole means of support, and hence, Iago's invective disparages not only Cassio's masculinity but also his professional stature. See Fiona McNeill, *Poor Women in Shakespeare* (New York: Cambridge University Press, 2007), esp. 31–34.

31. See, for instance, Paster, *The Body Embarrassed* , esp. 64–112 and Susanne Scholz, *Body Narratives: Writing the Nation and Fashioning the Subject in Early Modern England* (New York: St. Martin's, 2000), esp. 15–38.

32. Burton, Anatomy of Melancholy, 655.

33. For a further discussion the split between mind and body circulating in early modern medical texts see Sugg, *Murder after Death*, 130–159.

34. Jonathan Sawday, *The Body Emblazoned: Dissection and the Human Body in Renaissance Culture* (New York: Routledge, 1996), 29.

35. Burton, *Anatomy of Melancholy*, 29. Though William Harvey published "On the Motion of the Heart and Blood in Animals" in 1628, most of the work for it was completed in 1616. Gail Kern Paster describes the understanding that preceded Harvey saying that "In the conceptual linking of blood flow, both arterial and venous, with neural transmission, blood, spirit, and sensation become nearly indistinguishable in action and properties," indicating that blood was not merely the purveyor of nutriment but the substance of identity. Gail Kern Paster, "Nervous Tension: Networks of Blood and Spirit in the Early Modern Body" in *The Body in Parts: Fantasies of Corporeality in Early Modern Europe,* eds. David Hillman and Carla Mazzio (New York: Routledge, 1997), 107–25, esp. 113.

36. Michael Neill, *Issues of Death: Mortality and Identity in English Renaissance Tragedy* (New York: Oxford University Press, 1997). Patricia Parker, "Othello and Hamlet: Dilation, Spying, and the 'Secret Place' of Woman," in *Shakespeare Reread: The Texts in New Contexts,* ed. Russ MacDonald (Ithaca : Cornell University Press, 1994) 105–46.

37. Rose, "Othello's Occupation," 308.

38. For a discussion of English anatomical studies in the sixteenth century see C. D. O'Malley and K. F. Russell, introduction to *Introduction to Anatomy 1532: A Facsimile Reproduction with English Translation and an Introductory Essay on Anatomical Studies in Tudor England,* by David Edwardes (Stanford, CA: Stanford University Press, 1961), esp. 24.

39. *Thomas Geminus: Compendiosa totius anatomie delineation A Facsimile of the First English Edition of 1553 in the Version of Nicholas Udall with an Introduction by C.D. O'Malley* (London: Dawson's of Pall Mall, 1959), A.6.

40. Tellingly, Katharine Park points out the heart rather than the brain was the locus of selfhood until the eighteenth century. Katharine Park, *Secrets of Women: Gender, Generation, and the Origins of Human Dissection* (New York: Zone Books, 2006), 264. For the significance of the heart, see also William Slights, *The Heart in the Age of Shakespeare* (New York: Cambridge, 2008).

Reviews

Street Scenes: Late Medieval Acting and Performance, by Sharon Aronson-Lehavi. New York: Palgrave Macmillan, 2011. Pp. 183 Hardcover $84.00.

Reviewer: BOYDA JOHNSTONE

This book takes its title from an essay by Bertolt Brecht, "The Street Scene: A Basic Model for an Epic Theatre," which, according to Sharon Aronson-Lehavi, envisions a method of acting that highlights the tension between performing actor and enacted character rather than blurring and eliminating it. Aronson-Lehavi's most useful contribution to medieval drama studies might be her use of modern non-illusionist performance theory and examples to elucidate medieval theatrical practices, thus opening up her book to a potentially wide-ranging audience of performance theorists and medieval scholars alike. According to the author, medieval drama assumed a theory of performance, namely that the division between performing and performed must always be highlighted rather than suppressed for medieval players, "always emphasizing the signifying function of the theatrical event and never concealing its theatricality" (3).

Strangely enough, some of Aronson-Lehavi's most convincing evidence for the existence of medieval performance theory appears in her Introduction, in which she surveys early modern responses to (and disdain for) earlier drama. As she argues, the early modern period saw the birth of the aesthetic ideal of verisimilitude, the need to "Suit the action to the word, the word to the action" (8–9); Hamlet himself famously ridicules cycle drama when he states he would have a fellow whipped for "o'erdoing Termagant. It out-Herods Herod" (3.2.13–14). She also treats this and other early modern examples as case studies for the "new kind of humanist drama being written," which reacts against non-illusionistic (and medieval) stage practices (13). That Renaissance authors used such theatrical methods as foils for their own imitative or illusionistic theatrical concepts suggests that there was indeed an existing concept of medieval drama, even if that concept was only fully articulated post Middle Ages.

While this Introduction establishes a convincing case, unfortunately some of the rest of the book loses steam, partially because of its limited scope. Two of three chapters focus extensively on the late-medieval polemical text *Treatise of Miraclis Pleyinge* (*ToMP*) as a piece of aesthetic criticism of medieval theater. This text, composed between 1380 and 1425, objects to religious drama because it trivializes holy or serious events, and engages participants in a fleshly experience that could detract from the "real" or "efficacious" experience of Christ's works (17–18). Aronson-Lehavi thus opens up a conversation regarding the possible dangers of performing the divine that we usually associate with the Renaissance, and in this sense her intervention in the field is important. However, it remains unclear how pervasive the aesthetic attitudes the *ToMP* carries really were, since the text appears in only one manuscript. A more sustained discussion of the implications of the text's manuscript context, as well as its Wycliffite or Lollard associations, would have been welcome.

Even so, Aronson-Lehavi provides a meticulous discussion of this fascinating text, surely the most thorough to-date. Particularly useful is her analysis in chapter 1 of *ToMP*'s key terms, and her theoretical examination of how the *ToMP*'s objections to drama reveal its socially disruptive potential: by casting rigid prescriptions over how biblical material should be portrayed (namely without associating it with "bourding" or playing), *ToMP* underscores the ways in which drama is "susceptible to contingency and indeterminacy; meaning constantly threatens to escape the structure of the performance" (25). Occasionally, however, her own meaning becomes elusive, as when she concludes that "a 'game' or a 'play' in late medieval terminology is a performative event where something *real* happens *really*" (50, emphasis in the original). And as she frequently reminds us of the *ToMP*'s belief in the utter division of spirit and flesh, she herself loses sight of the possibility that this condition may not always have been the case, and that the flesh could potentially operate in the service of spiritual ideals. She argues, for example, that the actor's fleshly presence and use of the vernacular tamper with the removed and abstract voice of God (61). Many scholars might argue the opposite—that such elements aided devotion, drawing viewers into a closer relationship with higher truths.

In the final chapter of the book, Aronson-Lehavi more consciously applies her theoretical concepts to the plays themselves, discussing moments in the York cycle that highlight the ontological duality between the "here" of the play and the "then" of scripture. In this chapter, Bertolt Brecht's influence can again be felt, as Aronson-Lehavi adopts his notions of "epic acting" and "total acting." Epic acting intentionally exposes or draws attention to the theatrical mechanisms, such as when an actor's mask is alluded to, or when a character becomes a mold to be refilled by different performers, rather than a stable and singular psychological presence. In the phenomenological realm of total acting, the laboring and suffering body of the actor potentially distracts from or supersedes meditation on the character's divine signification, such as when the tranquil Christ is being hoisted onto the cross by the loquacious and clumsy soldiers in the York *Crucifixion*.

Inevitably, some of her dramatic examples are more convincing than others: while it seems clear that specific conditions of production, such as the performance of Noah by the Shipwrights' guild, would have called attention to the material production of the pageants, it is less clear how God the Father's statement that "I am gracyus and grete, God withoutyn begynnyng" may have represented a deliberate effort to emphasize the division between actor and character, rather than to extinguish it (88). How else would the actor have articulated his role as God? Or, to put it a different way, how could an actor ever *not* call attention to his humanity on some level? If even first-person dialogue refers to the play's artificiality, it is difficult to envision any possible alternative.

Despite some gaps in her argument, Sharon Aronson-Lehavi's attentive reading of the under-studied *Tretise of Miraclis Pleyinge* in tandem with the York cycle plays, and her enthusiasm for the theories, mechanics, and lived experience of performance—both medieval and modern—make this book a valuable contribution to medieval drama studies. It may be particularly useful to young scholars, or those unfamiliar with Middle English, as it consistently supplies modern translations of Middle English texts—including the *ToMP* in its entirety in an Appendix. Future scholars might test Aronson-Lehavi's theory of divided consciousness on other plays or genres, such as morality drama. And all of us would do well to learn from her enviable practice of combining modern theories with medieval plays, and modern plays with medieval theories.

The Language of Space in Court Performance, 1400–1625, by Janette Dillon. Cambridge and New York: Cambridge University Press, 2010. Pp. 292. Hardcover $129.95.

Reviewer: HEATHER C. EASTERLING

The field of early modern studies in recent years has seen the development of a robust critical interest in the city, most notably London, as a site and space of immense theatricality that complexly interacted with the popular theater that emerged there in the period. Drawing especially on the work of Michel de Certeau and Henri Lefebvre, critics have queried the significance of many place- and space-based forms that emerged or notably evolved with London's early modern transformation into an unprecedented urban environment. Alongside such reframing and re-theorizing of the city and its spaces as performed and performing, it has been perhaps more obvious and thus less worthy of sustained investigation that court culture at this time was even more highly theatrical. Critical interest in the court masque and in the masque culture of the Jacobean court has revealed the importance of the performance- and the audience-space for these spectacles, of the choreography of the aristocratic players, and of the often purpose-built venues where masques were performed. But apart from this work and intermittent interest in occasions such as royal entries, there has remained a substantial gap in critical attention to the precise and manifold theatrics of court life and court events. Janette Dillon's new book, *The Language of Space in Court Performance, 1400–1625,* thus makes a timely and valuable contribution to filling that gap. Dillon's introductory first chapter alone is noteworthy for its broad attention to the under-theorizing of court culture as theatrical, and for its rehearsal of the pertinence of contemporary place- and space-theory for helping us make sense of the early modern English court's "intense concern with the precise way that movement takes place within a given space" (2). She goes much further in this highly scholarly project, however, using seven additional chapters to present deliberately Geertzian "thick descriptions" of the many and varied performances of late-medieval and early modern court life, specifically royal entries and coronations (chapter 2), royal progresses (chapter 3), meetings with ambassadors (chapter 4), court revels (chapter 5), tournaments (chapter 6), trials (chapter 7), and executions (chapter 8).

Over the book's eight chapters, Dillon's analytical and rhetorical method varies. At times she surveys a range of instances of a kind of court performance—royal entries, for example—and focuses only briefly on one or two instances. In other chapters, such as chapter 3, on royal progresses, and chapter 8, on executions, she uses all or most of the chapter to explore just one significant event: Elizabeth I's 1575 Kenilworth progress, and the execution of Mary, Queen of Scots, respectively. Dillon does not articulate her rationale for determining which approach is more appropriate for the different classes of ceremonial events she treats, but the zooming-in and zooming-out effect keeps the reader highly engaged. In addition to her use of de Certeau, Dillon draws on other grounds for her analysis of movement in space and the body's performance of and in space, most strikingly dance theory, in her chapter on royal entries, and its interest in bodily "amplitude," "direction," "focus," "shape," and "grouping" (33), and precisely how these help create spectacle in not just visual but highly kinesthetic ways. The author also is careful to address the potential for controversy—both ethical and critical—in her inclusion and analysis of trials and executions as performances: these are not occasions of "play" by any means, of course. But, Dillon reminds us, most participants in these events, even if—or perhaps especially if—unwilling, "understood themselves to *be* players at [these] key . . . events" (11, emphasis original).

I found this to be a fascinating and important book. Dillon's central claim concerning these diverse rituals and the existence of a powerful and subtle "syntax" involving bodies, space, and "code[s] of movement, stance and gesture that operated within any given place" (17) itself is not groundbreaking; in our current critical climate it feels unsurprising to be told that the court was a deeply theatrical place and that elaborate bodily uses and production of space were essential to this. It is in support of this claim that Dillon provides something much more valuable: a formidable amount of primary research coupled with sophisticated and inventive analysis, all of which becomes compelling evidence of a courtly semiotics of place and space. There are some omissions as well as awkward inclusions worth noting with the book. Chief among the omissions is some kind of conclusion after seven highly focused chapters; I also found it odd that the book did not include a conventional index, relying on an "index of names" only. As for inclusions, chapter 1 employed far too many scare quotes around terms and concepts. This, along with a somewhat labored discussion of the terms "space" and "place" in current criticism, lent an awkwardly pre-emptive or self-conscious air to parts of the introduction that was unnecessary given the project's overall merits and achievements. In sum, this is an exciting new archive for reading the early modern court and assessing the possibilities of material critique.

Actors and Acting in Shakespeare's Time: The Art of Stage Playing, by John Astington. Cambridge: Cambridge University Press, 2010. Pp. 269. Hardcover $124.95.

Reviewer: LLOYD EDWARD KERMODE

It is not long into the introduction of John Astington's *Actors and Acting in Shakespeare's Time* before the reader understands that this book is going to be fascinating and frustrating by turn. While portraits of John Lowin and Richard Perkins and definitions of the "well graced" or not-very-good player suggest it will be a short road before we arrive at the essence of historical individuals and their special modes of performance, Astington's discussion of the contemporary praise for protean (rather than actor-specific) acting styles and his acknowledgment of the incompleteness of the historical record, especially in the sixteenth century, warn us that recovering consistent evidence for the technique or development of an actor's style and thereby perhaps something of the actor himself might be a wild goose chase. For some readers of this book, however, the landscape of the hunt will provide thrill enough.

The first chapter deftly weaves a carefully historicized study of acting terminology—making a "face," "gesture," and "accent"; "presence," "action," and "imitation"—and a wish for a sort of affective appreciation of human stage interaction. Astington moves fairly freely (and sometimes rapidly) between close textual readings, anecdotes, ironic asides, and suppositions about manners of playing. As the book progresses, this medley style at once gives the impression of a great wealth of accumulated material brought to bear on each section's study of an actor or company or performance while the reader—this one, anyway—does not always feel as if their understanding of the *art* of playing has been significantly advanced. To clarify, this is a result of the type and extent of surviving evidence, not of Astington's extensive collation of material and mode of presentation.

The second chapter on playing and education does an exquisite job of laying out the role of dramatic activity in the boys' schools in Shakespeare's time. Astington explains the differences (and interactions and mergers) between singing schools that happened to include dramatic pieces, academic institutions that used drama for rhetorical and elocutionary training, and dedicated centers for training young actors. He is also concerned to expand his study briefly to consider the probable practices in education outside London and to note when the schools were using public performance as part of their curriculum. As he moves on to discuss university performance, Astington contrasts the possible effects of a cast of similarly aged boys in a school production versus that of tertiary students ranging from their early twenties through thirties, as well as clarifying the further contrast with a slightly older demographic of the English-language-playing Inns of Court performers.

The third chapter is, to my mind, the best. Its multiple mini-biographies of apprenticeship tell imperfect and incomplete, but wonderful, tales of boys placed with adult actors and lays the foundation for one of Astington's main purposes in the book, and that is to establish that "groups of actors functioned as larger families, taking seriously the word 'brotherhood'" (84). In spite of the confession that it is "difficult to be confident about describing any normative pattern of theatrical apprenticeship" (85) (some seeming to be fleeting, some three years or so, others longer; all probably getting the young apprentice on stage and in front of audiences as soon as possible), this chapter really conveys the hard work of the constant cycle of learning, teaching, and playing. Astington manages to piece together several useful generalities about apprentice practice, for example, how the dramatic student apprentice would process through his career starting in female roles; how the master-and-boy relationship seems to have worked in the early years of their engagement; and how physical development affected playing style/choices for a youth. The dust jacket blurb claims that the book is "perfect for courses," and with this in mind, I wanted some subheadings and tighter organization here, as Astington does helpfully in chapter 2. (I have indeed brought Astington's ideas into the classroom, but selecting clear, short sections for non-specialist students to read was difficult, and I ended up summarizing main points dotted throughout the text.)

Any reader still wanting to find a definitive "method" and style for a specific actor—in spite of what we think we know about a blustering Alleyn in Marlovian parts—will finally have their hopes dashed in chapter 4, "Playing many parts." Beginning with a survey of some of Alleyn's various roles, this chapter emphasizes the versatility of professional performers in the period, from developing young minor actors to those whose names have become familiar to the academy and theater practitioners. If we tend to look back and slot players into a few representative and similar parts, Astington argues, we are doing early modern players and company and audience expectation a disservice. Alleyn and Burbage surely demonstrated breadth in their abilities, and the play texts themselves reveal that a single, star comic in a troupe, for example, could hardly hold down the fort either in terms of playing multiple fools (when more than one appear on stage) or by sticking to single, lead comic roles when a play demands several roles of "folly." "One should not make too much of a fetish of the leading comic performer within early modern playing companies," concludes Astington (120). The summary of possible role adaptation in this chapter is praiseworthy, although I can't help feel that, as elsewhere, the quick survey of what little we know about named actors in named roles leave us unsurprised by the conclusions: players were good at what they did, and they didn't overspecialize if their company required them to spread their thespian wings. However, this chapter continues to historicize well, and, in the vein of work such as Alan Dessen's book on stage conventions and modern interpreters, Astington reminds us of conflicts between our modern sense of performance possibility and early modern practice. For example, our attraction to thematic doubling (Astington uses the example of the Fool and Cordelia in *King Lear*) is a practice that would be "out of the question for the actors of the King's men" (125); major actors (in this case Armin) take lead comic or serious roles and apprentices or "youths" (up to their early twenties) would take the female roles.

Astington's final chapter, "Players at work," is anchored in two case studies of plays for which we have early seventeenth-century cast lists. This approach traces details of players in parts, which again describes history more than it enlightens us about the art of playing. But this chapter also does a rather impressive job of democratizing the history of players; thus the short-careered and short-lived contemporaries John Thompson and John Honeyman get a moment in the spotlight next to the established older John Lowin in Astington's detailed pseudo-reconstruction of rehearsal and performance moments of Massinger's *The Roman Actor*. This chapter also demonstrates in action several observations and claims Astington made earlier in the book on apprenticeship and multiple roles—the probability of small-group rehearsal; the company as fraternity, as symbiotic machine where old and young are necessary for each other's success; and the relationship of actors working together or replacing each other as fellows and substitutes rather than always as rivals—the latter being a dynamic we tend arguably to privilege.

The conclusion remains tentatively confident of the book's achievement. Things are still "probably . . . partly . . . supposedly" known and events and relationships still "must have been . . . must have been . . . must have taken . . . would have been" (184) a certain way; those (non-) commitments in a conclusion confirm the book's courageous and semi-satisfying course from studying parts and probabilities of evidence and meaning to producing useful hypotheses and deductions. The book's appendix includes a very good biographical list of significant players 1558–1660.

Staging Spectatorship in the Plays of Philip Massinger, by Anne Rochester. Burlington, VT: Ashgate 2010. Pp. 172. Hardback $99.95

Reviewer: CHARLES PASTOOR

Metadramatic performances provide a unique and valuable window into the world of early modern drama. In a period when discussions regarding the purpose and value of drama and its probable effect on its audience were narrowly circumscribed by questions regarding its moral function, the actual onstage depiction of audiences and dramatic performances gives us a much clearer sense of how the playwrights themselves viewed that relationship. And of all the playwrights whose work features such dramatic insets, Philip Massinger is perhaps the one who most explicitly deals with the relationship between the stage, its critics, and its audience in one of the period's most metatheatrical plays, *The Roman Actor*. While considerable attention has been given, especially as of late, to this play, Joanne Rochester's *Staging Spectatorship in the Plays of Philip Massinger,* the seventh published work in Ashgate's "Studies in Performance and Early Modern Drama" series, is the only book-length study of on-stage spectatorship in Massinger's work.

The Roman Actor begins with a spirited though thoroughly conventional defense of the theater through its main character, the actor Paris. Much of the scholarship devoted to *The Roman Actor* addresses the question of whether the subsequent inset plays featured in the play support this defense or undermine it, with more recent critics tending towards the conclusion that it does the latter. This failure is frequently ascribed to the manner in which the Emperor Domitian co-opts the stage to serve his own ends, with fairly obvious parallels to the political use of the theater during the Stuart regime. Rochester acknowledges the political dimension but places it within what she calls the "interlocking set of [the play's] interpretive gazes" (18). The result is an analysis that is both trenchant and thoughtful and that addresses Massinger's interest in the precise relationship that drama bears to its audience. Massinger, Rochester points out, is offering the audience a kind of "experiential lesson" in the role it plays in creating drama, and in contrast to the angry and pessimistic playwright seen by other critics, she discovers in Massinger one who is "realistic," "practical[,] and practiced" and who "insists his audience take their work seriously" (50).

In the second chapter, Rochester turns to the masques within four of Massinger's other plays: *The Picture, The Duke of Milan, The Guardian,* and *The City Madam.* She begins by summarizing the various forms of masques (Jonsonian court masques, masques performed at the Inns of Court, and country-house masques), and then proceeds to lay out the various dramatic and dramaturgical functions of masques-within (dramatic triggers, emblematic illustrations of themes or concepts, structural dramaturgical elements, and allegorical satiric mirrors), before turning to the masques within Massinger's plays. In these she finds a balanced representation of the masque: whereas the masque within the tragicomic *The Duke of Milan* illustrates "the court's pleasure in morally dubious outward show," Massinger's comedy *The Guardian* features masques-within that are both satirical and celebratory.

Most of the second chapter, however, is given over to analysis of the masques within *The City Madam,* Massinger's most metadramatic play after *The Roman Actor.* And, as with her reading of the other insets, Rochester's treatment of *The City Madam* points toward a playwright who fully understands both the limitations and the potential of dramatic art. In contrast to Martin Garrett, who argues that Massinger treats the masque with something akin to contempt, Rochester finds something else—an awareness of the deceptive nature of the masque but also an belief in its transformational power as satire, and its ability to challenge the viewer "to see beyond surface appearances to the truth beneath" (92). And masques wield that power, in part because, unlike the typical practice of early modern play-acting, masques offered entertainment that made the spectator not merely an observer but an active participant in the spectacle. Thus, Rochester writes, "the 'astounding' power of the visual—can be beneficially wielded by Massinger's art, so that the dangers of spectatorship become a facet of the powers of theatre" (93).

The third chapter shifts from dramatic performance to the staging of spectatorship of visual art in Massinger's plays. The chapter begins with a brief survey of various approaches to interpreting visual art in the seventeenth century, as well as the uses of painting and sculpture on the Renaissance stage, before turning to their presence in Massinger's plays, including *The Renegado* and *The Emperor of the East,* but focusing especially on the use of the miniature in *The Picture.* Here Rochester finds spectatorship presented in its purest form, since the audience cannot see the miniature portrait of Mathias's wife, which supposedly indicates her fidelity to her husband, or lack thereof. Instead, they see only Mathias's response to that art. And in this response, Rochester finds further evidence of Massinger's "ongoing interest in the larger question of how viewers interpret what they see" (123).

The Picture ends with a staging of the repudiation of art, and, like other plays featuring "magical images," points to the theater as pollutive and "a place of grave danger" (105). If this is the case, it would be helpful if Rochester would explain how such a view of the theater squares with her assessment of Massinger as a playwright who attempts to "inculcate lessons, explore moral, social, and intellectual problems, and . . . analyse the meaning and function of drama itself (140). Nevertheless, *Staging Spectatorship* makes a valuable contribution to scholarship on Massinger; furthermore, it is a valuable addition to the growing number of works dedicated to exploring meta- and paradramatic inclusions in early modern drama. By examining a range of such inclusions together, Rochester offers a more complete picture of Massinger as a playwright than the many articles that explore *The Roman Actor* and other plays individually or in smaller subsets. Of most interest will be the chapter on *The Roman Actor,* since, by Rochester's own admission, Massinger's use of masques-within, while more frequent that his use of plays-within, is less innovative or central to his dramaturgy. And the analysis of visual art in *The Picture* and other plays largely supports the intriguing assertions and compelling arguments made in previous chapters.

Ornamentalism: The Art of Renaissance Accessories, edited by Bella Mirabella. Ann Arbor: University of Michigan Press, 2011. Pp. 342. Hardcover $75.00.

Reviewer: ERIKA T. LIN

Physical artifacts have long been studied by art historians, but in the last decade or two, interest in early modern material culture has experienced its own Renaissance in literary scholarship as well. The thirteen essays included in this lavishly illustrated book focus on that subset of objects deemed "accessories": jewelry, gloves, handkerchiefs, ruffs, shoes, veils, pearls, and many other fascinating adornments to the body. The collection demonstrates that, far from extraneous or unnecessary, these items were essential to early modern subject formation and social life. Moreover, the volume explicitly interrogates what counts as an accessory by including investigations of objects not usually understood as bodily ornaments: scissors, busks, codpieces, dildos, document seals, and even boys. Tracing the social life of things and offering new readings of both canonical and less well-known literary accounts of objects, *Ornamentalism* usefully explores the production and circulation of accessories and their textual representations.

The book is divided into five sections. Part 1, "Dressing Up," centers on questions of fashion and beauty. The opening chapter, by Evelyn Welch, studies the increasing popularity of perfumed gloves, earrings, buttons, and other scented accessories in Renaissance Italy. Historicizing smell and making a case for early modern anxiety about the permeability of the body, this essay serves as a useful introduction to the volume as a whole since it connects the study of ornament to issues that have animated recent scholarship on the senses. Eugenia Paulicelli's chapter builds on and elaborates this account of accessories by describing the history of the veil in cinquecento Italy. Once linked to the Madonna, the veil later came to be associated not with chastity but with sexual seduction. The third and final chapter in this section takes up and extends these questions of female social status. In her account of the handkerchief in early modern England and Italy, Bella Mirabella traces the napkin's contradictory cultural meanings as both a mark of refined good taste and a receptacle for bodily fluids associated with the lower classes.

Part 2, "Erotic Attachments," explicitly foregrounds issues of gender and sexuality in objects that were detachable. In "Busks, Bodices, and Bodies," Ann Rosalind Jones and Peter Stallybrass describe the rigid supports inside ladies' undergarments on which verses were inscribed by men to those they courted. Women, in this account, are both the readers and the wearers of intimate love poetry. Will Fisher's fascinating examination of codpieces, originally published in his 2006 book, maps out the ideological implications of material forms. Bag-type genital coverings, he demonstrates, evoked the scrotum and were associated with earlier notions of manhood as based in reproduction and lineage, whereas later codpieces were stiffer, phallic protuberances that corresponded to emergent discourses of masculinity as requiring sexual dominance over women. Liza Blake's analysis of dildos rounds out the essays in this section by showing that early modern strap-ons were not prosthetic penises but independent instruments of pleasure, whose textual representations mirrored their material function through the literary pleasures they produced.

Part 3, "Taking Accessories Seriously," considers the political and emotional power of accessories. Opening this section is Karen Raber's essay, which continues the feminist investments of previous chapters by demonstrating how Elizabeth I mobilized traditional associations of pearls with chastity even as she established a subversive counterdiscourse linking them to female self-determination. Catherine Richardson usefully expands the conversation to nonelite experiences by examining the varied ways in which jewelry exchange was crucial to both social identity and interpersonal affective ties among the "middling sort." This interplay between public status and private life is evident also in Joseph Loewenstein's engaging chapter on document seals as technologies of authentication and privacy. His analysis of their material history in relation to representations of sealing in Shakespeare's plays point to the malleability of early modern subjectivity and the ways it was produced.

Part 4, "From Head to Toes," is structured around accessories decorating two bodily extremes. Natasha Korda's account of the material production of starched linen demonstrates the centrality of immigrant women from the Low Countries in the manufacture and maintenance of elaborate ruffs, collars, and bands. Her characteristically rigorous and intelligent analysis traces the impact of this form of female skilled labor on dramatic representations in *The London Prodigal, Patient Grissill,* and a short Cambridge play titled *Band, Ruffe, and Cuffe.* Michelle A. Laughran and Andrea Vianello's chapter turns to the opposite end of the body. Shoes in Renaissance Italy, they argue, were only sometimes visible in public and were thus associated with the hidden and the private. When displayed, poulaines worn by men and chopines worn by women could serve as provocations akin to lingerie, aimed at strategically drawing attention to precisely that which it supposedly conceals.

The collection concludes with two essays that do indeed address, as the final section's title suggests, "Unlikely Accessories." Adam Smyth's "What We Talk about When We Talk about Scissors" explores a crucial theoretical question at stake in all new materialist scholarship: What is the relationship between discourses about objects and their actual physical properties? By examining the curious impressions left in books by rusty shears, spectacles, and other objects used as tools for reading, Smyth considers the methodological challenges that inform recent strands of "thing theory." Amanda Bailey's chapter offers a strong conclusion to the volume as a whole by analyzing early modern notions of boys as accessories that secured the social status and masculinity of upwardly mobile gallants. Her careful and detailed account of the legal and economic conditions of boy actors raises important questions about how bodies can become objects and what happens when those objects become commodities.

Most striking about the collection as a whole are the broader theoretical questions raised by connections between essays from different sections of the volume. New materialism has been especially influential with regard to the history of the book, and a number of chapters deal explicitly with overlaps between items worn on the body and those used for reading and writing. Because of the collection's explicit emphasis on accessories, this critical conversation about textual production and reception is here recast in terms of corporeality and subjectivity. Doing so not only emphasizes how discourses and bodies are mutually constitutive but also underscores the centrality of gender and sexuality: these are not simply topics of study, the volume seems to assert, but rather ideologies and epistemologies through which the cultural life of objects and their consequent meanings are produced. Such questions are most clearly brought to the fore in the second section, but even in essays where such matters seem at first to be irrelevant, it quickly becomes clear that social practices and textual forms are fundamentally structured through and by logics of sexual desire and difference.

Moreover, *Ornamentalism* gestures toward the varied ways in which commodity culture is itself implicated in conceptions of the gendered and sexed body. In its particular emphasis on objects that were deemed—or became—luxury items and status symbols, the collection implicitly suggests that feminist and queer analytical frames are crucial to understanding the growth of capitalism. Although such concerns are not stated up front as part of the underlying goal of the project, the volume does admirably raise these issues through its juxtaposition of these particular essays. Indeed, we might say that the collection thus embodies the very questions so many of its chapters investigate: if the textual production of meaning depends on its particular material forms, then the form of this volume performatively enacts the dynamic relationship between physical things and the discourses that surround them so as to render the sum even greater than the parts. *Ornamentalism* thus serves as a useful addition to recent scholarship not only by examining the blurry boundaries between bodies and the objects that adorn them but also by materializing the study of accessories as itself essential to the corpus of material culture studies.

The Chemistry of the Theatre: Performativity of Time, by Jerzy Limon. Houndmills, Basingstoke: Palgrave Macmillan, 2010. Pp. 246. Hardback $84.00.

Reviewer: THOMAS P. ANDERSON

In *The Chemistry of the Theatre: Performativity of Time,* Jerzy Limon attempts to integrate cognitive studies, performance studies, and literary analysis to make an argument that theater is an artistic medium "governed by a system of multifarious rules or formulas" (3). Limon's book, then, is a spectator's guide to theater spectacle with the singular purpose to allow a discerning audience to "discover the rules" (4) or "know the rules" (5) that "explain and justify" the shape and force of theatrical spectacle. In the book's extended metaphor, these rules together comprise the chemistry of the theater—"a sequence of compound signs, heterogeneous amalgams.... These blended amalgams create meaning through a network of relations, such as the rule of equivalence, based on similarity or contrast, and the rule of contiguity, or, a 'theatrical syntax'" (8).

What emerges in Limon's dense analysis of the rules of performance is a type of theatrical structuralism in which theater is structured like a language, possessing the same power to shock and surprise as Lacan's notion of the unconscious. Central to Limon's thesis is the education of the spectator, who actively participates in the chemistry of the theater in a "cognitive retort" (11)—a response to the theatrical experience that, according to Limon, links spectator and performance in "blended spaces" (11). Limon's performance- and cognition-based analysis of the theater is a complement to other recent studies that seek to make literary analysis responsive to the material of the theater. Jonathan Gil Harris's innovative *Untimely Matter In the Time of Shakespeare* (University of Pennsylvania Press, 2011), along with his co-edited collection of essays with Natasha Korda, *Staged Properties in Early Modern English Drama* (Cambridge University Press, 2006), has established crucial links between the materiality of a play's staging and the way audiences might understand its significance. In addition, Andrew Sofer's book *The Stage Life of Props* (University of Michigan Press, 2003) offers a related study of the special way that the deep history of a particular stage item insinuates itself into the immediacy of a performance and affects audience reception, and Kent Cartwright's *Shakespearean Tragedy and Its Double: The Rhythms of Audience Response* (Penn State University Press, 1991) uses textual and historical evidence to make the case that a play's theatricality functions contractually to wed spectators to the effect of theatrical spectacle, making the audience an active participant in a play's performance. In contextualizing the book's scientific metaphor, "[a]s in chemistry, also in theatre" (47), with recent developments in cognitive studies, Limon too seeks to untangle the mystery of audience response. Limon expresses the link between cognitive science and performance studies in describing the migration of meaning of a stage prop, in this case a bowl of soup, in a staged performance: "It is not only the imagined plate of soup that is the intended meaning of the scene: what counts is how the meaning is created, what substances are used and how they are modeled. In cognitive science it is even more important how the blending process affects the body and mind of the recipient" (46).

Limon describes this process of cognitive blending as "theatrical osmosis" (60), and he resists understanding theater as a fictional mirror held up to nature; nor is the audience perception of a play simply a mirror image of what is implied on stage. The experience of the theater, for Limon, is much more complicated: indeed, it is transactional, an act of "communication in action" (64). In expressing the complexity of this communication loop between theater and audience, Limon's book takes considerable rhetorical risks. For example, in describing the function of the actor in the communication loop of the theater, Limon writes, "We, the spectators, take the input spaces of the actor and the figure signaled, and blend them in cognitive responses, creating an imagined figure, which may be treated as the resultant structure of the process. This then is related back to the stage and, again, back to the spectator, and so on, in a communication continuum" (158). Limon's analysis of the chemistry of the theater is filled with many of these moments in which his attempt at scientific clarity runs the risk of producing the opposite rhetorical effect.

The Chemistry of the Theatre is organized in three parts: the first is a three-chapter introduction of how Limon is using cognitive science and performance theory to establish a new way to understand the enduring appeal of theatrical spectacle. The second part of the book is a four-chapter exploration of how the mechanics of the stage and the process of cognitive blending in the audience coordinate to produce the force of theater. Limon offers chapters in this section on "Sculpting the Space," "Sculpting the Time," "Sculpting the Language," and "Sculpting the Body" in the performance. The book's final two chapters examine the theatrical conventions of soliloquies and asides and the play-within-the-play, followed by a brief, helpful conclusion that synthesizes the book's major claims about the force of time as the catalyst to artistic theatrical experience. For Limon, "the study of the different functions of time structures employed in theatre is fundamental in uncovering the ways in which the medium works, the complex and distinctive ways in which meaning is created" (210).

Limon's interest in arguing for time's paramount importance in a new science of the theater means that at times the specific contours of his argument are muted by the scientific discourse that he deploys to makes his case. While it is clear that the relationship between the infinite, fictional time of the staged play offers a rich contrast to the bounded time of the actors and spectators in the theater, the major implications of this relationship never fully crystallize in Limon's earnest study. This criticism of the book notwithstanding, Limon's vast experience as a teacher of theater infuses the book with its most pleasurable and informative moments. Although *The Chemistry of the Theatre* only minimally redresses the gap that separates current literary analysis from rigorous performance-based criticism, the examples that Limon marshals to prove his claims about theater's chemistry are fascinating accounts from years of play-going, seeing major European and American productions as well as small but remarkable local plays. Whether he is describing a production of *Two Gentlemen of Verona* at the Bristol Old Vic in 1952 or Roberto Ciulli's recent production of *King Lear* performed at the Teatr Wybrzeże, Limon's readings of interesting moments in staged plays are imaginative and full of rich insights. Perhaps my own biases that privilege the theatrical imagination inform my desire for more of the rich descriptions of staged plays culled from Limon's life dedicated to the theater. At the very least, these rich descriptions anchor the book's more scientific discussions and balance Limon's interest in "chemistry" with a sense of theater's "rough magic" that resists quantitative analysis. More significantly, perhaps, Limon's book exploring the power of dramatic performance and existing alongside of text-based accounts of drama reveals how little the two approaches actually speak to one another.

Supernatural Environments in Shakespeare's England: Spaces of Demonism, Divinity, and Drama, by Kristen Poole. Cambridge: Cambridge University Press, 2011. Pp. 304. Cloth $90.00.

Reviewer: **D. K. SMITH**

In this thought-provoking and impressive book, Kristen Poole extends the study of early modern cartography in fascinating new directions, carrying an examination of the period's increasing geodetic awareness into the realm of the otherworldly. In a marked break from recent approaches, which have set up a clear division between religious views of the world and the shift toward scientific and mathematical precision, Poole examines the way that cartographic epistemologies may be seen as embedded within a fundamentally theological cultural view.

New religious ideas in the wake of the Protestant Reformation, along with changing ways of thinking about physical space, produced a series of competing ideas about the structure of the universe. Even as it was becoming more precisely measureable and fixed, the world in early modern England remained a fundamentally religious space, and the experience of a person's place in that physical space was closely tied to her understanding of the supernatural and religious order of things. In this light, the increasing concern with how physical space could be measured and organized co-existed with ongoing concerns about demonic and supernatural manifestations in the world.

For Poole, the spatiality of the theater—its staging of characters moving through the world—offered an area for the representation of these competing physical and imaginative experiences. In a series of varied and intriguing chapters, she considers how an array of early modern dramas—Marlowe's *Doctor Faustus* and Shakespeare's *Othello, Hamlet, Macbeth,* and *The Tempest*—can be seen to highlight this ongoing negotiation between spatial and supernatural epistemologies.

The first chapter, "The devil's in the archive: Ovidian physics and *Doctor Faustus*," considers the nature of the physical world, which was increasingly seen in fixed and measureable terms, but which also had to make room for the fluidity of demonic and divine intrusion. This was a world in which Satan moved freely, a world in which supernatural occurrences were, if not common, at least well accepted. And to accept Satan's actions in the world was to accept a reality of unstable and shifting materiality, a world in which imagination and physical reality had equal play. To convey the imagined experience of this period, Poole introduces the intriguing concept of *Ovidian physics:* an epistemology of material reality that allows both for a fixity of space and for the destabilizing experience of sudden metamorphosis. This is a far cry from the modern understanding of the world, but by reading *Doctor Faustus* through this epistemological lens, Poole allows us to consider the lived experience of a character whose view of the world simultaneously encompasses these shifting extremes.

In her second chapter, "Scene at the deathbed: *Ars moriendi, Othello,* and envisioning the supernatural," Poole examines the supernatural environment that would have felt most immediate and universal to the play's audience: the imaginative and physical space of the deathbed. She explores the complex understanding of the experience as represented in *ars moriendi.* In this literary form, the dying figure is seen to argue against an invisible host of demons, recounting for the audience the lived experience of this spiritual trial, and highlighting the simultaneous experience of the physical and spiritual worlds. With this as her starting point, Poole reads Othello's murder of Desdemona in their marriage bed as a dramatization that both echoes its audience's eschatological understanding of the world and destabilizes the relationship of earthly and spiritual places.

In the third chapter, "When hell freezes over: The fabulous Mount Hecla and *Hamlet*'s infernal geography," Poole turns her attention to the existence of purgatory and its understanding at a time of both shifting religious doctrine and increased spatial precision. In the wake of the Reformation, concerns about purgatory included questions not just about its spiritual existence but about its precise physical location as well. The relationship of this world and the next became a geographical, as well as a spiritual, concern. In her examination of *Hamlet,* Poole explores the way spiritual understanding bumps up against the newly evolving understanding of geodetic precision, revealing a new geography that strives for spatial specificity in a universe saturated with the divine and the demonic.

The fourth chapter, "Metamorphic cosmologies: The world according to Calvin, Hooker, and Macbeth," considers the very different spatial understandings of the universe generated by the doctrines of John Calvin and Richard Hooker. In a fine analysis, Poole reveals the way that considerations of the nature of God must necessarily be reflected in an understanding of the material world. Where Calvin's God is the micromanager—unpredictable and illogical—Hooker's God establishes a divine order and than adheres to it. In her examination of *Macbeth,* Poole explores what she sees as a staging of these two competing views of the divine cosmos. In this light, the play offers the vision of a universe both stable and radically contingent, and Macbeth becomes a character clinging to the hope of cosmic order within a shifting and unpredictable universe.

The final chapter, "Divine geometry in a geodetic age: Surveying, God, and *The Tempest,*" carries the idea of a divinely shaped cosmos into the earthly sphere. Poole examines the connection between surveying and theology, exploring a world in which God was not simply in the details, He was in the geometry itself. In this context, the increasing importance of land surveying worked to tie together human beings, space, and the divine. Geometry itself became a theological discourse, and the study of geometry came to be seen as the means of understanding God's role in the fundamental ordering of the world. In Poole's study, *The Tempest* reflects this relationship of the land, the supernatural, and its human occupants. As she argues, a geodetic sensibility runs through the play, but even as it offers an awareness of mankind's attempts to order the world, it suggests the limits of human understanding and the immanence of God's presence in the spatial understanding of the landscape.

Drama and the Succession to the Crown, 1561–1633, by Lisa Hopkins. Burlington, VT: Ashgate, 2011. Pp. 188. Hardback $99.95.

Reviewer: JOHN E. CURRAN, JR.

Having this chance to review Lisa Hopkins's new offering, *Drama and the Succession to the Crown, 1561–1633,* is most welcome, for it gives me leave to declare openly what I have thought for a long time now: she is one of our very best scholars writing on Shakespeare and his contemporaries. While *The Shakespearean Marriage* stands out, being a magisterial as well as original treatment of that weighty subject, any random selection from her staggering output is bound to impress the reader with one rare insight after another. Her recent series of books from Ashgate, each well focused but all mutually reinforcing, deals with political topicality in the drama, and *Drama and the Succession,* building on *Shakespeare on the Edge* and *The Cultural Uses of the Caesars,* is the strongest member of the family so far. Packed like the others with the distinctive, penetrating readings and correspondences only Hopkins's vast knowledge and unique vision can produce, *Drama and the Succession* has a sharper argument than the others and lays out that argument's foundations more clearly.

Her thesis is that succession is a preoccupation in the drama not only where we expect it, such as in history plays, and not only at times when we expect it, such as Elizabeth's final years. Instead, succession worries—and fantasies—obtain in many odd places, like *A Midsummer Night's Dream, Measure for Measure,* and *The Broken Heart;* they invoke a number of different problems, referencing a dizzying array of possible candidates for the throne; and they subsist well past the point when the question would seem settled. The issues are genealogical, stretching back to John of Gaunt and branching out in multiple directions: foreign and domestic, legal, with Henry VIII's will going against the Scottish line, and geographical, there being great "ambiguity about what exactly was being succeeded *to*" (1). And understanding them as Hopkins does is an accomplishment in itself. The risk she runs, here as in her other books, is that her readings might seem a little too subtle, a little too hard to come by. But Hopkins does not merely rely on the fact that figures perhaps obscure to us, like Lady Catherine Grey or Sebastian of Portugal, were not so at the time; she also explains that not only obscurity but also imprecision would naturally mark these plays, as they do not systematically handle succession problems but unsystematically "glance at" them, to use a favorite term of hers. This owes to fear of trouble from the government, of course, but also and more interestingly to a lack of definitiveness on the playwrights' parts as to what would be the ideal succession scenario and even what the principle of succession ought to be. *Henry V* cannot plainly deal with the succession questions it raises, both because they are too "explosive" and because the Salic Law problem intensifies and complicates them, and so the play "performs a carefully sustained dance around them" (87). The Duchess of Malfi functions as a "fictional avatar" for several real-life royals, including Sebastian and Elizabeth, as well as for Arabella Stuart, and if this seems confusing, it speaks thereby to the confusing feelings Webster is expressing about Arabella's plight, about female rule, and about who would inherit and what would be inherited after James (113–14).

Throughout the book Hopkins is in this way able to make a virtue of complexity as she weaves together all her various connections: we are convinced that succession issues resonate in the drama, and that playwrights and audiences alike would have been alive to and conflicted about them. The chapter on Marlowe makes for a good representation of the whole, as Hopkins pulls together different threads of meaning in his work, and also in its descendants, to argue not that Marlowe advances a particular "monolithic" succession scheme but that he consistently provokes thought on the "wider questions of rule," which involve succession "inextricably": with *Tamburlaine* Marlowe "inevitably invites us to ask the same question as *Leir* and *Lear*: which of these three children is best fitted to succeed their father, and on what basis should questions of succession be decided" (34–35). Not always are the links Hopkins makes securely fastened; the link between Romans and Fairies as succession figures seems a bit tenuous, with the author perhaps putting more weight on Oberon's supposed descent from Julius Caesar than this small though interesting point will bear. But here too she is able to put her findings in perspective, suggesting that Romans and Fairies do similar thematic work, as they "mystify succession by their inherent stress on continuity rather than change," even as they represent how change has a "momentum of its own" (56). Moreover, given the enormous wealth of unusual and fascinating associations she has gathered, as she whirls from play to play and point to point, there are in my opinion remarkably few stretchers.

Part of this persuasiveness is due to her superior command of up-to-date scholarship, from which she selects expertly to corroborate and clarify her discussion. Readers of *MaRDiE* will appreciate the challenges of staying current with the scholarly literature and drawing on it judiciously, and at this no one is more skilled than Hopkins. With the Robin Hood plays, for example, she derives much of her commentary from existing work, but this is cleverly marshaled to allow us to see the valences Robin Hood had as a succession figure, in ways we had not before.

There are other strengths to the book, such as incisive readings of much overlooked works like Warner's *Albion's England* and Drayton's *England's Heroical Epistles*. But the book's main value lies with Hopkins's offering a bevy of fresh ideas at matter she has commented on so authoritatively before: the anxieties and the nostalgia over female rule; the ramifications of the prospective blurring of boundaries between Scotland and England; the politically charged meanings in Ford. *Drama and the Succession* is a worthy addition to Hopkins's oeuvre, one that has much to teach us, and at the same leaves us anticipating where she will take us next.

Shakespeare's Foreign Worlds: National and Transnational Identities in the Elizabethan Age, by Carole Levin and John Watkins. Ithaca, NY: Cornell University Press, 2009. Pp. 259. Hardcover $65.00

Reviewer: **PATRICIA PHILLIPPY**

In this "collaborative monograph," historian Carole Levin and literary critic John Watkins each contribute three chapters on three Shakespearean plays to a book intended "to serve as a metacommentary on the current dialogue between the two fields" of history and literary criticism (6). Demonstrating rather than theorizing this metacommentary, the authors situate "the distinction between historical and literary studies itself at the dawn of the modern era" (7) by studying Shakespeare's engagement with a number of demographic, mercantile, legal, social, and cultural shifts that attended the changing conception of the foreign in the latter years of Elizabeth's reign. The decision to write on Elizabethan plays—*1 Henry VI, The Merchant of Venice,* and *The Taming of the Shrew*—rather than the predictable works emerging from England's expansion of trade and exploration results in six fascinating chapters that investigate the "prehistory of [Shakespeare's] invention of the foreigner as a portable category within European society itself" (10).

The choice of plays in different genres enriches this project as well, since it enables the authors to treat the foreign as a multifaceted category central not only to English nation-building at the dawn of modernity but also to their own view of Shakespeare's Elizabethan plays "as a medium to reflect upon the plasticity and permeability of the English nation" (7). In section one, Levin approaches Shakespeare's Joan of Arc as a foreigner in social, sexual, and religious terms. Her reading of the character as a case study among others derived from chronicle history, Foxe's *Book of Martyrs,* and archival sources in which women pleaded pregnancy in order to defer or avoid execution illustrates the porous borders of drama and "religio-political actualities" (27) as sites where the crisis of nation building was played out. Locating gender at the heart of Shakespeare's oscillations between the native and the foreign in *1 Henry VI,* Watkins brilliantly "de-nationalizes" sixteenth-century history by tracing the play's displacement of a diplomacy grounded in dynastic marriage to a foreign policy dominated by English Protestant national interests; a new order in which the female monarch's dynastic concerns were canceled by the notion that "diplomatic outreach threaten[ed] to infect the English with the effeminacy and cowardice that define[d] the foreign for Shakespeare and his Elizabethan audience" (62).

Each of the book's three sections is prefaced by a co-authored summary of the issues addressed in the two chapters following, and each adopts the same format of Levin's contribution, followed by Watkins's. Levin's discussion of Jessica's conversion in *The Merchant of Venice* sets this event in relation to the conversions of Jewish women in Elizabethan England, arguing rather unsurprisingly that English suspicions of these women's residual religious identities—their "natures"—mitigated the successful integration of Jewish converts into English society. Watkins follows with a reading of *Merchant* that brilliantly explores the "intertextual drift" between the play and its Florentine source to show how Shakespeare assuages Elizabethan fears of the inevitability of the mercantile rise and fall of nations, on the Venetian model.

In section three, Levin draws a comparison between the marriage of Petruchio and Kate in *The Taming of the Shrew* and that of Henry VIII and Katherine Parr as recounted by Foxe, widening her discussion to suggest that Kate and Bianca are both "symbolic daughters" of the queen (176). Watkins finishes the volume by thinking about the rival claims as native and foreign of two Continental imports into England, Renaissance humanism and Protestantism, and goes on to argue persuasively that Shakespeare complicates his source for *The Taming of the Shrew* to cast Italian women's rights to own material property in their retention of their dowries and to acquire intellectual property through humanist education as distinctly foreign to the native English wife-taming plot which the play ultimately endorses.

The structure of the book is an apt reflection of its central idea and, as such, it is both engaging and challenging. In its best moments, *Shakespeare's Foreign Worlds* has the effect of a concert consisting of three duets, expertly performed by two strong musicians. At other times, however, it is easy to imagine that one has wandered into a panel at a scholarly conference at which papers are presented around a theme or topic but do not clearly engage each other. The structure is challenging not only for the reader but for the contributors as well. It is not clear why Levin performs first in each section. (Why not switch roles, and would it make a difference if Watkins led off rather than Levin? Is history somehow a preface to literary criticism, or literary scholarship a footnote to history?). And despite hopes to the contrary, the performance by one and then the other author in each section invariably invites comparisons not only of the methods but also of the value of one chapter as opposed to the other. (In light of this fact, it is especially unfortunate that all of Levin's contributions revisit previously published material, while Watkins's appear here first—giving the obviously counterproductive impression that they respond to and may aim to supplant Levin's earlier publications.) No one would argue with the authors' concluding claim that their "double readings of each play, and the ways [their] chapters interact with each other provide multiple perspectives of the central themes of the foreign" (208). By sidestepping a direct, theoretical engagement with the nature and implications of their interdisciplinary metanarrative, the authors cast the reader as respondent to their contributions. Their closing sentence, indeed, issues this invitation directly: if "the literary scholar and the historian can bring together a confluence of approach and method as well as a respect for the differences inherent in their approaches as well as the similarities, the foreign worlds will be home to all of us" (209).

Few books make so direct and so remarkable a demand on their readers—but why should not more do so? *Shakespeare's Foreign Worlds* risks much, but also gives a great deal, and promises much more in return. Surely readers *should* be respondents in the way that Levin and Watkins imagine them to be, and it is invigorating to be asked to rise to the challenge of reading by engaging the provocative questions this volume sets out. Which reading of *The Shrew* is the "better" one, and why? Whose is the more convincing Joan of Arc? And, perhaps most emphatically: How can we make this project less a contest and more a mutual search for meaning? The self-reflection that accompanies the reading of *Shakespeare's Foreign Worlds* is a risk that we all should take.

English Revenge Drama: Money, Resistance, Equality, by Linda Woodbridge. Cambridge: Cambridge University Press, 2010. Pp. 348. Hardcover $100.00.

Reviewer: STEPHEN DENG

In *English Revenge Drama,* Linda Woodbridge challenges the common belief that revenge in early modern England was universally condemned by theater audiences as an unchristian response to injustice. Instead of isolating "revenge tragedy," which as she notes "has helped obscure the prevalence of revenge across many genres," Woodbridge expands the scope to the category of "revenge plays" in order to analyze "the cultural work that literary revenge performs" (5). As a result, she finds revenge to be a vital concern within several plays in various genres (she mentions, for example, that all but two of Shakespeare's plays include the term "revenge") and concludes that revenge ultimately constitutes a justifiable solution to systemic economic, political and social unfairness (3). While "everyone talked" about this unfairness, "revenge plays did something about it. Many revengers are disempowered people, unjustly treated, who step up and take control" (6). Although critics several decades ago had dismissed Tillyard's Elizabethan world picture as "establishment ideology," conventional wisdom has maintained the view that "Elizabethans abhorred revenge because the establishment told them to" even though "ample evidence attests that [audiences] resisted propaganda from the state church, and revenge plays' huge popularity is part of that evidence" (17). "To say that Christian audiences flatly disallowed revenge," Woodbridge concludes, "does not bear scrutiny" (36).

The extent of unfairness felt within the culture could actually be quantified using new methods of accounting, especially the technique of double-entry bookkeeping recently imported from Italy. Revenge plays utilize the language of bookkeeping generously, particularly in response to economic frustration. Even an exact "bilateral symmetry" emerges in plays such as *Titus Andronicus,* which "features, on each side of its vendetta, two decapitations and the deaths of six major characters" (15–16). Faced with "unfairness, disorder, and imbalance," revengers respond "with a mad bookkeeper's parody of order," channeling in their actions "the methodical minds of accountants, whose ledgers register not pounds and pence but amputated body parts" (43, 61). A key term connecting bookkeeping with revenge was *debt,* the sense that "the imperative to avenge a relative was . . . analogous to money owed" (84). Considering revenge in light of Craig Muldrew's work on debt within an "economy of obligation," Woodbridge argues that both debt and revenge "involved duty and promises of action; both were dangerous and could lead to ruin; both could produce satisfaction. Both were all about paying back" (96). Moreover, she identifies an increasing conflation of the figures Fortuna and Justitia, the latter of whose "bilaterally symmetrical scales, like an accounting ledger" offered a potent image of the need for equality especially between the privileged and the dispossessed (106). Although Justice should not be subject to whims of Fortuna, "the bestowal of Fortune's blindfold on Justitia and of Justitia's scales on Fortuna bespeak a horrific suspicion: under that blindfold, Justitia and Fortuna were the same goddess" (115). It is not surprising, then, that revenge on the stage seems to mimic Tudor law, "where 'condign' penalties suited crimes—thieves' hands were cut off, scolds' tongues bridled" (6), "provocatively appropriating state justice" (17), even as the state attempted to maintain revenge's status as the illegitimate "evil twin" of the judicial system (9).

Moreover, according to Woodbridge, the sense of injustice went beyond the personal to the political, especially when the problem of tyranny became a central concern for resistance theorists and stage revengers alike (130). She finds a key link between the two in translations of plays by Seneca, whose Roman republicanism and resistance to tyranny performed "cultural work" similar to resistance theory (131) while offering the translators, whose "biographies suggest political motives" (150), "oblique tactics" of resistance by translating "that bard of tyranny" (163). In addition to the defense offered by translating classical texts, the "outlandish gore and fantastic plots made ideal camouflage" (170). What appears the work of "cheap sensationalists" could in fact have constituted the staging of "violence in the service of resistance" (185).

Ultimately, Woodbridge argues, revenge plays are concerned with justice for the oppressed; they might even be compared to revolutionary movements promoting social leveling and communism (251). The villains of these plays "embodied all that kept [the underprivileged] from getting what they deserved" (19). "Where the powerful can oppress and humiliate," Woodbridge concludes, "revenge asserts honor and dignity; against oppressive authority, it asserts personal agency. In a world of inequity—economic, social, political and legal—revenge is a blow for equality" (253).

Woodbridge's exhortation to reconsider injustices represented within revenge plays is well taken, but several points in the book warrant expansion, especially the connection to double-entry bookkeeping. As she notes in referencing Mary Poovey, the very idea of "balance" in balanced books is a pure fiction driven by adjusting levels of profits or loss on one side: "balanced" does not mean zero-profit accounts or "breaking even." Indeed, Woodbridge points out that positive profit, and not a break-even level, is what revengers (and bookkeepers within companies and nations) really want: "revengers sought not a tie game but victory" (16). If revenge is not about "getting even" but *profiting* from those who have wronged them, what then is the nature of this profit? And if profit and loss might inhere within what appears to be a "balanced" structure, does that not suggest the possibility that double-entry bookkeeping might *promote* systemic unfairness or at least provide another potential site for its development? Moreover, Woodbridge might expound more upon relations between personal, state-sanctioned and divine revenge. For example, she notes, "That God, the Chief Justice, and the man who kills his wife's lover were all 'revengers' may imply queasiness about the violence of God and the Chief Justice, or a claim to divine or official prerogative for private avengers, or both" (21). I think it would be more productive to open up contradictions like these rather than merely use them as evidence in arguing for revenge as a legitimate response to injustice in the period. Despite these limitations, however, Woodbridge's book importantly helps us to reassess the moral territory of revenge within early modern English drama more broadly construed.

Shakespeare Only, by Jeffrey Knapp. Chicago: University of Chicago Press, 2009. Pp. 256. Cloth $38.00.

Reviewer: JAMES P. BEDNARZ

Shakespeare Only concerns the question of what sets Shakespeare apart as a writer, and to this end Jeffrey Knapp presents two main arguments. To clear space for his main focus on authorial self-representation, he begins with an incisive polemic against the claims by contemporary scholars that either there were "no authors in Shakespeare's world" (x) or that drama itself was primarily anonymous and collaborative, identified chiefly with acting companies rather than particular poets. He then uses this critique as a platform to delineate his theory that Shakespeare conceived of himself as a commercial dramatist working in a degraded medium who paradoxically assumed that he could achieve "rareness" and "glory" by "aspiring to seem 'common' too" (xiii). His model of "dramatic authorship" can only be understood "*in relation* to mass entertainment" (4). Authorship, Knapp asserts, shaped "mass entertainment," just as "mass entertainment" shaped Shakespeare's conception of authorship. He becomes the many-in-one.

Reviewing criticism of the last two decades of the twentieth century with Knapp, one can now easily detect the extreme ideological assumptions concerning "the death of the author" that led influential theater historians to make surprisingly misleading claims about the nature of dramatic authorship in Shakespeare's age. Knapp is most effective in demonstrating how the drive behind such criticism "to celebrate collaboration *in the moment before the individual*" (12) now seems tendentious. He can do so because in the interim more sophisticated efforts to articulate the interrelations among overlapping modes of composition, such as coactivity, collaboration, and rivalry, have supplanted more suspect forms of analysis that deliberately exclude human agency. Indeed, despite Knapp's critique, those scholars who misread theatrical history in the light of Foucault and Barthes are now regularly exonerated for introducing a profitable paradigm shift away from naïve assumptions of "sovereign authorship" that ignored the literary and theatrical networks in which early modern writing developed. Yet nothing that Knapp reveals advances beyond the more cogent presentation of this matter offered by Brian Vickers in "Appendix II: Abolishing the Author? Theory versus History" of *Shakespeare, Co-Author* (2002). So that as much as I am convinced that Knapp's critique is justified, at this point it adds nothing significantly new to an already exhausted debate.

Asserting that single-authored plays provide the central paradigm for the discussion of dramatic composition in the early modern period, Knapp sees Shakespeare as an author who defined himself as a poet-playwright-actor by accepting theater's low status. Instead of aligning himself with the "literary," as Ben Jonson had done, Shakespeare, according to Knapp, discovered an "empowering debasement" (52) in mass entertainment. "It is this peculiar readiness to shame himself," Knapp writes, "that makes the speaker seem distinctive in his own eyes" (53) not only in the *Sonnets* but in representative characters that reflect obliquely on his art. Shakespeare is thus said to be involved in an "autobiographical fantasy" in the Henriad as Hal seeks to incorporate the common, although, according to Knapp, with one main difference, since Shakespeare felt no corresponding need to banish Falstaff from his enlarged domain. The playwright is equally figured in the Duke from *Measure for Measure* who manages the play's seedy plots to secure his theatrical ends. In the book's later chapters, Shakespeare's metatheatrical analysis is said to be expressed in allegories that detail (in diary style) his ambivalence about working with George Wilkins on *Pericles* and John Fletcher on *The Two Noble Kinsmen*. Since there are no controls on this method, any passages from the canon picked at random might be similarly mined for authorial self-reflexivity.

Despite this elaborate positioning, however, the model of authorial self-explication Knapp proposes largely issues in a clichéd dichotomy contrasting Shakespeare as a populist who accepts the "common" nature of "mass entertainment" and Ben Jonson as a self-styled "master-poet" who defines himself "in opposition to the theater" (68). Yet Shakespeare and Jonson change their nuanced perspectives so radically in different contexts and during successive phases of their careers that one despairs of positing unalterable principles or positions to cover the wide range and shifting bases of their speculation. Just as Jonson occasionally treats commercial dramatic performance as the perfect medium for his art, Shakespeare exhibits a more ambiguous attitude toward the "common" than Knapp suggests, and it was never his sole means of authorial self-reflection. Self-abasement was a Chaucerian inheritance that Shakespeare merged with the Plautine *plaudite,* and as such should not be mistaken for autobiography. It was intended to be balanced by the impressive quality of the work itself which, by winning its audience's approval, paradoxically revealed the author's true status. One of the greatest accomplishments of Robert Weimann's *Shakespeare and the Popular Tradition in the Theater* was its even-handedness in concluding that for Shakespeare "native theater" and "humanist-inspired poetry" were "inseparable" (xviii). I miss this balance in *Shakespeare Only.* Early in his book Knapp cites the motto, from Ovid's *Amores,* that Shakespeare emblazoned on the title page of *Venus and Adonis* in 1594: "*Vilia miretur vulgus; mihi flavus Apollo / Pocula Castalia plena minister aqua*" ("Let common people admire common things; may golden-haired Apollo serve me cups filled with Castalian water"). But while Knapp views Shakespeare's career as a repudiation of this attitude of sovereign singularity, my own suspicion is that it forms part of the complex elision of elite and popular culture that characterizes his work. His drama was apparently successful in addressing both elite and mixed audiences, and one might see the cannon as consisting of a series of negotiations between both constituencies, instead of an exaltation of the stigmatic. Knapp states that Shakespeare "never disowned mass entertainment for some more high-toned or exclusive pursuit" (147), yet the brilliant assimilative power he brought to the stage enriched it with literary resources that at times, such as in *A Midsummer Night's Dream,* seem temporarily to obliterate the difference between low and high. Rather than identifying with his "rude mechanicals," Shakespeare plays an intricate game of teasing out the similarities and differences between art at its most singular and common, and Knapp's study succeeds as far as it can address this paradox.

Shakespeare's Errant Texts: Textual Form and Linguistic Style in Shakespearean 'Bad' Quartos and Co-authored Plays, by Lene B. Petersen. Cambridge: Cambridge University Press, 2010. Pp. 330. Hardback $171.95.

Reviewer: HUGH CRAIG

Petersen's book has two main elements. There is a discussion of the importance of oral and memorial transmission in early modern English play texts. This is allied to an argument that the changes that result from this transmission can be seen as a movement towards a set of patterns common in orally transmitted texts such as ballads and folk tales, rather than simply as degradation from an authorial original. Then there is a statistical analysis of a large set of play texts aimed at assessing the degree to which textual transmission affects the reliable attribution of texts to authors.

Petersen has a real point in her warning that attributionists working in early modern English drama have too often ignored the nature of the texts they rely on. If, as generally assumed, texts were copied, printed, reconstructed from memory by actors, and possibly copied in shorthand by audience members, all with little regard for preserving what the author had written in his "foul papers" or working draft, then it behoves anyone relying on their style for ascription to be cognizant of all the non-authorial sources of variation in the writing. Stylistic analysis must take account of "how the features quantified ended up in the texts in the first place" (199). Petersen is the first to make this point at length. She points out that the existence of multiple varying texts alone creates uncertainties about which text to use (4–5). Her book is a forceful reminder of an often overlooked ground zero for stylistics and authorship in this area, i.e., that canons may be unstable (13n), even the term *canon* may be inapplicable in this period (19), and "internal mutability" or "fundamental indeterminacy" may be the best way to understand the textuality of Elizabethan drama (28, 209).

The *Zielform* hypothesis is that folk tales, ballads, and other popular oral forms move in a common direction as they are repeatedly transmitted, towards simplifying action, removing elaboration in description, and using more formulaic expression, for example. This is an engaging, persuasive idea, well described in the book. One kind of shorthand for this is to think of the Pyramus and Thisbe play in *Midsummer Night's Dream* as the *Zielform* of the action of *Romeo and Juliet* (64). Petersen offers lots of detailed instances. She freely admits that there are alternative explanations for the variations between versions that she highlights, like specifically theatrical adaptation (71–72), censorship, or simply poor memory (78). For this reader the *Zielform* idea remains a distinct possibility in the cases she discusses, but does not ever appear the only possible explanation.

Petersen thus gathers the evidence that plays were changed by the processes of transmission. She raises the possibility that these changes are of a kind and to a degree that they need to be taken into account in attribution studies, also an important contribution. The second phase of her investigation is to test these ideas in a quantitative stylistic study. Here I think she misses an opportunity. To my mind these tests should have been designed to identify an effect connected with changes attributable to transmission. However, she sets up a broad test for the interaction of authorship and categories like "Good Quarto," "Bad Quarto," and (in Shakespeare's case) "Folio," achieves confused results, which, if anything, show that authorship classifications survive any differences between "authorial" and "orally transmitted" texts (177, 216–17) and then concentrates on individual cases of classification to or away from the expected authorial group or transmission type.

The performance of the model in assigning whole plays to authors, after all due optimization, is given as 65.4 percent (187). (This number is depressed by the fact that the largest canon, Shakespeare's, is divided into competing cross-authorial Quarto and Folio groups, but there is no way of removing that factor from the results, so this is the result that obtains.) This modest success rate suggests that authorship is indeed a factor, but also that many plays are being mis-assigned, for all sorts of ultimately unknowable reasons, so that we cannot assume, as Petersen does, that any particular failure of classification is somehow "interesting" and informative.

This is of course different from showing that there is no transmission effect. A different set of measures might reveal it. We might hold that different forms of transmission must affect the style of plays, and we just haven't yet found the right way to detect this effect. But with this model, it is not evident, and so anything else the model tells us about individual cases is of doubtful utility. We are left with an important precautionary principle but with no additional support for it from the quantitative side.

In one test, Petersen uses her system to classify *Hamlet* and *Romeo* Bad Quarto, Good Quarto, and Folio scenes into their respective parent categories. With *Hamlet* the success rate is 42 percent, with *Romeo* it is 15 percent (230, 233). This is to be compared with the 33 percent we could expect with a purely random allocation. Even with the *Hamlet* test, if we were hoping to classify scenes of unknown provenance into Petersen's three categories, we would expect to get it wrong 58 times in 100. Petersen goes on to discuss individual cases of correct and erroneous classification, but since the evidence of her test is that the "signal" of transmission differences is weak, if audible at all, these classifications hardly seem worth considering. One might think that it was too much to expect any strong effect from oral transmission, since this sort of resemblance has to compete against all sorts of other likenesses between scenes, like overlapping content, but this was the question Petersen asked. The answer she got was that there was at best a weak effect, and it obtains more in the *Hamlet* texts than in the *Romeo* ones.

Petersen concludes from the absence of any strong clustering of orally transmitted texts as against authorially transmitted ones that the latter share the unreliability attributed to the former (216–17). This is fallacious, in my view. The right conclusion is that the tests have failed to show any difference, and thus, of themselves, give no reason to think that transmission matters for authorial attribution. They leave us precisely where we were before in relation to the question of ruling in or ruling out given markers for attribution on the basis of what we know about the textual transmission of particular texts.

Petersen raises questions, which are important and timely, but doesn't go on to answer them in an empirical way. She mentions that plagiarism software finds "formulaic phrases," often associated with oral or memorial transmission, in Folio *Hamlet*. She wonders if this means that even Folio-type texts are "not authorial *enough*" to be reliable for authorship studies (195). The answer is, it may, or it may not. These phrases may confound authorial classification; they may make no difference to authorial classification; or they may make good authorial markers because authors may use them at distinctive rates. A well-designed study could determine which of the three options fits the existing texts best. Petersen doesn't carry out this study, and focuses purely on the first option.

Petersen refers to her set of 257 texts as "plays" (e.g. 175, 264) but the list in Appendix III shows that this set contains masques and non-dramatic verse as well. The labels in Figure 10 (215) indicate that for this trial several additional prose and verse works have also been analysed. This mixing of non-dramatic verse and prose with plays is not discussed in the text as far as I can see. The discussion of Figure 10 refers to its corpus as "playtexts" (213). Analysing masques and non-dramatic works alongside plays introduces an undesirable extraneous element of variation. Breton is the outlier in Figure 8, as Petersen notes (181), but this probably tells us only that he is represented by poems while the other authors are represented by plays. Petersen remarks on the "notable separation between plays" in the Beaumont group in Figure 9 (191), but this gap may well be explained by the fact that one of these plays is in fact a masque, as Appendix III reveals. Two of the non-dramatic works in Figure 10 are the outliers along the First Component.

In her conclusion, Petersen remarks that quantitative stylistics in this case leaves us with "the openness of possibilities, not the closure of answers" (237). I agree, but feel that this is disappointing, rather than reassuring, given that scholars generally turn to computational stylistics hoping it will resolve some questions, at least in its own narrowly defined terms. This book makes a substantial contribution by presenting a case on traditional grounds that transmission matters for authorship work—by offering lots of good reasons why this might be so—but its statistical testing of this hypothesis is unsatisfactory.

Index

Adams, John Cranford, 192
Anderson, Thomas P. 279–81
Anne, Queen, 27–28, 35
Arden family, 214
Ariosto, 23
Aronson-Lehavi, Sharon, 267–69
Ashmole, Elias, 144
Astington, John, 271–73

Bacon, Sir Francis, 79, 213, 214
Beaumont, Francis, 102
Bednarz, James P., 290–92
Bellarmine, Robert, 85
Blackfriars playhouse, 100
blood, 241–63
Boar's Head, 132
boy actors, 34
boys' companies, 100, 131
Briant, Alexander, 48
Bridewell Court Books, 106
Brooke, Ralph, 138, 139, 141, 144
Browne, Robert, 131, 132
Burton, Robert, 242–43, 245, 255

Calvinists, 84
Camden, William, 140
Campion, Edmund, 48
Carew, Sir George, 28, 30, 36
Carleton, Dudley, 20, 33
Carr, Robert, 220
Catholicism, 75–96, 171, 219
Cecil, Sir Robert, 29, 55
Cecil, William, Lord Burghley, 55
Chamberlain, John, 20
Chambers, E. K., 215
Chapman, George, 97–119
Charles I, King, 100
Children of the Queen's Revels, 35, 100
Christian martyrdom, 43–59
clown(s), 49–50, 128–29
Cotton, Roger, 138–39, 141–42, 144–45

Council of Trent, 85
Courtesans, 60–74
Craig, Hugh, 292–95
Crompton, Richard, 138, 141, 142, 144
Curran, John E., 283–85

Daborne, Robert, 217–18
Daniel, Samuel, 17–42
Davenant, John, 85, 86
debt, 75–96
Dekker, Thomas, 44, 62, 99, 120–35
Deng, Stephen, 288–90
Deticke, William, 148
Devereux, Robert, Earl of Essex, 218
Dillon, Janette, 269–71
Dodsworth, Roger, 143
Downton, Thomas, 185
Dugdale, Sir William, 144–45
Dutch Courtesan, The, 60–74

Earl of Worcester's Men, 107, 132
Easterling, Heather C., 269–71
economic elements, 75–96, 98–99
Edward III, 143
Elizabeth I, Queen, 32, 120, 156–83
Elizabethan state, 54–55
embedded masque, 97–119
English Civil War, 77
eroticism, 100–101, 105–7, 112–13

Feather, Jennifer, 240–63
Field, Nathan, 106
Fletcher, John, 102, 103
Florio, John, 29
flying equipment, 189–93
Ford, John, 62
"Fortunatus" plays, 120–35
Foucault, Michel, 56
Foxe, John, 46, 143

Germany, 120–35
Globe Playhouse (First and Second), 189–90, 192, 196–98

297

INDEX

Gray's Inn, 108
Green, John, 131
Greene, Robert, 188, 195

Habib, Imtiaz, 207–39
Hall, Edward, 142, 157, 165–71, 175, 176
Hall, George, 132
Hampton Court, 20
Henry VII, King, 156–83
Henry VIII, King, 164, 171
Henslowe, Philip, 120, 125, 130, 136, 186, 189, 191, 192, 195, 199
Herbert, William, Earl of Pembroke, 35
Herford, C. H., 121
Heywood, Thomas, 184–203
Hooker, Richard, 85
Hopkins, Lisa, 283–85
Hoy, Cyrus, 123–24, 126

identity, 240–63

James VI and I, King, 35, 98, 107, 178, 220, 226
Johnstone, Boyda, 267–69
Jones, Inigo, 31
Jones, Richard, 132
Jonson, Ben, 23, 31, 99

Kempe, Will, 214, 215
Kermode, Lloyd Edward, 271–73
King's Men, 194, 199
Knapp, Jeffrey, 290–92
Knolles, Richard, 220

Lambeth Palace, 148
Levin, Carole, 285–88
Limon, Jerzy, 279–81
Lin, Erika, T., 276–79
Lord Admiral's Men, 120, 185
Lord Chamberlain's Men, 145
Lord Strange's Men, 136–55
Louvain, 87
Low Countries, 63
Lucy, Sir William, 138, 141, 142, 145, 149, 150, 225

Manley, Lawrence, 136–55
Mann, David, 184–203
Manwaring, George, 207–39
Marlowe, Christopher, 67, 130, 195, 197

Marston, John, 60–74, 108
Martyred Soldier, The, 43–59
martyrological narrative, 43–59
masque, 17–52, 97–119
Massinger, Philip, 44, 75–96, 97–119
May, Thomas, 108
Middleton, Thomas, 62, 99
Mirabella, Bella, 276–79
Mirandola, Pico della, 23
More, Sir Thomas, 157–60, 162–65, 167, 169, 174
Mountjoy, Marie, 28, 30, 33

Nashe, Thomas, 136
Nicholl Charles, 28

Ottoman history, 207–39

Pastoor, Charles, 274–76
Petersen, Lene B., 292–95
Philip II, King of Spain, 24
Phillippy, Patricia, 285–88
Pitcher, John, 17–42
Plato, 65
Poole, Kristen, 281–83
projecting booth, 189
prospective glass, 25–27
Protestant economics, 75–96
Protestantism, 75–96, 171, 219

Queen Anne's Company, 107, 199
queen consort, 156–83

racial ideologies, 240–41, 243–63
Red Bull Playhouse, 189, 198
Reynolds, George, 194
Richard III, King, 145, 156–83
Robinson, Richard, 147
Rochester, Anne, 274–76
Rose Playhouse, 187, 189, 192, 197

Savernake Forest, 36
Schlueter, June, 120–35
Scott, Sarah K., 60–74
Shakespeare family, 213–14
Shakespeare, William, 146, 149
—Plays: *Cymbeline,* 197; *Hamlet,* 149, 198; *Henry IV* plays, 149, 225; *Henry V,* 253; *1 Henry VI,* 136–55, 191; *3 Henry VI,* 197; *King Lear,* 43; *Measure for Measure,* 61; *Merchant of Venice,*

67; *Midsummer Night's Dream,* 107; *Othello,* 207–39, 240–63; *Sonnets,* 213; *Taming of the Shrew,* 56; *Tempest,* 197; *Titus Andronicus,* 120, 129, 130; *Twelfth Night,* 215
Sherley, Sir Anthony, 208
Sherley, Robert, 208
Sherley family, 213–14
Sidney, Sir Philip, 188
Sidney, Robert (Baron), 29, 30
Smith, D. K., 281–83
Smith, Matthew J., 75–96
Stanley family, 136–55
Stanley, Ferdinando. *See* Stanley family
stage properties, 185, 191
staging, 43–59, 97–119, 189–99
Swan Playhouse, 189, 198

Talbot, Gilbert, 138
Thorpe, Thomas, 213
Tillyard, E. M. W., 54–55
Tilney, Edmund, 32, 35
translation issues, 128–29
traveling players, 120–21
Tudor historiography, 156–83, 219–21

Underhill family, 213–14
usury, 79

Vandals, 44
Venetian Catholicism, 89
Venner, Richard, 198
Vergil, Polydore, 145, 157, 160–62, 166, 167, 169
Villamediana, Conde de, 24, 25
violence, 43–59, 240–63
Vision of the Twelve Goddesses, 17–42
Volksbuch, 121
voyeurism, 100–101, 105–6

Walsingham, Sir Francis, 55
Watkins, John, 285–88
Whitefriars playhouse, 100
Williamson, Elizabeth, 43–59
Wilton House, 35
woman: "fallen," 60–74
women: characterization of, 60–74, 156–83
Woodbridge, Linda, 288–90
Wotton, Henry, 214

York, Elizabeth, 156–83

Ziegler, John R., 97–119